An Introduction to
NEW TESTAMENT
THOUGHT

An Introduction to

NEW TESTAMENT

THOUGHT

By

FREDERICK C. GRANT

ABINGDON PRESS

NEW YORK   ●   NASHVILLE

AN INTRODUCTION TO NEW TESTAMENT THOUGHT

Copyright MCML by Pierce & Smith

Library of Congress Catalog Card Number: 50-8047

New Testament quotations not otherwise designated are
from the Revised Standard Version, copyright 1946 by the
International Council of Religious Education. Old Testa-
ment quotations not otherwise designated are from the
American Standard Version, copyright renewal 1929 by the
International Council of Religious Education.

PRINTED AND BOUND AT NASHVILLE,
TENNESSEE, UNITED STATES OF AMERICA

Preface

A GLANCE at the table of contents of this book may suggest that it is one more work on "New Testament theology" for technical theologians. It is not so intended. It is only, as the title states, an introduction to New Testament thought. There is a question, of course, whether or not the New Testament contains a theology—that question is dealt with in one of the early chapters of this book. Many scholars deny that there is a New Testament theology; others take it for granted. The term "New Testament thought" does not settle the controversy but only draws a larger circle to embrace the whole disputed area. Even if there is no New Testament theology, the thought of the New Testament is certainly moving in the direction of theology, and its first efforts in that direction are profoundly interesting as well as of profound importance for the whole later development. Much of the thought of the New Testament is concerned with the interpretation of the Old. Much of it is, we might say, artistic rather than speculative —as the New Testament writers search through the Old Testament for answers to their questions, and come upon "Christ in the Old Testament" in most unexpected places.

The quotations from the New Testament are usually from the Revised Standard Version, though I have not hesitated to use other versions or to make my own translation. After all, the New Testament is a Greek book, and no English version can do more than approximate its original meaning. Some verses and passages are cited more than once. Such repetition was unavoidable. I have not attempted to force each verse of the New Testament into a neat pigeonhole of classification. Some words, verses, and passages are keys to whole areas of thought—or rather, they are like revolving beacons which throw a great shaft of light in all directions and illuminate many surrounding areas. Or, to change the figure once more, the map is not like a jigsaw puzzle which requires only to be fitted together without remainder; in-

5

stead, we have a series of spot maps, which always show some of the surrounding territory. They must do so, if they are to have meaning and value, but the consequence is a certain amount of overlapping when we lay them down side by side. Such a text as our Lord's saying, "If I by the finger of God . . . ," has a relevance to a dozen different aspects of his teaching, and to the early church's view of the kingdom of God, and to Christology, and to the doctrine of the Spirit, and so on. The repetition of this text is inevitable if we are to study it in these various relations. As we shall see, there are a number of such texts, each with an important significance for more than one subject of New Testament thought.

I wish to thank the editor of *Christendom* for permission to reprint the substance of an article which appeared in Volume IV (1939), Number 4, on "The Significance of Divergence and Growth in the New Testament." This article forms the basis of Chapter III in the present book.

F. C. G.

Contents

CONTENTS

I

The General Pattern

THE thought of the New Testament is religious, from beginning to end. There are no "secular" books in the New Testament canon, as there are in the Old Testament (Ruth, Song of Solomon, Esther, for example—though these books have a religious-nationalistic relevance), nor are there any secular passages in the New Testament books. A high seriousness pervades the whole volume, a solemnity of tone, an austere beauty of religious devotion, which, by a purely literary test, is rarely reached elsewhere in the world's religious literature.

At the same time it is a realm of thought which is in closest relation to human life. The characters are as completely human as those of the Old Testament; even the divine character which dominates the whole is still human—the evangelists lay special emphasis upon this feature. Luke especially stresses it: he represents Jesus as friendly, human, sympathetic, a model religious character, and an approachable human teacher, albeit divine. Matthew does the same, though more formally. So does Mark. John, whose Christology is the highest in the Gospels, nevertheless goes further than the others in emphasizing the human limitations under which the incarnate Son of God was content to live; for John was faced with the perilous theory of Docetic Gnosticism—that Jesus was not really man but a phantom, a divine being whose "flesh" was only a thin veil which he laid aside before the first nail was driven into the cross. The early Christian religion was plowed deep into history. It was no self-sufficient metaphysical system (like Hinduism or Neo-Platonism) seeking for a point of contact with human life, for a demonstration of its truth on the level of ordinary experience —like a stratoliner cruising aloft until the opening comes for a perfect three-point landing. Early Christian thought grew out of early Christian experience, but that experience was not "secular" or scientific. It was a religious experience, and it followed the pattern of religious experience already created by a particular, specific religion.

Ancient Judaism with its sacred book, the Old Testament, and with its pattern of received ideas, aspirations, thoughts, prayers, ethical and religious norms, and its religious vocabulary, was the matrix within which primitive Christianity took form. Or, as a better figure, it was the old olive tree into which the new branch was grafted—though Paul, who invented this figure, recognized that the process was "contrary to nature" (Rom. 11:24). Not only Palestinian Judaism, which is the appropriate, and the only appropriate, historical background for the interpretation of the life and teaching of Jesus, but also Diaspora Judaism provided this indispensable pattern—Diaspora Judaism, without which Paul is an inexplicable figure in history, without which the swift and steady expansion, the vocabulary, polity, organization, ministry and prayers, and the very literature of early Gentile Christianity cannot be accounted for. Beyond the borders of Judaism, but already influential within the synagogues of the Diaspora, lay the whole wide realm of Hellenistic religious thought and experience, and this too shared in providing the pattern of religious thought for the early church. It was not just the mystery religions, and not even mainly the mystery religions—the period of their widespread *floruit* came later, in any event—but the ordinary everyday piety of earnest "god-seekers" throughout the Greco-Roman world. These people likewise had an inherited, age-old, but now somewhat re-oriented and re-emphasized pattern of religious thought, and this too helped to provide the medium for the expression of early Christianity. It was part of what the Greek fathers called the divine "preparation for the gospel" in Hebrew and Jewish religion, Greek philosophy, and Roman law. Only, the contributions were all religious. The philosophy which influenced early Christianity was religious philosophy, and the Roman contribution was not so much law—at first—as it was a modification of the Hellenic heritage of religious thought and philosophy under the stress of conditions prevailing after the establishment of the empire.

But among all these antecedent and preparatory stages and elements in the preliminary pattern, it was the Old Testament which exercised the greatest influence. From the first, tension existed between church and synagogue, with the result that the Christians appealed from empirical Judaism to ideal Judaism, from the existing synagogue, temple, sanhedrin, or body of scribal teaching to what the Law and the prophets had said. An interpretation of the Old Testament was therefore indispensable from the start. Even while they were engaged in taking over the Bible of Diaspora Judaism, the Septuagint translation of the Old Testament, and adapting synagogue prayers and even the synagogue type of ministry and organization, the Christians—who looked upon themselves, at least in many circles, as the true Israel—appealed to a higher and truer interpretation of the Old Testament than was common in orthodox Jewish circles. The earliest type of Christianity was a modified Judaism, Judaism with a new orientation and emphasis; only, unlike other movements of reform within Judaism both before and since, what resulted in the end was not something that could still be called Judaism, but a *nova res,* to which Judaism was thought to be only preliminary and preparatory. The gospel—that is, Christianity—was the true "fulfillment" of the old religion, of the Law and the prophets, all of which had looked forward to Christ. Hence the Old Testament really belonged to the Christians; the Jewish claim to it had been forfeited or had lapsed. This is a strange phenomenon in the history of religion, not without parallels—as in Zoroastrianism, Manichaeism, the sects of Islam, and elsewhere—but nowhere with such far-reaching consequences. A wholly new religion claimed to be the old fulfilled—continued and completed. The scriptures of the old religion were simply taken over (taken away!) from the mother religion, and interpreted in a new and different sense from that prevailing in the old faith.

There was considerable justification for the claim. We can say this without accusing first-century Judaism of having perverted the religion of the Old Testament and grown sterile, formalistic, and moribund. The line of development followed by first-century Judaism was still the old line of national cult; the line followed by Christianity was the critical, prophetic one, for which the national cult was of minor and passing importance. What emerged in Judaism, after the catastrophes of A.D. 70 and 135 when the Jewish state lay in ruins, was a survival of this old cultic, national religion, retaining as much as possible of the old forms, hoping still for a restoration when the full practice of the cultus would once more be possible, and adapting itself to the stern conditions of the second and following centuries. For primitive Christianity, on the other hand, the loss of the cultus had been anticipated. The destruction of the temple in the year 70 and of the entire city of Jerusalem in 135, accompanied by the total disappearance of a Jewish political state in Palestine—none of these dire events had any religious consequences for the Christians. By this time the majority of Christians were Gentiles anyway, but from the beginning the destruction of the temple and the eventual cessation of the sacrifices had been anticipated— Jesus himself had looked forward to this. It is far too simple an analysis to say that in Judaism the legalistic, cultic, nationalistic element triumphed, while in Christianity the prophetic, ethical, universalistic elements predominated. For the truth is, all these features or elements were to be found in both religions, and are still to be found in them. But the dependence of early Christianity upon the Old Testament (which is the point now under discussion) is obvious, ubiquitous, and indisputable. Christianity came into the world with a sacred book already provided; all it needed to do was interpret it—and supplement it with its own writings, the books of the New Testament.

The pattern of religious thought taken for granted in the New Testament is still that of the Old—with modifications. Quite distinctly from the patterns of other religions (Hinduism, for example, or Greek religion, or ancient Babylonian or Egyptian), the Old Testament pattern may be summed up briefly under a very few headings.

1. God, the creator of the world, has graciously revealed himself to man.
2. This revelation included the statement of what is required of man by God and of the blessings of obedience.
3. But man in his weakness and folly refused to respond and obey the divine revelation.
4. The natural consequence of disobedience is punishment—God "judges" mankind and punishes sin.
5. But because God is gracious and loving, his judgment is remedial— God restores and saves in the end, after man repents and turns from his sin.
6. The final salvation designed by God, the state of the individual and of the world, destined to be subject eventually to the divine reign, is to be

one of utmost bliss—whether upon this present earth, in a world transformed, or in a golden age to come.

The simple but dramatic stages of this pattern are presupposed throughout the Bible, in Old Testament and in New. The utter humanness of it, the understandable simplicity of its few but sequent steps (none of which may be omitted), the possibility of its further and wide amplification, the points at which supplemental ideas (for example, the covenant, or demonology, or messianism, or the atonement) may be inserted or attached, the way the pattern lends itself both to mystical interpretation (the drama of the private soul!) and to philosophical or theological elaboration (as by Augustine)—all this is clear from the subsequent history of Christian doctrine and may also be illustrated by parallel movements in Judaism (which had mystical and philosophical aspects, as well as the Talmudic expression). The pattern embraces past, present, and future, and implies a philosophy of history: God created the world and man and revealed himself, in the past; man sinned and suffers, and God judges and redeems, in the past and in the present; God judges and redeems and brings his salvation to pass, in the past, the present, and the future. Finally, it may be noted, the pattern is related to earlier religious beliefs than those of the Bible. It has affiliations with the religious conceptions and practices of mankind in many far-flung areas. Older writers on the history of religion, like Sabine Baring-Gould, pointed to the evidential value of this fact— the Bible is the fulfillment of the religious longings of all mankind. I think there is still a good deal to be said for this view. Christianity is not merely one religion among many, or the final religion in a long course of religious evolution; it is the fulfillment or realization of "the hopes and fears of all the years," of which the older faiths of mankind were the various and manifold expression. What Christianity "fulfills" is not merely the thought pattern of ancient religion, but the spiritual yearnings of which that pattern was the age-old symptom and manifestation.

Viewed outwardly, Christianity began with the preaching of one more village prophet, who arose among the *anawim* of Galilee and proclaimed the approaching end of the age and the establishment of the perfect reign of God upon earth. In spite of his crucifixion at the hands of the Romans the movement continued. His followers were convinced that he had risen from the dead as the glorified Messiah, who was about to hold the judgment and set up the divine reign in all its majesty. Deeper mystical meanings were found in his death and resurrection—especially his resurrection—as soon as the new faith spread beyond the borders of Palestine, or rather as soon as the Gentile or Hellenistic pattern of religious thought came to be applied to these events. It was chiefly Paul who gave to the new faith its new form, though the Hellenization of Christianity began even before Paul, indeed almost from the first preaching of the new faith in Jesus, the servant of God who had died for our sins and had been raised from the dead as Messiah and Lord.

That is one way in which the process may be viewed. But there are different levels from which the facts may be viewed—from which *any* facts, including facts of history, may be viewed. Judgments of value, as well as judgments of fact, are involved. For Christian faith this simple explanation of the rise of Christianity, true as far as it goes, does not go far enough. Behind the facts—or the "event" of Christ, as Professor John Knox says—was the act of the living God, revealing himself fully and finally to mankind, and effecting the redemption of man from sin. In Christ God was "reconciling the world to himself," as Paul said (II Cor. 5:19). Just as in the Old Testament the bare facts or events of history were more or less the same as those found elsewhere in the world's life—for example, God had called other nations from afar and settled them in their homelands, even as he had called the Israelites out of Egypt and located them in Palestine (Amos 9:7) —so in the New Testament it is not some startling difference between the gospel story and all others that gives it uniqueness, but its divine significance. God was using this method for purposes which men could at first sense only dimly, but its significance grew upon them as they contemplated the fact and began to see its relation to other facts, and found that somehow it was related to human sin and divine forgiveness, to the further realization of God's purposes for the world and the final coming of his kingdom.

From this point of view, then, the thought of the New Testament is essentially a continuation and further development of the thought of the Old Testament, with a new orientation and emphasis which were completely to distinguish it from the contemporary but divergent development of rabbinic Judaism. For a rounded view it is necessary to take into account the Old Testament thought on every point. The Old Testament is even more important than the apocalyptic literature, important as that is, though some scholars at the present time incline to rate the book of Enoch, for example, as more significant for the New Testament than anything in the old canonical scriptures. So true is this relation between the two Testaments that one might almost take a book on Old Testament theology and merely substitute New Testament references and illustrations for those which it cites. And the same is true of the apocryphal and apocalyptic books; they too are dependent upon the Old Testament, and much of their best thought is derived from reflection upon the old scripture. One thing is certain—the New Testament writers presuppose the Old Testament pattern of thought, phraseology, and conceptions a dozen times for every reference or allusion to apocalyptic. Even the apocalypse of John is far more dependent on the Old Testament than upon the "apocalyptic literature" of the period. This is not a popular view today, but from the religious and theological standpoint it will, I am confident, be confirmed ever more thoroughly as research proceeds. The exaggeration of apocalyptic in our day is due in part to the fact that it is a recent discovery. By another generation, perhaps, it will have fallen into proper perspective.

In brief, what we call New Testament theology is chiefly derived from the Old Testament as read and interpreted by the early Christians. The other factors, drawn from their own religious experience and their reflections upon it, affected the interpretation, not the data.

II

Is There a New Testament Theology?

1. *The Origin of the Term*

B IBLICAL theology was, in its origin, a product of "Protestant Scholasticism." It undertook to systematize the theological data of the Bible, which was the Protestant source of authority, as distinguished from the ecclesiastical system of dogma and theology which on the continent had reached its culmination, soon after the middle of the sixteenth century, in the Canons and Decrees of the Council of Trent (1564) and in the Roman Catechism (1566).

The basic assumption underlying biblical theology was the existence of a single consistent set of doctrines, either plainly stated or presupposed, in the scriptures as a whole—from Genesis to Revelation. God, who cannot lie (Heb. 6:18), the Holy Spirit, who never contradicts himself, was the guarantor of the truth of this whole system; the scriptural revelation was a unity, from beginning to end. Hence whatever in the scriptures might at first glance appear to be inconsistent or irrelevant must be studied more carefully. The old presuppositions of ancient Jewish (that is, rabbinic) biblicism were still assumed, as were its methods, logical, typological, allegorical, and so on. The early Protestant interpreters of scripture were as familiar with these methods, though they preferred a better one, as ever the rabbis, the church fathers, or the medieval schoolmen had been. The great principle of Augustine, "What is latent in the Old Testament is patent in the New," was universally recognized. Even in his own time, the formula was not unique or wholly original, except perhaps in the wording; it summed up the usual patristic method of interpretation. Naturally a kind of development was observed in the scriptures—nothing, of course, like our modern "evolution of religious ideas," but rather the slow schooling and education of the chosen people in preparation for the Coming One until finally the promise of the Law and the prophets of the Old Covenant was "fulfilled" in the full glory of the revelation and redemption in Christ and the inauguration of the New Covenant. At first the many words of prophet, seer, and lawgiver; at last the full and final One Word, which is Christ.

So large a part of this theory of interpretation—namely its central presupposition—was directly continuous with earlier patristic and medieval views that there may remain some doubt as to how consciously and purposefully biblical theology was set in opposition to the ecclesiastical system. Not in respect to its central affirmations, surely, but in respect to a second presupposition—that the Bible is complete in itself, apart from ecclesiastical tradition, and without any need for an authoritative external organ of interpretation. The *testimonium Spiritus sancti internum* was sufficient, without any need to rely upon creeds or decisions of councils, which only defined the teaching of scripture. This principle set the Bible free from its late entanglement with medieval, scholastic exegesis, much of it strained and artificial, some of it absurd and ridiculous. The way was thus cleared—though perhaps no one realized it at the time—for a more adequate historical and literary, as well as for a sounder theological, interpretation of the scriptures.

The earliest biblical theology was a theology of the Bible as a whole. It was several generations before "Old Testament theology" and "New Testament theology" were sharply distinguished—and even then the assumption continued to be made that each was still part of a larger whole (surely a sound enough view, as far as the New Testament is concerned). New Testament theology was simply "biblical theology of the New Testament," and so Bernhard Weiss entitled his great work. Only more adventurous spirits like Ferdinand Christian Baur, Willibald Beyschlag, and Heinrich Julius Holtzmann wrote on "New Testament theology" as an independent subject.

But even this final step in the nineteenth-century advance has been questioned since then. In the twentieth century we fully recognize the right of "New Testament religion" to a separate treatment—separate, that is, from "the religious development of the Old Testament." But a New Testament "theology"—that is the question! Everyone now recognizes that neither Old Testament nor New Testament contains a *systematic* theology. Systematic theological thinking was totally foreign to Hebrew religion, which was no philosophy, no product of a school. It was foreign likewise to ancient Judaism (despite rabbinic efforts at harmonization), and foreign also to early Christianity. For systematic theology is fundamentally philosophical, and in its organization of ideas works aprioristically, not inductively; its texts are proof-texts, adduced in support of—or to correct—the deductions drawn from axioms or the inferences made from first principles; its aim is to arrange truth *more geometrico* and with mathematical precision.

Not only the twentieth century but Protestant theology generally since the Reformation has been moving away from this conception of theology—especially since the end of the eighteenth century and the close of the era of "Protestant Scholasticism." Yet one may wonder if the pendulum has not swung too far, and if there is not really a greater unity in scripture, especially in the New Testament, than the atomistic, purely exegetical, purely historical interpretation of "New Testament religion" takes for granted. Certainly religious thinking presupposes some pattern or arrangement of ideas, some basic set of convictions, some more or less consistent outlook upon the world—and also a more or less logical sequence of thought. Hence a New Testament theology may be *implied,* though not stated in so many words, in the New Testament writings. The presupposed pattern of thought may not have been philosophical, as it was in increasing measure for the later development of Catholic theology, beginning with the apologists and the Alexandrines. More likely, as Ethelbert Stauffer assumes, it was found (at least primarily) in contemporary Jewish biblical interpretation, which was partly apocalyptic—though the influence, in some slight degree, of Platonic and even of Stoic patterns may be discerned in Hebrews and in Paul.

The logic is another matter. It was not the logic of the schools, but of immediate religious apprehension and inference, a logic of devotion and of piety, nurtured on the old Hebrew scriptures, now in Greek dress (the Septuagint), and of direct religious experience. As Johannes Weiss described Paul's theology as "a theology of conversion and of mission," so also was the theology of a large part of the remainder of the New Testament. It drew inferences from two sources, or rather from three: from the Old Testament, now freshly interpreted from a new point of view; from the history of recent events, which had supplied that point of view (the life, death, and resurrection of Christ, and the continuing activity of the Spirit); and from the ongoing religious experience (the new life in Christ) of the whole Christian community, shared in different ways and with various emphases by different individuals, faced with various problems. This logic was "dialectical," in the ancient sense. That is, it worked by way of question and answer, problem and solution, not aprioristically. Each question that arose received, as a rule, an answer—one answer or more. (Sometimes questions were asked for which no answer could be found, but in such cases they were often asked again, sometimes in a different form.) And as each answer was found, the center of thought or of interest moved forward, and new questions were asked, new answers sought—and found—in scripture, as a rule, or in the sayings of Jesus, or (in the latest stages of the New Testament) in the earlier apostolic writings, especially the letters of Paul. The progress of thought was like the game of dominoes, where each added block sets a new problem, inspires a new quest. Four matches four, but now a three must be matched by another three, or a five by a five, and so on. The logic of New Testament theology is the age-old logic of religion, with its insatiable, inspired demand to know, and not merely to feel, to relax, to be rapt to bliss on flowery beds of ease. Certainly this is the quest which Western religion has always set itself, even though a roomy enough place has often been found for mysticism, for transcendental, alogical devotion. And the New Testament, we cannot remind ourselves too often, is really a *Greek* book, a collection of small Greek books, the earliest surviving literature of *Gentile* Christianity.

2. *Incipient Theologies*

But to return, now, to the presupposed pattern of thought. There are, as a matter of fact, not merely one but more nearly a dozen distinguishable patterns in the New Testament. As the late Canon Burnett Hillman Streeter pointed out in his famous chapter on the "Rise of Christianity" in Volume XI of the *Cambridge Ancient History,* there are at least six or seven distinct panels or outlines of religious thinking—interpretations of the meaning of Christianity, incipient "theologies"—represented in the New Testament. One might suppose, then, that our problem is simple: first of all to distinguish these separate patterns, and then to arrange them in chronological sequence. The result will be a reasonably complete genetic account of the rise of Christian doctrine. But the problem is not that easy of solution. For one thing, the patterns overlap. John will share fifty per cent of Paul's view of redemption, and then go on with something new and unique, which throws Paul's whole scheme out of balance. Or the two longer Synoptics will take over Mark, but then add, each in its own way, sufficient additional material to give an entirely different resulting picture. Or Ephesians, or the Pastorals, will draw upon most of Paul's teaching, but give it an entirely new "slant," one that is appropriate to new scenes, new conditions and requirements. And the problem is not simple for still another reason. The data are too scanty, and are in fact far from complete. In order to write a satisfactory account of the rise of Christian doctrine we should need not only these 500-odd pages of the New Testament, but probably ten volumes more. And not only sermons, homilies, epistles, or gospels, but diaries, notebooks, records or memorabilia of the earliest preaching of the apostles (far more complete than in the opening chapters of Acts), and above all autobiographies—something like Wesley's voluminous *Journal* for the rise of Methodism, something like Luther's eighty-one volumes for the rise of Lutheranism, or Calvin's fifty-five volumes for the rise of Calvinism, or the fifty-five volumes of the Parker Society Library for the earliest period of Anglicanism.

Moreover, as a third reason for despairing of an adequate genetic account, we cannot be sure enough of the *terminus a quo*. It is customary to find this in the "messianic consciousness" of Jesus, and to derive all that followed from this one source. But even granting that he possessed such a consciousness (I myself would prefer a better term than "messianic" for it), what form did it take? There are reflections, even within the Gospels, of more than one type of Christology. It will not do simply to run them together and say that Jesus harmonized all these diverse tendencies within his own mind, and thought of himself alternately, or simultaneously, as Son of David, Son of Man, Messiah, Lord, Son of God, and so on. There are some views that are simply incompatible: the kingdom of God is either coming here on this earth or not; the Messiah is either "Prince of the House of David" or not; the Son of Man is either Ezekiel's lowly prophet, or Daniel's supernatural figure riding on the clouds, or the everyday Aramaic term meaning "this man" (that is, "I myself"), or something else—he cannot possibly be all four and more rolled in one. We really must take seriously Ernst Lohmeyer's distinction between the Lukan "Christos" of Judea and the South and the Marcan or Q "Son of Man" of Galilee and the North. It will not do to say "Son of Man–Messiah," for "Messiah" meant Israel's glorious future monarch who was expected to reign here upon this earth, while "Son of Man" meant (presumably) the wholly supernatural, wholly transcendent, heavenly figure coming from heaven to hold the last assize of men, angels, and demons. Traits and attributes sometimes got carried over from one to another, it is true, but the essential character of each was distinct; and it was only in later Christian thought and devotion, not in origin or in the common usage of words in Jewish Palestine, that the Messiah "fulfilled" all these descriptive titles— and more.

It may be said, of course, that if we grant that later Christian thought, even in the New Testament, identified all these terms, brought their deepest meanings together into one, and found the "fulfillment" of them all in Jesus of Nazareth, why could not he himself have done the same? Why should not the identification of the Suffering Servant of Isaiah 53 with the Son of Man of Daniel 7, for example, have existed in Jesus' own mind? But if that identification took place in Jesus' own mind, why is not the gospel tradition more unanimous and consistent on this point? Or if he "reinterpreted" all the prophetic "titles" of the Coming One, how could he continue to use them, or permit others to use them (especially his own disciples), without pointing out this fact of reinterpretation? A more reasonable view, it seems to me, is that the titles are partly later in date, partly the ascriptions or explanations made by other persons, and now survive in that selection from the extensive and varied body of early Christian tradition which got incorporated to some extent in the New Testament and in other early Christian writings. Back of the literature, back of the tradition, was a purely religious figure—no Mahdi, no Zealot, no self-deluded false Messiah, but one who lived so close to God that the full and final establishment of the reign of God appeared to him as already beginning ("realized eschatology"!), one who is much more adequately described in the language of the later creeds than in that derived from contemporary Palestinian apocalyptic. The earliest titles and categories were only temporary, in any case; before the New Testament itself was complete, they had been left behind, and the category of incarnation substituted in their place.

3. *Areas of Thought*

But if a genetic organization of the theological data is out of the question, there is another arrangement that is really more serviceable for the purposes of theology, an arrangement by "areas." Our standpoint, it scarcely need be remarked, is that of the New Testament as a whole, the finished product—a Greek book, as we have said, whose earlier sources cannot always be recovered and set in their true sequence or relationship of dependence. The areas are accordingly for the most part Hellenistic or Gentile, not Palestinian Jewish or Semitic. These areas of thought are partly chronological, no doubt, and partly geographical, but neither chronology nor geography provides the real clue to their significance. The area of religious thought addressed—and represented—in John, for example, with its peculiar problems, outlooks, questions and answers, was not necessarily later than the Synoptics, or even than Paul (contrary to the usual view!). Nor was it exclusively centered in Ephesus or Antioch or Alexandria, but was to be encountered wherever and whenever the peculiar world outlook, the quasi-philosophical or quasi-theosophical area of religious speculation and devotion represented by John came in contact with the Christian gospel. Its affiliations are far more intimate with the type of thought we find in the Hermetica, for example, than with that represented by the Mishnah, say, or even by Philo or by Fourth Maccabees—not to mention the tradition upon which the Synoptics are based. John's theological thinking is done in an area much closer to Gnosticism, which it repudiates, than to Paul or Second Peter or the Didache, not to mention the Apocalypse. Paul's theological area is much more nearly related to some type of partly Hellenized Diaspora Judaism (whose precise outlines we cannot entirely make out) than it is to rabbinic Palestinian Judaism—certainly the Palestinian Judaism of a century later with which we are far more familiar.

Thus primitive Christian theology or religious thought did not advance in a straight line, from Jesus to the primitive community to Paul to John, but moved out simultaneously in all directions. It is not like a series of telegraph poles or of piers in a bridge or of arches in an aqueduct, but is like the concentric ripples produced when a stone is dropped in a pool, or like the expanding universe described by modern astronomy. Or it is "like leaven which a woman took and hid in three measures of meal, till it was all leavened" (Matt. 13:33; Luke 13:21)—as Frank Vial explained it, the three measures were Jewish, Greek, and Roman! How distinct these different New Testament areas are is clear from the contrast in outlook of John and the Synoptics, for example. In Mark, Jesus' ministry is largely devoted to exorcism—he came to "destroy the works of the devil" (I John 3:8), as a later New Testament writer put it—but in John there are no demons. It is as if, according to John, all unclean spirits had fled from the presence of the Incarnate Logos, as the rising sun banishes the shades of night and melts away its miasmic exhalations—though the devil remains. Nor is there any trace of Jesus' exorcisms in Paul's echoes of the gospel tradition. Instead, there are the rebellious cosmic spirits, blind in their antagonism to God's Son and determined to destroy him; while back of all this, in Paul's thought, looms the dim outline of the elemental, perhaps precosmic revolt of those angels who, unlike the Son of God, did attempt to seize "equality with God."

It is the interpretation of Christology in terms of these antecedent and presupposed patterns, in different areas of primitive Christian thought, which sets the task for present-day New Testament theology. Again, it will not do to run all together and talk about "apocalyptic Judaism" or "Jewish apocalyptic" as if it were the *omnium gatherum* adequate to account for everything. The task requires more subtlety, patience, and skill than that! The same holds good for the ethics. "All who take the sword will perish by the sword" (Matt. 26:52) runs counter to "Sell your coat and buy a sword!" (cf. Luke 22:36). "I have not come to bring peace" (Matt. 10:34) cancels out "Blessed are the peace-makers" (Matt. 5:9). Some of these detached sayings simply cannot be understood or explained—as is often the case in traditional literature, not to mention plenty of cases in classical literature, and in English, where sometimes words, phrases, or whole passages have to be left without any explanation. Nor will it do to follow only one line and make Christology the clue to everything else; the ethical element is simply not to be left out of reckoning, nor is the institutional. It is one among several outstanding merits of Professor Millar Burrows' recent *Outline of Biblical Theology* that the author pays full attention to these other factors. Nor can the church, at least as ideal community, be ignored. If New Testament theology is basically Jewish theology with a change of emphasis and orientation, we must recall that for Judaism there were two foci to the ellipse—one God, and the covenant of God with his people.

4. *The Task Before Us*

New Testament theology, in brief, must be based upon a thorough study of history and exegesis, literary criticism and analysis, and sound textual criticism as well. It cannot stop with these, or merely gather up the results of these preliminary disciplines; it has its own new, fresh, distinctive task of correlation, insight, and interpretation. But it cannot dispense with these. Textual criticism, lexicography, exegesis, literary and historical criticism, source analysis, tradition criticism— all are indispensable. The student of New Testament theology must also understand religious psychology, especially the various types of religious experience to be met with in the Jewish and the Hellenistic world of the first two centuries. He must know ancient historiography before he presumes to pronounce upon the validity of the tradition underlying the Gospels, so different from our canons of historical tradition or writing, so inferior—and so superior. He must know what the world looked like in the first century: a flat earth, three or four thousand years old, but "old" at that, peopled with invisible spirits as well as with animals and men, and, above all, above the highest of three—or perhaps seven—hemispherical heavens, God and his angels, God not remote but in constant communication with earth, and ruling all by wisdom perfectly.

In a word, there *is* a New Testament theology, or perhaps several theologies, contiguous, partly overlapping—like the spheres or monads in certain pluralist philosophies. And it, or they, can be recovered, reconstructed, explained only by the utmost skill of the interpreter, who must take all New Testament learning for his province, and then, having done all, pray God to add to his equipment the indispensable gift of spiritual understanding and intuition. For the task is, first, last, and all the time, a task not so much of description as of interpretation. The New Testament is the most important book in the world. Its great variety, and even to some extent its divergence of thought, appeals to the most varied types of religious thought and aspiration, finds men where they live, and speaks to their condition. It is no collection of obscure and occult oracles, nor is it a set of rules and regulations for the religious life; yet it contains words of inexhaustible meaning—words whose full meaning has never yet been fully made out, for they are understood only by way of a similar profound experience. It also contains rules for everyday living which the simplest-minded can take to heart and put in practice. It contains no philosophy, yet it deals with and brings closer to us realities which every philosophy worthy of the name must take into account and attempt to deal with in adequate fashion. The task of the interpreter of New Testament thought, the New Testament theologian, will accordingly never be finished. It is a lifelong calling, but one that grows ever more rewarding as the years pass by.

The principles underlying or controlling the study of biblical theology are those already described. And the study can be carried further, as the New Testament was succeeded by the early fathers and apologists, the creeds and liturgies of the ancient Catholic church. Under the guidance of God the Holy Spirit, the doctrines and dogmas of the faith came to expression—as further questions came to be asked and answered, still under the control of scripture, history, and vital religious experience.

The chief danger implicit in biblical theology is the one pointed out at the beginning of this chapter. It is the danger of treating that body of thought which we find in the Bible as if it were unrelated to history and were somehow suspended in thin air. It is a defect of Karl Barth's theology, for example, that he does not really take history seriously, but severs the connection between things human and things divine—

too radically, it seems to me, to leave any basis for the Incarnation, and certainly in a way wholly foreign to the New Testament itself. After all, the New Testament is the church's book; and it is the church, not a printed volume of 500-odd pages, which is the repository of divine revelation. The danger of some Christian thinking may be an overemphasis upon the church, the institution, the living body through which the Bible came, but the opposite danger of pure biblicism is that the church may be minimized, and the Bible, especially the New Testament, treated as if it had suddenly come "out of the nowhere into the here"—without preparation, without warning, without any connection with or antecedents in the religious history of mankind, and without any psychological contacts with everyday religious life and thought. For this reason I myself earnestly hope that Anglicans, Lutherans, Calvinists, and others who share a "high" view of the church will take their part in the current revival of biblical theology, for we have something to contribute as well as to gain from the study.

III

The Meaning of Growth and Variety

1. *Unity in Diversity*

There are varieties of gifts, but the same Spirit: . . .
There are varieties of service, but the same Lord; . . .
There are varieties of working, but it is the same God
Who inspires them all in every one. (I Cor. 12:4-6.)

THIS Pauline statement of the doctrine of unity in diversity
ought to be inscribed as a motto over all our study of the New
Testament. It should point the final goal of every approach to the
sacred literature of our religion. But not in the traditional sense,
for as commonly applied the principle has too often emphasized unity
at the expense of a full recognition of diversity. Diversity has been
limited, one might say, to choice of language; aside from a superficial
difference of expression, Paul and the author of Hebrews, John and
the Synoptists, Peter and the editor of the Pastorals, the Apocalyptist
and the author of Acts were all made, in intention, to say the same
thing. *Multae terricolis linguae, coelestibus una.* All the writers of the
New Testament were assumed actually to speak the multiform language
of earth, but in thought, meaning, and intention to imply and suggest,
at least, the one language of heaven, the language of the Holy Spirit
whose voice was heard among them.

Such was the traditional view—unity in the midst of diversity—
and it is of course fundamentally true, though it may easily be exaggerated. There is real unity in the New Testament presentation of the
Christian religion under all its diversity, in its view of God, of his
revelation, of salvation, of the finality and absoluteness of Christ. As
contrasted with the Old Testament, and with the sacred writings of
some other religions, the New Testament has a marked unity and

homogeneity. It is the surviving literature of a distinct religious and ethical movement at a specific period in the world's history. Its subject matter, its technical religious terminology, its general outlook and expectation are all more or less the same throughout. As an inspired literature, and therefore inspiring, it is thus fitted to reach men in different circumstances, to speak to them at different levels of religious development, and to say what they need to hear in order to grasp the significance of its central message, the good news about God and what he has done in sending Jesus Christ. There is a real unity in the New Testament—we must never lose sight of that.

At the same time, the diversity is deeper and more important than was recognized in the traditional view. It is not limited to choice of language, as if the New Testament writers all meant the same thing but selected different words for saying it. The diversity involves some of the basic ideas of New Testament theology; the religious attitude, ethos, and approach of quite different groups; and also a variety in practice, in organization, and in types of Christian activity, which the studies of the past generation have made so clearly evident that no fair-minded student can ignore them. Unless he is obsessed by a preconceived theory, ecclesiastical or other, he will be compelled to reckon with this genuine and far-reaching diversity in the religion of the New Testament. It also includes New Testament ethics, both the basic theory and outlook of the Christian way of life and also the practical admonitions, standards, precepts, and tests of Christian behavior—though here too the fundamental unity is unmistakable and must not be ignored.

2. *Literary Variety*

First of all, the literature itself is diversified in type. There are religions that start with a purely oracular literature—the Quran is an example, the Hermetica another. But the New Testament oracles are enshrined in a collection of biographical narratives, anecdotes, letters, sermons, apocalyptic material, expositions of scripture, even some early liturgical matter. Much of the literature, apart from the letters, is traditional and was handed down orally for one, two, some of it for possibly three generations before taking written form. No doubt other early Christian literature was once in existence, even first-century literature; what we have in the New Testament is a survival and a selection. Moreover, the New Testament is not to be set off sharply from what went before and what followed. The earlier Jewish literature is indispensable for its interpretation, while certain second-century writings, some of them once included within its covers (even in the great fifth-century codices), are almost equally important—Clement, Hermas, the Didache, Barnabas, the Epistles of Ignatius. In brief, what marks off the New Testament is its quality and its contents; it is not distinguished by its form. Quality and content came gradually into general recognition as definitely superior to those of other related writings. The history of the canon, of the "canonization" of the New Testament books as sacred writings, is the history of the application of a pragmatic test of use by the church. These particular books were found to be supremely valuable for the purposes the church had in mind: edification, instruction, reading at public worship, the record of the origins of the Christian faith, and the combating of strange, erroneous, subversive doctrines such as those of the Gnostics. But, like the Old Testament, the New was full of human diversity. Its treasure was in "earthen vessels." It was no collection of unset jewels, no portfolio of timeless oracles, like Mohammed's sheaf of messages from heaven or the "Golden Sayings" of Pythagoras. The oracles were there—chiefly the sayings of the Lord, in the Gospels—but they were still in their human, historical setting, as Jesus had delivered them in the synagogues and on the hillsides of Galilee. That is perhaps the first thing that impresses us in the New Testament—its perfectly human mediation of the divine. Religion is not set off from the rest of life, which is thereby made secular and "worldly." Its variety is the many-faceted variety of life itself. And its supreme doctrine, the incarnation of the Word, is completely consonant with this principle.

3. *Theological Variety: Christology*

An equal variety is to be seen in the theology of the New Testament. It ranges all the way from the rigid Jewish messianism of parts of the Apocalypse of John, the "Little Apocalypse" embedded in Mark 13, and of passages in Paul's epistles to the Thessalonians, to the exalted Hellenistic mysticism of the Gospel of John and of the Epistles to the

Colossians and Ephesians. Between these extremes, one can make out other levels or stages, in which messianism is abandoned in principle though not in form, and where the "high" theology—or Christology —of the Pauline-Johannine type has not yet been reached. I refer to the Gospel of Luke and book of Acts. Indeed it would appear as if some of Luke's documents or sources of tradition (chiefly his gospel source, L) had not yet reached the out-and-out messianic Christology of the Synoptics as a whole. Jesus was "a prophet mighty in deed and word before God and all the people," who "went about doing good," and was unjustly put to death, whereupon "God exalted him at his right hand" as the appointed Messiah, the one chosen by God "to be judge of the living and the dead" (Luke 24:19; Acts 10:38; 5:31; 10:42; cf. 2:33). It was Mark, apparently (that is, whoever was responsible for the "form" of the gospel tradition as we have it in Mark), who took the crucial step of reading back Jesus' exaltation into his earthly life. If he was Messiah after his resurrection and exaltation, he must have been Messiah before, and in Mark we can see how the evangelic tradition is edited and revised to make this as clear and unmistakable as possible. The demons recognize him as divine; his exorcisms and other mighty works proclaim him as "the Son of God"; his disciples, or at least Peter, confess their faith in him as Messiah; the Voice on the Mount affirms his divine Sonship; Jesus identifies himself with "the Son of Man" in speaking to his disciples of his approaching sufferings, and before the high priest he makes the unequivocal claim; even the heathen centurion at the cross acknowledges him "a Son of God."

This Marcan Christology was a great step forward in the development of the New Testament doctrine of Christ; indeed, it was the step of crucial importance. It leaves the Christology of the primitive community definitely behind it—that reflected in L and the speeches of Acts 1-12. And it lays the foundation for the later development. Matthew, for example, only elaborates and underscores the Marcan emphasis and interpretation of the earthly life of Jesus, while combining with it his conception of Jesus as the New Lawgiver and Founder of the New Israel. In taking over Mark, Luke adopts this Christology, even though it does not harmonize with that of his own peculiar source, L. And John—John's Christology is simply incomprehensible as a historical phenomenon, apart from the interpretation of Jesus which the author of the Fourth Gospel (or the group he represents) found in earlier Gentile Christianity, in the "Son of God" Christology which is to be seen in Paul, Mark, Hebrews, and elsewhere.

Of course, a "Son of Man" Christology is also found in Q, the other great Synoptic source which supplied the non-Marcan material common to Matthew and Luke; but it is not interpreted in terms of Jesus' earthly life to the extent that it is in Mark. The Son of Man in Q is still the future judge coming on the clouds of heaven. Of course he is this in Mark also, but in Mark he has already walked and talked in Galilee, incognito, though recognized by only the exceptional few. Where this view is reflected in Q, it is the result of a parallel development to that in the Marcan tradition—parallel, or prior. For although Mark has probably been influenced either by the Pauline, or more probably the pre-Pauline, "common" Gentile interpretation of the Gospel, we can never go back to the view that Mark is only a biographical version of Paulinism. Mark seems to echo Q more than once, probably not as a document but, like his other traditions, for example the parables, as an oral collection of Jesus' sayings. And the identification of Jesus with the expected Son of Man is already evident in Q, in the sense that Jesus was not only destined to become the Son of Man at some future date, but was already identified with the Son of Man during his life upon earth. There are sayings in Q in which Jesus distinguishes between himself and this heavenly, supernatural being (e.g. Luke 12:8; 17:26); there are others in which he apparently identifies himself with this apocalyptic figure (e.g. Luke 6:22; 9:58; 11:30). The latter identification, we cannot help suspecting, is probably the result of Christian reformulation of the tradition. It is an example of "oral" editing of precisely the same kind as Matthew's "literary" editing of some of the sayings, where Jesus' first person singular becomes "the Son of Man" in either the first or the third person (e.g. Matt. 16:13). Where this transformation took place we cannot tell. The theory of Ernst Lohmeyer and Robert H. Lightfoot, that there were Galilean Christian communities as well as Judean and that these communities looked upon Galilee as the predestined land of revelation, the center of the future kingdom, seems quite probable. Moreover, the emphasis upon the Son of Man Christology in Matthew, which is probably a North Palestinian or Syrian writing, and the undoubted location of the Parables of Enoch in the North likewise point in this direction. Mark's traditions are mainly Palestinian, though the Gospel itself is no doubt Roman in provenance; most likely, his traditions are mainly Galilean in origin, even including some of those to which he has given a setting in Judea or Jerusalem.

Nor is Paul to be explained without reference to those who "were in Christ before" him (Rom. 16:7). In the excitement of controversy Paul makes strong and sweeping assertions of his independence of the Jerusalem church authorities, but he does not say where he obtained his knowledge of the life and teaching of Jesus. It has sometimes been assumed that his knowledge came solely by vision, even including his account of the Last Supper, though his own language suggests quite the opposite—oral tradition. And much has been made of his refusal to know "Christ after the flesh" (II Cor. 5:16 K.J.V.), thanks to the mistaken older translations; what he said was that he no longer regarded Christ "from a human point of view" (R.S.V.). Perhaps Paul himself is in a measure responsible for this interpretation. But the researches of Frank C. Porter and others have made it clear that Paul had very definite information about the historical Jesus; one of the best summaries is to be found in Chapter III of Maurice Goguel's *Life of Jesus*. Paul knew much more about Jesus than the occasions of his letters or the exigencies of his controversies required him to set forth. Where then did he derive this knowledge? We must admit that here is one of the dark areas in New Testament history, about which we should like to know far more than we shall ever be able to discover. But the clear statement of the book of Acts that Paul was visited by Ananias, a disciple in Damascus, that he was cured of his blindness and was baptized and received the Holy Spirit and then remained for a time "with the disciples at Damascus" (Acts 9:17-19)—all this points in one direction, especially when taken in connection with the references to Arabia and Damascus in the Epistle to the Galatians (1:17) and in Second Corinthians (11:32-33).

But how did Christianity reach Damascus or "Arabia"? Was it taken thither by those who fled the persecution following the death of Stephen (Acts 8:1, 4; 11:19), even as it was taken to Samaria, Caesarea, Phoenicia, Cyprus, and Antioch? Or was this a result of the slower spread of the faith from more adjacent territory, for example from Galilee? We do not know, but I suspect it was the latter. And if so, I believe that Wilhelm Bousset and others are right in holding that the faith Paul embraced at Damascus and elaborated at Corinth already centered in a "high" messianic Christology. Jesus was the heavenly "Son of Man," and the only adequate equivalent of this title in Hellenistic religious terminology was *Kyrios,* Lord. In other words, the Christology with which Paul began his career as a believer was not that of L or even of Q, nor was it that of the speeches in "First" Acts (chs. 1–12); it was the more advanced Christology which lies at the basis of the Marcan formulation (or reformulation) of the traditions of Jesus' ministry of healing and teaching.

There is diversity, then, and growth in Christian doctrine and belief reflected throughout the New Testament, not only as a finished collection of early Christian writings and thus in a broad general sense, but specifically in respect to the cardinal doctrine of all, and from the very earliest period, and reflected in the very sources underlying the New Testament writings. There was growth in the oral tradition before ever an apostle or evangelist took pen in hand to write narrative or epistle.

4. *Theological Variety: Atonement and Grace*

We have taken the doctrine of Christ as the main illustration of this principle of diversity and growth; we might have taken other beliefs or doctrines—for example the Atonement, or the doctrine of Grace.

It is well known that Luke has no doctrine of the Atonement, or at best has a very undeveloped one. For example, he introduces the Ethiopian treasurer reading the fifty-third chapter of Isaiah, but never hints that the sufferings of the one "as a sheep led to the slaughter" were vicarious, or effective in the "removal of transgressions" (Acts 8:32-33). And he goes all the way around to avoid Mark's ransom saying (Mark 10:45), offering in its place the saying—which some think more probable—"I am among you as one who serves" (Luke 22:27). It is commonly supposed that Paul is the one who gives us the most fully articulated doctrine of the Atonement, but the truth seems to be that Christian theology owes far more, on this score, to the Epistle to the Hebrews than it does to Paul. Just what the debt of the author of

Hebrews is to Paul is not easily answered; certainly he owes something, but he owes perhaps more to the Alexandrian school of "mystical" exegesis of the Old Testament, not to Philo, perhaps, but to Philo's predecessors in Alexandria, and to the school he represented. But then Paul too owed something to this school, so that the sources of the doctrine are complicated here likewise.

There is variety, and growth, from the very outset. Indeed, variety and growth are complementary characteristics; you cannot have growth without a resulting variety, and you cannot have variation except as a product of growth. It is the full proof of the human and historical quality of our religion—the revelation comes in human terms and God is revealed in history, not in abstractions, not in dogmas, not in a set of infallible oracles. Though often rationalized in the course of Christian thinking and exposition, the doctrine of the Atonement is really rooted in human experience and is mystical to its very core. It represents the attempt to set forth in reasonable terms of the intellect, and with appeal to analogies found in law or in the ancient ritual of sacrifice or elsewhere, an experience of release from sin and of reconciliation to God which is essentially beyond our comprehension, ineffable, passing all understanding. As set forth in Hebrews, it is not merely the death of Christ that effects atonement for sin, but his whole life of obedience to the will of God, the sacrifice of his own will. He was made "perfect through suffering," and "learned obedience through what he suffered" (2:10; 5:8). *Virtus in infirmitate perficitur* ("my power is made perfect in weakness," II Cor. 12:9). Here is growth in insight, a vaster view of the purposes and the ways of God in dealing with man; but the experience that lies at the heart of the doctrine was unquestionably the Christian experience from the very beginning of the new movement. "Repent, and be baptized every one of you in the name of Jesus Christ for the forgiveness of your sins; and you shall receive the gift of the Holy Spirit" (Acts 2:38). But also, "Christ died for our sins in accordance with the scriptures" (I Cor. 15:3).

The doctrine of Grace, on the other hand, is undoubtedly Pauline. If Paul can claim any New Testament doctrine as specially his own, it is this—though he himself would be the last to claim a "Gospel according to Paul." Certainly the later expositors of the doctrine of Grace looked to Paul for their material and their authority—Augustine, Luther, and all their followers. But the emphasis upon Grace which we find in Paul is partly the result of his own agonizing intellectual and emotional struggle over the Law and its observance, and partly the result of his great effort to state clearly the Christian principle —as he understood it—of freedom from the burden and demands of the Law. Partly, also, he found it emphasized in the Old Testament (e.g. Ezek. 36:16; 37:28). Other men no doubt solved the problem in other ways. The author of Hebrews finds values in the Law perhaps unsuspected by Paul, though he is equally certain of its transitory nature. The author of James suffuses the whole conception with a new light; for him the very gospel is still "the royal law," "the law of liberty"! And Matthew—or his source M—retains the current Jewish estimate of the Law, but insists upon its supplementation and "fulfillment" in the gospel, so that the disciple of Jesus not only keeps the Law of Moses but more than keeps it (5:20), by a nobler Pharisaism than that of the scribes and Pharisees themselves, with a "hedge about the Law" which is "in spirit" (5:3) rather than in the letter.

And yet every Christian from the beginning knew the grace—the "graciousness," the "gracious favor"—of God; without that, salvation would have been impossible and unreal. Eternal life was the "free gift" of God, not something earned by merit, though "Strive to enter by the narrow door" was one form of Christian exhortation, and "This is eternal life, that they know thee . . . and Jesus Christ whom thou hast sent" was another statement of the same truth (Luke 13:24=Matt. 7:13; John 17:3). More strictly Pauline is the language of another late New Testament writer, though the terms already sound somewhat "catholic" and second-century: "When the goodness and loving kindness of God our Savior appeared, he saved us, not because of deeds done by us in righteousness, but in virtue of his own mercy, by the washing of regeneration and renewal in the Holy Spirit, which he poured out upon us richly through Jesus Christ our Savior, so that we might be justified by his grace and become heirs in hope of eternal life" (Tit. 3:4-7). And he adds, Let "those who have believed in God . . . be careful to apply themselves to good deeds" (vs. 8). Here the Pauline language is no longer metaphor, but technical theological terminology; indeed, for Paul himself the language of metaphor had soon become technical terminology—though Adolf Deissmann was undoubtedly correct in describing its origin as metaphor, one among several means which the powerful religious genius of the apostle seized upon for the purpose of making clear the full meaning of the new life in Christ.

5. *Variety in Organization and Practice*

There is variety likewise in the forms of organization, in the ministry, and in worship as reflected in the New Testament. The late Canon Streeter was certainly right in the main thesis of his book *The Primitive Church*. Instead of one universally recognized type of organization, instead of one most primitive type from which the rest were derived, what we see in the church of the first century, say from A.D. 30 to 130, is a number of quite different types—all the way from the primitive Palestinian, modeled probably on the synagogue or Jewish community organization, to the Hellenistic religious society in Corinth and other cities of the Aegean basin. In ministry these churches varied all the way from the "apostles and elders" type in the Jerusalem community through the various charismatic or "pneumatic" ministries to the "bishops and deacons" type found at Philippi and in the early second century. The Didache seems to picture a community with "prophets" as its settled clergy, and with "apostles" as "visiting missionaries"; at the end (15:2) the "bishops and deacons" are urged upon the faithful as if they were something new, and deserving as much recognition as the prophets received! In the Pastoral epistles we meet still another type of ministry; we may perhaps call it the "apostolic delegate" type. In the epistles of Ignatius the "monarchial" bishop makes his appearance; Ignatius is so ardent and indefatigable in urging his rights and claims that we suspect he cannot have been very long established in his supreme position of authority, even in his own church at Antioch.

All along the way, then, there is divergence and growth in the conception of the church and its organization and ministry, and in the actual practice of the church in administration and worship. What would a sober Palestinian Jewish Christian community have made of the wild "glossolalia" or speaking with tongues at Corinth? There were prophets in Palestine, of course, but we suspect that the spirit of the Jewish Christian prophet was more completely "subject" to the prophet (I Cor. 14:32) than was the case with the Corinthian enthusiast with his "tongues." Paul's stern rebuke, and the distinction he draws between "prophecy" and "tongues," and his clear preference of the former (I Cor. 12:1–14:30)—all this must reflect the attitude of Jewish sobriety and earnestness, the attitude we should expect to find more common in Palestine. And if the Didache may be cited in this connection (its liturgical passages are clearly modeled upon Jewish prayers) it is obvious that a certain sobriety and earnestness, gravity and decorum, and deep Jewish seriousness and reverence for the things of God characterize these men. Farther to the West, say in Corinth or, a few generations later, in Phrygia, it was not ever thus; the Hellenistic prophet was less restrained, his spirit less under control.

There is variety also in the motivation of the church's work. We are struck by the divergence found even within the pages of the same book. The Gospel of Matthew ends with the great commission, "Go therefore and make disciples of all nations, baptizing them . . . , teaching them to observe all that I have commanded you" (28:19-20); but it also contains the command, "Go nowhere among the Gentiles, and enter no town of the Samaritans" (10:5), which absolutely interdicts the Gentile mission of Paul—and of others before him, according to Acts. How can this contradiction be explained? The traditional explanation is that Jesus' words referred to the brief temporary mission of the disciples to their fellow Jews in Palestine during Jesus' own ministry and prior to his last journey to Jerusalem (cf. Matt. 10:6 and 15:24). But the saying later in the chapter (10:23) points away from this interpretation, "When they persecute you in one town, flee to the next; for truly . . . you will not have gone through all the towns of Israel, before the Son of Man comes." Throughout the mission discourse of Matthew, the author has in mind not the local, temporary mission during Jesus' lifetime, but the later mission of the church, after the resurrection and exaltation of the Lord—a point, incidentally, that Albert Schweitzer overlooked to the vitiating of his whole interpretation of the life of Jesus. Instead, therefore, of explaining this command as historical, from the lifetime of Jesus, it seems far better to regard it as derived from the document—or strand—M, which, as Streeter has shown, bears the marks of the Jerusalem controversy over the admission of Gentiles. Here is an oracle of some prophet, speaking in the name of the Lord, but speaking on the other side—perhaps using some saying from the current tradition of Jesus' words, but expanding it to cover, now, the mission of the church, and limiting it to Jewish towns. There was little enough time, anyway, and the Parousia would take place before "all the towns of Israel" had been evangelized! But if this be the source of the saying that forbids the Gentile mission, how did it ever get into the "universalistic" Gospel of Matthew? The answer is simple. The Gospel is a "traditional" book, not the free literary composition of a self-consistent author. The author—or editor— was one who, like the compilers and copyists of the Old Testament and of other sacred literatures, aimed to "gather up the fragments . . . , that nothing may be lost" (John 6:12); he was himself a "scribe who has been trained for the kingdom of heaven, . . . who brings out of his treasure what is new and what is old" (Matt. 13:52)—later prophetic interpretation as well as older and unquestionable tradition. Above all, as a Semitic compiler of religious tradition, he was very uncritical. This is fortunate; otherwise we should have had one man's poor selection rather than the rich and varied church tradition of his time.

6. The Permanent Significance of Growth and Divergence

We might illustrate the growth and divergence found in the New Testament from other angles—say from the ethical, where views range all the way from blind, furious hatred of Rome (e.g. Rev. 17–18) to the acknowledgment that the "powers that be are ordained of God" (Rom. 13:1 K.J.V.). In the latter passage Jesus' counsel, "Render to Caesar . . . and to God" (Mark 12:17), appears already to be taken as a blessing upon the two empires, thus anticipating Dante and Aquinas by twelve centuries, and Ambrose by three, Constantine by two, Melito of Sardis by one. Some of the New Testament ethics is frankly world-renouncing, apocalyptic, eschatological, either ascetic or at the least an interim ethic; but not all—other passages are as completely unmotivated by eschatology or by asceticism as anything in Epictetus or the Jewish wisdom literature. Both attitudes have influenced the transmission of Jesus' ethical teaching. On the one hand, it has been heightened, in the eschatological, otherworldly, ascetic direction (e.g. Matt. 5:21-26); on the other, it has been flattened into a prudential code—in places little more than rules of etiquette (e.g. Luke 14:7-11). Both tendencies—or rather all three (eschatological, ascetic, and prudential)—have been at work, and must be reckoned with, especially in connection with Jesus' so-called "social ethics." Was he a revolutionist, or an apocalyptist, or neither—or both?

But enough has been said to indicate the range of variation and the rapidity and vitality of the growth displayed in the New Testament. What is the significance of it all for us today? "The wind blows where it wills" (John 3:8); you hear its sound, but cannot tell whence it comes or whither it goes. And so it is with everyone "born of the Spirit." There is no confining the movements of the Spirit within the prescribed courses of conventional religion, nor does the New Testament provide us with a set of blueprints covering every future development of the Christian Church to the end of time. Of course it is not enough merely to claim that the Spirit "saith" so-and-so "unto the churches." The proof of the Spirit's guidance must be forthcoming in "the fruits of the Spirit," in the enrichment and extension and illumination of the church's life, and in the transformation of human motives, bringing every act and thought into subjection to the leadership and inspiration of Christ.

But surely we can now see that the New Testament is the record of a tremendous upsurging movement of spiritual vitality which "made all things new," took a fresh view of human life and its possibilities, broke "the power of sin in the flesh," set men free from despair, launched them upon a new course of spiritual discovery and adventure, and opened up wholly new avenues of moral and religious attainment. It is more than a record of the past. The New Testament is a book throbbing with present achievement and hope for the future. Even the life of Jesus and the stories of the early apostles are told, not as history, but from the vantage point of present reality. The Jesus of the Gospels is the one who now stands at the right hand of God; the Spirit outpoured in Jerusalem is still active in the church. The so-called "historical" books of the New Testament are quite as much documents of contemporary faith as they are records of that faith's antecedents and beginnings. Its history is "history of salvation" (*Heilsgeschichte*) —and the salvation is present and future, not merely past. Indeed, the New Testament might be called the testament or revelation of the Holy

Spirit, supplementing and bringing to its destined climax the testament or revelation of the Law and Prophets. With such a book in its hands, the church cannot fail to be adventurous, to "undertake great things for God, expect great things from God," and be prepared to see new things in our time, great and wonderful and unexpected, as the Spirit leads us on where he will. We must have tests and criteria of judgment, of course, as the New Testament itself warns us (Rom. 8:2-30; I John 4:1-6); but we must also expect variation, and seek for unity in the midst of diversity rather than for a dull and static uniformity. Above all, if we are to be true to the New Testament, we must have faith in the guiding Spirit of the Living God, who is still, and evermore, intimately concerned with human affairs, and has never—will never—abandon his church.

But what then of the unity of the New Testament, of its thought, its theology? If this was exaggerated in the past, when it was an axiom of biblical theology that a single unified system of thought was contained in the whole Bible, today the danger is that we may overemphasize the diversity by ignoring the unity. The fundamental outlook of the primitive church was certainly consistent and increasingly homogeneous —and yet this consistency and even homogeneity were compatible with considerable variety and even divergence. And so it has always been, wherever in Christianity—or in other religions—theological thinking has found a place. The fundamental doctrines of the Christian church are few in number; the "dogmas" (the officially defined doctrines) have been fewer still. The history of Christian doctrine and theology is a history of diversity and even of conflict, from the first century to the present. The faith is one; its intellectual expression and exposition—not just its language—are various and manifold. It could not well be otherwise, since theology is the result of rational thinking, or of philosophy, as it attempts to deal with the given data of revelation and of religious experience.

IV

The Scope of New Testament Thought

1. *Religious Thought and Theology*

THE title of this book reads "New Testament Thought," rather than "The Thought of the New Testament," and is meant to suggest that it is the thought rather than the history or the interpretation of our collection of sacred books which is the subject of study. It may seem an undue refinement, but the words "New Testament" in this phrase are meant to be descriptive; the stage or period in Christian theology here presented is that which is reflected in the New Testament. Other stages followed it, in the course of history. New Testament thought is Part I, or Book I, in every history of Christian doctrine, or perhaps is only an introduction to that first division of the history. In other words the choice of the title is meant to rule out the older view that "New Testament theology," as the second division of "biblical theology," is somehow final and complete in itself, and can be understood without reference either to what went before or to what followed after.

This does not mean a repudiation of the finality of the New Testament for Christian doctrine, as the canonical and authoritative collection of early Christian writings and as the source containing the data for Christian dogma. Theology is not identical with either dogma or doctrine, but is the statement of Christian teaching in terms of a thought-out structural relationship. As thus defined, theology is found in the New Testament in an early, inchoate, pristine state, not yet worked out in full co-ordination, system, and harmony. Theology is not divine revelation, nor is it even formal doctrine (that is, teaching, *didachê*), let alone officially defined and formulated dogma (which came much later). Instead, it is the human attempt to think out and to state clearly

43

the principles and presuppositions of Christian belief. As such it is a purely human and entirely individual process. A clear distinction can be drawn, for example, between the theology of Augustine, say, or of Calvin, or of Bishop Andrewes (or between Augustinianism, Calvinism, or Anglicanism) and the doctrine or teaching of the church in their time; as also between these theologies, or the current doctrine taught by the church, and the official dogmas of the great councils—the formal definitions set forth by ecclesiastical authority. An equally clear distinction can be drawn between, say, the theology of Thomas Aquinas (or any of the Schoolmen) and the commonly held doctrine or doctrines of the Western church at that time and later, and also between these and the official dogmas of the church set forth at Trent and elsewhere. It only leads to confusion to use the terms "theology," "doctrine," and "dogma" interchangeably, as if they were synonymous; they must be carefully distinguished and used accurately.

At the same time it must be recognized that this later terminology cannot be forced upon the New Testament. The dogmas of the church were as yet unofficial; the only "conciliar" pronouncement is the one in Acts 15, which is practical and moral rather than intellectual or creedal. The doctrine of the church was steadily increasing in extent, as the original *kerygma* (or proclamation of the gospel) became the settled *didachê* of the church's teachers and pastors and was enshrined in its growing liturgy, catechetical instruction, and the collection of sacred books. It might even be urged that there was as yet no theology at all, in the sense just defined; indeed some writers have stated categorically that there is no theology in the New Testament—that is no intellectually wrought-out co-ordination and systematization of doctrine in terms of current philosophy or the commonly accepted world view.

But we must not be rigorists, even though we try to speak accurately. There is certainly an increasing theological tendency observable in the New Testament. There is certainly a theology implicit in Paul's writings, in Hebrews, and in the Johannine literature, sometimes coming to clear expression, sometimes latent and presupposed. In fact, as we have seen, there are several theologies in the New Testament—ten or a dozen distinct patterns of Christian thought, as the common faith got itself expressed from different points of view and in relation to various intellectual or moral (practical) problems. We may hesitate to describe

Jesus' teaching as theological, but there was certainly a theology implicit in the thoughts and beliefs of the earliest Palestinian Jewish Christian community and in those of the early Gentile Christian communities (that is, in the scanty sources for the thought of these two all-important primitive groups), in Paul's letters, in the Synoptic Gospels (indeed, each writer had a more or less distinct theology), in the Epistle to the Hebrews, the Epistle of James, in the Pastorals, in Ephesians, in the Gospel and Epistles of John, in the Apocalypse, in the Petrine epistles, in Jude.

If we could distinguish them all, there might turn out to be eighteen or twenty different theologies reflected in the New Testament, theologies implicit or incipient, as various writers undertook to set forth the common faith in terms of their own understanding and interpretation of it. Yet all of them were dependent upon the one unique source of divine revelation which the New Testament reflects and presupposes. Our Christian sacred book is like a spectrum, spreading out a beam of pure white light into its various colors, or like life itself, which,

> like a dome of many-coloured glass,
> Stains the white radiance of eternity.

"The true light that enlightens every man was coming into the world" (John 1:9), and each in his own way reflected or transmitted that light. The theologies of the New Testament did not create that light, but only reflected it, refracted it, displayed it, as it spread abroad, each one bearing its "witness" to the light.

2. *The Unity of the New Testament*

The most significant thing is, of course, not the variety in New Testament theology, with each type to be studied in isolation, but (as we have seen) the consistency, the unity, the unity in and through variety, the consentient testimony, what might almost be called the "catholicity" of the New Testament. For its main body of doctrine is *kath' holon* or at least *di' holou,* found—or presupposed—everywhere, and held by all; and its theological expression contains few, if any, dissentient and incompatible elements.

This is the result, not of later conformation or selection (as by ruling out books or views incompatible with orthodoxy, when the canon was drawn up), but of loyalty and fidelity to a common origin in the apostolic proclamation of the gospel, and of participation in a common religious outlook rooted and nurtured in the Old Testament, in a common inheritance of thought and language from Judaism (chiefly in the Diaspora), and in a common hope and faith. The ominous threat of Gnosticism, which was destined to become the most serious danger to Christianity in the latter part of the second century, already looms upon the horizon of the New Testament, but it scarcely affects the unity or integrity of New Testament theology. The Gospel of John is probably anti-Gnostic, certainly anti-Docetic, and there are accents or echoes of the Christian reply to various forms of Gnosticism in Paul and even in Matthew; but the full battle with this multiform "theology of syncretism" (as Paul Wendland rightly described it) had not yet been joined in the New Testament period.

Hence in spite of the manifold variety in the thought of the New Testament we can continue to speak of a New Testament theology, a varied and yet on the whole a unified religious outlook, based upon a common faith and sharing a common world view, a common interpretation of the meaning of life. Its variety, as we have seen, was the natural and necessary expression of its vitality. Without being philosophical, it is nevertheless a philosophy; it at least presupposes a religious philosophy, and justifies Dean Inge's remark that our religion has been from the first "a philosophical religion," one that takes thinking seriously, and assumes that it matters profoundly what view one holds of God, of the world, and of human destiny. But this philosophy was by no means a system of speculation. Contrary to a widespread assumption, it is not possible to trace the "development" of Christianity or of Christian doctrine *ab initio et ab origine* in the New Testament. Instead, as we have seen, the New Testament presents us with a stage—or a group of related stages—already well on its way toward the "Catholicism" of the second century. It is already the literature of a "religion of redemption." The older evangelical view, which finds "the gospel" in the epistles of Paul, like the Catholic one, which identifies "the gospel" with the New Testament as a whole, is really sounder than the popular modern Protestant view which either distinguishes too sharply between the "religion" of Jesus and the "faith" of Paul, or else—as among conservatives—attempts to show that the main principles of Pauline Christianity were already set forth in the teaching of Jesus. But the religion of Jesus was Judaism—a high, distinctive, very individualistic kind of Judaism, echoing in many ways the thought of the prophets, but building upon their work, and going beyond it (Matt. 5:17). What, precisely, Jesus taught or thought upon many points in religious teaching can never be known—there are no available sources. But for the New Testament this does not greatly matter; the real significance of the "historical" Jesus lay not in what he taught but in what—or who—he was, and in what he did, or rather, in what God did through him.

Our standpoint, in the study of New Testament thought, is, as we have said, that of the finished product, the New Testament as a whole —a Greek book or collection of books dating chiefly from the latter half of the first and the early decades of the second century. (Few present-day scholars would date even the latest New Testament writing beyond A.D. 150.) In some instances we can, it is true, trace lines of development, or of interrelation: from Paul to the deutero-Pauline writings, or from Mark to Luke-Acts and to Matthew (not to John— as Percival Gardner-Smith has shown, John is not dependent upon the Synoptics—nor from Matthew to Luke or Luke to Matthew). In some cases we can trace back the connection between Paul and the primitive community, reading between his lines and drawing inferences as to what was original with him, what was shared with those "in Christ" before him, and what was common ground between him and other representatives of contemporary Gentile Christianity. Occasionally we can distinguish between the Synoptic or the Johannine "portrait" of Christ and the "Jesus of history," but this is only rarely, and with considerable difficulty, and largely by hypothesis. For New Testament thought, the Jesus of history is the Christ of faith; or rather, the other way around, the Christ of faith *is* the Jesus of history, the only "historical" Jesus the church knew or cared to know. The apostles and their companions, the missionaries and heralds of the gospel, the "ministers of the word," the earliest teachers and writers in the church were not historians but evangelists, preachers, propagandists, pastors. True, their aim was to make Christ known, yet not as a man who had lived some years ago in far-off Palestine, but as the Man by whom God

47

"will judge the world in righteousness" (Acts 17:31). The detailed events of his life upon earth, and even the details of his teaching, were not the subject of careful historical research. A general picture of his career sufficed (as outlined in the Christian *kerygma*) and could be adapted, varied, and supplemented as circumstance required. It is impossible to fit the data, even of the first three Gospels, into any satisfactory chronological scheme, while the Johannine data present insuperable difficulties, whether viewed in relation to those of the Synoptics or examined in isolation.

The same situation is found in the accounts of Jesus' teaching. Only a general outline of its main content is possible, and the divergence between the sources (for example between Q and Mark and John) is most remarkable. One has to choose between the various strands in the Gospels, and to recognize that something more than mere selection from a vast body of tradition has been at work. In John, for example, the teaching of Jesus has been completely restated—for the benefit of readers influenced by the incipient Docetism or Gnosticism of the late first or early second century. Much of the language used here is that of the heavenly, exalted Christ addressing his church in a new and quite non-Jewish environment, and only faint echoes of the old "Galilean accent" are heard from time to time. But the same holds true, in some degree, of the Synoptic account of Jesus' teaching; it has been selected and adapted to meet the needs of the church a generation or more after Jesus' lifetime—needs for propaganda, edification, even liturgy and catechesis.

This is not to say that the needs of the church *created* the tradition of Jesus' teaching. Instead, that tradition was gathered up and handed on—in many parts, in various places, in different ways, by many different persons—because it was normative, and was understood to be determinative for Christian teaching (*didachê*) and practice. Christian conduct, ideally viewed, was "life in accordance with the teachings and commandments of the Lord." But the teaching was not gathered up from a historical point of view or with a historical or philosophical motive, as Arrian put together Epictetus' discourses or Porphyry those of Plotinus. There was no attempt to give an exhaustive account of the "discourses" of Jesus, or even a complete and comprehensive account of his teaching. If we were to suppose that our salvation depended upon recovering the exact lineaments of the life and teaching of the "historical" Jesus, for purposes of a modern biography, let us say, or at least of a major article in some "Dictionary of Universal Biography," the outlook would be hopeless. Fortunately, neither the first-century church nor the ecumenical church in any age since has ever assumed that our salvation depends upon the historicity of every detail in the Gospels. A general view is all that is possible—or necessary. The books of the New Testament are all written "out of faith" and "to faith," or "through faith for faith" (cf. Rom. 1:17), and the Christian faith begins, not with a chapter or a volume of modern scientific biography, but with the revelation of God in Christ, the manifestation of his power, his wisdom, his goodness and love in the Man whom he has "appointed" to judge the living and the dead; "and of this he has given assurance to all men by raising him from the dead" (Acts 17:31).

3. *Limitations of the Historical View*

The problem of history is most important for any interpretation of New Testament thought, as it is for the interpretation of the New Testament and of primitive Christianity as a whole. It has become more serious in recent centuries, with the rise of modern historical research into the past, and especially as a consequence of the view that such research is an end in itself—once the records of the past have been accurately deciphered, this is all that needs be done about the matter. Expert modern historians can write as if history had no "meaning" or "pattern," never "repeats," and has no "lessons" to teach us, a view totally contrary to the one assumed in the Bible and throughout Christian theology. The influence of this view upon modern theology has been all the greater as a result of the "biblicism" which has characterized large areas of religious thought since the sixteenth century—since the decline of Scholasticism—in the West, especially within Protestantism. Here the assumption has been that the "truth" of the Bible was identical with its historical accuracy; if any part of the biblical revelation could be shown to be false (including dates and names and accurate detailed reporting of events), then, in Bishop Butler's famous words, "let scripture, in the name of God, be given up!" Earlier generations, with their allegorism and manifold "senses" of scripture, while not questioning the accuracy of the record, laid less stress upon it and made no such identification. But the sixteenth and especially the seventeenth century threw out allegorism and along with it much of the super-historical, artistic—and even some of the theological—interpretation of scripture current since the days of the Greek fathers. By the nineteenth century the theory had come full circle and was complete; theology became purely historical, and "historicism" (*Historismus*) triumphed over "metaphysics." This may be seen in the vast flood of nineteenth-century lives of Jesus, with their eager pursuit of a purely historical reconstruction of his career, his personality, and his teaching. They ended (though they did not cease to appear) in 1900, as Albert Schweitzer pointed out, face to face with the insoluble dilemma of thorough skepticism (Wilhelm Wrede's *Messianic Secret in the Gospels* appeared in 1901) or thoroughgoing eschatology (Schweitzer's own *Mystery of the Messiahship and the Passion in the Gospels* was also published in 1901). Since then fewer lives of Jesus have appeared—form criticism, on the one hand, now being content to study the tradition underlying the Gospels, and conservative scholarship, on the other, taking the Gospels as they are, without trying to write the biography of our Lord.

It is not to be hoped that we can ever come into possession of sufficient material to write a satisfactory life of Jesus. The best we can expect to do is to arrange the existing sources in as probable a historical order as is possible—though here the subjective element is inescapable —and to view them, not as a modern secular biographer would, but as the early church itself (to which we owe their preservation) viewed them, as the records of what Jesus "began to do and teach" during his earthly life (Acts 1:1). The "truth" of the gospel (Gal. 2:5) is not a mere accurate record of historical events, which could be interpreted in a dozen different ways or not at all, but is the meaning these events have for the salvation of men, for the coming of God's kingdom, for the fulfillment of all the purposes of God in creation, redemption, and "the glory that is to be." In a word, the truth of the gospel, as Martin Dibelius said, is *übergeschichtlich,* suprahistorical; not so much "beyond" history (after the end of this present age, when the past will come clear and fall into its true pattern) as "above" history, outside time and place, in the ever-present "now" of eternity—in the mind of God. As compared with such a view, which is the primitive Christian, our modern quest for accurate biography, and our refusal to credit what cannot be proved or documented by reliable sources, seems poor and barren—certainly from the religious standpoint. As Francis of Sales insisted, the only tense that matters for religion is the present tense. It is the urgent, imperative present, moving swiftly into the awe-inspiring future, that dominates all New Testament thinking and theology. In a word, New Testament thought or theology, from beginning to end, is eschatologically conditioned.

4. *Limitations of the Systematic View*

It is important at the same time to recognize that of purely philosophical or metaphysical theology, working with the "categories of the understanding" and arriving by a logical, inductive, or aprioristic method at adequate definitions of things divine, or moving on steadily from doctrine to doctrine in a systematic exposition—of this there is almost no trace in the New Testament. At the stage of Christian theology reflected in the New Testament the outlook was still practical and nonspeculative. The New Testament theology is deeply concerned with actions, attitudes, behavior, worship, the whole round of the moral and religious expression of Christian faith. The hope is centered upon the coming Kingdom of God, the Parousia of Christ as messianic Judge and Lord, and the approaching Day of Judgment. In such a situation there was little occasion or opportunity for theological speculation; the eschatological outlook stood in the way. Moreover, in part as a result of the church's Jewish inheritance, pure speculation made little headway in the first three or four generations; and when it did begin (in Gnosticism), the results were not encouraging. The early Christians (in spite of Justin!) were not a school of philosophers but a sect of devotees, of saints, a purely religious group. Hence the theology of the church during this period was anything but inductive or aprioristic, with logical solutions of all problems and a close-knit correlation of all doctrines; instead, as we have seen, it was dialectic, in the correct original sense of that much overused word.

Faith came first: faith in God the creator and sustainer of the universe; faith in Christ who revealed and represented God the creator;

faith in the salvation promised and effected by Christ—effected chiefly by his death upon the cross and by his resurrection from the dead. But at once questions arose: How can God, who is good, permit evil? Above all, how could he permit his Son to die on the cross? But if he purposed to set forth his Son to die, how had this mystery been kept secret? Why was not Jesus recognized as the Son of God? But he *was* so recognized; more than that, he had even been foretold as the one who was to suffer and die for the sins of his people. On the other hand, if his death was thus foretold in prophecy, how had Israel failed to recognize him, save only for a handful of disciples? At least Israel should have known, if not the nations of the world!

So it went. Each question that found an answer (a few were asked but never answered!) was followed in turn by another question or series of questions, to which the very answer had given rise. Instead of moving out logically and uniformly in all directions from a central affirmation of faith, instead of proceeding geometrically—like Spinoza's *Ethics*—from axioms to theorems to proofs and demonstrations built upon those that preceded, instead of any such systematic procedure, New Testament theology moves only in certain limited directions—though not at haphazard. As we have said above, the procedure is like a game of dominoes, and the illustration is still useful. There is a limited number of questions and answers matching each other, the new answer each time giving rise to new questions, and these in turn to new answers, as Christian thought explores the fresh field of religious experience, insight, and conviction opened up by divine revelation.

5. *The Importance of Scripture for New Testament Thought*

There is a further preliminary observation which it is important to make, and to bear in mind as we proceed with our study. It is closely related to and helps explain the two just put forward—the New Testament view of history, and the absence of speculative or metaphysical theology in the New Testament. There are really two foundations upon which New Testament theology rests, history (or tradition) and present experience. A third foundation must also be included, the Old Testament, interpreted now from the point of view of Christian faith and hope. We have already seen its importance in another connection; here too it is of paramount significance. It might be thought that the Old Testament belongs with history or tradition, as indeed it does; but it functioned in another way as well, for the Old Testament view of God, of creation, of man, of history, of sin, of salvation, and of human destiny acted as a catalytic agent in precipitating and crystallizing the ideas of the apostolic church. It not only preserved and carried over many of the major doctrines of Judaism, but helped to give form to the new ideas and doctrines that sprang fresh and unique out of Christian experience. It was not only during the earliest period, while the church was still a sect within Judaism, that this process took place; it continued throughout the whole New Testament period, and indeed for long thereafter—as Adolf Harnack clearly demonstrated in his *History of Dogma.*

Yet it is not enough to describe the early Christians as another "people of the Book" (the Old Testament). The history recorded in scripture was sacred history, the record of God's dealings with men, but it had not ended with the establishment of Judaism; its true culmination was the appearance of Christ, his death and resurrection, the inauguration of the New Age, the spread of the church, the continuous outpouring of the Spirit. The whole series of events which formed the distinctive Christian history and tradition, and which were still continuing as current history, was now steadily leading on, at long last, to the divine consummation of all human history, the Last Judgment, the general resurrection, the full realization of the Age to Come. Christian tradition was thus connected up explicitly with the long past of Israel, God's own "people"; but it was no isolated series of events in the past which this tradition recorded, for it led on without interruption into the contemporary scene, whose events were now simply moving forward to the culmination of the whole world history. Men were indeed living in "the latter days" foretold in prophecy; they were those "upon whom the end of the ages has come" (I Cor. 10:11; cf. Heb. 1:2).

Thus history and tradition, including both the ancient past of Israel —indeed the whole history of the world since its creation—and also the recent past of Christ's life, death, resurrection, and the spread of the church, were continuous with present experience and with the anticipated denouement in the near future. History or tradition taken alone becomes legalism, the palsied hand of the past (true mortmain!) restraining all fresh and independent growth of insight; experience taken alone becomes fanaticism, *Schwärmerei*—such is the general and consentient testimony of the world's religions. Primitive Christianity combined the two, and, owing much to the religious life and thought of Judaism, preserved a balance; it was born with a definite historical perspective, a specific philosophy of history, and at the same time it cherished its present experience of God as the vital and determinative principle in every relation of life.

6. *Religious Experience*

Thus neither a philosophy nor a historical tradition is the central factor in New Testament thought, neither Greek "wisdom" nor Jewish tradition (I Cor. 1:22) but *the new life in Christ*. "If any one is in Christ, he is a new creation" (II Cor. 5:17). Like the flood of light which flowed from the newly created sun (II Cor. 4:6), this life, originating in Christ or mediated by him (John 1:4), had come into the world (John 1:5), and behold, all things were new (Rev. 21:5). Here is to be found the new and unique principle of Christianity, which distinguished it from all human philosophies and all "traditions of men." The source lay in God himself. "Only God can reveal God," as Emil Brunner maintains, and the whole phenomenon of early Christianity—including its rich and varied religious experience, its reorientation of religious thought, its new concepts and its revitalizing of older ones, its explicit doctrines and its implicit theology—is the consequence of what the New Testament writers can think of only as a new and unique act of God. This was one more of his "mighty acts" like those of old, only now it is the mightiest of all, and final. God is already taking his "great power" and is about "to reign" (Rev. 11:17) finally and forever, and absolutely, over the world. God is known, not by human speculation, but through his self-revelation in deed and act. Goethe was right in his interpretation of the first chapters of Genesis and of John: *Im Anfang war die That*—"In the beginning was the Deed" (Faust I). New Testament theology is theology of revelation, of God's own self-manifestation to the world. The initiative is his, not man's. Every New Testament writer takes this for granted, and without question.

Again, New Testament theology—as contrasted with Greek "theology," which dealt with the nature of the gods, the origin and destiny of the soul and of the material world (purely speculative matters)— was concerned very largely with the fact, and to some extent (especially in Paul) with the problem, of *sin*. The reason for this is not, as some modern writers have assumed (especially in the heyday of "scientific" liberalism before the two world wars), that it was a survival from Judaism. Ancient Judaism was not, as a rule (except for two late first-century, *post bellum* apocalypses), greatly concerned with the problem. Nor is the reason the one advanced by certain other writers, that it reflected the all-pervasive influence of Paul, with his abnormal private spiritual experience, for Paul's influence was really not all-pervasive in primitive Christianity. Nor that it matched the ethos of surrounding Hellenistic religion in the first and second centuries, for this deep concern over sin existed long before the church came into close contact with Neo-Pythagorean, Orphic, or "mystery religion" ideas—which ideas, moreover, were not so much concerned with sin as with ignorance, or mortality, or the vile muck of matter which had contaminated the soul. Instead, the reason for this grave concern with sin, reflected in the early Christian literature, is that New Testament theology is fundamentally religious and not speculative, moral and not philosophical, and is centered upon the act of God in revelation and redemption. The chief obstacle in God's way, so to say, is not human ignorance or the "blind" matter of which the physical universe is composed; it is sin, both human and demonic. Sin is even viewed by some writers, for example by Paul, as cosmic in its origin and extent; its beginning long antedated the creation of man, when certain of the angels fell from their first estate, or when—in more "Hellenistic" terms—the cosmic rulers, the starry spirits set over various nations or over different provinces of the universe, revolted against the supreme authority of their Creator. All of human experience, all thought of the world as a whole or of the various orders in creation, was affected by the sense of sin which men discovered in the depths of their own inner consciousness. In the first century (and the same is true still) a deeply religious philosophy or theology like that reflected in the New Testament simply could not view sin with anything but the profoundest seriousness.

This grave outlook is not limited to Paul, or the Epistle to the Hebrews, or the Gospel of John; it is implicit in the teaching of Jesus and in his activities, not least in his ministry of healing and exorcism. "If it is by the finger of God that I cast out demons, then the Kingdom of God has come upon you" (Luke 11:20), for the demons were the "unclean spirits" who led men into sin and disobedience, and inspired that revolt against the reign of God which necessitated the work of redemption before God's kingdom could be fully established. Restoration to health was accompanied by the injunction, "Go, and sin no more" (cf. John 5:14).

It will not do to dismiss all this as "primitive superstition," for we cannot get very far in understanding the New Testament until we accustom ourselves to take seriously what the earliest Christians took seriously, and learn to see the world through their eyes. It is true that Paul lays no stress upon the exorcism of demons or the healing of the sick in Jesus' earthly ministry (he might well have done so, some writers hold, in such a chapter as I Cor. 15); but the great conflict between Christ and Sin, Death, and the disobedient, malevolent *Stoicheia* ("elemental spirits") of the cosmos—the conflict from which Christ emerged or shall emerge victorious (for the conflict is still going on)—is the dramatic pattern fundamental to Paul's whole theology. Nor will it do to caricature the New Testament theology as "hamartocentric" (sin-centered). It is genuinely Christocentric, or rather theocentric, but it is undeniably a theology of redemption. The revelation takes place not in thought or idea but in act. It is a manifestation of divine power, wisdom, goodness, and love, in which God himself naturally takes the sole initiative, and in the course of which the main obstacle in the way, sin, has to be removed, its force and influence crushed, its ill effects obliterated, and its surviving traces swept away. Only then can the reign of God come in its full power and glory, and the final purposes of God be completely realized.

It is this magnificent conception that lies at the very heart of New Testament theology. It is not pessimism (the "pessimistic world outlook of later antiquity" of which we hear so much) but utter realism, on the religious level. It is really optimism; for as it views the world situation, the case is not hopeless—something can be done about it. Something is being done about it; God himself has set moving the process that will eventually bring order once more out of chaos and restore his creation to its pristine state, when the Creator "saw everything that he had made, and behold, it was very good" (Gen. 1:31). Nay, even more than this, for a still greater glory shall be revealed when the Creator crowns his triumph with the coronation of his Son, the Redeemer (Phil. 2:9-11), or when the now enthroned Lord is seen.

As over against the religions of escape, current in the opening centuries of our era, there is no disguising the unique and unpredictable freshness of this upsurging confidence in divine power and goodness, in "the goodness and loving kindness of God our Savior" which had "appeared" (Tit. 3:4) in Jesus Christ and was still manifest in the movement which he had set going—which God had set in motion through him—in this sad and disillusioned world. Primitive Christianity took sin seriously, but that was not the last word. *God* took it seriously, and was doing something about it. And if God was engaged in the conflict, there could be no doubt of the outcome. What men could not do, in their impotence (the consequence of the very sin that infected them!), God would do, and was already doing, in Christ, to redeem and restore. It is this faith, and this faith-inspired hope or confidence, that throbs at the heart of every book of the New Testament.

7. A Theology in Transition

The theology of the New Testament is a theology in transition. One could probably maintain the view that vital theology is always engaged in this process, as each freshly won insight discovers new horizons, as each affirmation leads on to others. By the very necessity of being understood, religious thought has constantly to adapt itself to the changing milieu of the general intellectual outlook of men. No theological system continues long in one stay; a "final" theology inevitably gets left behind, after a generation or two. But the New Testament theology is far from final; the great systematizers—Origen, Augustine, John of Damascus, Thomas Aquinas, John Calvin—were not to be born until generations and centuries had elapsed. Nor had it attained more than the outlines of the relatively finished systems of Irenaeus and Tertullian. Nevertheless the transition represented by the New Testament was the greatest ever to take place in Christian history—a transition from the fundamentally Jewish outlook of the first disciples to that of the vast surrounding world of Greco-Roman thought, with its age-old inheritance of classical philosophy and its religious traditions of a wholly different order from those in Jewish Palestine. True, the transition was never completely made; the church never wholly abandoned its Jewish, Old Testament heritage. But the movement was already under way toward the compromise with Greco-Roman, late-classical, Hellenistic modes of thought which may be seen, for example, in the later Catholic conception of God as absolute, and of ethics as including the "law of nature" expounded by the Stoics.

In brief, the New Testament theology is fundamentally a Jewish theology whose center of gravity is being shifted, whose twin foci, to change the figure, of (a) monotheism and (b) the covenant with Israel are being changed for (a) monotheism (now conceived more classically and philosophically, less personally and "biblically") and (b) the church with its sacraments, ministry, and liturgy (in place of the old Israelite priesthood and sacrifices). True, once more, the transition was never complete—for the church never abandoned the living, personal God of the Bible for the "One," the Absolute, of the philosophers, the Supreme Idea of Plato, the Unmoved Mover of the Peripatetics, or the "Nature" of the more popular Stoics, nor did Christ ever become a mystery god, pure and simple. But the transition from Judaism to later Gentile Catholicism was none the less a genuine change in orientation or center of gravity, and carried with it a shift in loyalties. Take for example the great change that took place in the church's attitude toward the Mosaic Law—a change which was never wholly completed. It was the change from the Law, viewed as final and to be interpreted on "Christian" principles, to the frank abandonment of the Law, or of most of it, and the substitution in its place of an ethic based partly on the Sermon on the Mount and partly upon Stoic-Cynic standards. This process, curiously enough, was helped forward by Judaism itself, which in its far-flung western Diaspora had already created a religious-ethical vocabulary, Greek in origin but impregnated with Jewish ideas—a vocabulary and a set of religious concepts which the early Gentile church did not hesitate to take over and make its own.

8. *A Summary*

Thus the New Testament is primarily a book of religion, not of theology; yet a theology (one or more!) is certainly presupposed by it, as a rational co-ordination of the data of revelation and of religious experience. There is truth in the dictum that the Christian faith has been a "philosophical" faith from the beginning—the writers of the New Testament certainly "thought out" their religion. If we may speak of the "theology" of the Lake Poets, or of the early Greek philosophers, or of Tannaite Judaism, we may certainly speak of a theology of the New Testament. The Lake Poets were not theologians (Coleridge was one, more or less), and the ancient Jewish tannas were not dogmatists or *Systematiker;* but they thought about their religion, they formulated it in intellectual terms, up to a certain point, and they co-ordinated and interpreted its data as best they could. Now this New Testament theology is a theology in transition; it is a body of *Jewish* religious thought with a new emphasis, orientation, and center of gravity, but retaining as much as possible of the ancient and inherited language and concepts (via the Greek Old Testament, for the most part). Added to this were certain influences from the Greco-Roman world, influences which had already begun to affect Judaism, especially in the Diaspora, but which were destined to affect the church far more than the synagogue. The question is, How great was this influence? A generation ago, many scholars were prepared to attribute almost the whole of Gentile Christianity to the influence of Hellenistic religious thought and practice; today the tendency is to recognize the far greater importance of Judaism. Was Gnosticism already in the air when Christianity crossed the borders of Palestine and entered the broad world outside? Had it already begun to influence Judaism even before Christianity began? Was it, in fact, as Paul Wendland held, simply "the theology of syncretism"? These are among the important questions that confront the student of New Testament theology at the present time.

All that has been said thus far is preliminary to the real purpose of our study, which is to examine the specific thought out of which arose the great doctrines of Christianity. We can summarize it rather briefly in a few paragraphs which express the fundamental theses underlying all that is to follow:

1. New Testament theology was the theology of the growing Christian church, as reflected in the New Testament, not a finished product but a theology in process. Hence its variety and even divergence—the necessary condition of growth.

2. It was the theology—or the "religious thought"—at first, of a Christian Jewish group, which soon became overwhelmingly Gentile in its constituency. Hence the theology was a Christian Jewish theology in transition, steadily moving in the direction of Hellenistic (Greco-Roman) thought, and adopting to a considerable extent its presuppositions, terminology, and outlook.

3. But it never gave up the great heritage of the Jewish scriptures, though these were constantly reinterpreted from new points of view.

4. The fundamental importance of Christian experience, both for the reinterpretation of the Old Testament and for the formulation of new and specifically Christian views, must always be recognized. Worship and piety and the growing institutions of the church were central in importance, rather than a merely logical or ideological development of thought.

5. It is not possible to reconstruct the lines of advance from one position to another in full detail, for lack of sufficient documentary evidence. Instead, the various types of New Testament theology must be studied as reflections of different areas of thought, attitude, and practice.

6. Though Christology was central from the start, and became ever more important in early Christian doctrine (down through the patristic period), it was not the only center of importance for New Testament theology. Ethics and the growing institutional life were also fundamentally important.

7. Although the apocalyptic type of Jewish eschatology provided the earliest pattern or framework for theological thinking, this was gradually abandoned, and even before the New Testament period was over it had been set aside for a profounder and more philosophical pattern.

8. The antecedents of the various types of Christian thought represented in the New Testament (Pauline, Synoptic, Johannine, that of the Epistle to the Hebrews, the Pastorals, the Catholic epistles, even the Apocalypse) are not exclusively Jewish. Paul's antecedents are to be looked for in a type of Diaspora Judaism already influenced by

Hellenistic syncretism. "John's" antecedents include the logos philosophy current in Egypt and the Near East and reflected in such literature as the Hermetica, as well as in Philo and the Stoics. The Gospels are all of them Gentile-Christian books. Hebrews presupposes a school of thought somehow affiliated with Philo, but familiar with the Old Testament as a book read (in Greek) by Christians, rather than as the lectionary of the synagogue. The Apocalypse contains Jewish material, but also pagan—for example certain age-old Oriental myths now reinterpreted in a Christian sense.

9. The dominant, central tendency of the New Testament as a whole is Christological. It was the Pauline and Johannine types of thought which contributed most to the later evolution of Catholic dogma. For it was essentially the doctrine of Christ which distinguished Christianity both from Judaism and from the competing cults of "lords many and gods many" abroad in the Roman empire, from the time when Christianity first began its missionary propaganda and expansion until the official victory over paganism in the fourth century. It was this conflict with paganism (even more than the contest with Judaism) which forced the church to formulate its dogma of the God-Man, so sharply distinguished from conceptions of apotheosis (the imperial "Man-God"), of temporary epiphanies of savior-gods, of "divine men," of purely discarnate cult deities (Isis, Osiris, Dionysus, Mithra, and the rest). What was distinctive and unique about Christianity was seen to be inseparably bound up with the Incarnation, with the actual appearance of God upon earth, with the complete and wholly real and genuine assumption of human nature by the Son of God; and the importance of this fact was already beginning to be recognized before the New Testament was complete.

Since this book is only an introduction to New Testament thought, that is to say an introduction to its study, it is important to point out that our major aim must be a *total* view of the subject. It is not enough simply to arrive at the correct exegesis of a few key passages, or properly to appraise the views of two or three main types of New Testament thought. The early Christian religion was primarily a faith, and its theology was a faith in search of a satisfying intellectual expression, a *fides quaerens intellectum*. To that end it not only made use of religious concepts already at hand, but also created new ones. There was a freshness and vitality about this emergent new faith which cannot be accounted for by merely collecting analogies, parallels, and antecedents—important as these are for sound exegesis, whose aim is to ascertain what the New Testament writings meant when they were first written. There was also a homogeneity and unity in this early Christian faith amid all its diversity of expression, a uniqueness which cannot be explained as a synthesis of antecedent elements, Jewish, Hellenistic, Greco-Jewish, or Oriental-mystical. Hence the student must constantly try to find the terms, conceptions, or principles which set forth the master ideas or motives which bind together, correlate, and explain the rest. The conception of Christ, for example, must be one which will account for the range and variety of eschatological, metaphysical, and even moral ideas and attitudes, expressed not only in the plain prose of description or exhortation, but also in hymn, prayer, and liturgy—and likewise in personal devotion. Only so can a *total* view be obtained, adequate to comprehend the full range and ramifying development of early Christian thought in the various areas into which it entered and within which it freely moved.

V

Revelation and Scripture

1. *The Authority of a Divine Revelation*

WHAT does the New Testament have to say of its own authority as an inspired book? What conception or conceptions of revelation does it take for granted? In what ways is it assumed that divine revelation has taken place? The answer to these questions is not to be found in any one text or passage, but must be gathered from the collected early Christian writings as a whole.

It is assumed without question that the Old Testament is inspired—this view is shared by the early church with contemporary Judaism. Indeed, throughout the Hellenistic world at that time many ancient books were looked upon as oracular, as setting forth a deep or hidden wisdom which required special skill, training, or insight for their interpretation. It was even assumed that the more ancient a writing, or the more obscure, the more certain it was to contain hidden wisdom. The New Testament writers did not all take this extreme view of the Old Testament; certainly the interpretation of the Old which is generally taken for granted in the New is more historical, less pedantic than, let us say, either the Stoic allegorization of Homer or Philo's exegesis of the hidden sense of the Hebrew scriptures. But the fact of the inspiration of the Old Testament, and its source in divine revelation, is everywhere taken for granted in the New.

This led in the course of time to the view that the New Testament is equally inspired, equally based upon divine revelation. But the authors of the New Testament books were not, as a rule, consciously writing inspired works. And yet a distinction must be made—the words of the Lord (the sayings of Jesus) were from the first looked upon as inspired and absolutely authoritative. Not only do the Gospels so represent them, but Paul quotes and refers to them in this way. Moreover, the apostolic writers (especially Paul) on occasion speak with final authority; in deciding certain questions Paul is solemnly conscious of having the "mind of Christ" (I Cor. 2:16). The utterances of early Christian "prophets" probably belong in the same category. The possession of, or possession by, the Holy Spirit was sufficient guarantee of the authority and validity of the prophet's words. In a real sense New Testament prophecy was a continuation, or rather a revival, of the older Hebrew prophecy. Some scholars have thought that in the apocalyptic sections of the Gospels, as well as in the postresurrection sayings of Jesus and in the messages of the Spirit to the churches in the book of Revelation, we have the recorded utterances of some of these early Christian prophets. The authority with which an apostle orders his letter read to the congregation (Col. 4:16) is not necessarily of this kind; he speaks more with the pastoral or paternal authority of a bishop than with the direct and immediate voice of divine inspiration. Paul draws a clear distinction between his personal authority and what he writes upon the authority of the Lord (I Cor. 7:25).

Thus there exists a considerable variety in the view of inspiration as reflected in the various parts of the New Testament: (1) the Old Testament scriptures are inspired, and presumably infallible; (2) the words of Jesus are infallible; (3) the words of Christian prophets—probably including the apocalyptists—are directly inspired by the divine Spirit; (4) the quoted words of Jesus as remembered and interpreted by his representatives, together with legitimate inferences from and applications of those words, are also inspired; (5) in the latest parts of the New Testament the apostolic writings are beginning to be placed on a par with the sacred scriptures of the Old Testament, and are being read at public worship in addition to the selections from the Law and Prophets.

This means that, as the second-century apologists were not backward in affirming, the Christian revelation began, not in Jerusalem a few years earlier, nor yet in the villages of Galilee a few months earlier still, but ages ago. The Christian revelation took its origin in the days of the Hebrew patriarchs; indeed it could be traced back before Moses, before Abraham, practically to the beginning of the world. God had never left himself "without witness" (Acts 14:17) in any age, in any part of the world. Since God had been known from of old, and since God could be known only by making himself known, it followed that revelation, "at [many] times and in divers manners" (Heb. 1:1 K.J.V.), had been continuous since the time of man's creation. What Christians saw in the revelation in Christ was the culmination or "fulfillment" of a continuous process from the very beginning. Indeed they were led to stress the antiquity of the origin of the Christian revelation not only by its appeal to Gentiles in the Hellenistic world (for whom antiquity was a strong argument in favor of validity) but also by their own effort to present it as superior to Judaism; the religion of the Law was later in date than the original religion of promise. Paul had advanced this argument in his Epistle to the Galatians and elsewhere (the gospel is older and more all-embracing than Mosaism), and it is also found in the Epistle to the Hebrews (Melchizedek's priesthood is older and higher than Aaron's) and in John (e.g. 1:17). The authority of such a divine self-revelation, as old as creation and culminating finally in the life, death, and resurrection of God's own Son (Heb. 1:1-4), was absolute and universal (Heb. 2:2; 12:25; Gal. 3:19).

2. *Inspiration and Revelation*

But what is "inspiration"? "Holy men of God spake as they were moved by the Holy Ghost" (II Pet. 1:21 K.J.V.). This surely does not mean that every word which they uttered was inspired, but only the words spoken when they were "moved by the Holy Spirit." It may be inferred from this that the record, so far as it provides a setting for the words spoken, contains considerably more than the words which were actually inspired. Inspiration was occasional, not continuous. Thus the priests who gave decisions at the ancient oracles, or decided cases for which no other provision was made by law; or prophets moved to utterance in the name of God upon the occasion of great national or social crises, speakers for God and from the point of view of the divine judgment and purpose; or wise men in their teaching; or the sweet singers of Israel with their inspired songs of praise to God—these were all "holy men" of old. In the midst of their judging and deciding, their preaching and prophesying, their teaching and their singing, would come a divine word, a word of direct and immediate inspiration. They might themselves be aware of this, or it might be recognized only by others as inspired; in fact, some words were recognized as inspired only by posterity. The inspiration was occasional, not constant; and it is pure rabbinism and bibliolatry to claim that every word in the Bible is inspired —the Bible itself makes no such claim.

And not only holy men of *old,* for the New Testament is full of a sense of present inspiration—the ministry of Christ, the work of the apostles, the whole life of the church represented an "outpouring" of the divine Spirit. Hence inspiration included the present utterances of the Spirit. This was the theory, apparently, of the author of Acts, who locates the initial "outpouring" of the Spirit on the day of Pentecost; he shows that it was promised by Christ (and even earlier—in fact long ago—by God through the prophet Joel) and implies that it was followed by other and similar phenomena in the early "witness-bearing" church (Acts 2:1-36, 40-47; 4:31, etc.). Not only by the author of Acts, but by almost every New Testament writer, the "gift of the Spirit" (inspiration) is attributed to the Christian group, usually as the result of Christ's resurrection and exaltation (Acts 2:33; 10:45; Matt. 10:20; Luke 12:12; John 7:39; I John 3:24; Rom. 8 *passim;* Eph. 1:13, etc.).

The doctrine of inspiration goes a long way back in the history of religion, including Hebrew religion. The prophets of the Old Testament were descended from a long ancestry which reached back to the primitive diviners, seers, and *nebhiim* who were common among all the Semitic peoples, and were also to be found elsewhere in the ancient world. When these men fell into a trance, or when a strange mood of ecstasy and exaltation came over them, or when "the spirit came upon them," they uttered words not their own—that is, not their normal speech or conversation. The words uttered at such times were looked upon as "inspired," as coming from the spirit which had "come upon" or "entered" them. Not all such inspired words were good or true, for a "lying spirit" rather than a true one might come upon a prophet, deceiving him as well as his auditors. The psychological phenomena of false prophecy, both external and internal, were apparently identical with those of true. It was the ethical or religious content of the words uttered, and their confirmation or refutation by later events, which provided the criteria for distinguishing true prophecy from false. And the frequent falsity, or at least the uncertainty, perhaps even the triviality of the seer's or prophet's deliverances led one of the greatest of the Old Testament prophets, Amos, to refuse the title: "I was no prophet, neither was I a prophet's son; but . . . Jehovah took me from following the flock and . . . said unto me, Go, prophesy unto my people Israel" (Amos 7:14-15 A.S.V.). Here the prophet of Tekoa clearly distinguishes his own calling from that of the ordinary *nabhi* of the day. (The implied criticism of the diviner's trade is like that which some of the philosophers heaped upon the Greek *mantis,* as in Plato's *Euthyphro.*)

But the criteria for distinguishing between a true prophet's call and the claims of a false one were never satisfactorily established, not in the Old Testament, and not in the New. The existence of false prophets is still taken for granted in the New Testament, and even beyond the New Testament, in the Didache (11, 13) and later. For the prophet himself the test was one of certainty, resting on his own experience and reflecting its vividness, permanence, or compulsion. For others the tests were various: Was the man self-seeking? (Didache 11:8-12.) Did his words tally with the revelation contained in scripture? Was he one who spoke easy and comfortable words, reassuring his hearers with impossible promises in the face of doom? Did he say things like those which the great prophets of the past had foretold were to be spoken by the false prophets of the latter days? But none of these tests was satisfactory or decisive. The only real criterion was the test of time: Did his words come true in the end? But this required an afterview, from the vantage point of later events, perhaps even of later generations. And so the direct inspiration of the prophet—that is, of the man himself at the time of his utterance—came to be viewed as the inspiration of his *words,* written down by him or his disciples and perhaps "sealed up" for posterity to read (Isa. 8:16), when the prophecies would "come true."

In the New Testament, as in the later periods of Old Testament religion, there are both kinds of prophecy, oral and written. The theory of inspiration applied to *written* prophecy was much the same as that which was applied elsewhere in the ancient world, for example in Greece; it was the theory of verbal—oracular—inspiration. The "words" of the prophet were like the words of an oracle, such as the Pythia at Delphi, though they likewise required "exegesis," as even

Apollo's utterances had to be expounded by the professional "exegetes" attached to the shrine. At the same time this oracular view was widened to include other writings in the Old Testament. The Law was no longer a series of codes descended from the long past, but was looked upon as the "words" addressed by God to Moses (who was "the" prophet, par excellence, even for later Judaism—for example for Maimonides, in the twelfth century). They were accordingly viewed as inspired, even in the last and least detail. At the same time this view of the Law had a counter effect upon the interpretation of prophecy, and the prophet's words, even to the tiniest letter and corner of a consonant (Matt. 5:18), came to be viewed as law. (In its fullest sense Torah included the Prophets as well as the Pentateuch.) Other parts of the Old Testament were similarly viewed—the Psalms were also looked upon as inspired. In fact, so large a place in Hebrew and Jewish religion was occupied by the "words" of God—that is, by the concept of God's message to his people—that inspiration and revelation came in time to crowd aside the old and equally primitive concept of the relation to God through the cult. Not that the two were incompatible (as in much nineteenth-century interpretation of the Old Testament); even as late as John Hyrcanus the high priest is also a prophet, and so is Caiaphas in the Gospel of John (Josephus *War* I. 68-69=I. 2. 8; John 11:51).

But with the steady growth of an intellectual approach to religion—especially in later Judaism, which came to be a religion of "the Book" and found its highest exercise of piety in the study of scripture—revelation came to be viewed as "the imparting (by a mysterious and unspecified method) by God to man of a series of propositions of absolute truth and universal reference" (J. N. Sanders). This "propositional" view of revelation, growing out of the oracular, is also to be found in the New Testament, though the major view is still the one expounded by the prophets themselves, that God had revealed himself not only in words but in deeds, in his mighty acts in nature and in history—a view quite as strongly supported by some of the psalmists as by the prophets.

There are, accordingly, three views of revelation to be found in the New Testament, lying side by side—just as in the Old Testament:

1. God reveals himself in mighty acts, in nature (the creation of the world) and in history (the exodus of Israel from Egypt), not only in

the past but now once more and emphatically in the present—chiefly in the resurrection of Christ, which is the supreme "mighty act" of God in both nature and history and marks the definite beginning of the New Age, even as the redemption of Israel from Egypt had marked the inauguration of an age of special revelation long ago.

2. God reveals himself in words as well as deeds. John the Baptist's work ("the Baptism," Mark 11:30; Acts 10:37) was "from heaven"—that is, it had divine authorization, *exousia*. Jesus' own ministry was of equal authority (at least). His words were "with authority," "with power" (Mark 1:27), and it was therefore the duty of every Israelite, and of all men everywhere, to accept his teaching. Even the later apostolic message was "with authority," and the "signs that attended" its preaching (Mark 16:20) provided the evidence of divine authorization, for it was the Spirit who wrought the deeds and likewise uttered the words, through the media of the apostles and of "prophetic men" whom he inspired. These words were not merely "propositional" or informational, but mandatory, and were stated not in the indicative but in the imperative mood.

3. God reveals himself in written words as well as in the oral utterances of men inspired by him. Just as in some parts of the Old Testament the "word" of the Lord is almost hypostatized and has an independent, substantial existence apart from the divine Speaker, separated from him after being spoken (for example it does not "return" to him void—Isa. 45:23; 55:11), so in the New Testament the words of Christ have a similar independent existence. This is noticeable as early as Paul (Col. 3:16), but is especially marked in the two latest Gospels. In Matthew, Jesus' "words," whether written or oral—that is, repeated in the tradition—are almost a body of supplemental law. A Christian may either keep or not keep, do or not do, "confess" or be "ashamed" of Christ's words (Matt. 7:24, 26; 28:20a; cf. Mark 9:38), while the Lord's sayings introduced by the formula, "I say unto you" (especially in the Sermon on the Mount), have practically the force of a new and supplementary Torah. In John the words of Jesus are "spirit and life" (6:63b). It is not only their subject matter which provides new revelation; the very words themselves (John 15:3) are a revelation; they are the testimony of the Heavenly Witness during his sojourn

upon earth (3:11); they are the *logoi* of the divine Logos tabernacling among men and manifesting his glory to the world (2:11).

Already the Christian life is understood to be life in accordance with the sayings and commandments of the Lord, as in Matthew and the Didache, where the "words of the Lord" are not only the Old Testament words of the Lord—of *Adonai, YHWH*—but also the words of the Christian Lord, *Kyrios,* Christ. The distinction is not drawn, and both are equally authoritative. In John, which is even more "Hellenistic" in outlook, the words of Jesus have become more "propositional"—they are still imperative enough, but they are more didactic, and imply a system of facts and principles, inferences and insights, which we can scarcely refuse to call a "theology." Christ is *himself* the Light of the World, the Resurrection and the Life, and the Way, the Truth, and the Life, the Bread of Life, the Water of Life, and so on. He is the Judge at the last judgment, who already judges, even now; yet his judgment is not his own—the words which he has spoken judge men, he judges no man (John 12:48). All this paradoxical statement and counter-statement, affirmation and modification, is to be understood as an attempt to set forth the present meaning of Christ for the church and for the world; and in making this attempt the author views the person of Jesus and the words spoken by him as two distinct entities, two and yet one, separate and yet identical. It is evident that the words of Jesus are now a body of traditional (perhaps already written) sayings through which the later church, and the world, can come to know Christ and so become his disciples, and, though not having seen him, love him (I Pet. 1:8). The words of Christ are divine words, as truly the utterance of God as were the words spoken of old through Moses and all the prophets. And in them men have "eternal life" (John 6:68; 10:28), even as the Jews searched the scriptures in pursuit of the same end (5:39).

How men were to recognize the voice of God speaking to them through Law and Prophets in the Old Testament, or through the Lord and his apostles in the New, is not clearly stated in the New Testament. Presumably a life of responsiveness and obedience to the *already* revealed will of God would enable one to recognize and accept (obey) the new word when it came. "To him who has will more be given." (Mark 4:25.) But this carries the problem back to a very early stage in history and in the religious development of the individual. Israel's response at Sinai, when the Law was first proclaimed (Exod. 24:3), was viewed by all Jews as the acceptance of the divine Covenant and the beginning of the nation's special relationship to God. The Gentiles, not having the Law, were to have been taught by God's revelation in nature (Rom. 1:18-23) ; only, alas, they did not respond, but turned the truth of God into a lie, worshiping the creature rather than the Creator (Rom. 1:25) and plunging into the depths of idolatry, superstition, and vice, until God's wrath (judgment) upon them could no longer be delayed. But the presupposition, even of this somber and exaggerated view of paganism (perhaps borrowed from conventional Jewish polemics), is surely that the nations might have responded and obeyed, and thus have been led to the truth. Not only was it a common theory in Judaism that the "Noachian" precepts were binding upon all mankind, but it was the common Christian view that God had not left himself "without witness" anywhere in his world (Acts 10:35; 14:17; 17:22-37). This view was eventually formulated in the high doctrine of the Prologue to John, that "the true Light that enlightens every man" had all along been coming into the world in Christ (1:9). It was not another light than the light of conscience, or than that of the primordial self-revelation of God to the world, or than that which inspired the age-old quest of the nations for the true God (Acts 17:27) ; it was the very same light, only now fully and finally manifested in Christ (cf. Heb. 1:3). It may be argued that the outlook of Acts and of John is more favorable to paganism, or at least less severe, than what we find in Paul. This is probably so, for they are more "Hellenistic" in their general tone and attitude; nevertheless there are other texts in Luke-Acts and John which must be considered, texts which modify the apparently overfavorable view (e.g. Luke 7:4-5; 18:20; Acts 1:8; 15:19-21; 16:3; 14:18-19; John 4:22). But on the point now at issue it may be said that the New Testament generally takes for granted a capacity to know and obey God, and to respond to his revelation of himself, which revelation is equally binding upon Jews and upon Gentiles. The capacity carries with it an inescapable obligation. Those who refuse and disobey can only await the inevitable divine judgment—it will overtake them in the end.

How such responsibility was possible, how mankind could be held accountable for its rejection of the divine revelation if man's nature is wholly corrupt and alienated from God and incapable of obedience (as has been held in certain later types of Christian theology, and notably in one which is widely current today), the New Testament nowhere makes clear—for the simple reason that the New Testament does not accept the premise of total corruption. There were religious thinkers in the first century, especially among the apocalyptists (e.g. Fourth Ezra), who had pondered deeply and somberly over such statements as Gen. 6:5-7: "And Jehovah saw that the wickedness of man was great in the earth, and that every imagination of the thoughts of his heart was only evil continually. And it repented Jehovah that he had made man. . . ." Their conclusion was that human nature, per se, is utterly corrupt. There were thinkers among the Christians who shared their views—not only Paul, but others as well, such as the author of First John (see 5:19, "The whole world is in the power of the evil one"). But this was not the only view, and if Christian theology is to be based on the *consensus* of scripture, other views must also be taken into account (for example those cited above from Acts and John). In this case it turns out that there is *no* consensus, and the total corruption of human nature cannot be pressed as the uniform and consistent teaching of the New Testament. The "broader" view is likewise to be found in the Old Testament, where God is "loving unto every man, and his mercy is over all his works" (Ps. 145:9 B.C.P.), and where also he is "the confidence of all the ends of the earth, and of them that are afar off upon the sea" (Ps. 65:5). This is not to say that mankind by their own seeking could have found out God, or by their own strength could have obeyed his will. Instead, it is to recognize that God wills to make himself known to all men, to Ninevites and Egyptians as well as to Hebrews, and that his grace is illimitable, promising not only his favor, but his help. The Bible already points in the direction of a doctrine of "prevenient" grace—the grace available *before* the coming of specific revelation and of Christ the revealer and redeemer. In fact, apart from the logical detail and supporting argument of the later scholastic definition, that doctrine in principle only gathers up the clear indications of scripture, in both the Old Testament and the New.

It may be difficult for us to recover, in imagination, the outlook of the first century and to realize the full meaning of revelation as it was understood by the earliest Christians. But the effort must be made.

Our theology is naturally propositional; we have inherited from the ancient church fathers and the councils, and especially from the Schoolmen and from the Reformers who succeeded them, a conception of theology which demands accurate, exhaustive definition, and which insists that truth must be stated in the form of propositions—statements of fact and principle which can then be subjected to the fullest examination, attack, and defense by human logic. But theology of this kind did not exist among the early Christians. It was on its way, but it had not advanced, in the New Testament, beyond an inchoate and simple stage. Adolf Harnack was probably right when he said that theology in its proper sense began with the apologists, or when he conceded once, in conversation, that it began "when the first Greek was converted to Christianity." Theology is an intellectual process, and its ferment requires a certain infusion of the yeast of philosophy, or, to change the figure, the pearl requires the irritation of a hard grain of sand within the soft tissues of the oyster!

The New Testament is pre-eminently a book of religion, not of systematic theology; its intellectual outlook, its patterns of thought, its presuppositions (certainly in regard to inspiration and revelation), are still those of the Old Testament. It is full of *data* for theology, but those data are not yet systematized or cast in the mold of propositions, and the logic is still only the elementary dialectic, as we have already said, of question and answer, and of further question. The great concern of the New Testament is not orthodoxy of profession—though false professions are clearly repudiated (e.g. I Cor. 12:3; Matt. 7:21) —but repentance from sin, acceptance of the gospel, and obedient response to all that God had declared to be his will. The transition is beginning to take place in some of the later writings of the New Testament, such as John and First John ("This is his commandment, that we should believe in the name of his Son Jesus Christ and love one another"—I John 3:23), but the inevitable tension is also apparent—a command to believe is something very different from and quite beyond a command to obey, to do, or even to accept as authoritative. It was probably the stress of the times, and the impending conflict with Gnosticism, which explains the tension and the transition, as it also explains the whole second-century-and-later insistence upon orthodoxy of belief.

3. *The Inspiration of Scripture*

"All scripture is inspired by God and profitable for teaching, for reproof, for correction, and for training in righteousness, that the man of God may be complete, equipped for every good work" (II Tim. 3: 16-17). This translation is preferable to that of the American Standard Version, "Every scripture inspired of God is also profitable. . . ." For the aim of the passage is not to distinguish between inspired and uninspired scripture; that distinction has already been made (vs. 15, "the sacred writings which are able to instruct you for salvation through faith in Christ Jesus"). At the same time it is quite possible that the true reading of vs. 16 is preserved in the Clementine Vulgate; it is found in one old Latin manuscript (*f*), in the Peshito, and in Ambrosiaster, where the conjunction "and" is omitted: "All scripture, inspired by God, is profitable for teaching. . . ." The point of the statement is that the sacred scriptures, which Timothy has known from childhood, are sufficient both for his own instruction and for his work as a teacher and guide of others. These scriptures are of course the Old Testament, which the early church took over from Diaspora Judaism and read in the current Greek translation. Along with the book the church took over the methods of interpretation, though both the Greek-speaking church and the Diaspora synagogue were dependent upon methods of interpretation in use in Palestine.

The idea of a sacred book or literature, though foreign to classical Greek religion, was one which had steadily grown during the Hellenistic age. Not only the Neo-Pythagoreans, who revered the recorded (ostensibly) teaching of their founder, but even the Epicureans reverenced "the Book," which in their case contained the dicta of Epicurus—or sayings selected from his writings. A papyrus document of the second century refers to the sacred writings which it was a pious and responsible task to translate (*Oxyrhynchus Papyri* VI, 1381). The wisdom of Zoroaster, Orpheus, Hermes, and other legendary or semilegendary teachers was enshrined in writings, not always translated and not always made public. But none of these examples could compare with the sacred literature of the Hebrews, which possessed a far greater authority than Homer or Hesiod had ever enjoyed in the Greek world, and was far more widely known than any of the philosophical texts or scriptures of other Eastern religions. Both Jewish and early Christian apologists made much of this point, and also of the priority of the Hebrew Bible to all other collections of wisdom, of the great antiquity of the Mosaic writings, and of the inspired character of this collection, evident from the unquestioned "fulfillments" of its prophecies. As we have already observed, the Jews were by this time almost the "people of the Book," as Mohammed described them; and the early church, entering upon its inheritance, tended likewise to merit the description—though Christianity, throughout its history, has never become a religion of a book to the extent that both Judaism and Islam have been.

The passage quoted from Second Timothy is the most explicit statement of the doctrine of biblical inspiration to be found in the New Testament. But its view of inspiration is not more advanced than that of any other part of the volume, as an examination of the passages cited in a concordance (*s.v.* "scripture" and "written") will show. Everywhere it is taken for granted that what is written in scripture is the work of divine inspiration, and is therefore trustworthy, infallible, and inerrant. The scripture must be "fulfilled" (Luke 22:37). What was written there was "written for our instruction" (Rom 15:4; I Cor. 10:11). What is described or related in the Old Testament is unquestionably true. No New Testament writer would dream of questioning a statement contained in the Old Testament, though the exact manner or mode of its inspiration is nowhere stated explicitly. The statement in II Pet. 1:21 comes nearest to such a definition: "No prophecy ever came by the impulse of man, but men moved by the Holy Spirit spoke from God" (or, "holy men of God spoke"). But even this is no explanation of the *writing* of scripture. The writing was presumably the writing down of the spoken prophecies—as Isaiah's disciples treasured his utterances, and as Jeremiah wrote (and rewrote, with Baruch's help) the oracles of the Lord delivered by him. The Mosaic books were presumably written by Moses; the "earlier prophets" (histories) by the prophets themselves; the Psalms by David; the Hagiographa (the "writings") by various authors.

Under the circumstances it is all the more extraordinary that Jesus should criticize the Old Testament, and that the evangelic tradition should hand down his criticism. Like Philo, Jesus distinguished the original intention of God (the real Lawgiver) from the concessions to human weakness allowed by the earthly legislator. It is not, "For your hardness of heart *God* allowed" divorce, but, *"Moses* allowed" it. So the criticism, or rather the deepening, of the Law in the Sermon on the Mount is introduced by the phrase, "You have heard that it was said to the men of old" (Matt. 5:21, 33), where we might expect the statement, "God said," or "Moses said." The point is of course the contrast between the new and the old interpretation; according to Matthew (5: 17-20) Jesus had not the slightest intention of abrogating the Law, but meant to deepen and widen its application, thus "fulfilling" or completing it. He then proceeded to reinforce this deeper interpretation and wider application both with the authority of the original Lawgiver (God) and with his own messianic authority as well. For Matthew, Jesus is the "Second Moses," the true "Prophet" who was to arise and supplement the Law. Nevertheless, the reinterpretation implies a criticism not only of the current scribal exegesis but also of the Law itself, taken *verbatim et litteratim*. It is only the authority of Jesus, as conceived by those who handed down and formulated the tradition, which can account for the survival in early church tradition of his criticism and revision of the sacred Law. No one else—in that period—ever dreamed of criticizing it. Paul might reinterpret it or allegorize it, but he felt sure he was only unfolding the hidden sense of the original— though as a rule he uses the Greek translation. The saying in John, "You search the scriptures, because you think that in them you have eternal life; and it is they that bear witness to me" (5:39), reads like an early Christian apologetic statement (Christ is to be discovered through the Old Testament), though the words "you think that in them you have eternal life" are only a rough approximation of what the study of scripture meant to the Jews. (The "you think" is far too skeptical, or sarcastic, and it goes with the author's intolerance of Judaism.) It was not the *study* of the scriptures that guaranteed eternal life, but "he who does [the commandments] shall live by them" (Gal. 3:12; cf. Rom. 10:5; Luke 10:25-28).

The question has often been raised as to whether the early church viewed the scripture as possessing an authority in and by itself, apart from the church (that is, Israel, or the people of God, or the New Israel, the Christian church). The suggestion that it was either Israel or the church which guaranteed the scriptures and gave them their authority would have been as abhorrent to a first-century Christian as the notion that either Israel or the church had produced them—and that in spite of the fact that the "canon" was in each case the work of representative bodies of men.

We are not concerned with the full and final establishment of the Old Testament and New Testament canons—the former taking place about A.D. 100 at the Jewish Council at Jamnia, the latter by various steps and stages from the first collection of Paul's epistles to the Festal Letter of Athanasius in 367. Nor are we concerned with the various conciliar actions which preceded and followed that latter date. Our concern is with the first century and a half of our era—to about A.D. 150, the probable date of the latest New Testament book, Second Peter. During the earlier part of this period the accredited and authorized books of the Old Testament were generally recognized by Christians, as they had been by Jews even prior to the meeting at Jamnia. (There is no evidence, until much later, that the decisions at Jamnia had any influence upon Christian use of the Old Testament.) As for the books of the Apocrypha, they were undoubtedly read by the Christians; Paul seems to have been reading the Book of Wisdom shortly before writing his Epistle to the Romans, while the early Christian interpolations found in the Testaments of the Twelve Patriarchs, First Enoch, and other writings seem to show that the "Pseudepigrapha" were also read, and prized. But the whole idea of canonicity in this period—both the Jewish and the Christian idea of it—needs closer scrutiny. The process of selecting books fit for use in public worship, and the choice of those which were unquestionably inspired, was not to be effected by human authority, whether of rabbis or of bishops. It was a process of determining which books were *already* authenticated as divinely inspired, and then singling them out from the others, not of supporting by ecclesiastical authority a well-considered choice among the numerous good books in current circulation. For the Jews this meant deciding which books "defiled the hands" (Mishnah Yadaim 3:3-5), which books were sacred and could not be treated as common or secular. For the Christians it meant distinguishing those which were genuinely "apostolic" and inspired from those, usually pseudonymous, which claimed—but unfairly—a like authority. Yet even these criteria belong to the late second century, not to the first. As late as Hermas, or the Muratorian Fragment, or even Codex Sinaiticus in the fourth century, it was assumed that a postapostolic writing *might* be inspired and authentic, but only if it was a directly inspired prophecy addressed to the contemporary church.

Thus it was not the sacred society—Israel or the church—which gave authority to scripture, though there was certainly a close connection between the religious group and the scripture. God had given his people a Law, and had sent them prophets, and had raised up wise teachers among them, and had inspired the sweet singers of Israel, the psalmists. The scripture was not addressed to all the nations of the world, but to God's own people, who had heard his voice from Sinai and had promised him their entire obedience. Similarly the church looked upon the Gospels and the epistles as peculiarly its own sacred scripture, though with varying degrees of recognition (cf. II Pet. 3:16).

4. *The Canon of the New Testament*

The term "canon" means (among other things) a measure or rule; as applied to the Bible it means the list of recognized, authoritative books, authorized for use in public worship. Presumably this list includes the inspired books which contain the record of the divine self-revelation. An example of this use of the term may be seen in the thirty-nine "Articles of Religion" of the Anglican Church, where Article VI reads:

Holy Scripture containeth all things necessary to salvation: so that whatsoever is not read therein, nor may be proved thereby, is not to be required of any man, that it should be believed as an article of the Faith, or be thought requisite or necessary to salvation. In the name of the Holy Scripture we do understand those *canonical* Books of the Old and New Testament, of whose authority was never any doubt in the Church. [Then follows the list of thirty-eight books of the Old Testament—not thirty-nine, as Lamentations is presumably included with Jeremiah; Ezra and Nehemiah are given as First and Second Esdras.] And the other Books (as Hierome saith) the Church doth read for example of life and instruction of manners; but yet doth it not apply them to establish any doctrine; such as these following. [Then follows the list of fourteen Apocrypha; the phrase "such as these following" might be interpreted as permitting the use of still other books, for example the Testaments of the Twelve Patriarchs, or the

Epistle of Barnabas.] All the Books of the New Testament, as they are commonly received, we do receive, and account them *Canonical*.

Much debate has been occasioned by the use of the term "canon" in the church (its earliest use for a list of the books of scripture was apparently at the Council of Laodicea in A.D. 360). But the debate was unnecessary; the church's application of the term *kanôn* was simple and natural, since it was already in use in a similar sense by teachers of rhetoric and of philosophy in the Greco-Roman world. The sifting of the treasures of ancient literature, to which we owe those that have come down to us, affected the choice of the works which we know as the "classics." These were the works which were used in schools, and hence set the standard of taste and education. A list of such standard works which every student should know—the "great" books, from Homer down, with which all educated men were familiar—was called a *kanôn*, and the writings were looked upon as "canonical."

In the Hellenistic period the Alexandrian grammarians Aristophanes of Byzantium and Aristarchus of Samothrace drew up a list of pre-Alexandrian poets and prose writers which were to be read in schools. (Cf. Quintilian X. 1. 54: "Apollonius [of Rhodes, author of the *Argonautica*] was not included in the list drawn up by these critics, since neither Aristarchus nor Aristophanes would include a contemporary"; cf. I. 4. 3.) From the agreement between what Cicero says about the most worth-while books and authors in the fragments of his *Hortensius* (which dealt with education) and what Dionysius of Halicarnassus, Quintilian, and Dion of Prusa (*Orat.* xviii) say, it is evident that they were all indebted to this list. To these writers should also be added Petronius, *Satyricon* 5. It was the works of these canonical writers that provided the material for the observations upon which classical grammar was founded. Moreover, some of the lists themselves have survived and come down to us. J. A. Cramer published one which he discovered in the Bodleian Library, and Bernard de Montfaucon edited one which was found in the library of the Duc de Coislin (now in Paris). The older part of Montfaucon's list is as follows:

Five Epic Poets: Homer, Hesiod, Peisander, Panyassis, Antimachos;
Three Iambic Poets: Simonides, Archilochus, Hipponax;

Five Tragedians: Aeschylus, Sophocles, Euripides, Ion, Achaios;

Seven Poets of the Older Comedy: Epicharmus, Cratinus, Eupolis, Aristophanes, Pherecrates, Crates, Plato;

Of the Middle Comedy, two: Antiphanes, Alexis Thourios;

Of the Newer Comedy, five: Menander, Philippides, Diphilos, Philemon, Apollodorus;

Four Elegiac Poets: Callinus, Mimnermus, Philetas, Callimachus;

Nine Lyric Poets: Alcman, Alcaeus, Sappho, Stesichorus, Pindar, Bacchylides, Ibycus, Anacreon, Simonides;

Ten Orators: Demosthenes, Lysias, Hyperides, Isocrates, Aeschines, Lycurgus, Isaeus, Antiphon, Andocides, Deinarchus;

Ten Historians: Thucydides, Herodotus, Xenophon, Philistus, Theopompus, Ephorus, Anaximenes, Callisthenes, Hellanicus, Polybius.

The canon of the ten Attic orators does not, however, go back to the Alexandrian grammarians; it seems to have been drawn up by Caecilius of Calacte. The Egyptian papyri show clearly enough that all kinds of noncanonical works survived till late antiquity, but that the canonical writings were the most widely read and copied. However the enormous mass of Hellenistic literature in the field of science, which failed to meet the taste of the era of classicism, was compressed into compendia, lexica, and scholia. (See Wilhelm von Christ, *Geschichte der griechischen Litteratur* [5th ed., München, 1911], Vol. II, Pt. 1, pp. 21-22.)

The canon of the Old Testament was established, not by rule or decision of council, but by constant use in the synagogue—the Council at Jamnia only set the final seal of approval to the choice already made. It arose in three stages: the Pentateuch, the Prophets (including the "Earlier Prophets," the older historical books, and the "Later Prophets," those which we recognize as the works of the writing prophets), and the Writings (including the Psalms). The final decision as to which books belonged in this category and were to be viewed as sacred was, as we have said, not finally reached until about A.D. 100. Meanwhile, in the Greek-speaking Diaspora, chiefly at Alexandria, other books were in use, some of them translations from Hebrew, some of them original compositions in Greek; these were never adopted into the Jewish canon, which was limited to Hebrew and Aramaic writings, but were taken over by the Greek-speaking Christian church, and are to this day included in the Bible of the Roman and Eastern churches.

(There were still others, commonly referred to as the "Pseudepigrapha" —though many other books deserved the name!—which never got into any canon, Hebrew, Greek, or Latin.) It was as a still further supplement to the scriptures that the New Testament arose and was made canonical in the Christian church; it formed the Christian supplement to the Greek Old Testament (the Septuagint), which was the original Bible (*ta biblia,* "the books") of the Greek-speaking Christian church.

The importance of this well-known fact is sometimes overlooked. The New Testament canon did not arise independently, as a Christian "collection of sacred books," somewhat as other religions have produced and treasured their own peculiar scriptures, without reference to any other body of sacred literature. The New Testament presupposes the Old, every step of the way from the first writing down of gospel traditions or of apostolic letters to the finished treatises that crown the literature: the Epistle to the Hebrews, the Gospel of John, the great two-volumed historical apology contained in Luke-Acts, and the marvelous artistic-didactic work known as the Gospel of Matthew. No New Testament author imagined for a moment that he was writing a book which would someday be included among *ta biblia,* as part of the church's Bible. To be conscious of writing scripture is a serious handicap—as modern writers of gospels, epistles, and apocalypses ought to know! It was the simple and natural process of writing down what needed to be presented—a necessity which even the apocalyptist felt (Rev. 1:11)—or of writing when direct communication by speech was out of the question (I Cor. 11:34*b*), which led to the production of the New Testament. The later process of canonization was equally simple and natural. These books were no independent body of oracular literature, but the writings necessary for a full knowledge of the truth, for the proper interpretation of scripture, for acquaintance with the life and teaching of Christ, for "instruction in the faith," and for the full knowledge of salvation. But they did not form an independent collection of scripture; the Septuagint was the church's Bible, from the first, and these were added to it as its crown and completion. The much later distinction between "Old" Testament and "New" Testament, useful and valid as it is for many purposes, and for ordinary use today, has no place at all within the New Testament itself.

5. *Early Christian Exegesis of the Old Testament*

A religion with a sacred book (or books) cannot do without exegesis. As time goes on, the meaning of ancient scripture becomes obscure— words change their meaning, references to contemporary events are no longer recognized, the historical setting and relevance of a book or a passage is lost—and both learning and skill are required in order to ascertain the original significance. But the need for exegesis went beyond this natural requirement, in the early church. Among the Jews, and increasingly among the Christians as their religion became more literary, the scripture was looked upon as a divine revelation in which every "jot and tittle" had a meaning. It was a body of inspired books, and it could be studied as a collection of divine oracles; the whole truth lay behind every statement, and one uniform, consistent system of ideas or of doctrine was presupposed throughout. What God had declared to the later prophets had been in his mind from the beginning; the divine plan of history could be inferred from Genesis as well as from Isaiah or Daniel.

This view of the Old Testament was, as we have observed, an inheritance of the early church from Judaism, the main difference being that the early church read the Old Testament in Greek, not in Hebrew (except for a few Christians in Palestine). Along with the scripture itself the church also inherited the methods of exegesis which had been worked out in the Jewish schools. Except for Paul, in the first century, it is doubtful if much attention was paid to these rules until the time of Origen and the great biblical scholars of the third, fourth, and fifth centuries. But the influence of Jewish methods of interpretation upon Paul had been great enough to secure admission of their general principles and presuppositions in almost all early Christian study of scripture, especially since the Jewish methods of studying the Old Testament were matched, to a certain extent, by pagan study of Homer and other ancient writers. The seven rules of Hillel (early in the first century) had marked a beginning of scientific scriptural exegesis; the thirteen rules of Rabbi Ishmael were a further elaboration of these. The aim of these rules was to regulate the appeal from one text of scripture to another, and to insure that nothing would be added, nothing taken away, from the requirements laid down in the divine Torah. Especially in the Tannaite period, exegesis was severely practical and (contrary to the view popular in modern Christian circles!) nonallegorical. It was a far later period, that of the Zohar (thirteenth century), which summed up the four types of exegesis under the word *PRDS* (*paradise,* or "garden") :

P for *peshat,* "simple"—that is, the literal sense
R for *remez,* the search for suggestions contained in the text
D for *derush,* the familiar homiletic interpretation
S for *sôd,* the theosophical interpretation—that is, the uncovering of mysteries hidden beneath the letter

One might match this system with the principles laid down by Christian exegetes, for example Origen, or by the great Alexandrian allegorist Philo—though in both instances the fourth division (the search for theosophical wisdom) would be left without much to parallel it. But the same would likewise be true of first- or second-century Judaism; this theosophical or cabalistic type of Judaism was a much later development.

A most thorough study of rabbinic exegesis and a comparison of rabbinic and Pauline methods is to be found in Père Joseph Bonsirven's recent work *Exégèse rabbinique et exégèse paulinienne.* It was characteristic of the rabbis, he shows, that their major interest was legal; that they had a profound knowledge of the letter of Old Testament scripture; that they viewed the oral law as on a par with the written and therefore turned naturally from the oral to the written for a confirmation of views already established; that their view of scripture was atomistic—every verse, every phrase, every single word could stand by itself, as an independent oracle or medium of revelation; that to their skill as jurists in finding support in scripture for principles or decisions already arrived at was added their fertility of imagination as haggadists and popular preachers. It was this defect of their good qualities—their excessively dialectical method, appropriate to the jurist and the casuist concerned with *halakah,* and their unrestrained fancy in haggadic "expositions"—which was their chief limitation and stood in the way of any genuinely historical interpretation of the Old Testament. For them everything in the Old Testament centered in Moses or Abraham, the election of Israel, the covenant, the Law, or the temple —matters which were of first importance to these religious lawyers.

(Parallels can easily be found under modern conditions—for example clergymen who preach nothing but church dogma and the seven sacraments and tend to find these subjects reflected—or assumed—everywhere in scripture, or the "evangelistic" type of preacher who sees nothing in scripture but the "message of the cross," or the gospel of "sin and salvation.") Thus literalism, legalism, and unfettered private fancy went hand in hand in this oldest rabbinic exegesis—a part of which survives in the halakic interpretations of the Mishnah and Talmud, and another part in the haggadic Midrashim.

It is generally held that Paul learned the principles of biblical exegesis as he sat at the feet of Gamaliel in Jerusalem. But we do not know very much about this phase of Paul's career, nor anything in particular about the teaching of Gamaliel. If Paul went to Jerusalem at an early age, say twelve or fourteen, his study of the Old Testament must have been mainly rabbinic; but the usual chronology does not allow him many years for study with Gamaliel—he is almost at once engaged in persecution of the Christians. If, on the other hand, he came to Jerusalem as a young man, his study of scripture must have been rather far advanced before he arrived, and this is the impression we gather from Paul's own letters. His exegesis of the Old Testament is, like the rabbinic, a search for confirmation of views already established; and these views were not the normal rabbinic, as far as we are able to make out, but include more mythological elements, derived (who knows how?) from the surrounding Greco-Roman world but already united with Jewish ideas—for example the roles of "Sin" and "Death" as reflected in the first two chapters of Genesis (these are personal beings, not personifications), or the Messiah who descends "from heaven," or the "clothing" of the risen saints with bodies already prepared for them. As Ethelbert Stauffer says, quite rightly, Paul presupposes a *post*biblical Jewish exegesis; the only question is, Was this exegesis Palestinian, or Diaspora—or his own?

Characteristically, in argumentative passages Paul presents his exegesis of the Old Testament (he has no real "Old Testament theology") as readily to his Greco-Roman, once-pagan, readers as to Jews. This presupposes a real familiarity with the Old Testament and its interpretation on the part of Gentile converts, which some scholars have thought impossible. But it should be recalled that many of these converts had formerly been the "God-fearers" attached to the synagogue and were thus somewhat familiar with the contents of the Old Testament, and also, perhaps, with Jewish methods of interpretation—which were not very different in any case, as we have seen, from the common Hellenistic methods of interpreting other ancient sacred books. It should also be noted that there is evidence, as Charles H. Dodd has pointed out in Part II of his *The Bible and the Greeks,* for knowledge of the Old Testament on the part of religious-minded pagans, quite apart from the synagogue and mediated solely through the reading of the Septuagint. He shows the evidence to be found in the Hermetica, for example; to this might be added Pseudo-Longinus' *On the Sublime* (ch. ix), Virgil's Fourth Eclogue, the Sibylline Oracles, and other works.

One of Paul's great principles of exegesis (not common among the Tannaite rabbis) is the eschatological one—the events which are to take place at the end of the age will repeat those at the beginning. Another "exodus" will take place, another "wilderness wandering," another "conquest" of the Holy Land, another building of the "temple," and so on. The "restoration of all things" would even include a new Eden and a new race, united in the Second Adam as the present race is one in the first. Only, "the second man is from heaven" (I Cor. 15:47), not the earthly Adam made from the dust of the earth. Thus by a kind of reversal, and not a mere repetition, all things would be "summed up in Christ," and the new creation take the place of the old. This form of the theory of the two ages of course affected all of Paul's study and interpretation of the Old Testament, which was "written . . . for our instruction, upon whom the end of the ages has come" (I Cor. 10:11). Adam was only a type of him who was to come (Rom. 5:14); indeed Israel "after the flesh" was only a foreshadowing of the true Israel "after the spirit" which was to follow, and which is destined to be realized in the new supernatural age now beginning. This is of course *eisegesis,* not exegesis—no Old Testament writer would have recognized the ideas attributed to him (or rather to the Old Testament as a whole), though the later prophets with their doctrine of the "remnant" might have come to understand Paul after a little study. But then, as Père Bonsirven quotes from August Clemen,

No one ever asked how the Old Testament writers understood their own words, or how their contemporaries understood them. All that mattered was what use the Holy Spirit made of them, what the Spirit meant to teach through them—not only in addressing the writers themselves and their contemporaries, but all future generations. (P. 273 n.)

In general it is quite clear that Paul exercised far more liberty in dealing with the Old Testament than was claimed or exercised by any Jewish rabbi. He did not hesitate to paraphrase, to substitute one term for another when synonymous and clearer or more useful to his argument, and in general to disregard the exact wording of the Old Testament text—a feature perhaps to be explained by his use of the Septuagint, which was ordinarily his "Bible," but which he recognized was only a translation; the sacred text was in Hebrew. It is sometimes proposed to explain Paul's freedom in his use of the Old Testament text as due to his rabbinic education; but, as Père Bonsirven points out (pp. 336-37), this is not a rabbinic characteristic, but the opposite. Nor can it be due to failure of memory, or to variant readings in the Septuagint translation, or to that carelessness of the letter of scripture which Jerome pointed out as characteristic of the apostles and evangelists. Instead the alterations Paul makes seem deliberate, and to be based upon his typological theory; he at least does not set out intentionally, like the rabbis, to find his views supported in scripture, at whatever expense to the literal meaning. In the words of Père Bonsirven,

St. Paul receives the deposit of the Old Testament with the respectful liberty of a son of the house, master of the inheritance from his fathers. He sees in it, not the rule of his faith, which for him is derived from Christ, but the *paedagogus* who has prepared the reign of the divine Wisdom and the faithful witness charged to attest the Christian truth. When he expounds the gospel message, his memory, nourished by the sacred writings, supplies him amply (especially on the more controversial points) with the depositions of the ancient witness which illustrate and confirm his statement. He uses them freely, substituting, when necessary, in place of the traditional words certain equivalent terms which set in sharper relief the profound meaning of the sacred document, and not hesitating to combine texts whose testimony was in agreement and provided mutual support. (P. 338.)

6. *The Bible in the Church*

Millar Burrows has persuasively demonstrated that the authenticity of the revelation contained in the Bible cannot be established by any external testimony, nor by its own claim to be inspired, nor by the unique mode of its deliverance—since the mode was really not unique —but only by its own inherent truth and value. This is a matter of faith and of insight, the inner testimony of the Holy Spirit in the individual, as Calvin said. In other words, the scripture must "find" me and speak to me, to be true for me—a testimony as old as the *Theologia Germanica,* at least, and one strongly emphasized by Coleridge and other Christian thinkers of more recent date. But of course this does not deny the church's right, exercised in the choice of the canon, to select and approve a body of sacred literature which is appropriate for reading at public worship, which is authoritative as setting forth the true, original Christian faith, unsullied by heretical accretions or by Gnostic or other misinterpretations, and to which appeal may be made in the attempt to settle or define the numerous doctrinal questions which emerged at a later date. Something like this must be allowed those churches which adopt an "authorized" version of the Bible: the Septuagint in the Greek church, the Latin Vulgate in the Roman, Luther's translation in the German, the King James Version in the Anglican, and so on. These are "lectern" Bibles, and are used at public worship; they are the canonical texts, the legally adopted, official, definitive versions. The "authorized" English version was—at least was intended to be—"authorized for reading in churches." It would be impossible to insist that the Hebrew Bible (Kittel's *Biblia Hebraica,* for example) and the Greek New Testament (say Nestle's or Westcott and Hort's) must appear on every lectern in the Anglican communion, though the sacred text is studied by Anglican scholars in these critical editions. Something like this is true of the Roman authorization of the Vulgate; the Roman church certainly encourages its scholars to study the original texts.

We must be clear as to what a Bible is, and what it is expected to provide. Churches, like other institutions, have laws and rules of procedure. The old-fashioned Protestant view that every detail of scripture (even the punctuation points, some argued!) was inspired and infallible, that its primary message was to the individual in the privacy of his own chamber, where he meditated and was still, and that his salvation depended upon strict obedience to the very letter of scripture—all this, while profoundly moving as an example of piety, not only has passed away in much of the modern world, but must be recognized as something quite different from the historic position of the great churches of Christendom. It is in truth not the original Protestant position at all, but a pietistic view, stemming from the devout scripture-centered religion of seventeenth- and eighteenth-century Germany; it has little regard for the cultic and institutional use of holy scripture, which was the purpose, nevertheless, for which the scriptures were collected in the first place, both in the Jewish synagogue and in the early church. It may be true—it is true—that the individual finds in the scripture an illumination and a guidance which he finds nowhere else; at least he finds *more* illumination here than in any other literature. But this is not a sufficiently broad base upon which to establish the authority of scripture as inspired, as the record and vehicle of divine revelation. As we see the process taking place before our eyes in the New Testament, and in the writings of the early fathers, say down to the fourth century, it is the *church's* use of these books which gives them their sacrosanct character; and if we still insist that it was their power to reach and speak to the individual that lay behind this use, we must at least recognize that it was not the individual in his solitariness but as caught up within the fellowship of the church that made the choice and selection effective.

The modern historical view of the Bible enables us to see more clearly what should have been obvious on any view, what in fact the New Testament as well as the Old (Heb. 1:1-4; Exod. 3:6; Dan. 9:2, etc.) presupposes—that the revelation was progressive, that interpretation and reinterpretation, or what Julius Bewer has called "progressive interpretation," characterized the entire course of its long history. Its successive stages of canonization (three stages in the Old Testament, followed by a supplemental one for the Christians, which included the New Testament) reflect the gradual institutionalizing of religion, its authorization or crystallization about fixed norms. Gradually and steadily the faith, worship, and practices of religion were hedged about with divine sanctions. First the Law was set apart as unquestionably of divine authority. This was followed by the writings of the prophets, both the Former and the Latter; their teaching was supplemental to the Pentateuch, and in the Jewish view there was no conflict between law and prophecy, each taking the other for granted. Finally, in Judaism, the Writings were added, some of them selected for reading at the festivals, some for instruction and edification, some—like the Psalms—for use in worship; and none of these was thought for an instant to be incompatible with the original Torah. In fact, in one view, and that a common one, the whole Bible was Torah, divine instruction or teaching; for by this time Judaism had, as we have seen, become very largely a "religion of a book." The Christian supplement, the Greek New Testament, was added by the church as the completion, the true interpretation of the Old Testament and the classical documentation of the church's own faith and practice. It is impossible to account for the growth and canonization of the Bible apart from the use made of it in the Jewish synagogue and the Christian church.

The process must not be conceived too rigidly. The freedom with which the evangelic tradition was formulated, and reformulated, is evident from even a brief study of the Synoptic Gospels; and if it is clear from written gospels, it must have been the practice before the Gospels were written. The older view that the Gospels merely supplemented one another, and may be "harmonized" by a process of skillful interpretation and interweaving, must be given up. Each Gospel was meant to be *the* Gospel, the complete and final formulation of the tradition. This is especially important in studying the relation of John to the Synoptics, but it also covers the relation of Matthew and Luke to Mark.

Moreover, the importance of the institutional factor in the composition of the Gospels, as well as in their preservation and selection for the canon, is deserving of note. This is clear enough in the case of Matthew, which records the institution not only of the Eucharist but also of Baptism, the appointment of the apostles, the conferring of authority upon them, the establishment of the church (16:18), and the codification of the New Law (chs. 5–7, etc.). It is also clear in the case of Mark, which is addressed to a martyr church and both gives a clear statement of the disciple's duty in time of persecution and sets forth the assurance of a speedy end of the tribulation—the time is at hand, this generation will see it, the signs of the end are already apparent, and those who have sacrificed their all in this age will receive a hundredfold in the age to come. Luke's "institutionalism" is less apparent, but his is a gospel for the Gentile church and forms an apologetic statement of grounds for official tolerance not merely of individual belief but of the harassed body of Christians throughout the empire— a feature which it shares with the second volume of his work, the Acts of the Apostles, and which must be interpreted in the light of the total composition. The extraordinary situation in John, which seems to run counter to the generalization made above, is probably to be explained by the situation in which that Gospel arose. To some extent the institution is taken for granted but not stressed; the apostles receive power, but their authority is overshadowed by that of the "other Paraclete" who functions in Christ's name. In other ways the institutions of the church are peculiar. Baptism is recognized, but it is essentially baptism by the Spirit, a new and second birth, from above. The Eucharist is recognized, but what is important is receiving the Bread of Life, the "flesh" of Christ, the spiritual "manna from heaven"; and in lieu of the Pauline "Do this in remembrance of me" the rite of foot washing seems to be instituted for apostolic observance. The quasi-Gnostic milieu of the author, against which he is reacting strongly in favor of historical, traditional, institutional Christianity, has nevertheless colored his outlook. If we only knew what the church was like where he lived and wrote (Alexandria? Ephesus? Antioch?), we should understand somewhat better what he is saying—though we might be considerably surprised to find such a church in existence in the first or early second century.

The preservation and canonization of Paul's epistles, presumably as a result of the publication of the book of Acts (if we follow Edgar J. Goodspeed), was obviously an "institutional" step, though we must beware of reading into the word "institutional" the associations of the fourth or the eleventh or the sixteenth century. The other epistles, as apostolic writings, were likewise included on account of their usefulness as well as because of their presumed apostolic authorship. What Second Peter says of Paul's letters (3:15-16) doubtless applied to others; there were some things hard to understand in them, but for all that, Second Peter does not question the "wisdom" which God had given to the apostle. As for the Apocalypse, the very difficulty it experienced in entering the canon supports our view, since its eventual acceptance depended upon its interpretation in a sense favorable to the institution, the church. For it was now viewed as the church's divinely inspired and revealed program of world history leading up to the consummation when the church itself should be the Bride and the Dwelling Place of God, the New Jerusalem, the Heavenly City come down to earth and taking the place of this transient scheme of things. This interpretation, we may assume, had something to do with its admission to the canon. While chiliasm and Montanism held forth, and as long as the interpretation of the Apocalypse was tied to old and inherited apocalyptic views, there was little hope of the acceptance of the book within the canon— certainly not in the East, where the burden of chiliasm and apocalyptic schemes was felt most acutely. It was the West that saved the Apocalypse for the canon—and it was the West that early developed a strong institutional conception of Christianity, and interpreted scripture in accordance with this view.

What we see in the New Testament is a body of literature whose origin lay in the practical sphere. Gospels were written, not to supplant, but only to safeguard the original oral tradition of Jesus' words and deeds; and they arose in the Gentile church, not the Jewish, where oral tradition was rarely committed to writing. The epistles were equally practical; as the Gospels contained the "words and commandments of the Lord," so the epistles contained the admonitions and directions of his apostles. And what we see, beyond this, is a body of literature which is gradually becoming aware, we might almost say, of its own sacredness, a quality derived in part from the words of the Lord and the authoritative directions of the apostles and in part from the Old Testament, which it supplemented in public worship and in religious teaching. As the Old Testament gradually became a sacred collection, through a process spreading over hundreds of years, so the New became such a collection, in the course of perhaps one hundred years. The process was greatly accelerated, as we have seen, by the fact of the existence of the Old Testament in the Jewish synagogue (especially of the Greek Old Testament in the synagogues of the Diaspora), and also by the fact that early Christian "institutionalism" was to some extent ready-made. The church simply took over the worship, organization, and scriptures of the synagogue, reinterpreting the latter and revising and modifying the former. However, the Christian Bible was neither a legacy from Judaism nor a creation *de novo;* it was the legacy revised and reinterpreted—and supplemented. Our New Testament came out of this process; it was a supplement to the Greek Bible, and it was a collection of books which by use, interpretation, repeated copying, and constant reference were gradually becoming as sacred as the Old Testament scriptures to which they were added. As late as the fourth or fifth century the process was not complete—Barnabas and Hermas are still part of the New Testament in Codex Sinaiticus. In fact, the process has never been finished, in a sense; it is quite conceivable that, as Luther rejected the Epistle of James, so an ecumenical council might someday segregate the Apocalypse and form about it a kind of New Testament Apocrypha—at least this is the hope of some students, especially those who think of holy scripture as limited to the most indubitably and directly inspired words of God.

7. *Modern Interpretation*

The Bible contains the record of a divine revelation. It was written by men who were guided by the Holy Spirit. Its underlying tradition was derived from persons whose utterance had been inspired by God. Thus the inspiration was an inspiration of men before it was the inspiration of a book. How then is the teaching of the Bible to be interpreted and applied in after generations, especially today?

This question states one of the gravest problems for religion and points to one of the most difficult areas of tension in Christianity, both theological and practical. To begin with, the authority of the church to interpret the scriptures is balanced today by the claim of historical, scientific exegesis to be heard. Antecedently it might be assumed that the institution, whose sacred book it is, ought to be the proper authority for its interpretation. In the broad sense this is certainly true. Christianity is not a book but a life—a new kind of life shared by countless multitudes throughout the world, and spanning the centuries since its origin. That life is still in contact with the original inspiration. The Holy Spirit still guides the church. The primary authority for the interpretation of the Buddhist sacred scriptures is the Buddhists themselves, through the centuries, of the Quran the Moslems, of the Hebrew Bible the Jews, and so on. Yet even here it has been found that other scholars than Buddhists, Moslems, or Jews can throw light upon the original meaning of these writings, and a similar situation exists in regard to the Christian sacred writings. Objective scholarship may lack some of the requisite qualities for the thorough understanding of a sacred book, but it can often supply something very precious and indeed indispensable for the exposition of its original meaning. Moreover, in the case of the Bible, most of the objective, scientific scholarship of modern times has in fact operated within the church, though there have been scholars whose allegiance to historic Christianity was rather attenuated. The tension nevertheless continues between scientific historical scholarship, on one hand, and literalism (fundamentalism), sectarianism, or private interpretation, making capital of a few selected texts, on the other.

Examples of the danger involved in the literal interpretation are not far to seek. The backwoods cult of snake handling, as proof of the power of the gospel and of the convert's faith (based on Mark 16:18), is a current example. The simple-minded adherents of these groups in the mountains of West Virginia and Tennessee have never questioned the "Longer Ending" (16:9-20) of the Gospel of Mark, though it is certainly no part of that Gospel but an appendix added, probably in the second century, in an attempt to supply Mark with an account of the resurrection. Other examples are the numerous cults of faith healing, based on such texts as "Heal the sick, raise the dead" (Matt. 10:8). Extreme pacifism may also be cited as an illustration of pure literalism, or the refusal of certain groups to take oath in court, or the attempt of the millenarians to discover the future course of history from the apocalyptic writings. So are the endeavors of many worthy people to introduce "Bible economics" into our modern industrial-commercial society, ignoring the wide contrast between the primitive agricultural economy of ancient Palestine and the vast, complex, and somewhat less humane organization of modern capitalism. One cannot but respect the earnestness and sincerity of such people; at the same time one cannot help wishing that they were more critical of their own views, and that they had a better knowledge of the conditions—social, economic, and religious—of the world in which the Bible was written. It is usual among Protestants to view fundamentalism as a noble affirmation of the truth of the Bible, somewhat narrow and fanatical, of course, but nevertheless on the whole deserving of commendation. But we should distinguish between the loyalty or the zeal of religious people and their intellectual competence. Even the most godly and devout may be hopelessly mistaken on questions of fact, of interpretation, of history and exegesis. We need not impugn their zeal or orthodoxy, though it may not be "according to knowledge."

One of the most tragic results of a literal interpretation of the New Testament is the support which has been derived from it for antiSemitism, one of the blackest and most ineradicable blemishes upon the modern world. Anti-Semitism is very old, indeed pre-Christian, as all historians recognize. The shame of the church is that it has permitted anti-Semitism to survive within its own ranks. The causes, like the origins, of this disgraceful and dysgenic social attitude certainly lie outside the New Testament and are shared by Jews and non-Jews; but that the Christian sacred scriptures got infected with the virus, that the poison survives there to this day, that the church has hitherto done very little to counteract the infection—all this is inexcusable. To this day Jews are accused of being "Christ killers"; reactionary and halfeducated preachers heap abuse upon them as a people cursed by God for rejecting the gospel; and appeal is made to texts of the New Testament in support of this fanatical and inhuman prejudice. The Jews themselves can hardly be expected to distinguish between the literal fundamentalist interpretation of these texts and the interpretation which is common among liberal scholars. Fortunately many of them do, nevertheless, recognize the difference.

The worst of these texts is John 8:44, "You are of your father the devil." It is simply inconceivable that Jesus of Nazareth ever said these words. For one thing, he was himself a Jew, though it is "the Jews" who are addressed in this passage. It has been proposed to translate by using the word "'Judeans" rather than "Jews" in this and similar passages, but this will not do—the whole Gospel of John is a polemic against Judaism. The book is not a historical record of the life and teaching of Jesus, but a dramatization of the meaning Christ had come to have for the church at the end of the first or the beginning of the second century. It reflects the strained and bitter feelings which attended the separation of the church from the synagogue.

Many Christians, at first, were thorough Jews, were in fact Christian Jews—Jews who added to their practice of Judaism the conviction that the Messiah was Jesus, risen from the dead and glorified and soon to come again. Others looked upon the Law and the gospel as fundamentally antagonistic, and viewed the Law as temporary and now superseded—approximately the view of Paul. Controversy with orthodox or conservative (non-Christian) Jews was common, and the New Testament reflects the situation in more than one passage. Christians were excommunicated, their "names cast out as evil"; parents were betrayed by children and brothers by brothers; they were beaten in the synagogues; they were sometimes even put to death when mobs became violent. It is not likely that the Christian minority was in any position to retaliate; they took their revenge, as the Old Testament psalmists took revenge upon Babylon (Ps. 137:8), in a literary way. The story of the death of Christ was retold in such a way as to exonerate the Roman authorities and shift the blame upon the Jewish sanhedrin—in spite of the unquestionable fact that Jesus was crucified, not stoned to death, and that the resulting story violated the Jewish rules of legal procedure at a dozen points. The teaching of Jesus was likewise modified in an anti-Jewish direction, even during the oral period before the Gospels were written, though the climax of the process was not reached until the Gospel of John appeared.

The earliest Gospel, Mark, already (about A.D. 68) displays an anti-Semitic bias; it was a Roman gospel, and Rome was familiar with anti-Semitism and had been familiar with it for two centuries. Matthew is a strongly colored document. Though it is traditionally described as "the Jewish gospel," this is only because its chief sources for the teaching of Jesus are Christian-Jewish documents or traditions (Q and M). It is Matthew who gives the awful story of the self-invoked curse upon the Jewish people, "His blood be on us and on our children" (27:25). Luke might with more justice be called Jewish, for he was familiar with the actual Jewish religion of the first century as well as with literary Judaism—found chiefly in the Septuagint, whose diction and style have deeply influenced his own. But the Gospel of Luke is only Volume I of a two-volumed work, Luke-Acts, an apologetic treatise designed to show that Christianity was not inimical to public law and order, and that Christians ought to enjoy the same privileges that Jews enjoyed: free exercise of their religion, release from military duty, exemptions from the requirement of sacrifice as a test of loyalty, and so on. Naturally Luke did not stress the antagonism between Jews and Christians, though he records examples of popular opposition in Acts, and follows perforce the Marcan passion narrative in the Gospel.

Paul's position was more difficult. Though he recognized that the Law was "holy and just and good" (Rom. 7:12), he also realized the conflict between the gospel and the Mosaic code. His solution was to view the Law as temporary but useful and valid, up to a point and for a limited time. Its purpose, in the providence of God, had been educative and disciplinary. It had been useful in bringing out an awareness of sin, in making sin even more sinful—somewhat as old-fashioned doctors brought a fever "to a head"—and its ultimate value in God's purpose was to show the weakness of the "flesh," of unaided human nature, apart from the grace of God. Thus it was designed to throw men entirely upon the mercy of God, and to make them realize that their salvation must be by divine grace, through faith, and not by works. Though he also realized the seriousness of the antagonism between Christianity and Judaism, and the dire consequences of the conflict as they were already working out in contemporary history, he nevertheless believed that the ultimate solution lay within the divine purpose. Eventually "all Israel would be saved"; he believed this as devoutly as any other Jew of his time or since (it is still emphasized in the Jewish Prayer Book). The long discussion of the problem in Rom. 9–11 is Paul's contribution to its solution, and involves his whole theodicy, for the final factors in the problem and also in the solution involve God and his plan for the salvation of mankind. Israel's rejection of the gospel was only temporary; it was a "hardening of heart" like that of Pharaoh and other instruments of God's will in the Old Testament. But after the Gentiles had been brought into the church (or the kingdom of God), then the Jews would in their turn acknowledge Christ and so be "saved." His illustration of the wild olive grafted into the cultivated stock (Rom. 11:24), though confessedly "contrary to nature"—since cultivated trees are grafted into wild ones—is a clear exposition of his meaning. Hence Paul can say that his heart is torn by the struggle; he writes in "great sorrow and unceasing anguish." Whereas today many Christians accuse Paul of having "Judaized the Christian religion," while many Jews look upon him as a most unrepresentative Jew, a traitor and apostate to the religion of his fathers, the truth lies somewhere between these two extremes. This is one of the features in Paul's theology that justifies its characterization as "dialectical." He was aware of the truth on both sides of the argument, and he affirmed both, without arriving at a position where both could be embraced within a larger unity, axiomatic and logical and irrefutable.

What Christians can do, today, to stem the tide of anti-Semitism in the modern world may not seem of much consequence, but it certainly ought to begin with a frank acknowledgment of the seriousness of the situation within the New Testament itself. In the choice of lessons for reading at public worship, and of material for use in religious education, sermons, and confirmation instructions, the clergy and other leaders of the church should realize how far-reaching are the inferences people draw from the passages heard or read at church, and how serious are the practical consequences of our acquiescence in the inherited prejudices which the New Testament seems to support. We do not hesitate to criticize (or to explain away) certain primitive or savage elements in the Old Testament; why should we be less ready to do so when they are found in the New? Moreover, we cannot escape our responsibility merely by saying, "It is in the Bible," for after all the Bible is the church's book, and the church is responsible for its translation, publication, promulgation, interpretation, and application. We do not hesitate to "explain away" the passages that seem to support slavery, or imperialism, or the subordinate position of women; why should we not do the same with passages that support hatred and prejudice and vindictive attitudes toward our fellow men? To say the very least, and to put the matter on an entirely different ground, there is no hope that Jews will ever be led to accept the gospel as long as these misrepresentations of their religion and the accusation of their responsibility as a people for Christ's death continue to be read in the New Testament.

Finally, if we are to use the New Testament at all, as a book of religious instruction, edification, and propaganda (and naturally I assume that we will continue to do so), then it should be accompanied by an interpretation. The scriptures should have brief notes, explanatory of difficulties, and stating the conditions under which the books were written, their purpose, and the background of the writers. The idea of an annotated Bible is very old, as is illustrated by the Geneva Version—a version that was still competing with the King James as late as the middle of the nineteenth century in some places, for example in Scotland. The reason for the omission of notes, as stated by the translators of the King James Version in their Preface, was valid enough at the time; moreover, the annotated versions were far too theological. But there is surely no reason why the Bible printed for popular use today should not contain a certain amount of comment and explanation, for the guidance of the ordinary reader who is neither a scholar nor a theologian. In such a Bible these far-reaching practical matters, as well as obscurities in the text, items of geography, law, or custom, and similar things, ought to be dealt with.

But the first question, and the last, is justice and truth. Literalism or fundamentalism has no way out of the impasse. Only enlightened historical scholarship can provide the interpretation needed—it is needed as much by the church for its own sake as it is by non-Christian readers, who are mortified and offended by the obviously unfair and prejudiced attitudes which certain passages reflect. Most of us Christians are scarcely aware how tragic this situation is, but a little imagination and a little more human sympathy will awaken us.

This is only one illustration—but a crucial one—of the importance of the proper interpretation and application of the thought of the New Testament. Our modern world hangs in the balance; civilization may survive, or it may disappear; brotherhood, justice, honor, and fair play may succeed, or they may vanish from the earth; the One World envisaged by modern idealists may become fact, or it may perish like a forgotten dream. Now we Christians must not secularize the outlook for religion by maintaining that the goal of a civilized society—or of social democracy—and that of the Christian faith are one and the same. A peaceful and prosperous human society here upon earth will not necessarily be the kingdom of God. But the immense responsibility of the Christian church in this present situation is none the less real. And the fulfillment of this responsibility must begin with a sound and realistic interpretation of our own sacred scriptures. We cannot leave it to others to distinguish within them between what is permanent and what is passing, between the central and the peripheral, the essential and the existential, the eternal and the temporal, between the divine revelation which they enshrine and the external, the adventitious, the phenomenal, the transient elements in the record of that revelation.

VI

The Doctrine of God

1. *Traditional Theism and the New Testament*

BELIEF in God is everywhere taken for granted in the New Testament. In only one or two passages is it even suggested that anyone might conceivably not believe in God. Even the demons "believe—and shudder" (Jas. 2:19). Those who come to God must believe that he is, and that he is the rewarder of those who seek him (Heb. 11:6). The desperate condition of those who are "without hope" is equivalent to being "without God in the world"—which may mean living in a world where there is no God, no thought of him, no faith, or may mean living in the world as if God did not exist (Eph. 2:12). Either condition is sufficiently hopeless and despairing. As a book of practical religion the New Testament is not concerned either with proofs of the existence of God or with definitions of his nature, person, or attributes—matters which belong to systematic theology. Widely throughout the Hellenistic world of the first century there was an undercurrent (as Paul Wendland called it) of belief in God; out-and-out atheists were in a small and decreasing minority. If anything, the Greco-Roman world was too religious, too uncritical in its faith, too credulous. Paul's compliment to his Athenian audience (Acts 17:22) was that they were "very religious"—the word *deisidaimonesterous* might be translated "most religious" and verges on the thought of "too religious." At least the world believed in divine beings, if not in the one and only God, and in this respect it was markedly different from our world, where many persons have given up all faith in either God or gods.

The idea of God taken for granted in the New Testament is the idea found in the Old Testament and in Judaism. This means, not the primitive ideas still surviving in parts of the Old Testament, but the

99

high and noble idea arrived at in the later books. God is absolutely sovereign, as in Second Isaiah and the Psalms; he is holy; he is invisible and mysterious—"a God that hidest thyself, O God of Israel, the Saviour" (Isa. 45:15). No one has ever seen him at any time (cf. John 1:18; I Tim. 1:17), though the old tales and legends recounted the experiences of men who had seen God face to face and—contrary to all expectation—had survived. He is all-powerful, all-knowing; even the inmost thoughts of men's "hearts" (minds) are laid bare to his sight (I Cor. 3:20, quoting Ps. 94:11). He is just, and the guardian of justice; he is loving, patient, long-suffering in his dealings with men, not only with nations but also with individuals. Since he is the creator of all things, and the ruler of history, in the end all creatures must own his sway; resist as they may, there is no final escape from the divine judgment. His care for Israel goes a long way back, to Moses and the exodus from Egypt; but even farther back than that, to Abraham, whom God chose to be the father of the faithful, of his own people. The special relationship in which Israel stands to God is one of privilege but also of responsibility: "You only have I known . . . therefore I will punish you . . ." (Amos 3:2 K.J.V.). In this exalted conception of God, henotheism (one god among many, supreme among his own worshipers, as other gods are supreme among theirs) has been left far behind; it is a pure and lofty ethical monotheism that we find in the later parts of the Old Testament and in Judaism. The theology of Second Isaiah and the Psalms is carried forward and enshrined in the liturgy of the synagogue, whose oldest parts are on the same high level. As for the gods of the heathen, they are but idols of stone or wood; it is Yahweh who made the heavens (cf. Ps. 135:15). Indeed, the gods of the heathen were often looked upon as demons, a view reflected in Paul's first letter to the Corinthians (10:20-21). A good illustration of this demotion of heathen deities is Beelzebul (not Beelzebub; the best manuscript tradition supports the former spelling). This wicked spirit is, in the first century, an archdemon, "the prince of the demons" (Mark 3:22), a powerful local spirit with an army of evil spirits under his control. But this wicked spirit was really what some of our anthropologists and historians of religion call a "faded" god—originally he had been a high god, "Lord of the Mansion," the mansion being either sky or earth or the underworld (or perhaps all three). But that had been long ago, as long ago as the Ras Shamra tablets (perhaps 1500 B.C.) ; and when the Hebrew religion, and later Judaism, triumphed in that area, the old northern deity had declined in honor until he was only a demon, though still powerful and dangerous.

There is a widespread popular view, at the present day, which pictures the Jewish idea of God, in the first century, as remote and inaccessible—too lofty and transcendent, too sublime, to be approached by men. Only the priests could approach him, and then only with the arbitrary formulas of prayer and sacrifice. Instead of dealing directly with his world he was surrounded with innumerable angels, who did his bidding; these were so numerous, in fact, that they were organized in armies and battalions, legions and cohorts, like the Roman armies. He was an Oriental monarch of the Egyptian or Babylonian type, dwelling in light unapproachable, never seen by his people, as in some palace of Mycerinus; only his angel, like a grand vizier, bore his messages and mandates to the serflike inhabitants of his realm. This caricature of the idea of God as held by ancient Judaism is probably to be explained as due to the reading of Philo by Christian scholars, and to the inference, without further investigation, that this idea prevailed throughout the Jewish world. The next step was to take the picturesque language of the apocalypses as normal, and to insert the Philonic dualism into their symbolic scenes. Along with this has gone the popular Protestant neglect of liturgy and of liturgical language, which often expresses the deepest as well as the commonest ideology of a religion. If one wishes to feel the very pulse beat of any high religion, it must as a rule be sought in its liturgy. And the truth is, as we study the liturgical literature of ancient Judaism we find that the idea of God which it expresses is almost identical with that of the classical prophets and psalmists of the Old Testament. There were additional emphases by the first century, as was to be expected in a living liturgy, one which really expressed the piety and devotion of a people. The messianic hope was perhaps more concretely conceived, though the language is still that of Isaiah and the Psalter. But the central emphasis and the fundamental "theological" idea is still that of the highest and noblest passages of the Old Testament.

When we turn from the liturgy to the midrashim and the commonplace books of ancient Jewish preachers and expounders of scripture, the same thing is true—even more true! If anything the ancient Jewish conception of God is too human, too *gemütlich;* God is too much like the old-fashioned Jewish *paterfamilias,* surrounded by a huge family, possessing quaint and endearing personal traits, and above all things a perfectly approachable person. If Jesus used parables which seemed (if allegorized) to represent God as an unjust judge, or a complacent cynic, we need not be surprised to find that the ancient rabbis did the same, and with a similar irresistible and sometimes almost irreverent touch of humor. This was the religious conception which the people were familiar with, at least a century or two later, and probably earlier as well, in the time of our Lord. It was no philosophical conception, not even much of a theological conception. But it was profoundly and thoroughly religious—and Jesus took it for granted. God, we might say, was still more thoroughly humanized in the thought of our Lord. To call God our Father goes a long way in this direction, and the Old Testament and the old Jewish prayers had already familiarized the Jews with this term.

The other most common term for God, both in Judaism (in the prayers) and in the tradition of Jesus' teaching, is King. Modern Christians—especially, perhaps, in democratic countries—infer at once that this term implies exaltation, remoteness, power and grandeur; and so it does, but not in the degree commonly supposed. The background and connotations of the term were not, for Judaism, the exalted office of the Persian Great King or the Egyptian Pharaoh, nor, certainly, the military monarchs of the West. Instead the old idea of kingship, rooted deep in the Jewish sacred literature and surviving in the synagogue prayers, was that of a local prince or king—the city kings of ancient Semitic times and of Homer. The king is a judge of cases at law; he is a farmer with unusually large estates; he superintends his own mowing of hay—one of the traditional taxes was still the "king's mowings" (cf. Amos 7:1); he rides in a chariot with horses, where other men rode asses or walked. Above all he is responsible for the welfare of his people, as the desert *shayik* is to this day. If they hunger, so does he; if they prosper, so does he. Even the brutal Herod the Great, when the Jews were faced with famine, twice sent his golden sconces from the palace walls and hocked them at the Alexandrian pawnbrokers' shops in order to buy grain for his people. Kingship of this kind, local, personal, familiar, was among the connotations of the term in its religious application. Jesus was probably never inside the palace of a king, but he knew what went on there, as did every other Galilean—people wore purple and fine linen and sang songs and feasted sumptuously every day, as in other rich men's houses (Matt. 11:8). The idea of a remote imperial administration, say that of Augustus with his heavy correspondence, or of Trajan examining the blueprints for aqueducts in Bithynia, or of Tiberius or Vespasian checking over the balance sheets of the provincial governors—no idea of this kind ever crossed the mind of anyone in Palestine when the word "king" was uttered. And in public worship the words, "God is my King of old. . . . The Lord sitteth above the water-flood, and the Lord remaineth a King for ever. . . . Thy kingdom is an everlasting kingdom" (Pss. 74:13; 29:9; 145:13 B.C.P.)—words like these connoted exaltation and majesty and power, of course, but not the power and majesty of a distant, unknown, perhaps arbitrary emperor, whose fiat could sentence a "million men, east and west," to instant and irrevocable doom. Of course God *could,* but God was not that kind of a king. To know him was to love him, as you might love a good king whose palace lay up the hill above your village, or more probably in the center of your walled city, and whose sons and daughters came and went and were seen every day. The notion of Immanuel Kant, that worship is the "court etiquette" appropriate at audiences of the heavenly King, is as far removed from ancient Jewish worship as the concept of God in modern idealist philosophy is remote from the naïve, traditional, but deeply religious thought of God in the piety of the synagogue.

It is this popular, untheological idea of God which the New Testament takes for granted, but only as its starting point. Among the New Testament writers we can observe the advance most clearly in Paul. Like other eschatologists he at least tends in the direction of dualism. He does not go the whole length of the apocalyptists, but that is chiefly because he thinks of God in terms of Christ, of Christ's revelation of God, of God's great act in Christ for the salvation of the world, and of Christ as a person. The Old Testament God is personal, and so is the God of the synagogue worship. The God of Jesus is supremely personal—no religious teacher in all history has made him more so. But Paul's God, though personal, is more abstractly conceived and is concerned with dark problems, chiefly the problem of saving a race in spite of itself, a race in which sin had now become ingrained and inherited, and for whom the remedy of the Law had proved not even a palliative —it merely intensified the fever in men's souls, so that more drastic measures were required. Not that Paul pictured God as wrestling with these problems, as a later rabbi might have done (some of them even represented God as studying Torah so many hours each day, like a model rabbi). Instead Paul is aware that God knows in advance what he will do and has the whole course of history, with all its involved contingencies, fully worked out in his own mind. What is mystery to mankind is clear as day to the divine mind; indeed, for Paul "mystery" does not mean a secret, but a secret disclosed, understood, shared, and proclaimed. But it was God's secret for a long while, "hidden for ages and generations," until at last it was declared in Christ (Col. 1:26; cf. Rom. 16:25). This secret, which surpassed the schemes of the apocalyptists with their rigorous schedule for history, was hidden even from the heavenly powers—the *archontes* set over the world. (Here Paul seems to breathe the air of Alexandria and think after the manner of Philo.) Some of these rulers of the world had rebelled against God and so could not be expected to share the divine plan. But the others had not—and yet God (as the writer of I Pet. 1:12 said) did not take even the angels into his confidence when he devised the plan of salvation.

In these writers, chiefly in Paul, the simple conception of God found in the Gospels and reflecting the views of Jesus has been left behind. They are not philosophers, but they are moving in the direction of a Christian philosophy. And yet their conception of God is after all essentially the conception of Jesus—and of Judaism. Only, God is now "the God of our Lord Jesus Christ, the Father of glory" (Eph. 1:17) —not so much the God about whom Jesus taught as the divine Father of Christ whose essence, being, and power Christ manifested or reflected. In John a still further step is apparently taken: "No one has ever seen God; the only Son, who is in the bosom of the Father, he has made him known" (1:18). Yet even this is not a metaphysical definition; but it is not far from it, and the later church was compelled to work out a metaphysical definition, or series of definitions, in order to safeguard both this statement and the monotheism fundamental to the whole biblical revelation.

It was—and still is—the central "dogma" of Judaism that God is one. The main affirmation of the daily Shema, "Hear, O Israel: the Lord our God is one Lord," meant originally, no doubt, "Yahweh is our only God." The point of the statement as it appears in Deut. 6:4 was undoubtedly, in those days, the denial of the right of other gods to the allegiance of the Hebrews. (Cf. Exod. 20:3.) Its immense importance for the whole history of Hebrew, Jewish, and Christian religion, and likewise for Islam, a "daughter" religion of Judaism, is perfectly clear. It was only natural that, as time went on and ever higher conceptions of God were expressed, especially by the prophets, the phrase "our only God" should be understood to mean "the only God." This is certainly the sense in which the affirmation was understood in New Testament times, and in all later Judaism and Christianity. From the days of Deutero-Isaiah, if not before, the affirmation had this meaning. From then on, as Ernst Sellin says, Hebrew practical monotheism became likewise theoretical monotheism.

But this does not mean that for the Old Testament prophets, or for ancient Judaism, or for primitive Christianity, God was conceived as living alone in the sky or in "heaven," as Heinrich Heine satirized the God of traditional belief as dwelling in loneliness aloft, or as H. G. Wells pictured the "infinite" God, contrasted with the "finite" God (Christ). In the Old Testament, as the late H. W. Robinson repeatedly pointed out, God is conceived as surrounded with a heavenly "company" or "court"—not only with heavenly or angelic armies who haste to do his bidding, but with a friendly Olympian society of the "Sons of God." The picture we see at the opening of the book of Job reflects a late conception of this heavenly society, but that the idea was really primitive and can be inferred back from Job to the days before the Exile is most probable. As time went on an enormous development of angelology took place in the apocalyptic circle of thought and also in popular, non-apocalyptic lore. Not only were the actual number and the importance of angels increased, but their character was changed. Instead of being creatures of God who could be formed *ad hoc,* created instantaneously for whatever mission was to be entrusted to them, or transformed once more into winds or flames of fire—the older conception (cf. Ps. 104:4; Heb. 1:7)—they were now viewed as permanent denizens of the invisible world. Instead of being wholly dependent upon God and entirely obedient to his will—whether at his bidding they flew upon errands, or only stood attentively about the throne, or engaged in perpetual adoration—some of them were now thought to be permanently disobedient, in revolt against the high will of heaven, and practically identical with demons. Satan, instead of being looked upon as the "accuser," the celestial state's attorney, permitted by God to test the virtues of the saints (as in the prologue to the book of Job), his presence in the heavenly court neither contested nor resented—Satan is now the "prince of the power of the air" (Eph. 2:2), the tempter to sin, himself in revolt against God, and the great "deceiver" (II John 7). His cohorts of rebellious angels form an army opposed to the forces of God. And although the victory in the end will certainly be won by the forces of light (as in Rev. 12:7-8), the struggle will be severe, and the whole world will feel the effects of the celestial contest.

The transformation thus effected in the old Hebrew belief during the period after the Exile, and carried to an extreme length by apocalyptism, is reflected not only in the New Testament but also in popular Jewish lore surviving in the midrashim and in the Talmud. The causes of this transformation are usually found in the enormous emphasis laid upon the transcendence of God during this period, especially by the apocalyptists, and in the widespread influence of Zoroastrianism, especially during the Persian period (538-332 B.C.). An exaggerated and one-sided emphasis upon divine transcendence widened the gulf between God and the world. The Persian religion with its angels and demons suggested that this gap should be filled with supernatural beings, while the actual constitution of the Persian empire, with its hierarchy of officials, viziers, satraps, messengers, and envoys, provided the pattern for such a celestial organization. The dualism inherent in the Zoroastrian faith, the picture of the world conflict between the two powers of light and darkness with their attendant hosts, the evil attributed to darkness, the final judgment, the assize of souls, the narrow path across the bridge from death to life—all this is called in to explain the transformation of the primitive court of heaven into the more elaborate scheme presupposed in Judaism and early Christianity. No doubt the influence existed, but the elements of the later faith were indigenous within Judaism itself. What took place was a development, not an importation. The counterbalancing elements were likewise present, for the Old Testament continued to be read, and the simple, older, indeed primitive concepts were deeply embedded in that sacred book. Hence Judaism never became dualistic, except in extremely one-sided and individualistic expressions (in Philo, for example). Nor does the New Testament reflect a dualistic outlook upon the world. That the danger existed is certain. The Johannine theology advances a long way in this direction (cf. I John 5:19), but the permanence of evil is nowhere admitted. "I saw Satan fall like lightning from heaven" (Luke 10:18)—the whole New Testament echoes this exclamation of confident faith. The "strong man" was already bound, and his armies were being routed, his castle was invaded, his prisoners were being released (Mark 3:27). If "the whole world is in the power of the evil one," nevertheless, "Be of good cheer, I have overcome the world" (John 16:33; cf. I John 5:19). The dualism is only temporary and transient; the ultimate victory of good is certain, and is now in sight. Hence the unity of God and his real sovereignty over the world are not in the least endangered or infringed by the ideas of Satan, the angels, or the hosts of demons.

It is a further question whether and to what extent the Zoroastrian religion as a whole directly influenced Judaism and, through Judaism, early Christianity. Of late years we have become more familiar with the general development of religion in the Hellenistic age. The existence of an "orientalizing" movement during this age, especially from the middle of the third century B.C. and increasingly until the time of the Syrian emperors, is undeniable. Within the vast syncretism and mixture of religions which then took place, the influence of Zoroastrian and also of Babylonian ideas was very marked—were not these religions already hoary with age, and therefore presumably more true than the younger religions of the West? Popular demonology throughout the Near East and the Mediterranean world was increasing steadily during the Hellenistic period, and it is perhaps more likely that the Jews were now influenced by this feature in the surrounding heathenism than that they had responded to a direct influence coming from Zoroastrianism during the preceding period of Persian domination. What the Persians did in the West during their two centuries of political control was to pave the way for the westward sweep of "Oriental" ideas after Alexander. During the Persian period the way was blocked—in Europe by the heroic Greeks, in Palestine by the poverty and privation and the religious zeal of the tiny Jewish community. But after Alexander's conquest of Asia Minor, Syria, Egypt, the Near and the Middle East, and especially during the existence of the Seleucid empire, which extended originally from the Mediterranean to the Indus, the way was clear for the westward movement of ideas. Many of these found ready acceptance in the West, for they really revived primitive notions which, though long suppressed (as in Greece) like a hidden fire, now burst into flame once more. In other words the growth of demonology was part and parcel of the whole tendency of religion in the surrounding world, and is not attributable to one source alone.

What is meant by "unclean" spirits is difficult to say. Presumably they were demons which prompted the unclean acts of those whom they possessed. Originally "demons" (at least in Greek thought) were neutral; the term *daimonion* could even be applied to gods and, at least in the vocative, as a term of address to a human being—like "sir" or "gentleman," as often in Homer (e.g. Iliad II. 190, 200; Odyssey IV. 774). In the course of time these were thought of as minor discarnate spiritual beings, something like "angels" in the Old Testament. In this process their neutrality was abandoned, and they were viewed as both good and bad. So important was the spread of demonology in the Hellenistic age that Wilhelm Nestle in his history of Greek piety devotes an entire chapter to the "demonizing of religion." Under the increasing influence of "Orientalism," and due to the lapse into more primitive ways of thinking, and especially as a concomitant of the growth of magic, belief in the malevolent activity of wicked demons became almost universal in the Greco-Roman world.

In the Old Testament we read of a "lying" spirit who comes down from the heavenly court to seduce and trick a Hebrew king (I Kings 22:19-23). Satan is the adversary, the tempter, the reviler and blasphemer. However, this is still no clue to the conception of "unclean" spirits. But as Jewish religion tended more strongly in a ceremonial direction, with the stern provisions of the P code against eating or even touching anything unclean—a tendency which was perhaps fostered by Zoroastrian dualism during the long period of Persian domination of the Near East—the behavior of those possessed by evil spirits came to be described in terms of "uncleanness." Added to this was probably the moral judgment, as a passage in the Clementine Homilies (9:19) suggests: "Having the desire for food and drink and intercourse, but not being able to partake because they are spirits, . . . they enter into the bodies of men." Such a judgment would be the more inevitable, in the popular thinking of that age, as the demoniacs themselves claimed the inspiration of spirits for their actions—that is, claimed to be the spirits who acted through them (e.g. Mark 1:24). (This feature of spirit possession was common among the witches and wizards of the seventeenth century, and made judicial procedure the more difficult and its decisions the more inevitable.) Add to all this the actual filth and obscenity of certain types of insanity, in which care of the body and even control of the natural functions has ceased, and the conclusion (in terms of popular first-century diagnosis) could only be that the person was possessed by an "unclean" spirit or spirits. If there was such a state as possession by "a spirit of infirmity" (Luke 13:11), then certainly possession by "a spirit of uncleanness" (that is, by an "unclean spirit") was equally possible, and even more disastrous. This would be understood as no figure of speech, meaning a general attitude or tendency, but in thorough earnest, with all the realism of first-century thinking on the subject.

It may also be noted that the tendency found in the later parts of the Old Testament and also in contemporary Judaism to hypostatize the divine powers is likewise reflected in the New Testament. God's spirit (that is, a spirit from God), his word, his wisdom, even his name have received in the Old Testament a degree of personification which passes over into distinct and separate hypostasis; they are conceived as existing more or less apart from God. Much of this is poetic imagination, no doubt; some of it is the primitive man's idea of the separability of the "soul" or other attribute from the person himself; some of it is a naïve attempt at a theology. Whether or not it is due to the emphasis upon the transcendence of God is not certain—such terminology is very old in human speech and thinking, especially in the Orient. But by the New Testament period there is little question of the hypostatization; the Word of God, the Wisdom of God, above all the Spirit of God, have a "substantial" existence and are no longer poetic metaphors. Too much has been made in Christian exegesis of the *memra* (word) of God found in the Targums of the third and following centuries—some of them much later. It is not impossible that the expression was used in the synagogues of Palestine, in translating lections from the Hebrew scriptures into oral Aramaic; but it cannot be proved. And even so, such a formula as "the word of the Lord said," in the place of the straightforward ancient Hebrew statement, "God said," does not carry us very far. Every intelligent worshiper at a Jewish synagogue would recognize at once that this was mere circumlocution, like the use of *Adonai* for the sacred tetragrammaton *YHWH,* and was motivated by reverence; he would not be likely to jump to the conclusion that *memra* was a supernatural being independent of God. Furthermore *no* being, however supernatural, was really independent of God. Even Satan, hardened in opposition to God and his saints, was not independent—God could terminate his existence in an instant if he chose. That he did not so choose showed that Satan served a purpose in the divine economy. Chiefly, as time went on, this was seen in his function as the one who "tried" (put to the test, rather than "tempted") the righteous. So with the rest, the good powers of God; they were used by him in the maintenance of the universe, in the guidance of the righteous, in the superintendence of various realms of activity (waters, storms, volcanoes, winds, stars, nations, lands). At any moment God could revoke their very existence; they existed only in dependence upon him; and for this reason it is idle to speak of a latent or merely suppressed polytheism in Judaism or the New Testament, or to represent it as a Hebraized version of Zoroastrian dualism. For all the poetic fancies tolerated on the periphery of Judaism, that ancient religion was now monotheistic to its very core.

This principle also holds good in the Christian development of Christology and pneumatology—Christ is still one with the Father, and the Spirit is still "the Spirit of your Father" (Matt. 10:20). Gentile Christianity eventually went beyond this, and the whole development of later trinitarian doctrine is the process whereby the fundamental conviction of the unity of God was safeguarded and preserved in spite of tendencies in the direction of Hellenistic pluralism. Within the New Testament itself the Pauline formula, "the love of God, the grace of our Lord Jesus Christ, the fellowship of the Holy Spirit" (cf. II Cor. 13:14), is still in closest contact with Christian experience, and betrays no suggestion of the later speculative elaboration of the doctrine of the Blessed Trinity. Even the late Matthaean formula (Matt. 28:19b),

while undoubtedly a part of the text of Matthew and not a later interpolation, is probably an addition to the postresurrection saying, which
accordingly ran, "Go therefore and make disciples of all nations, teaching them to observe all that I have commanded you." And yet even the
Matthaean formula, "baptizing them in the name of the Father and of
the Son and of the Holy Spirit," is to be understood in the light of the
early church's experience of revelation, and not as a piece of speculation. It was fundamental that God is the Father, not only in Jesus'
teaching but throughout the New Testament and all early Christian
thought. The Son was the one through whom the revelation and redemption had come, historically, and the one who was still present with
his church (vs. 20b). The Spirit was the present and continuing manifestation of God, of his presence and active power within the community, inspiring Christian prophecy, healing the sick, guiding believers, providing the language of defense of the persecuted when on
trial for their faith, and guaranteeing the final eschatological fulfillment of Christian hopes. As G. F. Moore remarked, the formula is a
thoroughly natural summary of Christian faith and aspiration in the
setting in which it properly belongs, that of the early Palestinian or
Syrian church, and does not require to be understood in the light of
fourth- or fifth-century theological speculation. What we should add is
that the later theological development of the docrine was equally natural
and necessary in its own time and place. And later still—even today—
the terms continue to safeguard elements of primary importance for the
whole Christian outlook and fundamental to the whole Christian experience and thought of God.

The earliest history of the doctrine of the Holy Spirit is, like that
of every other doctrine found in the New Testament, related to the
future; it is, as we say, "eschatologically" conditioned and orientated.
The Old Testament had prepared the way; the Spirit was the power,
the agent, the manifest presence of God, the instrument through which
God's "mighty acts" were effected. The approach of the new age was to
be marked by a special outpouring of the Spirit (Acts 2:17-18; 10:45);
the new age itself, wherever it was conceived as a supernatural order,
was to be the age of the Spirit. In the Gospels, in the ministry of Jesus,
the activity of the Spirit is evidence of the approaching "end of the
age," proof of "the powers of the age to come"—see once more Matt.

12:28: "If it is by the Spirit of God that I cast out demons, then the kingdom of God has come upon you." The same was true of the earliest apostolic church, as the book of Acts specifically states (2:15-18, 33). The supernatural manifestations which accompanied the rise of the new faith were evidence that the turning point had been reached, that the new age had dawned, and that "the day" was about to appear.

In Paul's teaching the work (or "fruits") of the Spirit was seen in the moral and spiritual life and conduct of believers, rather than in outward and obvious supernatural phenomena—such as speaking with "tongues" (Gal. 5:22-23). But these inner phenomena are, in Paul's view, equally supernatural. The "life in grace" or the new life "in Christ" could also be described as life "in the Spirit," or as "walking in the Spirit." But this also was eschatological in its orientation—like all of Paul's teaching.

Eventually, in the Gospel of John, the doctrine is formulated in terms of the divine "Counselor," "Advocate," or "Helper" (Paraclete) who has taken Jesus' place or acts as his representative in the Christian community (John 14:17; 15:26). He is specially active—as also in the Synoptics (e.g. Matt. 10:20)—in the testimony of Christians during persecution, in controversy with the "Jews" or in preaching to the unconverted "world" (John 16:13-14, 8-11), and also in the interior life of Christians, as in prayer (John 14:17, 26; cf. also Paul, in Rom. 8:26). It is obvious that by now, if not long before, the Spirit has come to be thought of in personal terms, as a person distinct from God and from Christ.

The doctrine of the Trinity, which attributed to the Holy Spirit the most explicit personal existence, was the result, as we have seen, of the church's attempt to combine all these data of revelation without infringing upon the doctrine of the unity or "oneness" of God. It was no example of "metaphysics," or of philosophy in general, invading the realm of faith, but of a vigorous effort to safeguard the truth of revelation. This was undertaken by means of a formula which, although strictly incomprehensible and beyond rational explanation, was nevertheless true. In this it is like some of our modern scientific formulas, which either describe facts or safeguard the statement of what they imply, quite regardless of the question whether or not we can understand either them or the formula. Until some formula is discovered or devised which will embrace both—or all—sets of facts (such as the nature of light, or of electricity, or the behavior of electrons), this tentative or dialectical combination of statements will have to serve. So it is with the doctrine of the Trinity. The Holy Spirit is God—yet he is not the Father, not the Son, and so on.

2. *The Old Testament Background*

The Christians were not the only ones who took the Old Testament for granted, and viewed their teaching as its completion or fulfillment and its correct interpretation. Pharisaism, Sadducaism, Talmudic Judaism, Essenism, the Damascus sect, the Alexandrine school, and other groups likewise built upon the Old Testament. But it was fundamental to the apologetic statement of the Christians, as reflected in the New Testament, that their interpretation of the sacred Hebrew book was truer than others—it was in fact the one true interpretation. This interpretation was made from the standpoint not only of Jesus' teaching but also of the theological ideas centering in his death, resurrection, and coming triumph (the Christian eschatological faith). The great theological ideas which the Old Testament had slowly but finally wrought out were all taken for granted. God is one, not one among others but the only God; God is spiritual, holy, the living God; he is exalted above creation, which is his work; he is self-sufficient, and in need of nothing, neither temples made with hands nor the offerings of men; he is eternal, all-powerful, omnipresent, all-knowing, all-wise; he is good and merciful, true and trustworthy, righteous, the God of judgment. His "wrath" is still conceived as a personal attribute, though in some passages "the" wrath of the divine justice seems to operate almost automatically, like Nemesis (e.g. I Thess. 2:16). He is loving and merciful, patient and long-suffering—only his regret, which the Old Testament frequently stresses ("it repented him"), is missing from the New Testament. The universe is the work, not of his "hands," as in the poetic or primitive language of the Old Testament, but of his word (e.g. II Pet. 3:5), or his wisdom—either he commands and the world is created, or he "thinks it into existence." He works continuously in maintaining it (John 5:17). Above all, he manifests or reveals himself, not only in physical phenomena or in the crucial events of history, but by special acts of revelation, through angels, dreams, oracles, ecstasy, tongues, prophecies, direct words to men, and above all through the words of his Son and his Spirit. His glory is revealed or at least reflected in nature (Matt. 6:28-30), and in many parts and in various ways—in dreams, visions, oracles, and so on—but supremely in "a Son" (Heb. 1:1-2). The media chosen by God for communication and for self-communication in the New Testament are the same, for the most part, as in the Old; indeed, they are the same as those to be found more or less the world over, and throughout the history of religion. In this respect the New Testament belongs with every other ancient religious literature. Its outlook is not philosophical, rational, subjective—like much of our present-day religious literature, which has to commend itself to the intelligence of modern man before it can gain a hearing. Instead, it assumes the naïve, realistic, ancient approach; God is the God who speaks and makes himself known. Far from being critical or suspicious of God's ways, the ancient believer (Hebrew, Jewish, Christian, or Greek) welcomed the revelation and "returned to his Lord right humbly." But it was the combination of this naïve realism and its data with the rational reflections of philosophy which made possible the later Catholic (patristic) theology. The problem of our present-day theology is that its right wing has collapsed, while its center and left are imperiled; perhaps the only safety, as in Foch's strategy, is to advance, to recapture once more the lost ground of the ancient, naïve, simple, realistic *piety* out of which the New Testament arose.

In studying the great doctrines of primitive Christianity we shall not follow the traditional order of classical dogmatics, which begins with God and the creation and ends with the "four last things," death, judgment, heaven, and hell. Instead we shall try to set the doctrines in the relation in which they stood for the early Christians, though every doctrine was of course related, more or less closely, to every other. The doctrine of God is naturally primary and fundamental, and certainly includes the doctrine of the divine sovereignty, the divine rule, God's reign over the universe, his "kingdom." But eschatology, the doctrine of the future full establishment of the divine reign, far from belonging at the very end of the series of Christian doctrines, belongs (for the New Testament) in the very closest relation to the doctrine of God. The doctrine of the coming kingdom is basic to all that follows—the doctrine of Christ, of salvation, of church and sacraments, and so on. A purely logical, scholastic arrangement of doctrines does not fully correspond to what we find in the New Testament. As the history of doctrine in the New Testament period must be written from the eschatological point of view, so the systematic exposition of New Testament thought or theology must be made from this point of view.

It is sometimes proposed that the discussion of New Testament theology should begin with the resurrection of Christ. It is true of course that the resurrection of our Lord is central for the New Testament, but that transcendent event was itself interpreted eschatologically. Moreover, its significance lay in the fact that it was the resurrection of Jesus, not just of any good man or saint. It was the resurrection of the one whose life had been completely dedicated to the purposes of God, and whose destiny was wholly bound up with their realization. It was he who had been the unique revealer of "the way of God" in truth (Luke 20:21), and his resurrection was looked upon as the final step in the fulfillment of the divine plan of the ages. Moreover, the resurrection, or the eternal life, of all other human beings was bound up with his; such was God's plan of redemption. It is still, therefore, the doctrine of God with which the New Testament begins—the God whose promises are all "Yes" in Christ, since they receive their full and final realization in him (II Cor. 1:20).

As we have already seen, the New Testament doctrine of God takes for granted the biblical, Old Testament, Jewish doctrine, rather than any Greek philosophical, mystical, or other outlook. Even though Greek philosophical terms came eventually to be used (e.g. Rom. 1:20; I Tim. 1:17), the basic concept is the traditional, biblical view (e.g. Acts 14: 17). God is the creator, superior to the created universe of angels, demons, men, and physical nature. Nowhere is he identified with the world, or with his creation, visible and invisible, though his "Logos" informs the whole universe (John 1:3). Nowhere is he limited by the world, or contained within it—as the Greek gods were thought to be; he is wholly sovereign over it. And yet his transcendence is not pushed to exaggeration, as in Islam, where the will of Allah is practically identical with fate. Nor is he set over against the world as the "wholly other," to be described (as by later Dionysian mystics) only in negative terms as "not this," "not that," and in his ultimate essence "beyond being." There is no dualism in the New Testament (as there is in Gnosticism, for example), though some phrases might—and did—lend themselves to such an interpretation. The thought of the New Testament, like that of the Old Testament and of contemporary Judaism, was more naïve, less reflective, less "philosophical" than either of these divergent philosophical and mystical views.

As in Judaism, which was the contemporary first-century form of the religion of the Old Testament, so in the New Testament God is the creator and sustainer of the universe (cf. the Shemoneh Esreh); he is also the God of history, who is in immediate, personal control of events and has repeatedly intervened for the sake of his people or in order to assure the final realization of his own gracious purposes; he is the revealer, who has not only declared what is the true way of life within his world and has therefore given a law to guide his people in the right way, but above all and as his supreme act of grace has revealed *himself*. He is the "King," the supreme ruler of the universe "to whom all things do bow and obey," whom "all dominions shall serve and obey" (Dan. 7:27). He is the savior, "the redeemer of Israel and his king" (cf. Isa. 43: 14-15; 44:6; 47:4), who has "bared his mighty arm" for the salvation of Israel repeatedly in the past, and will "bare it once more," and finally, in the latter days. It is this last note that brings in the ideas of eschatology, as we have seen. God's "kingdom" or "reign" is accordingly thought of in two ways: (*a*) God is the King "of old," from the creation of the world, and forever; "Thy kingdom is an everlasting kingdom, and thy dominion endureth throughout all generations" (Pss. 93:2; 145:13; cf. Dan. 7:27). At the same time (*b*) since God's rule has been rejected in large parts of his world by rebellious angels, by demons, and by men, it must be "established"—or re-established—there; and that is the heart of the eschatological hope. What has been observed of the "double" eschatology in the Gospels, and the "double" motivation of its ethics, is also true of Judaism. God's kingdom is eternal, and yet must "come"; the reason for doing the will of God rests back both upon his sovereignty and upon the very nature of man and the universe, but it also involves the "coming" of the kingdom, as in the Lord's Prayer:

Thy kingdom come,
Thy will be done
    On earth as it is in heaven.

It might even be said that the fundamental doctrine of the whole
Bible (Old Testament, Apocrypha, and New Testament) is the
sovereignty of God, the idea of God as King, and of his kingship
(which is what the Bible means by his "kingdom") over the nation and
over the whole universe, material and spiritual. As in the Nicene Creed,
he is "God the Father almighty, Maker of heaven and earth, and of
all things visible and invisible." Not only in the New Testament but
also in the Old, the connotations of the words for "kingdom" are not
so much "realm" as "reign"—kingship, sovereignty, the act and fact
of being king or absolute sovereign. This fact is amply supported by
the very diction of the Bible, and is true of all the words, Hebrew,
Aramaic, and Greek, which it uses for the purpose of conveying the
idea; their primary meaning, in every case, is "kingship." James Moffatt
quite properly translated the clause in the Lord's Prayer, "Thy reign
begin." In the Old Testament, God's reign (or "kingdom") is over
the whole universe, and is from everlasting and for ever. In later Judaism, as for example in the liturgy, God's kingship is stressed constantly. Men may even "make" God king by accepting him as their
Lord and Ruler. The common rabbinic expression "to take upon [one-
self] the yoke of the kingdom of Heaven" means virtually what a
Christian understands by "making an act of faith"; it can even be
applied to the saying of the Shema. The distinction peculiar to the
New Testament and not commonly found in the older Jewish sources
is apparently one which is made between the ordinary Jewish idea of
religious devotion and the eschatological conception—it is the reign of
God in the age to come which one may "enter." And yet the fundamental idea, common to both the gospel and contemporary Judaism, is
the idea of the reign or kingship, the sovereignty and dominion of God,
or of "Heaven," which is simply a reverent circumlocution for God.

As we have already seen, the "great king" idea—of a remote emperor
of a vast realm who could be approached only through subordinates,
his angels or "powers," through whom he exercised his sovereignty, an
idea fostered by the political experience of the Near East under Per-

sian rule and later under Ptolemaic and Seleucid—certainly left its impress upon the biblical literature and upon biblical religion. Yet it never supplanted the more primitive one in which God stands in close relation to his people and can be approached directly and immediately. Ninety per cent of the Old Testament stood in the way of the impersonal, imperialist idea of God; the examples of a purely transcendental conception are few and can be isolated (e.g. Dan. 7:9-10; Isa. 57:15). The same is true of the New Testament. Earth may be his "footstool," but Jerusalem is still "the city of the great King," as in the Psalms and elsewhere (Matt. 5:35; Ps. 48:2).

The *incorporeal* nature of God is strongly affirmed in the Fourth Gospel (John 4:24, "God is spirit"; cf. 1:18a, "No one has ever seen God"). This affirmation may be viewed as characteristic of the author of the "spiritual" Gospel; no other writer of the New Testament would have thought of making it. But it cannot be supposed that other New Testament writers believed in the corporeality of God. The very language of John's statement had already been anticipated in the Old Testament (Deut. 4:15; I Kings 19:11-12). Moreover, in each of these Johannine sayings the affirmation, positive in one case, negative in the other, is made as the premise to the further statement which fits the writer's argument: "Those who worship him must worship in spirit and truth." "The only Son . . . has made him known."

But this does not end the matter. Of course God is not corporeal, and has no "body, parts, or passions" (cf. Art. I of the Thirty-nine Articles), but this does not mean that he is incapable of manifesting himself through material media, for example through light, or of uttering his words through sound. Indeed God dwells in light unapproachable, but on occasion visible (I Tim. 6:16); he has no visible "body," but he is surrounded, as in the Old Testament conception (Jas. 1:17; I John 1:5), by a "cloud of glory"—the *doxa* of God is incorporeal but real, and to chosen persons on rare occasions was not only visible but even palpable. This was the ancient conception of divine "glory," a conception found also outside the New Testament. The shepherds in Luke's pastoral idyll "see" the glory of the Lord and are afraid (Luke 2:9); the Spirit descends upon Jesus "in bodily form" (3:22); in Acts, Paul is struck to the ground by the divine glory of the exalted Messiah (9:3-4; 22:6-7; 26:13-14). These features might be attributed to the author of that thoroughly Hellenistic, characteristically first-century book, Luke-Acts; but the conception is equally taken for granted by Paul, and nowhere more characteristically than in his doctrine of the resurrection body. Like the body of the risen Lord, that of the Christian is to be "glorious," "incorruptible," "immortal," and yet so completely real that a new terminology is required, almost a new philosophy, a spiritual realism in which "spirit" or "glory" (*doxa*) takes the place of matter—indeed *is* a kind of rarefied, subtilized, spiritualized matter (see I Cor. 15:35-54). No one who thought in such terms could be a Gnostic; Paul is no Gnostic, but an ancient Jew, nurtured on the Old Testament. The church has wrestled with his thought for nineteen centuries now, and has not yet found the way to define and maintain it consistently; perhaps Paul, were he alive today, could not do so either. Transubstantiationism, if only the Aristotelian-Scholastic physics were sound, would perhaps provide the ideal equivalent in Western thought for Paul's conception of "body." The inner "substance" of the "body" is first changed; its eventual transformation and glorification, when "it is raised a spiritual body," is the consequence of its earlier "redemption" in this present life. Something like this statement is required if we are to do justice to Paul's profound view.

Throughout the New Testament it is the "biblical" conception of the relation of God to the world as *creator,* and of the world to God as his creation, dependent upon him for its existence and maintenance, which is everywhere taken for granted. Such a problem as that which faced the Greeks, for whom "the eternity of the world" was all but a dogma, and for whom the termination of the world's existence was all but unthinkable, never arose for biblical thought. In other words the Christian (and Jewish) problem was never faced by Hellenistic thinkers, nor the Hellenistic philosophical problem by Christians of the first century. For Greeks and for those who shared the Greek outlook, the gods were inside the world; there was accordingly no possibility that one God alone had created all that is. Such a view would have been looked upon as we view the notions of savages that "Manitou" or some other "great spirit" made the universe—a perfectly childish answer to a childish question, a primitive "Just So" story. True, the gods had something to do with the regulation of nature, the rain and the weather, or with striking and unusual phenomena, comets and eclipses and the like (though Greek scientists explained them otherwise). But in general the gods were denizens of the world as men were; the only difference was their immortality, their invisibility, their supernatural power, though again it must be added that great poets and thinkers often held higher views. For Greek thought, then, there could be no problem of the creation of the world in time—or even "with" time, as Augustine was to explain it—nor of its maintenance by God, though *Pronoia* (Providence) came to hold an important place in later Hellenistic philosophy.

For the Hebrew, the Jew, and the Christian, on the contrary, the question was entirely different. It was the question of *theodicy*. Nurtured on the scriptural account of creation in Gen. 1–2, their problem was the more difficult one: How can God continue—or how long will he continue—to maintain a world in which his own purposes are often frustrated, or at least temporarily thwarted? Must he not sooner or later bring it to an end and destroy, or transform, what he has created?

The New Testament assumes that God created the world "by the word of his mouth," even as the Old Testament affirms. This "word" was more than the creative *fiat lux, fiat mundum* of the first chapter of Genesis, or the "breath" of the Lord described by the psalmist (Ps. 33:6). The word was *The Word,* the agent of God in the creation, like the figure of Wisdom in some of the later parts of the Old Testament (e.g. Prov. 8:22-31); it was the Logos, the reason of God, the uttered mind of God, acting for the Creator and carrying his purposes into effect. In him, the Logos, "all things hold together" (Col. 1:17); "all things were made through hm" (John 1:3; cf. Heb. 1:1-3). Not that this high Logos doctrine is found everywhere in the New Testament. The simpler, more naïve and unreflective, more traditional view is found side by side—even in Paul! (see Rom. 1:3-4; Eph. 1:22-23)— with the more advanced and philosophical. In the Gospels, God is himself the creator and sustainer of the physical universe, even as in the Sabbath prayer of the synagogue:

> Blessed art thou, O Lord,
>> The Most High God, Maker of heaven and earth. . . .
> Thou art mighty forever,
>> Thou sustainest the living.

Thus the New Testament takes for granted the great scriptural doctrine of the creation of the world by God, who said, "Let light shine out of darkness" (II Cor. 4:6), and who formed all things in accordance with his own wisdom. He has not left himself without witness; the regularity of the seasons and the abundance of the earth, providing as they do for human wants, are proof of his power and his goodness (Acts 14:17). Even more, his very nature is reflected in the order and splendor of the world: "Ever since the creation of the world his invisible nature, namely, his eternal power and deity, has been clearly perceived in the things that have been made" (Rom. 1:20); no Greek philosopher could have stated this more clearly. At the same time, "the things that are seen are transient, but the things that are unseen are eternal" (II Cor. 4:18).

The creation of the world included the creation of time—day and night, summer and winter, the circling seasons, and the succession of the ages (as in the creation story in Gen. 1). There is no metaphysical speculation upon the nature of time in the New Testament; the statement in the Apocalypse of John "that there should be time no longer" (Rev. 10:6 K.J.V.) means only, "There will now be no further delay." Augustine's view that time was created along with the physical universe would have satisfied any philosophically inclined Christian of the first century. The speculations of the apocalyptists regarding the sequence of the ages, as ten in number, or seven, or whatever number, from the dawn of creation until the end of the world, find no place in the New Testament, though the general idea of such a succession is clearly implied in more than one passage (Gal. 4:4; Mark 1:15; Luke 9:51; Rev. 1:3; etc.).

Oscar Cullmann's recent *Christus und die Zeit* (Zürich, 1946) has emphasized a fact which is of fundamental importance for the interpretation of the New Testament. The crucifixion and resurrection of Christ mark the culmination of the past—the Cross stands at the end of history, so to speak, and yet at the same time in the center of history—since when the new age has begun. If the new age is not yet fully realized or manifested, the delay will not be for long and can be explained as part of the divine plan. Yet signs are abundant that the new age is already on its way; the miracles or "mighty works" of Christ were the "powers of the age to come" (Heb. 6:5) already breaking in upon the old world (old and "ready to vanish away," Heb. 8:13), and these mighty works still continued to be wrought in the days of the apostles. These were indeed "the last times," the "latter days" foretold by the prophets (Acts 2:17; Heb. 1:2), and it would not be long now until the full and final realization of all the purposes of God should come to pass. But so little was the first-century church given to speculation that we cannot say that the consummation was conceived as the "end" of history. History, the sequence of time, would still continue—certainly as long as the universe lasted, which means forever. The philosophical concept of an eternal state (*totum simul,* or an "eternal now") lay far beyond the horizon of the early church, as it also lay outside the ken of the Jewish apocalyptists. True, God "inhabiteth eternity," as every Jew and every Christian knew (cf. Isa. 57:15); but this did not involve a philosophical concept of the relation of time to eternity. Eternity was thought of as endless time; there were "days of eternity" for Hebrew and Christian as well as for Egyptian and Babylonian poets.

It is because God is sovereign in creation that he is also sovereign *in history*. His miracles, as we call them, are his "mighty works," signs of his power, his presence, his purposes. The divine overruling includes all history, which is not the work of fate, or the cyclic repetition of a mechanical system of independent laws, or the product of chance. Neither *Tychê* (Chance or Fortune) nor *Anagkê* (Necessity) has any place in biblical religion. Controlling all events from the creation of the world is the age-old plan or purpose of God, hid in a "mystery" (Eph. 1:9-10; Col. 1:26) but partially unveiled to his servants the prophets (Luke 1:70; 16:16) and now finally disclosed in all its majesty and wonder in Christ (Col. 4:3). As in our modern hymn, so in the Bible, "God is working his purpose out, as year succeeds to year." Or in other language,

> There's a divinity that shapes our ends,
> Rough-hew them how we will.

That divinity is not blind destiny; it is the personal will of God our creator; it embraces nations as well as individuals, angels as well as men, heaven and earth and all that are therein. Quite as much as the Old Testament, therefore, the New takes for granted belief in the creation of the world by God—since the universe is not "eternal," as it was for certain Greek philosophers, early and late—belief in the calling of Israel, in the divine mission of Israel, and in the profound significance of Israel's history, and also belief in the final consummation of all God's purposes at the end of history.

This doctrine of the sovereignty of God and of his ruling power, his dominant will which is in control of the whole world and its history, underlies the Old Testament as a whole and the New Testament as well. The Law is the law given by God for the guidance and welfare of his people, "which I teach you . . . that ye may live" (Deut. 4:1). The Prophets supplement the Law, in the view of the New Testament as in the Jewish view, and are full of the doctrine of the divine sovereignty, especially as manifested in current and impending events. The Psalms are hymns of praise addressed to God the King, or if not addressed to God, they certainly presuppose his sovereignty. "The Lord is King, be the earth never so unquiet"—this is a major theme of the "hymnbook of the second temple." The Apocrypha also teach it, especially the histories (First and Second Maccabees) and the wisdom books, above all the book of Judith—its eighth chapter is one of the sublimest utterances of religious faith in all literature! And the New Testament equally presupposes it. For example, the earliest conception of the resurrection of Christ viewed it as God's great act in raising him from the dead and exalting him to be "Leader and Savior" (Acts 5:31; cf. 3:15). Or take Paul's conception of history as outlined in I Cor. 15: 20-28, or his theory of the function of the Law in the divine theodicy; as given by God, it must be "holy and just and good," and yet its function was limited, negative, and temporary (Rom. 7:7-25). God could use the Law, and then discard it when his purpose had been served, even as in the Old Testament God could "raise up" Assyrians or Egyptians to do his will, and then discard them.

Along with this cardinal doctrine of the divine sovereignty went two other doctrines which were closely co-ordinated with it: (*a*) the divine *self-revelation,* and (*b*) the divine *salvation,* which means both his preservation of Israel or of chosen individuals and also his deliverance of them when occasion required. This is the full meaning of *sôtêria* in the Bible, both in the Old Testament and in the New. It is as the preserver, who keeps alive, whole, well, or safe, that God is also the deliverer or savior (*sôtêr*) when danger threatens, or even after the blow has fallen, when he further manifests himself as the redeemer who "brings back" and restores. That is, God does whatever is necessary to achieve his ends; he removes whatever obstacles stand in his way. This is the clearest evidence of all for his real sovereignty and power—he is the God of grace, who as sovereign can even restore from the dead (Rom. 4:17; II Cor. 1:9). Nothing can thwart the will of God, in the end. "All things are possible with God" (Mark 10:27).

This is the biblical view, from beginning to end. Though the term is not always used, at least not in this sense, the biblical doctrine of the divine sovereignty is therefore a doctrine of divine *grace*. God uses his great power for gracious ends. In the midst of suffering, defeat, and desolation God is present with his people: "In all their affliction he was afflicted, and the angel of his presence saved them" (Isa. 63:9). In the midst of the fiery furnace, where the three servants of God were to meet their doom, a fourth was seen, a "son" of God—an angelic deliverer who represented God himself (Dan. 3:24-25). Thus it is impossible to say that there is no doctrine of grace in the Old Testament. In the New Testament it is affirmed repeatedly, as the full meaning of the doctrine is spread out, rich and manifold. It ranges all the way from graciousness (Col. 4:6) to favor (Rom. 3:24) to divine help or aid (II Cor. 12:9) to "strength to help in time of need" (cf. Eph. 3:16; Col. 1:11). This is not the later scholastic formulation, but it is the material out of which later theology fashioned the formal doctrine. Naturally it is not a metaphysical doctrine, but a description of the living God in his relation to his people, God manifest in his acts, in his unceasing care for men (Tit. 2:11). On the nature and person of God only those statements are made which are required by immediate religious experience, which spring out of such experience, and are fully illuminated by it: aspiration, faith, prayer, the realization of God's care, the experience of special deliverance and of the "effectual" working of God's grace (Eph. 3:7). This is not philosophy, or even philosophy of religion, but religion itself; yet without it theism and the philosophy of religion would not exist, any more than would systematic theology. Speculation for its own sake, for the sake of intellectual satisfaction, finds no place in the Bible, which is in closest touch with living experience. So it is with the doctrine of grace, which Augustine and the Schoolmen and the later Jansenists and others were to elaborate systematically, which Luther was to "rediscover" in his reading of the New Testament, and which Protestant theology as well as Catholic—though somewhat differently—was to view as one of the two controlling foci of New Testament revelation.

Thus creation, sovereignty, salvation, redemption, and grace are the great keynotes in the biblical idea of God and of his relation to the world. In fact, it is only in his relation to the world that the conception of God is elaborated. The thought of the Bible as a whole is oriented *eschatologically*—the purpose of God is what gives meaning to human history, and that purpose, originally dominant, later thwarted by angelic rebellion and by human disobedience and by the work of the evil spirits, must be dominant again, as all things are brought once more into submission to the divine will. This is the simple theodicy and philosophy of history presupposed throughout the Bible, in Old Testament prophecy and apocalyptic and everywhere in the New Testament, in Gospels, epistles, and apocalypse. The difference between the Old Testament and the New is not merely that between prophecy and its fulfillment, or between what is hidden and what is revealed—as in Augustine's dictum: "What is latent in the Old Testament is patent in the New." For prophecy is still alive in the New Testament, and the early church, living in the brief interval "between the times," looked forward to still greater things to come (John 5:20). The church existed "between the times," or rather, let us say, in the period when the two ages overlapped, not in some "no man's land" between them. There is really no indication of such a view as the latter in the New Testament. The modern view of Jesus' "ethics," for example, as "interim" ethics is, simply, a modern view. The difference between the Old Testament and the New is not that one is eschatological while the other is not, but that the eschatological view of history presupposed in the Old Testament takes the form of prophecy, while the same eschatological view of history presupposed in the New takes the form of apocalyptic. The difference is partly one of outward form, partly one of emphasis, partly one of content. In the New Testament, as in the later portions of the Old Testament, prophecy has often given way to apocalyptic.

3. *The Justice of God and the Problem of Human Suffering*

It might have been thought that the justice of God would have been questioned by the early Christians, in view of the martyrdom of Jesus and of some of his earliest followers. But here again the eschatological viewpoint was dominant—Christ suffered for a purpose; he even chose to die; far from being unconcerned in the event, God had "sent" or "set forth" his Son for the very purpose of dying. As for the Christians, the eschatological outlook absorbed and neutralized their difficulties; the sufferings of this present time were not fit to be compared with the glory of their eventual triumph (Rom. 8:18). Christ had not promised his followers an easy victory, but hardship, toil, pain, the loss of all things, even life itself—and in the world to come life everlasting. Whether we live or die does not greatly matter; the victory is within sight, and the living and the dead will share it soon.

In the Old Testament the problem of unmerited human suffering was approached from a religious and ethical point of view, but no real or just solution was found, not in Job, not even in the Psalms or in Second Isaiah. The problem is as clearly seen here as anywhere in religious or philosophical literature, and it is chiefly the problem of the sufferings of Israel and, within Israel, of the righteous. On the level of primitive eudaemonism (the theory that religion leads to prosperity) the facile, immediate solution of the problem was the simple inference that sin, either open and flagrant or secret but equally destructive, was its cause and occasion. The "Deuteronomic" explanation of Israel's reverses was a rereading of Israel's history in the light of this explanation—the kings and leaders had "made Israel to sin" through successive generations, until the mass of accumulated wickedness led to national destruction. Job's friends were similarly convinced that the pious sufferer must have committed secret sins which had at last found him out. But the solution does not satisfy. Job really *is* innocent, not guilty, and a prophet later than the Deuteronomists recognizes that Israel has received from the Lord's hand "double" for all her sins (Isa. 40:2).

The failure of this solution is an example of the general failure of prophetic religion to fathom the mystery of wickedness. The prophets had risen to influence during the conquest of Canaan, or the time of the Philistine menace, and under the early monarchy. It was their simple, primitive theory at this early period that the wicked, the enemies of Yahweh, were the heathen round about; once these were defeated, or preferably annihilated, Yahweh's people could then serve him without let or hindrance. Hence the importance of the prophets in rallying the forces of Israel and in unifying the nation during the earlier period. But when the main political problem became that of internal order and of survival within the hostile and threatening international chaos of the eighth, seventh, and sixth centuries B.C. and later, prophetism got beyond its depth and completely foundered. In the end the best that could be hoped was not the bare survival of the nation, nor even its restoration after a time, but only the survival of a remnant—and even this had, in the end, to be transferred to the age to come. Isaiah was no statesman (for all the Victorian changes on this theme in the 1890's!); he denounced the Syrian and Egyptian coalitions as futile, though these were only a temporary, negative expedient. What to do in the total situation, and vis à vis the advancing power of Assyria, lay beyond his comprehension—there was no solution. Whether guilty of sin or not, the nation was doomed. The same is true of Jeremiah, in the altered situation of his days. There was simply no future for a small independent nation occupying the land bridge between Asia and Egypt, once the great empires had risen to power and were demanding territory and tribute in the West.

The roots of the difficulty go far back in the history of Israelite religion. As modern Old Testament scholars reconstruct the origin of Israel's history and religion, there were two very different strands in that history, the northern and the southern. The primitive Yahwism which was brought into Palestine from the east, from the desert, in the fourteenth or thirteenth century B.C. was the cult of a god of storm, volcanic eruption (at Sinai), and war. In spite of the efforts of the prophets (chiefly in the North) this religion accommodated itself to the situation which it met in Canaan, with its Baalism, fertility cults, and thoroughgoing eudaemonism. The eudaemonistic element in later Hebrew religion presumably owed more to Baalism than to Yahwism. In the South, on the other hand, Yahwism had been mollified and strengthened by the influence of Moses and by contact with the settled community of Kadesh—Yahweh was not only the god of storm and tempest, earthquake and volcano, and of war, but above all the god of justice, *mishpat*. Not only were his own ways just, but he strongly favored justice between men and their neighbors, between tribes and cities and nations of men. This conviction, coupled in time with the eudaemonism natural to all primitive religion but now more strongly reinforced by the Canaanite element in northern Israel's religion, gave rise to the acutest form of the problem for Old Testament religious thought. Conceivably God may *not* intend people to be happy and prosperous—not even his own faithful and loyal worshipers. (For ages the nomads of the desert had been more concerned with survival than with further thoughts of opulence.) A god of storm and tempest may do strange things with a nation, and his ways continue to be "past finding out." A god of justice can insist absolutely upon the categorical imperative, "You ought, therefore you must," regardless of consequences, regardless of rewards. He may not be interested in the least in the establishment of a cult, or in the survival of any particular nation or nations, peoples or cities. "Nationalism" may even be anathema to him, his area of interest being world-wide. As he loathes the smell of slain beasts in a Canaanite cult (or in one modeled after the Canaanite cults), so he may also detest the claims of nationalism and exclusiveness, with the fawning demands of servile worshipers for peace and protection, good harvests, and sundry other benefits. (Quite conceivably essential Yahwism moved in that direction, or would have moved in that direction, concretely and historically, had it not been for the circumstance of Israel's settlement in Canaan and the consequent amalgamation with Baalism.) For such a view of God there is no "problem of human suffering." It is a primitive view, no doubt, but for it suffering does not count, death does not count—any more than it does in Homer. All that matters is that a man live, not valiantly, as in Homer, but justly and in obedience to Yahweh, whatever the consequences.

So neither the easy explanation of early prophetism (suffering is due to sin) nor the later (Israel suffers for the sins of other peoples) is a real solution; and the problem was one that did not really belong to Yahwism—it got forced upon Yahwism as a consequence of the intrusion of Baalism, with its primitive agricultural eudaemonism, into the equally primitive but far sterner religion of the desert.

It is chiefly against this background of traditional religious thought that early Judaism and early Christianity struggled with the problem.

There were various solutions. A good man is permitted to suffer in order that he may be prevented from falling into sin—since opulence and happiness are pitfalls for the pious and lead to manifold temptations. Or the heathen have their happiness now, and it is fleeting, while Israel has its happiness deferred, and it will last forever. Some thinkers, like Second Isaiah, rise to the height of the sublime concept of vicarious suffering, with the conversion of the nations in view; and from the same region of exalted insight came the affirmation that God, instead of meting out, or permitting, really shared the suffering of his people (Isa. 63:9). Nevertheless the usual solution of the problem was still eudaemonistic, and it only shifted to the next world, the new age, the blessings and benefits denied here and now. Even the doctrine of the kingdom of God (the actual term is rare in Judaism) came to be understood in this ultraeschatological or apocalyptic sense. And this was certainly the sense in which the term was understood by many of the early Christians, as Paul clearly implies when he tells the Romans that the kingdom of God does not mean "food and drink but righteousness and peace and joy in the Holy Spirit" (14:17). Hence Jesus' cures and exorcisms were looked upon as signs that the new age was on the point of arrival—had either already begun ("realized eschatology") or was about to arrive at any moment. Modern commentators have pointed out that in the Gospels the ministry of healing and exorcism is not portrayed from a "humanitarian" point of view but as a demonstration of supernatural power (this is probably not true of Luke the Hellenist; for him it is both). It is nevertheless arguable that for Jesus himself the motivation was both "humanitarian," as a ministry of mercy, and the demonstration of the powers of the age to come. "If it is by the finger of God that I cast out demons, then the kingdom of God has come upon you" (Luke 11:20). Since the age to come was to be a demonstration of the mercy and goodness of God, of salvation in the fullest sense, and since Jesus' mighty works were the demonstration of the power of God already operative here and now, the inference was obvious—the mercy of God and his salvation, to be fully realized in the age to come, were already at work in the here and now. His ministry was proof of the powers of the age to come; it was the already-realized salvation of God—and both were signs of the mercy and lovingkindness of God. The cures were not merely cures, good works which ought in any case to be done, and worth doing regardless of their religious or supernatural references; nor were they mere evidences—portents—of the approaching end of the age, as a secular phenomenon. The New Testament explanation is thoroughly biblical—that is, religious. God is in control of history, and whatever is evidence of his plans for the world partakes also of his character as the savior and redeemer of his people. The purely secular, even the humanitarian, conception of good works is quite unthinkable on the level of New Testament thought.

The solution, accordingly, of the problem of human suffering is not theoretical but practical and deeply religious—that is to say, profoundly eschatological. The evils of life may be inexplicable, incomprehensible; but God is solving the problem, by removing the evils. Moreover we are permitted to share in the task; we are God's fellow laborers (I Cor. 3:9); the cost, the price which God pays, "Christ's afflictions for the sake of his body, that is, the church" (Col. 1:24), can also be shared. So Paul speaks of his privations as "filling up what is still lacking" in his share of the sufferings of Christ—a mystical view which, to this day, sets forth the profoundest contribution Christianity has to make to the problem of human suffering.

4. *The Terms "God" and "Lord"*

It was generally known in the ancient world that the God of the Hebrews had no personal name—a strange, unique feature in that strange, exotic religion, whose only temple was a statueless shrine, where the inmost sacred holy of holies was a dark and empty room. "What a religion!" would be the perfectly natural remark of almost any pagan. On the other hand there were pagans for whom the very namelessness of God was attractive—the one to whom had been attributed many names was, in effect, unnamed. For many centuries Greeks had insisted that certain gods were "many-named"; with the spread of syncretism and the consequent identification of the Greek gods with foreign deities these "many names" steadily increased in number. But the Hebrews' refusal to name their God was something unusual. True, their scriptures did have "names" for God, *El Shaddai, YHWH* (never pronounced in later times), and so on; but these were not known to the world at large—excluding titles, the Septuagint had only two words for God, *theos* and *kyrios,* neither of them a proper name.

In the Hellenistic age the term *theos* was still (as long before in Homer) a generic term for a supernatural, superhuman, "divine" being. Either with or without the article (as in John 1:1) it denotes not so much *a* god or *the* god (the one referred to) as "the deity." When John 1:1 states, "The Logos was *theos,*" this does not mean "a god," but "God"—which is something more than "divine" (*theios*), for the noun is used attributively or predicatively, and the noun means "God." When the Septuagint translated the Hebrew *Eloah* and *Elohim* by *theos,* it was not expressing an exact equivalent for the idea of God conveyed by these ancient Hebrew names. On one hand the term *theos* was far more impersonal, and could lead to such abstractions as we find in Philo; on the other, the impersonal term "deity" could lead on to an appreciation of the personal religion of the Old Testament (such as that of the Psalms), as we see in Paul.

But it was the title *Kyrios* that marked the greatest advance in thought. This term was practically equivalent to *Adôn* in the Hebrew Old Testament; it meant lord, master, owner, ruler, and its correlative was slave. In religious usage the term *Adonai* ("my lord") had already come to be substituted for the sacred tetragrammaton *YHWH* (whose proper pronunciation, and meaning, were lost early in the second century B.C., if not before). Wherever the word *YHWH* appeared, the synagogue reader substituted *Adonai,* with the result that when the text eventually became vocalized (when the traditional vowels were added to it), the vowels supplied to the tetragrammaton were those of *Adonai* (*a, o, a*), a device perfectly understood in the synagogue but destined to lead to the impossible hybrid so popular in Puritanism, "Jahovah" or "Jehovah," which is a wholly artificial and meaningless word.

What lies back of this use of *Adonai* in the Jewish synagogue, and therefore back of the Septuagint translation of both *Adonai* and *YHWH* by *Kyrios?* The enormous researches of W. W. von Baudissin, *Kyrios as a Name for God in Judaism and Its Place in the History of Religion* (4 vols., 1926-29), have made it clear that in the Hellenistic age *Kyrios* was a divine title, especially appropriated to lordship of a cult. It was so named in the cults of Isis and Serapis, but the usage was much wider and included most of the cults, both Semitic and Greek, in the ancient Near East. The significance of this title for Diaspora Judaism and for early Christianity, both directly and as mediated through the Septuagint, was far-reaching. The total absence of any personal name for God in the Greek Bible and the use of the word *Kyrios* instead was really "a manifesto of monotheism."

This is as true of the use of *Theos* as of *Kyrios*. How the usage would impress a Greek is not difficult to imagine—let us say one who for the first time read the opening verses of Genesis: "In the beginning God made the heaven and the earth. But the earth was unseen and unorganized—chaotic—and darkness lay over the abyss. And a spirit [or a wind] of God swept back and forth above the water. And God said, Let light be. And light was. And God saw the light, that it was good . . ." A Greek reading these lines might have expected, in a "barbarian" Oriental book, to read that "in the beginning" the great god Marduk, or perhaps Rê, or Isis, "created heaven and earth"; but this said simply "god," or "the god"—or even "the deity." "How simple yet impressive," he would observe; and if he tended to be a monotheist, he might add, with the author known as Pseudo-Longinus, "How sublime!"

Along with this use of *Theos* and *Kyrios* as divine titles (not names, though they sometimes functioned as such) went a purging of the Old Testament anthropomorphisms, some of which were entirely removed, others softened and modified, and still others provided with substitutes. This tendency was parallel to what we can observe in the later Targums, for example "the voice [or "word"] of the Lord said" for "the Lord said"—though some examples of this are to be found even in the Old Testament (e.g. Ps. 29).

Greek-speaking Christianity fell heir to the Septuagint, as everyone knows. What is even more important, the Septuagint, and the Greco-Jewish writers in Alexandria and elsewhere who used the Septuagint and made it known to the Greek-speaking world, really provided the religious vocabulary for early Gentile Christianity. At least they provided its major terms, the terms about which the whole pattern of religious thought was built. This is conspicuously the case with the terms for God, *theos* and *kyrios,* which have just been considered. God, the supreme and only God, the one true God, was both *Theos* and *Kyrios*.

He was both creator and sustainer of the universe, the *Kosmokratôr* or *Pantokratôr*. And as the God of a special cult, as the God of Israel, he was the *Kyrios* of Israel, or the *Kyrios* of hosts, or the *Kyrios* of far-distant nations, "of them that remain in the broad sea" but have heard of the "mighty deeds," the "terrible acts" of Israel's God. It is especially in his relations to nature and to history that he is *Kyrios*—Lord, Master, Controller, Victor—for the simple reason that the Septuagint is a translation of the Old Testament, where *YHWH* is the special "name" for God in history, and where *Kyrios* is the translation of *YHWH*.

But how was the risen, exalted Jesus, the *Kyrios* of the Christian faith and cult, related to the *Kyrios* (God) of the Old Testament? How could Christology avoid infringing upon strict monotheism? Or how could the doctrine of Holy Spirit fail to do so? It was no easy step to take, in a monotheistic environment, to identify the exalted Lord Christ with the God of the Old Testament, and it was not, apparently, taken directly or immediately. We cannot imagine Christians in the earliest generation identifying the risen Christ directly with God; the language of Acts 2:36 ("God has made him both Lord and Christ") itself makes it clear that "Lord" is used in a subordinate sense, i.e. under God —even though Luke may have understood the terms in a later and more developed theological sense. The stages by which Christ came to be viewed and worshiped as *Kyrios* seem to have included at least the following:

1. By his resurrection from the dead Jesus "became" Christ, the heavenly Messiah, "exalted at God's right hand," and was expected presently to return in glory as judge of the living and dead. As head of a cult of followers, disciples, or worshipers he was addressed by them as "Lord." (*a*) The fact that this was the term used in the Greek-speaking Diaspora for *YHWH* or *Adôn* (or *Adonai*) made no difference, since the language of the earliest Palestinian-Christian communities was not Greek but Aramaic, and the term used by them was evidently not *Adonai* but *Mar, Maran,* or *Mari*—which was almost never used for God (see Ps. 110:1). They could address the heavenly, exalted Christ as *Maran* without in the least infringing upon monotheism. (*b*) The oldest surviving formula of Christian prayer, *Marana tha* ("Our Lord, come!" I Cor. 16:22; cf. Rev. 22:20; Didache 10:6)

makes it clear that prayer was directly addressed to the exalted Christ, and also that it was assumed that he could hear and respond. This was no longer the language of prayer addressed to God, who would "send" Jesus Christ at the proper time (Acts 3:20).

2. The second stage apparently followed soon after this point had been reached, and it was inevitable when the church became even partly Gentile and Greek-speaking. For the one word used to translate both *Mar* and *Adôn* into Greek was *Kyrios,* as a comparison of the three passages in First Corinthians, Revelation, and Didache cited above will show. In other words the heavenly Christ could be termed or even addressed as *Mar* by his Aramaic-speaking followers and cult members without infringing upon monotheism (though orthodox Jews would scarcely admit this); but one could not call him *Kyrios,* the term long used by the Septuagint to translate *YHWH, Adôn,* which were the "names" of God in the Old Testament, without doing so. In the Septuagint

$$Kyrios = Ad\hat{o}n$$

or *YHWH* of the Hebrew scriptures. But also

$$Kyrios = Mar$$

of the Aramaic usage. Therefore by a familiar axiom

$$Mar = Ad\hat{o}n$$

—that is to say, the use of the common translation *Kyrios* could lead to the identification of Christ, in some sense, with the God of the Old Testament. And this stage, I believe, had been reached long before Paul arrived at Damascus, or Antioch, or wherever he is supposed to have provided early Gentile Christianity with its chief christological term. The word was already in use, as applied to the exalted Christ, among the earliest Gentile Christians, even before Paul's conversion; and so also was the title "Son of God," which he took over and similarly enriched and deepened in meaning.

3. The third stage is reflected chiefly in the letters of Paul. The consequences of the use of the Septuagint term *Kyrios* for Christ, the

exalted, heavenly head of the primitive Christian messianic cult, are now fully drawn. And they are drawn in connection with the other title just mentioned, "Son of God," which was no Jewish messianic title at all, but came straight out of Hellenism and was especially appropriate for the divine head of a cult. Not that New Testament Christology was the result of an accident of language—far from it! The whole drift and tendency of the evidence thus far considered seems to support the view that the Christian faith was christological from the beginning. It was no accident that the name for the followers of "the Way" among Greeks at Antioch was *Christianoi*, "Christ-worshipers" (Acts 11:26), not "followers of Jesus," "Galileans," "Nazarenes," or what not. The roots of Catholic Christology evidently go down to the very oldest historical stratum of Christianity; Christ was worshiped as head of a cult from the very beginning, even in the most primitive Aramaic-speaking Christian communities.

What Paul did was to take the identification of the heavenly Lord (whom he, and probably other Gentile Christians, viewed as pre-existent) with the *Kyrios* of the Septuagint in full earnest. He could do so, as we have said, without absolutely identifying Christ with God (with "God the Father" in later Catholic theology), by viewing him as a divine being, subordinate to God, the "Son of God"—the one through whom God had acted, revealed himself, proclaimed his will, guided his people, who had now come to earth to redeem those who believed in him. The relation of Christ to God, in the thought of Paul, is best stated in the dramatic language of Phil. 2:5-11 or in that of I Cor. 15:20-28. This was not strict monotheism of course; but there were other Jewish thinkers who thought along similar lines, hypostatizing the "powers" of God or his "angel" or his "presence"—for example Philo. It was a view destined to vex the peace of the church—as when modalists and adoptionists undertook to defend the divine *monarchia* in the second century, only to be repudiated by later orthodoxy; or as when Marcion undertook to distinguish between the good (if unknown) God of Christ and the evil Creator-God of the Jewish Law—though the problem is not identical with Paul's, and the solution is far from his.

The view has sometimes been proposed that the God of the early Christians was not the one God of the Old Testament at all, but the cult

Lord, Christ, who, like other cult deities of the time, claimed absolute prerogatives and so became in effect the one and only God. This may perhaps have been true of some Christians here and there, even of certain groups of Christians, but it was scarcely the view of the New Testament (the evidence for it is found later). And it was a view certainly destined to be swallowed up in the resurgent monotheism of the third, fourth, and fifth centuries, when—now partly under the influence of Greek philosophical thought and of the general religious tendency toward monotheism and the "absolute" deity or sovereignty of one God —the great Catholic creeds were formulated, and place had to be found for Christ the Word within the very nature of the Divine Being.

4. There were other stages, but they were subsidiary—for example that reflected by the reading back of the title *Kyrios* into the gospel tradition, whether as a divine title used by or of Jesus during his earthly life (e.g. Matt. 17:4; Luke 10:1; John 6:68) or as an innuendo or implication from the ordinary Greek vocative *kyrie,* "sir," "master," "teacher." These are secondary usages and are consequential rather than causal in the developing Christian doctrine of God. It is interesting that such a title could be used along with the divine title; but there are plenty of examples of the same sort of usage, as in English "Lord," meaning either God, or master ("milord"), or a member of the upper house of Parliament. Ordinarily no confusion would result from it; the context or the situation would make the meaning clear. The fact of such variety in meaning must, however, be borne in mind as one reads the Gospels, for it affects the interpretation of more than one passage.

It is a striking and yet a perfectly natural phenomenon which we find in the New Testament; the terms *theos* and *kyrios* are repeated here— that is, continue in use—as if the Septuagint had set the standard for their occurrence. A pagan reader looking through the Christian supplement to the Septuagint—that is what the New Testament really was, at the time—might have noted the continuity of usage; only a more careful reading would have made him aware that although (*a*) in the original work (the Old Testament) the words *theos* and *kyrios* always refer to the same person, the god of the Jews, nevertheless (*b*) in the supplement the term *theos* still continues to mean this god whereas *kyrios* is now sometimes the title of this god, sometimes the title of the risen, exalted, glorified Christ of the Christians. This double usage would no doubt confuse our pagan reader somewhat, and he might easily assume that the Septuagint usage had itself suggested the distinction—*theos* could not be used of a man, *kyrios* could be used of either god or man (at least of a divine man, one raised by apotheosis to the level of deity). He might accordingly suspect that the familiar process, still common in the Hellenistic age and known almost everywhere in polytheism, had taken place here; that either (*a*) the two Septuagint terms had given rise to two separate deities, by projection, or that (*b*) a departed hero had now become head of a cult, and had taken over one of the older divine titles. But his first hypothesis would be wrong; the Septuagint did not provide the primary incentive to a developing Christology; it provided only the most readily available terms in which that Christology expressed itself. His second hypothesis would be nearer the truth, but it would require correction and elaboration from the history of the earliest Christian cult—as we have seen, Jesus was head of a cult before the Greek term *kyrios,* with all its Septuagint associations, came to be applied to him.

As *kyrios* could be applied either to God or to Christ, so it could also be applied to the Spirit; but this was a slow, and a much later, development. Only the slightest indications in the New Testament point in that direction (e.g. II Cor. 3:17). In the New Testament, especially in Paul, the formula is the widespread monotheistic one, *heis theos,* modified by the addition of the distinctively Christian formula, *heis kyrios*— "There is one God . . . and one Lord" (I Cor. 8:6). This usage continued for several generations in the Gentile churches and both explains and underlies the language and the theology of Justin, for whom Christ is the "second" God (*Dial.* 56:11), and also that of contemporary monarchians or adoptionists as well as that of the later Arians. The development was not purely theological, or academic, or exegetical (exegesis of the Septuagint), but arose out of Christian cult and preaching. Nor was it an intrusion of polytheism into the faith of the gospel, for it sprang directly out of the earliest Christian experience and conviction of the "place" of Christ in relation both to God and to his own followers, with whom he was invisibly present in prayer, sacrament, mighty work, and proclamation of his saving word.

5. *God and Christ*

The New Testament doctrine of God is summed up in the Pauline formula: He is "the God and Father of our Lord Jesus Christ" (II Cor. 1:3). That is, he is the God of Jesus—the one whom Jesus loved and adored and obeyed, whom he called "Father," or "my Father," whom he taught his disciples to address as "our Father," to whom he referred as "your Father"—and he is also the Father of "our Lord Jesus Christ," who is the Son of God. If the latter usage does not yet imply a "metaphysical" relation, it is certainly (in Paul's thought, at least) well on the way toward that implication. As we shall see, there is ground for thinking that the relation *was* metaphysical, though not in the full Nicene or Chalcedonian sense. Christ is a divine being who existed with God from the beginning. He is more than an angel, for Paul as for the author to the Hebrews and for John. God is his Father in a unique sense, as he is uniquely "Son" of God. Father and Son are not yet thought of as

> Consubstantial, Co-eternal,
> While unending ages run.

It is impossible to insist that any New Testament writer should recite the later creeds, though the language of the later creeds is no doubt a true interpretation and unfolding of the implications of the New Testament. Nor do the New Testament writers set forth the view of the "coequality" in nature of the Father and the Son (and of the Spirit) found in the later "Athanasian" Creed. The New Testament Christology, even in its highest flights, implies an original subordination of the Son to the Father—original, and permanent.

But it is the doctrine of God, who is "the Father of our Lord Jesus Christ," which is our present concern. Here it is not enough to say that the New Testament took over the traditional Old Testament doctrine, inherited from Judaism. For the Christian church took over the doctrine but modified it, gave it a different emphasis and a fuller, richer content, now that God was recognized to be not only the creator and sustainer of the universe, the Lord of history, the God of grace, mercy, and forgiveness, but also "the Father of our Lord Jesus Christ." His work of creation, revelation, and redemption reached its final consum-

mation in his last and greatest act, what he did in and through Christ—
the new creation, the fresh and complete revelation, the final and universal redemption. As early Christian teachers looked back upon the
past, especially upon the history of Israel, and studied the covenants and
"promises" set forth of old, they saw that the full and final unveiling
of God's purposes from the beginning of creation had been made clear
at last in Christ. Christ was the key to history and to revelation, and
without him both were left incomplete and truncated. He was the *telos*
of all earlier revelation (Rom. 10:4). All the past led up to him; all the
future was bound up with him. He came "not to abolish . . . but to
fulfill" (Matt. 5:17); all God's promises were "Yes" in him (II Cor.
1:20); God, who had formerly spoken through prophets and wise men
and a lawgiver, had at last spoken *en huiô*—through the agency of one
who was no less than his Son (Heb. 1:2; cf. Mark 12:6).

It has sometimes been argued (see above) that the God of the early
Christians was Christ, and then, by a process parallel to that by which
other gods became sole and exclusive deities (especially in the third and
fourth centuries, for example Helios, Mithra, Isis), Christ came to be
identified with the One God (*heis theos*). It is true, as we have already
admitted, that some such conception of Christ was perhaps to be found
here and there on the outer fringes of the Christian faith during the
first three centuries; but it was not the inner core of Christian conviction, which was too biblical, too monotheistic, too Jewish for that.
"Normative" Christianity was moving steadily in the direction of the
Catholic creeds. And the theory makes it all but impossible to explain
the difficulties faced and overcome in the christological tensions and
controversies of the second to fifth centuries. For if the Christian faith
had begun with Christ as *God,* those difficulties would either not have
arisen at all or would have taken a very different form. The New Testament knows nothing of the theory—it moves from the manhood of
Christ to his deity, not from his deity backward and downward to his
manhood. The same fact refutes the once-popular "Christ myth"
theories which made of him a "pre-Christian" solar (or other) deity
who eventually got identified with the historical Jesus of Nazareth.

Still another popular modern statement must be ruled out if we are
correctly to understand the New Testament—that the God of the early
Christians (and of Christianity all along, especially today) is "the

Christlike God." This view assumes that upon a basis of nineteenth-century agnosticism, with God the Great Unknown or Unknowable, or of twentieth-century crisis theology, with God the Wholly Other, was founded the religion of the historical Jesus—first of all the religion that Jesus of Nazareth taught and lived, and then the religion which centered in devotion to the Jesus of history, the purely human but also "human-divine" figure known from the Gospels. That is, upon a foundation of pure agnosticism was erected the "Jesuolatry" of sentimental attachment to a heroic and practically divine human figure— "practically" divine, since he had (and has) the "value" of God for Christian faith. How extraordinarily all this parallels the hymn of welcome and thanksgiving addressed to Demetrius Poliorcetes, the "liberator" of Athens in 307 B.C.!

> The other gods are far away—
> Thee we see face to face!

But the theory has no warrant from the New Testament, which is theocentric rather than Christocentric, from beginning to end. The New Testament assumes that there is a natural knowledge of God, either implanted in or open to every human being, since God "did not leave himself without witness" anywhere in his creation (Acts 14:17), and since his Logos or Word is "the light that enlightens every man" (John 1:9). Of course this "natural knowledge," available to everyone, with its corollary of "natural law" binding every human being and every nation, and of "natural theology" open to every person capable of rational thought, is something more than inference and speculation. It is itself revelation, since (as Emil Brunner rightly maintains) "only God can reveal God." God really *has* spoken "of old to our fathers" (Heb. 1:1), not only in the prophets but "in many and various ways," in nature and in history as well as through men. The very heavens "declare the glory of God," as the psalmist said (Ps. 19:1), and his rule over the nations has been apparent from the beginning. From the period of primeval chaos,

> The Lord sitteth above the water-flood,
> And the Lord remaineth a King for ever.
> (Ps. 29:9 B.C.P.)

His mighty works declared his existence even before prophets and seers were raised up to make him known as a person and to announce his will. The New Testament simply assumes the biblical, Old Testament view of God, his revelation, his self-disclosure "in many and various ways." Only, it insists, this continuous and constant earlier revelation in many parts has now reached its climax, since he "has spoken to us by a Son."

No, the logic of the New Testament theology is not that God is Christlike, which is only a still further and more paradoxical extension of the nineteenth-century formula, Christ is "like God," or "has the value of God." Rather it is that (a) God has revealed himself continuously since the dawn of creation (creation is the beginning of God's self-revelation and the primary manifestation of his goodness, for creation is not evil but good, as in Gen. 1:31), and that (b) he has finally and fully revealed himself in Christ. The God revealed in Christ is the same God who is revealed in nature, in history, in prophecy and law. As Athanasius correctly argued against Arius, the God of creation and the God of redemption are one and the same, in the Christian view. This also rules out Marcionism, Manichaeism, and other like errors with two gods or two ultimate principles at war in the universe.

That the Christian view as set forth in the New Testament must naturally lead (as it historically did lead) to the doctrine of the Incarnation is quite obvious. For what God did in Christ was not only to reveal himself by word and teaching, but to manifest himself in the person of Christ and to act in and through him for the redemption of mankind. He not only spoke *en huiô;* he acted. He is not only "the God who speaks," but the God who acts. In fact, throughout the Bible, his revelation is not only by word but by deed, by "mighty acts, and wonders, and signs" of his presence and power, setting forth his purpose and his will. His "word," in brief, is often learned in events, which are under his control, and his word is "sent" when he "raises up" Jesus, first as his emissary to the children of Israel and again as his Son—by resurrection from the dead (Acts 10:36), when Jesus is proclaimed, demonstrated, or set forth as Messiah and Son of God (Rom. 1:4). It is a total inversion of the New Testament or primitive Christian view when Jesus is represented as "the man who would be God," or "the man who became God." For although the line indeed runs from man to

God, from manhood to deity, the underlying principle presupposed all along is that the initiative came from God, who was thus revealing himself.

> This is the Lord's doing,
> And it is marvellous in our eyes.
> (Ps. 118:23 B.C.P.)

Not "Christ reveals God," but "God reveals himself in Christ." Not "Christ reconciles us to God"—let alone "reconciles God to us"!—but in Christ God was "reconciling the world to himself" (II Cor. 5:19). Not "God is like Christ," nor yet "Christ is like God," but God reveals himself in Christ, God acts in Christ, God reconciles us to himself in Christ, God saves us in Christ, God gives to us a new and higher life in Christ, God's gift to us in Christ is nothing short of eternal life, which is a life in himself and to himself. Indeed, in Christ, God gives us something of himself, so that we become in him "partakers of the divine nature" and sharers in his own immortality and eternity (II Pet. 1:4). The line from manhood to deity is real, but it is not the whole line, or the whole process; it is the part that *we* see, but the total line is one that runs from God to man and then back again. We see the return, not the coming forth, but the line from God to us is there *before* the line is drawn from us to God.

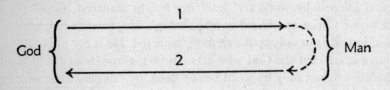

This concept is fundamental, not only to Paul's theology, or John's, but to the whole New Testament, and indeed to the whole of biblical theology, which is not man-centered, or even Christ-centered, but God-centered, from beginning to end. It is Christ-centered only to the extent that Christ stands on the side of God, not of man—though truly he is on both sides, and, as we have already observed, there is a real subordination of Christ to God not only in origin, nature, and essence (Phil. 2) but also in history, eschatologically and finally (I Cor. 15).

Thus the New Testament doctrine of God was not a new and revolutionary conception of God as Creator, Redeemer, or Father of mankind. These conceptions were all very old, in fact older than the oldest parts of the Old Testament. The great development given the doctrine in the Hebrew scriptures is taken for granted in the New Testament—God is the Creator of the whole world; he is the Redeemer of Israel; he is the Father of the nation and of the pious individuals in the nation. But the advance upon the older idea, which it "fulfills," is this: God is the Redeemer not only of Israel but of all men who put their trust in his mercy; the nation has given way to a smaller body, which in turn may become—is already becoming—universal, and will eventually embrace all mankind. The divine covenant with Israel fades before the divine covenant with all mankind, that is with those who respond to the gospel as Israel had once responded to the Law. God is the Father, not only of Israel, or of the king of Israel, or of the pious, but of all men; and in a special and unique way he is "the Father of our Lord Jesus Christ." Thus it is both a new emphasis which we find in the New Testament and also, as a consequence of this new emphasis, a new content. It was this idea of God which the early church presented to the world as the fulfillment of all its age-old dim longings for him, seeking and reaching out for him, "if haply they might . . . find him, though he be not far from every one of us" (Acts 17:27 K.J.V.; cf. 14:15-17).

VII

Miracles

1. *The Old Testament and Judaism*

AS in the Old Testament, so in the New, what we call miracles were looked upon as manifestations of divine power. The purpose of this manifestation was to reveal the will or the purposes of God or to effect judgment or salvation. Even where the miracle was a manifestation of the divine "glory" (*kabhodh*), it had the purpose of changing something or someone, reassuring the doubtful, overwhelming the enemies of God, aiding the persecuted, or declaring the law and commandments of the Most High. There was no motive of self-display, as a heathen god might grant an epiphany to his devotees, like an idle eighteenth-century monarch holding levee. The great miracle of the Old Testament was the deliverance from Egypt—replete with particular miracles, signs, and mighty deeds, and culminating in the giving of the Law on Mount Sinai. The great miracle of the New Testament is the resurrection of Christ, followed by the coming of the Spirit, the inauguration of the New Israel, and other related "mighty works."

The effect produced by the Old Testament miracles was as a rule the renewed conviction of God's holiness, at first a very primitive sense of awe at the presence of this unpredictable deity; and so it was in the New Testament—the demoniac infers that Jesus is "the Holy One of God," and Simon Peter exclaims, "Depart from me, for I am a sinful man, O Lord" (Mark 1:24; Luke 5:8). As time went on, the Old Testament conception had deepened; miracles were intended not only to aid and support—or to rescue and "deliver"—Israel, but to manifest God's power and goodness in relation to other nations and to win their allegiance to the only true God (this is especially

144

clear in Second Isaiah). But above all, the miraculous, inexplicable deeds of power by which God manifested himself were meant to prove that God was the ruler of history, in absolute control of the destinies of men and nations.

It is of course true that this high level was not always maintained. Just as in the West, in Greek and Roman religion, the Hellenistic age saw the resurgence of crude beliefs which had been buried and overlaid for generations, so in Israel the old, primitive beliefs and legends survived among the people and emerged again, after the period of classical prophecy had come to a close, in a wild miracle mongering. We see traces of this revival in the work of the Chronicler; we see more of it in the popular tales of rabbis and magicians in the Herodian and Roman periods. Popular Judaism, the religion of the rank and file, was by no means on the level of the prophetic religion nor even on that of rabbinic piety. It is this religion of the ordinary populace which is reflected in the Gospels—quite naturally, since contacts with rabbinic Judaism are either almost wholly lacking or are negative and polemical.

Just as in the Old Testament and throughout the ancient world, so here there are no "laws of nature" which stand in the way of miracles. God is in direct and immediate control of the world, and can use any occasion or event for the manifestation of his power. He is the "living" God, and instead of being remote and inaccessible, a distant sultan or pharaoh who communicates at long intervals and then only through intermediaries, God intervenes directly and frequently in the course of events. There was nothing like the deistic view of the world, save in a very tiny circle of skeptics who had fallen under the influence of Epicurean "atheism" or of the cold agnosticism of contemporary Roman philosophy; and of this influence there is scarcely a trace in the New Testament. God had not created the world and then left it to its own devices, or set it going upon the iron rails of rigid law; instead, he could—and did—interrupt its course from time to time, and there was no problem involved in his doing so. "All things are possible with God" (Mark 10:27; cf. 9:23). But his purpose in doing so, which men might infer, was either disciplinary or directive; and it was consistent. He was "working his purpose out," and the end in view was the eschatological goal which lay at the heart of all Hebrew, Jewish, and early Christian faith.

2. *The Modern Attitude Toward Miracles*

For the past two centuries and more, since the days of the deists in England and of the Enlightenment in France and Germany, there has been a persistent and continual effort to eliminate the miracles from the New Testament. For example glossolalia or "speaking with tongues," which in the early church was looked upon as miraculous, was explained as due to "enthusiasm"—of which contemporary religious excitement furnished examples, as among the Irvingites. Modern psychologists have studied this phenomenon, attributing it to individual or mass suggestion, to imitation, to the dim recollection of half-remembered, half-forgotten foreign languages, to reversion to "baby talk," to uncontrolled automatism, or even to injury of speech centers in the brain.

Other miracles such as exorcism of demons, healing of the lame, relief from fever, or the cure of blindness or deafness have been similarly explained as due to suggestion, and parallels have been found in modern psychotherapeutic practice, for example the treatment by hypnosis. Others have been recognized as the work of autosuggestion. Still others (such as the walking on the water, or the multiplication of the loaves or of the wine at Cana) have been accounted for simply as the growth of legend, or the borrowing of legends from other cults or from current folklore. Thus one theory will explain some of the miracles, but another theory is required for others. In general the psychological explanation is now the more prominent, and the legendary or "mythical" (as David Friedrich Strauss called it) is in eclipse. It may well be that both theories will contribute something to the final solution, if that solution is ever to be reached. The fundamental difficulty today is of course that in a scientific world, in a rational world, miracles "simply do not happen." The objection is reasonable, and very real.

But the presuppositions of much of our modern study of the miracles are really inadequate, both on philosophical or theological and on historical grounds. (1) On the philosophical side, our modern "scientific" view of nature as a closed system—however necessary for practical purposes—simply cannot claim finality. Philosophy demands a realm of ends, of values and of final causes, to which the natural order must be subservient. Even upon the "humanistic" (or naturalistic) view of the universe as "self-existent," it must have *some* meaning. If the universe has a meaning, then it cannot be a mere machine with no end or purpose beyond its own "self-stoking, self-repairing" maintenance. The possibility of novelty, of new and unpredictable "emergents," is inevitable for any but a purely "scientific" philosophy (which is scarcely entitled to the use of that queer and really indefensible name) ; and the miracles of the New Testament *may* be viewed as examples of such emergence of novelty, as human life rises above the level of the natural order, and God, the creator and sustainer of the whole universe, adopts new methods to suit further purposes in his creative work. As the Schoolmen insisted, especially Thomas Aquinas (*Summa Theol.* I, qu. 110.4), miracles may be not so much *contra naturam* as *supra* or *praeter naturam;* in God's eyes the ordinary and the extraordinary are equally *naturaliter,* and "miracle" is only our name for what transcends human explanation. In the will of God—which, as Augustine said, is "the nature of things" (*City of God* XXI. 8)—there is no natural and supernatural; or rather, the supernatural *is* the natural, and the natural rests back upon what is, in the divine transcendence, wholly supernatural.

Equally (2) on historical grounds the modern, Humian view that "miracles do not happen" is wholly inadequate, as is also the view that "original" Christianity, the "pure" gospel of Jesus, must be stripped bare of "legendary accretions." We simply cannot transfer our twentieth-century world view back to the first century and understand what is going on there. Any first-century religion which lacked miracles, we may confidently affirm, would not have survived long enough or have been sufficiently influential to leave behind any record for posterity. The world was full of miracles—at least of stories of miracles. Every religion, Jewish, pagan, Christian, had its share. Indeed there were miracles with no religious attachment whatsoever, and a whole literature was in circulation, in the Hellenistic-Roman age, relating these unaccountable phenomena. By the same token a miracle had not the same value that it would have for us who live in a "scientific" age. Miracles might even be false in purpose and intent, though valid enough as events—such were the "pretended signs and wonders" wrought by the demons or by men under their control (II Thess. 2:9). On the whole, however, "religious" miracles were veridical, though they often required interpretation. There is general truth in the common saying that whereas miracles were once the support of faith, now they are a burden to it. For the ancient world had no conception of the "laws" of nature, except for a few students of science or philosophy here and there—and some of them, for example Posidonius, were equally students of the occult and supernatural. But the real test of a miracle with religious value was, then as now, and as in every age, whether or not it supplied proof of the presence, the power, or the purpose of God. This criterion may be applied to the miracle stories of the Old Testament as well as to those of the New, and also to those reported in the Greek and Roman religions, and in every other. For religious men a "true" miracle must have religious significance; otherwise it is only a "wonder." It must be a sign (*sêmeion*) and "signify" something of religious importance; or, in the more usual biblical language, it must be a power (*dunamis*), a manifestation or "mighty work" of God; otherwise it was merely one of the "unaccountable things of nature"— a wonder (*thauma*), a portent or prodigy (*teras*) perhaps, but, except for Roman religion, not religiously significant.

3. *The Eschatological Interpretation*

But if our modern "scientific" presuppositions are inadequate for a proper understanding of the New Testament miracles, what presuppositions *are* required? The answer can be given in one word— the only adequate presuppositions for understanding and interpreting the New Testament miracles are *eschatological*. In the language of the Synoptic Gospels they are not "signs and wonders" at all, but "mighty works," powers, especially "powers of the age to come" (cf. Heb. 6:5) already active in the present age which is now drawing to a close. Not that they operated automatically—there was nothing automatic about the succession of the ages, for Christian thinking. It was entirely due to the divine initiative that the great change was coming to pass, as God was about to take his great power and reign (Rev. 11:17). The personal element was uppermost; the "mighty works" were works of the living God, and therefore mighty, and would have been wholly impossible without his initiative. They could not be used for self-glorification, either by Jesus or his disciples (Luke 10:20), nor even for self-preservation—so the temptation narrative (Luke 4:9-12). They were intended to "confirm" the word spoken, but they did more than that—they actually advanced the change which God was bringing about in his world; they drove back the forces of evil and led on the forces of the divine kingdom. Jesus flatly refused to work a "sign" to satisfy the curiosity or credulity (that is, the skepticism) of men (Mark 8:11-12); he would not "pass a miracle" (as *Green Pastures* used the phrase) in order to save himself from embarrassment or to extricate himself from danger; yet he affirmed with complete positiveness, "If it is by the finger of God that I cast out demons, then the kingdom of God has come upon you" (Luke 11:20; cf. Matt. 12:28). Granted that the sons (students) of the scribes could and did exorcise demons (Matt. 12:27)—and their work was not frowned upon—still the work of Jesus, though similar in outward form, had a different significance. While the intention of the saying was, originally, only to parry the thrust of the scribes and their charge of collusion with Beelzebul, for the evangelist and for those who handed down the tradition the words were emphatic: "If *I* by the finger of God. . . ." It was in the light of Jesus' mission and message, and of his person as the Messiah or Son of God, that his activity meant the coming of the kingdom of God. As Paul conceived it, Jesus was fighting the battle of God against the rebel spirits of the universe, the archdemons, and the crisis of that battle was his own crucifixion; after which he was even now pursuing his victorious way until every enemy of God should be destroyed or subdued (I Cor. 15:24-28)—and "the last enemy to be destroyed is death." Or as a later New Testament writer described it (I John 3:8), pushing the contest farther back and into the earthly ministry of the Lord, as the Gospels likewise did, "The reason the Son of God appeared was to destroy the works of the devil." Or as the Gospel of John described it (16:33), his career was one of winning a victory over "the world."

It has often been pointed out that Paul ascribes no miracles to the earthly life of Jesus, though he might well have done so in one or two passages (notably in I Cor. 15). The one great miracle of Christianity followed his earthly life—his resurrection. But the eschatological framework of Paul's thinking is obvious throughout his letters. Indeed, the evils in the world generally are ascribed to "enmity against God," to the "wickedness" and "blindness" which were characteristic results of demonic or Satanic activity. When Christians fell sick or grew feeble, and some died (before the Parousia), it was the result of profaning the body and blood of the Lord in the communion service (I Cor. 11:30), by partaking without self-judgment in anticipation of the judgment of the Lord (vss. 31-32), and perhaps also by communion with demons (10:21). True, this reflects the general ancient view of the relation between sin and sickness—the view which meets us in the first book of the *Iliad,* at the beginning of Sophocles' *Oedipus the King,* and throughout the length and breadth of the ancient world, and even of the modern world until very recent times. (In the English Prayer Book, in the Office for the Visitation of the Sick, the priest is still directed to admonish the sick man to confess his sins.) Even such a half charlatan, half saint as Apollonius of Tyana, when he foresees a plague about to sweep through Ephesus, orders a poor beggar to be stoned to death as a *pharmakon,* in order to avert the catastrophe—an act of fanaticism which resulted in the sage's trial before the emperor—though Philostratus tries to veil this feature. The reverse solution of this problem of suffering, for Hellenistic religion, is echoed in the lines of Ovid: "So it was fated; it was no sin of yours, but a god [brought this upon you]—what you suffer is not the due punishment for sin but the wrath of heaven" (*Fasti* I. 481-83). The difference between the Christian and the pagan view is obvious, though they share similar presuppositions—that suffering is the result of sin, and that sin is some spirit's doing (god, demon, devil, or vague *numen*). The final uprooting of evil and the end of sin and suffering will take place at the end of the age, when "the judgment of the Lord" takes place. That is to say the difference lies in this: the Christian view is eschatological—and the end is in sight. And it is the eschatological outlook of the early church which sharply marks off the New Testament view of miracles from that which prevailed in paganism. The miracles are simply harbingers of the new age, the age to come, when sin, suffering, and death will be no more. If there were no evils in the world, if there were no sin, then the will of God would always have been done (as before the Fall); all his acts within or upon the world would be "miraculous," but all would be perfectly "natural." Hence the importance of the present question of the relation of suffering, death, pain, and all other evils to human or demonic sin.

In the Gospel of John there are two passages which are often cited as either affirming or denying the explanation of suffering as due to sin, and both relate to miracles. When the disciples ask Jesus, "Who sinned, this man or his parents, that he was born blind?" the Lord replies, "It was not that this man sinned, or his parents, but that the works of God might be made manifest in him" (9:2-3). He then proceeds to give him his sight. The passage is sometimes cited as clear evidence that our Lord—or the evangelist—meant to repudiate the current and age-old view that sin and suffering (or physical evil) go together; but the view cannot be pressed, since for John the occasion of a miracle is, one might almost say, artificially created or utilized (cf. 11:4, 6, 42), and is looked upon only as a divinely provided opportunity for the manifestation of the power of God or the "glory" of the incarnate Logos (cf. 2:11). The motive of divine compassion or mercy is not stressed in John's accounts of Jesus' miracles (as in Mark 1:41; 6:34; 8:2; etc.), and here the disciples' question is simply brushed aside, in view of the "work of God" about to take place.

In John 5:14 the man who had been healed at the Pool of Bethzatha is told, "Sin no more, that nothing worse befall you." This apparently implies that illness or impotence is the penalty for sin—though it can be argued that, while the man's condition for thirty-eight years had been due to "natural causes," if he fell into sin something worse than physical suffering would happen to him. The argument is somewhat weak, in view of the words "sin *no more*," yet it is strange that the restoration takes place without any expression of the man's repentance. In vss. 8-9 the miracle is instantaneous, while according to vs. 7 the invalid's mental outlook was merely one of discouraged acceptance of his lot—neither faith, nor hope, nor repentance. But, again, the usual Johannine view of the miracles must be allowed for;

this is one of the seven great "signs" or epiphanies of divine power and glory recorded in that Gospel (cf. vss. 17-18). The miracles in John are differently viewed than are those in the Synoptics; they are "signs" (12:36*b*-43), not "proofs of the powers of the age to come" so much as proofs—or rather manifestations—of the *praesens sed latens deus,* the Incarnate Son of God. Yet this is only part and parcel of the whole transvaluation of eschatology in the Fourth Gospel. The fundamental motif is still in a broad sense eschatological—the conquest of "the world" which is under the dominion of Satan (cf. I John 5:19) and the defeat of the "prince of this world," its ruler—but as John views the miracles, it is their evidential and epideictic value (as proving Jesus to be the Son of God and manifesting his "glory," his true nature) which outweighs their importance in the scheme of eschatological salvation. That the view is a "later" or theologically more advanced one than the Synoptic goes without saying. And yet the basic assumption all along is really eschatological, as we have seen.

The healing of the paralytic in Mark 2:3-12 may be cited in this connection. When the paralytic is let down before him Jesus says, "My son, your sins are forgiven." There is no suggestion of the man's repentance, nor even of a specific connection between the man's sins and his condition, though homilists have laid great stress upon this. For some writers, like Bousset and Lohmeyer, the problem is solved—or disappears—upon the assumption that Mark has telescoped two stories. The repetition of the clause "he said to the paralytic" in vss. 5 and 10 is, on this theory, the double suture that holds the patch in place, the words "to the paralytic" in vs. 10 being viewed as editorial. One story related the healing of a paralytic (vss. 3-5*ab,* 11-12), a healing pericope of the usual kind; the other told of the Savior's pronouncement of forgiveness to a (presumably) penitent sinner (vss. 5*c*-10 are the fragmentary survival of this story). But the great difficulty with the theory lies in vs. 9: "Which is easier, to say to the paralytic, 'Your sins are forgiven,' or to say, 'Rise, take up your pallet and walk'?" This seems far too important to be a mere editorial clamp designed to hold the two stories together. It seems far better to recognize that Jesus viewed illness and suffering, like all the other evils of life, as due to sin—to alienation from God—

and since it was his mission to "undo the works of Satan," the first attack must be launched against the works of the evil one within a man's own heart. Even so our difficulties are not over, for the other narratives of healing do not involve repentance but only faith—and sometimes even faith does not seem to be prerequisite. Those who told these stories, in the process of handing down the evangelic tradition, apparently had no rigidly uniform or consistent theory to promote.

The sayings about the Galileans and the tower of Siloam in Luke 13:1-5 are sometimes brought forward as evidence, likewise for or against, the theory that suffering is the consequence of sin. *Either* these people were worse sinners than others, and hence were singled out for conspicuous punishment (a view entirely in harmony with ancient eudaemonism, cf. Pss. 35; 73; etc.), to which Jesus replies, "No, for the rest of men are equally guilty and deserving of the same dire punishment"; *or* there is no connection between suffering or disaster and the guilt of men, and these things might have happened to anyone—these unfortunates were no more and no less guilty and deserving of punishment than others, or than you. Unquestionably, I think, the former interpretation is nearer the truth, yet neither interpretation expresses the view of Jesus. For him the question of evil and the problem of suffering are both alike viewed in an eschatological setting, along with the miracles. The divine judgment impends above this sinful generation; if the judgment is delayed, it is only because God in his mercy is affording an extension of the time of grace, in the hope that men will repent. As the "mighty works" of Jesus are evidence of the oncoming power of God's reign, so the delay is evidence of his grace; and these "temporal" judgments, upon the Galilean pilgrims and the eighteen residents of Jerusalem, are a foretaste of what is to come. They are not merely test cases for an examination of the problem of the connection between suffering and sin, but loud warnings of the judgment which is about to take place: "Unless you repent you will all likewise perish." It is clear that the mind of Jesus (antecedent to his portrait in the Gospels and apart from the evangelists' interpretation) is not interested in philosophical problems; his mind is purely and thoroughly religious. Practical concerns are not only more important than speculative, but are alone

worthy of consideration; and his outlook is almost wholly eschatological.

If we found these sayings in the Quran, for example, there is no
doubt how we should view them: prophetic warnings, threats of
divine vengeance, stern denunciations of sin (sin in the abstract, not
specific sins—a failing of most denunciatory preachers, nurtured on
the Old Testament prophecies of doom!), with an obvious expectation of the worst, namely the divine judgment upon the prophet's
contemporaries. But when we find these sayings among those attributed to Jesus, there is a difference; they must be studied in the
light of his other utterances, where the grace, the patience, the goodness of God are more strongly emphasized (they are emphasized also
in the Quran, but more formally and without elaboration). As a
prophet, Jesus was aware of the approaching doom which overtook
his people in the catastrophies of A.D. 70 and 135. Whether we can
explain it or not, a similar sense of impending disaster was possessed
by the Old Testament prophets, by John the Baptist, and others. But
for Jesus—as for some of the Old Testament prophets, and especially
for Second Isaiah—this sense was balanced by another, an immediate
awareness of the goodness and mercy of God, an insight into his
purposes, a realization of his utter goodness, an anticipation of the
character of his divine reign which was about to be set up over the
whole earth. (We ought not to minimize the parallels to this in the
Old Testament; they are evidence of the truth of revelation.) And
instead of merely announcing the judgment of God and warning
men to repent, or even (like John) urging men to "bring forth . . .
fruits worthy of repentance" (Luke 3:8, A.S.V.—Q; cf. vss. 10-
14—L), Jesus was aware of a mission to *do* something about the
present situation. His ministry of exorcism and healing was more
than preparation for the coming of the kingdom; it was the proof
of the arrival of the kingdom, the first fruits or beginning of the
kingdom, the "reign of God" itself. Once more, "If it is by the finger
of God that I cast out demons, then the kingdom of God *has come*
upon you" (Luke 11:20; Matt. 12:28—Q). He was himself engaged in pushing back the frontiers of the realm of darkness, of
sin, Satan, and death; and his work was not so much proof that
the kingdom of God was about to come (Luke 10:9) as evidence

that the kingdom was already here, that the transition from this age to the next was already under way. This was the "sign" to his generation (Mark 8:11-12; Luke 11:29; Matt. 16:1-4; 12:38-39), the only sign that should be given, very different from any prodigy or portent such as the scribes and Pharisees and the populace demanded in attestation of his authority as a teacher or prophet (John 2:18; 6:30). Here was "something greater than Jonah" or "Solomon" (Matt. 12:41-42)—"something," the activity of the Spirit of God in Jesus' ministry, not "someone," the Messiah, upon which identification he laid no stress.

This is what is meant by the "eschatological" setting of the miracles of Jesus, still prominent in the Synoptic tradition and still presupposed, though given another orientation, in the Fourth Gospel. The full realization of God's reign here upon earth means the end of every evil: sickness, possession by demons, famine, pestilence, plague—the whole realm of "sin, Satan, and death," in the familiar Prayer Book summary. But the evils of life are already being overcome; they are in principle already vanquished, since Christ has bound the strong man (Mark 3:27). This is the whole point of the miracle stories in the oldest strata of evangelic tradition—namely, proof of the arrival or at least of the near approach of the kingdom of God. They are not even put forward, in the Synoptics, as evidence of the power or the divine nature of Jesus himself, though they do attest his messiahship (note the answer to John the Baptist in Matt. 11:2-6). The emphasis is all upon the coming kingdom; it is already "coming"; it is in process, rather than still "to come" in the sense of prophecy. For the New Testament there is no such question as that of the possibility of miracles—our modern question. The possibility of miracles is everywhere taken for granted, as it was throughout the ancient world. The only questions for the first century were: (a) the *evidence* (and the minds of most men leaned strongly in the direction of accepting whatever evidence was supplied—hearsay was often sufficient); and (b) the *interpretation* of the meaning, not of the evidence, but of the phenomenon reported.

The evidence for the miracles of Jesus is more than hearsay or common report. The very form of many of the stories shows this. Jairus' daughter was given food, thus proving her complete restoration

(Mark 5:43); the woman with a chronic hemorrhage was cured in the midst of a crowd of people (Mark 5:25-34); the blind man "saw everything clearly" and was sent home (Mark 8:25-26). The evidence for the greatest miracle of all, Jesus' own resurrection, is stated repeatedly—by Paul (I Cor. 15:3-8, the earliest list of witnesses), by Mark (16:6), by Luke (ch. 24), by Matthew (27:62–28:20), by John (chs. 20–21). And though this testimony is difficult to harmonize, a fact quite in keeping with its diversity (if one man had "invented" the story, the whole body of "evidence" would be easily harmonized and self-consistent), the amplitude and importance of it for the early church is not to be questioned. As for the interpretation, the significance of this greatest miracle of all is eschatological, throughout the New Testament. Jesus rises from the dead (or "was raised," by God, in the older form of the tradition) as the exalted Messiah (Acts 2:32-33), not as a resuscitated human being like Lazarus (John 11) or Jairus' daughter (Mark 5:21-43) or the young man at Nain (Luke 7:11-17), who were brought back to life only to die again, but as the "Son of God in power" (Rom. 1:4; cf. Mark 9:1, "with power"; Rom. 6:9). The immediate inference is that with him the New Age has finally come "in power" (Mark 9:1; Acts 1:6; even Matt. 27:51-53, which may very well be a quite primitive detail—the resurrection of the saints was to be one of the most important events in the anticipated drama of the eschatological salvation).

The interpretation of the miracle of the Resurrection only brings to a climax the interpretation of all the miracles of the Gospel, and its significance is entirely eschatological. It is not evidence of the possibility of "human survival of bodily death," or proof of the "immortality of the human soul," or even, at first, evidence that Jesus was divine (cf. Acts 2:24). Rather it is evidence that the whole mission and ministry of Jesus in the inauguration of God's kingdom is—far from ending in frustration and defeat—going on victoriously and successfully, and now with added supernatural power. This is what Paul, for example, takes for granted as the primitive and still universal Christian view when he describes Christ as the "first fruits," the beginning of the new creation of God (I Cor. 15:23). John views the miracles, including the resurrection of Jesus, somewhat differently, but only to the extent that a spiritual, cosmic, eternal order takes the place, in his thought, of the old-fashioned eschatology with its time sequence of the two ages. For him Jesus' death and his rising from the dead are the "hour" of his victory over the world, of his conquest of Satan and Death and the whole realm of "darkness" (John 1:5), and of his return to the Father (13:1; 16:28). The inauguration of the new order of life and light is—as also in the Synoptics and in Paul, though the language is different—brought to its climax in the Resurrection.

4. *The Importance of Miracles in the New Testament*

The attempt to remove all traces of "the miraculous" from the Gospels, though it has now been carried on for over two centuries, is a hopeless one. Explain away the miracles and there is little left of the evangelic record—not only of its outer fabric but of its inner substance and meaning. Not that the gospel story is a "tissue of miracle tales." Here was a religion, or a religious movement, primitive Christianity, which was "supernaturalistic" to its inmost core. True, there are traces of the growth of legend, even of "myth" (in the true sense of that word), in the Gospels; perhaps, indeed, as in the story of Lazarus, or of the wedding at Cana, or of the exorcism of "Legion," there are traces of borrowing from external sources, or even—as it has been suggested—of the influence of other cults. Perhaps some of the miracles can now be "explained" as due to suggestion or to other psychological procedures (which does not leave them any the less miraculous in the first century); but the puerile nineteenth-century explanations— for example of the feeding of the multitude (the noble example of a little boy sharing his meager lunch) or of the walking on the water (Jesus was really walking "along," not "upon," the lake, and they saw him only through the mist)—such "explanations" had better be given up. The Resurrection itself no doubt requires to be understood more strictly in accordance with the earliest evidence for, or interpretation of, that event (see pp. 227-30). But none of this effort at interpretation or reinterpretation helps us in the least to understand the religion or the theology of the New Testament. The Gospels must be read as first- and second-century books, not twentieth; their underlying tradition must be studied against the background of the time in which it arose and was handed on, prior to the writing of the Gospels. Whether we can "explain" the miracles or not—and I doubt if we can "explain" them to the satisfaction of the mind of our generation—they had better be left as they stand, as an indispensable element in the gospel story, and as the evidence (for the first century) of the stupendous power and true nature of the oncoming kingdom of God, the proof of "the powers of the age to come" (Heb. 6:5) and the assurance that the ministry of Jesus and, continuous with it, the spread of the church was not human in origin or devising, but was the mighty act of God for the salvation of men.

It must be remembered that the Gospels were written to recount what Jesus "began" to do (Acts 1:1), and that the wonders of the apostolic age were continuous with those of the Lord's earthly life—as, for Catholicism, the miracles of the saints have been continuous with these. Furthermore, the miracles related in the gospel tradition were the "mighty works" wrought by the one who was even now "at the right hand of Power" (Mark 14:62) and at the same time in the midst of his elect community, the church. He who had been able to save his perishing disciples in the storm on the lake (Mark 4:35-41) and to heal the sick in Galilee was still powerful to save and to heal; "where two or three are gathered," there he would be, in the midst of them—and that to bless (Matt. 18:20). The stories in the gospel were illustrations of his saving power, or of the saving power of God effective through him. Hence cures and exorcisms undertaken in his name (Mark 9:38) were successful, even when undertaken by some who were not members of the Christian community—or perhaps by schismatics separated from the apostolic group (Mark 9:39-40; contrast Acts 19:13). Moreover, as in later Catholicism great saints were sometimes privileged to be the agents through whom were wrought miracles closely similar to those in the gospel story, so it was in the early church, even within the New Testament period. The parallel between the miracles of Peter and those of Paul, as recounted in Acts, has often been pointed out. But even more important is the parallel between apostolic miracles and those of Jesus. This fact is also important for our understanding of the theological significance of the New Testament miracles, both those "wrought by the Lord" and those of the apostolic period. His miracles were the signs of the arrival of the kingdom of God; the later miracles were the "signs that attended" (Mark 16:20) the preaching of the gospel. (The examples given in this longer second-century appendix to Mark [see vss. 17-18] are not altogether normal and representative. Exorcism and speaking with "new tongues" are characteristic of the apostolic age, and even of later times; handling serpents and drinking poison are late and legendary and, at the best, wholly extraordinary and thaumaturgic. The incident at Melita [Acts 28:3-6; cf. Luke 10:19] may have suggested one, and the legend of John's experience at Ephesus the other; but they really belong with the most extreme of the later ecclesiastical miracles, such as St. Patrick's banishment of snakes from Ireland or the exploits of St. Denys.)

VIII

The Doctrine of Man

1. *The Old Testament View*

LIKE other New Testament doctrines, the doctrine of man is based almost wholly on the Old Testament. There are traces of post-biblical Jewish "psychology," but none of scientific (philosophic) Greek or Roman terminology. Paul uses certain Stoic terms—not always in the exact Stoic sense—but these are popular terms, and no more connote a philosophical schooling than the use of such a term as "evolution" implies, today, that one has taken a college course in biology.

According to the biblical view, man was made of the dust of the earth and was formed in the image of God; whereupon God breathed into his nostrils the breath of life, and man became "a living soul" (Gen. 2:7). In this statement later biblical theology found a difficulty: How could man be formed "in the image of God," since God has no "form" or "likeness" (Exod. 33:20; Deut. 4:15; cf. John 1:18)? The solution of Philo was along the lines of his Stoicized Platonism and allegorism. But this solution reflected the views of Philo and the Alexandrian school, no more. The general assumption of the New Testament, wherever the problem appears in the offing, is that "image" and "likeness" are synonymous (as indeed they probably are, in the Hebrew Old Testament); the later scholastic distinction, referring "image" to man's spiritual "nature" and "likeness" to his original state of moral innocence, is completely remote. The Old Testament account of the creation of man implies that it is man's rational and spiritual nature which distinguishes him from the other species and entitles him to "lordship" over the lower creation. It is this quality in man which is the divine image in him, not his physical form, though the original story, long prior to Genesis, may possibly have assumed that gods and men are alike in shape. As it stands, the creation story has left such primitive conceptions far behind.

Another problem lay in the word "soul," which in Greek (*psychê*) could mean "life" as well as "soul." In the creation story Gen. 2:7 simply meant that man became "a living thing," "came to life," or "became alive." It was the Septuagint translation which introduced the idea of "soul." For in Greek, not only of the New Testament period but generally from the days of Homer, *psychê* meant soul (indeed Homer restricts it to the "souls" or ghosts of *dead* men, as in *Iliad* I. 3, etc.; the living are not described as "souls" but as men) completely in contrast to Hebrew usage. Hence the confusion of meaning, or at least the possible double meaning, of such a passage as Mark 8:35-37 (cf. 10:45).

Now it is not to be thought that any strict system of psychological terminology, explicit or implicit, underlies or is implied by the New Testament—which is certainly not a textbook in psychology, ancient or modern. The general meaning and connotation of terms is all that can be made out, all that we have a right to expect to make out.

Psychê is the vital principle, "life," "soul."

Pneuma is that same principle of vitality seen on its inner side, as related (or relating the individual) to God. Hence it may be, and is, "given" to men; men can share in the *pneuma* of Christ or of God.

Sôma is the outward manifestation of the individual life or "soul." Man "has" a body just as the animals have—or the stars (I Cor. 15: 40-41?).

Sarx is the Old Testament (Septuagint) term for "flesh," for lowly human nature, mortal and frail, in contrast to the divine nature. But Paul also uses it for the material out of which the *sôma* is formed, whereupon it becomes the seat of sin—not because matter is evil, but because flesh is "weak," the poor stuff out of which the physical body is made. Paul is no Gnostic, though he might have had a harder time not to be one if he had lived in the second century rather than in the first. Nor is he a fifth-century Manichee. But he has combined Old Testament language with ordinary *koinê* Greek in such fashion that his very terminology leads him some distance in the Gnostic or Manichaean direction—the more so since both heresies are deeply rooted in Greek thought and go back through subterranean but genuinely historical channels to the Orphics.

In most of the New Testament the terms which are used bear their ordinary, everyday meanings. Man has a dual nature, body and soul. It is the soul which thinks and feels and is in general the living principle within the body, so that the question in Mark 8:37 may be translated either, "What can a man give in return for his *soul?*" or "for his *life?*" And yet both soul and body are in danger of being "cast into the fires of Gehenna" (that is, hell; Mark 9:42-48). On this level of naïve, popular speech no distinction is drawn between "soul" and "mind"; in the language of the Bible, deriving from primitive Semitic usage, "heart" is used where we (or an ancient Greek) might have expected "mind" (cf. Mark 7:21). It is a mistake to read into such language the exact distinctions of scientific psychology, and to view the "heart" as the seat or source of affective or emotional life—as if the saying, "Out of the heart are the issues of life," implied that a man's life is entirely ruled by his feelings. (Cf. Mark 7:14-23.)

When we turn to Paul, a richer terminology at once confronts us. "Flesh" is used as well as "body," while "spirit," "thought," and "mind" are used as well as "soul" and "heart." Paul's terminology is fundamentally biblical (derived from the Old Testament), where "flesh" (*basar*) and "spirit" (*ruach*) or "soul" (*nephesh*) are set in strong contrast, where "flesh" often stands for human nature, with its mortality, its finitude, folly, and futility (e.g. Job 34:15), while the "spirit" in man is either the animating principle, or the breath, or—in certain passages—the divine afflatus by which man was called into existence and by which he continues to live. But crossing this traditional terminology with its ancient and even primitive connotations is another set of words, derived from popular Greek usage: "body" (*sôma*), "soul" (*psychê*), "mind" (*nous*), "spirit" (*pneuma*), the last-named carrying with it certain overtones not found in the Hebrew Old Testament. Here again it would be a mistake to represent Paul as a scientific psychologist, using his terms with accuracy and precision. For him the "body" is the physical, material vehicle of man's "soul"; it is made of "flesh," and as flesh it is peculiarly susceptible to the corruption of sin (the Old Testament connotations of "flesh" are retained, and carried further). The body is the form taken by flesh during a man's natural life—this is his emphasis, rather than the Platonic view of the body as the form taken by the soul. The term "spirit," on the other hand, is sometimes used interchangeably with "soul," especially for the inner life, sometimes with "mind," sometimes in connections where we should say "persons" or "personality," and sometimes with reference to the divine Spirit or even to Christ the heavenly Lord. Since Paul is no psychologist, we cannot insist that his language implies a threefold (trichotomistic) view of human nature, as "body, soul, and spirit"; for his language is still popular and approximate and, as we have said, represents a blending of ordinary Greek with traditional biblical (but equally ordinary) Semitic terminology.

2. *Spirit, Soul, and Flesh*

As we have seen, the "anthropological" terms "spirit," "soul," "flesh," "body," and "mind" are used in the New Testament in a popular, nontechnical sense whose background is partly scientific and philosophical (so far as Greek philosophy had influenced popular usage) and partly—since the New Testament writings are religious—the usage of the Septuagint, the Bible of the early Gentile church. Since these two influences were quite diverse in origin and character, we are not surprised to find the New Testament usage to be basically that of the popular, everyday *koinê* Greek, but crossed and deflected by that strange, originally Semitic influence which moves through the whole thought and vocabulary of the New Testament.

1. Originally, and throughout classical Greek, *pneuma* (spirit) was a physical term meaning air, wind, breath, breath of life; more rarely it meant "life" or "soul substance," yet never with a definitely individual or psychical or religious sense. On the other hand, *psychê* (soul) from Homer onward is the term for life, whether of plants, animals, or men, for the individual man, living or dead, and therefore for the seat of intellectual, moral, or emotional activity, the basis of individual, personal character. The term *sarx* (flesh) is merely the soft, yielding part of the human body, as contrasted with its bony structure, though often it is used synonymously with body. It has no psychical or ethical connotations. *Sôma* (body) is the term for the outward, visible, concrete manifestation of the individual person. *Nous* (mind)

is the intelligent or "intellectual part"—though, as John Burnet has shown, it should often be translated "spirit" in the fragmentary passages which have come down from the earlier Greek philosophers.

2. In the Hebrew Old Testament the term *ruach* (spirit) was, like the Greek *pneuma,* originally a term for wind, air, or breath; but from an early time it also had a religious connotation, as the invisible power by which God was active in the world (cf. Gen. 1:2; 6:3), or as the presence of God himself in the world—but never as a hypostasis separate from God. Indeed, as E. DeWitt Burton argued—in his valuable work, which is still of very great importance, *Spirit, Soul, and Flesh* (University of Chicago Press, 1918)—the meaning "spirit" came *before* that of "breath," and its application to God preceded that to man—a reversal of the popular modern view which views the divine spirit as an anthropomorphism. At first the inspiration of the spirit of, or from, God was seen in extraordinary actions or activities of nature or of men—in the whirlwind in the wilderness, the mountain tempest, the destroying east wind; in the inspiration of the dervish or the *nabhi,* the ecstatic behavior of the primitive prophet or soothsayer. Only later was it used to explain the skill of a great artist or craftsman (e.g. Bezalel, Exod. 31:3), the religious inspiration of the poet, or the spiritual insight of the writing prophet or seer (e.g. Isa. 61:1). But the term "spirit" never lost its objective connotation; it was still a substance, however refined and immaterial, and not a mere metaphor for spiritual intuition or enthusiasm or skill arising within the man himself. It was a divine, supernatural stuff or substance, like light, or "glory," or breath—not a mere figure of human speech for a purely human and subjective phenomenon.

Nephesh (soul), on the other hand, is a psychological term, denoting man's life or vitality, that which distinguishes him from the material world. It is not a substance, like *ruach,* but the individualized vital center of a man's emotional or intellectual life, the seat of his appetites and the part of him that survived in Sheôl, the realm of the dead. One could speak of the *nephesh* of a dead man, but never of his *ruach.* He might be only a "shade," after death, but so far as he retained any vitality whatsoever, he was a *nephesh.*

Basar (flesh) is the term for the physical part of man, which is animated, as long as he lives, by his *nephesh.* The term has no mental, moral, or religious qualities. It stands in strong contrast to spirit—throughout the Old Testament it connotes weakness, frailty, mortality (e.g. Isa. 31:3, "The Egyptians are men, and not God; and their horses flesh, and not spirit"). As for "body," the term *basar* includes this meaning and is practically identical with it; there is in Hebrew thought no approximation to the Greek philosophical Orphic-Platonic distinction between soul and body, with an open possibility that soul preceded body, or that

> Of the soule the bodie forme doth take:
> For soule is forme, and doth the bodie make.

The closest approach to this idea is the use of *nephesh* as "a ghost, so to speak, within an embodied living being." This is not far from Homer's usage, for example in the opening lines of the *Iliad*. But neither the old Hebrew religion nor the old Greek (except for the Orphic and Pythagorean sectaries and the Platonic philosophers) ever arrived at a consistent or generally accepted view of the immortality of the soul. *Basar* like *sarx* is a purely physical term, usually including the "body" or identical with it. The term "mind" was used of a function of the individual, one of the manifestations of his *psychê* or *nephesh;* its distinct separation from the inner vital principle, and its occasional description as superior, come much later.

3. Later Greek speculation strongly affected ordinary Greek usage—especially, the view of *pneuma* as air, or fire, or "fiery ether," or (whatever it was) the primal substance out of which the universe was formed, a view fundamental to the Stoic physics. Posidonius was apparently the first to use *pneuma* as a predicate of God, though for him as for the other Stoics *pneuma* remained a substantial entity. Though the term was applied both to God and to the human soul, it was still a material stuff, infinitely refined and subtle, no doubt, but material and therefore perishable, in the repeated cyclic *purôseis* or universal combustions of the cosmos. *Sarx* is certainly an uncommon word in pre-Christian philosophy, and has no more ethical connotation than the words for meat or fat or bones.

4. It is in the Jewish-Greek writers of Alexandria, especially Philo, and in the Greek translation of the Old Testament that the change in

usage leading to the New Testament begins to take place. The old usages survive—*pneuma* is still wind, for example—for they are embedded in the Old Testament and in common usage, but the shift in connotation begins to appear. Philo endeavored to express Hebrew religious ideas in terms derived from or cognate with Greek philosophy, and in doing so he naturally modified both the Hebrew ideas and the Greek terms. He was fundamentally a dualist—though this is sometimes denied—and his philosophy was dependent upon Plato, the Stoics, and the Neo-Pythagoreans. For him God and matter were the two fundamental and final realities, even though matter (which was as "dead" for him as it was for Aristotle or Democritus) depended for its existence upon God. Matter is eternal, as for many a classical thinker; yet its eternity depends upon that of God, who is the active principle in the universe, the Creator. He uses *pneuma, psychê,* and *sarx* in the same way in which the terms are used in the Old Testament. But, as in the Old Testament, the spirit is now usually the Spirit of God or the "divine" spirit; the dominant part of the human soul is also *pneuma,* and indeed divine *pneuma.* Even the soul is for Philo, as for the Stoics, a part of God, a divine spark, a seed implanted by God and from his own substance. Yet nowhere is it said that matter is evil, or that the soul is caught and entangled in the thicket of physical existence, or that salvation consists in escape from the body or from matter. Nor is *pneuma* raised above *psychê* (by an anticipation of the later theory of trichotomy), nor is there any sharp metaphysical antithesis between *sarx* and *pneuma,* such as we find in Paul. The way is opening toward the New Testament usages, but the Jewish-Greek writers still closely adhere to the language of the Septuagint and its connotations. *Pneuma* is still a substance, as it is for the New Testament too—the stuff, so to speak, of which the soul was made, not some *tertium quid,* neither soul nor flesh, either outtopping or embracing both. As a philosopher Philo prefers the term *nous* to *pneuma.* The *pneuma* is (as in the Greek Old Testament) the *pneuma* of God; see his *Allegories of the Sacred Laws* I. 31-42 (= chs. 12–13).

5. Within the New Testament itself the usage of most writers is the ordinary, everyday usage of *koinê* Greek. It is Paul who is distinctive. For him *pneuma* never means wind, breath, or air, but always spirit, either the human spirit or the divine. Why Paul singled out this particu-

lar Old Testament meaning and made it central and normative, we do not know; Burton suggests that in the mind of Paul himself, or in some circle of thought by which he was influenced, something had occurred to exalt the importance of the term. Whether this was Paul's conversion, or his experience as a Christian, or certain earlier experiences as a "pneumatic," or contacts with some group of such "spirituals" we do not know. But the fact is striking. For Paul the human spirit and the divine are analogous; what the "spirit" of a man is to the man, this the Spirit of God is to God (I Cor. 2:11). As in the sentence "The Lord is the Spirit" (II Cor. 3:17), so here in I Cor. 2:11 the logic seems to require the practical identification of the Spirit with God; the Spirit is *within* God, not an external power or attribute. Moreover the divine Spirit is active in human life and upon human beings, rather than upon external things—though glossolalia, prophecy, and similar phenomena are only temporary (I Cor. 12–13). More important than signs or wonders, or tongues, or even prophecy, is the growth in the new life, the manifestation of the "fruit of the Spirit" (cf. Gal. 5:13-25; Eph. 5:9), or the words spoken for the edification of the hearers (I Cor. 14:1-5).

Further, the Spirit of God is identified with the risen and exalted Lord Christ. Either may be described in terms of the other (cf. Rom. 8:3-11; II Cor. 3:17). The two terminologies are in origin quite distinct. The Spirit terminology is as old as human thought and language since the days of animism. But the Christ terminology is Paul's own, and the Gentile church's, and has grown up, partly under the influence of the Greek Bible, but more largely under the direct influence of personal experience and, not least, doubtless, in Christian worship. It was the experience which furnished the key for interpreting the Bible. Finally, as Burton notes, the apostle never entirely abandoned those forms of thought and expression which had come down from the early Old Testament period, when the Spirit of God was thought of as more or less impersonal ("it," not "he"), and even in quantitative terms. He appears reluctant to identify God and the Spirit, without qualification; yet for him, as Burton says, the Spirit is "the personalized power of God, operative in the spirits of men, not distinguishable, in experience at least, from the heavenly Christ. At the same time he uses *pneuma* for discarnate spirits (*pneumata*) and also for the "spirit in man."

His use of *psychê* was the ordinary one, found in earlier Greek thought, in the Hebrew Old Testament (*nephesh*), and in the Septuagint. Thus " 'the first man Adam became a living being'; the last Adam became a life-giving spirit" (I Cor. 15:45). That is, by his resurrection from the dead Christ became "spirit," able to make alive, to raise and restore the dead (cf. Rom. 1:4). *Pneuma* is still the substance of which the soul is made, upon which it rests, by which it exists—not some third entity, apart from the soul, but "stuff of its very stuff." It is because Christ is now purely and wholly *pneuma* that he can, and does, give life to the dead, even in this life and before the death of the body (I Cor. 15:45).

It is his use of the term *sarx* that provides the most distinctive, and most baffling, example of Paul's creative contribution to Christian thought. Sometimes he thinks of it as physical, almost as identical with the body (e.g. Rom. 7:5; 8:10); at others, and prevailingly, he thinks of it in ethical connections. And yet he nowhere betrays the outlook of the metaphysical dualist. Neither matter, nor the body, nor the flesh is essentially evil. As in the Old Testament the flesh is weak, but not in itself sinful. It provides the "occasion" for sin (cf. Rom. 7:8, 11), the point at which sin finds lodgment in a human being. But this is not to say, with the later Gnostics, that the body is the seat of sin; for the seat of sin is in the will, in the consent of the mind, in the "weakness of mortal flesh"—in our common human *nature,* which, as in the Old Testament, is opposed to the divine spirit and its leadings or strivings (cf. Rom. 8:3-8). As such, as our inherited human "nature," the flesh is the source not only of weakness but also of inherited tendencies to evil—to which, however, we still do not need to consent and yield, but to which as a matter of observable fact we usually do yield. And so the inborn tendency—the *yeçer ha-ra'*, as the Jewish teachers later called it (cf. Gen. 6:5)—became a settled habit, and the "mind of the flesh" turns out to be "at enmity with God" (Rom. 8:7, "for the mind that is set on the flesh is hostile to God").

The evidence is against the view that Paul found in the flesh as a physical thing a compelling force for evil. The flesh that makes for evil is not the body or matter as such, but an inherited impulse to evil. This force is not compulsory, but can be resisted by the power of the spirit. The body is not an evil, but a factor of the best life. The inherited evil impulse is, of course, related to the bodily life. The body is inferior to the spirit and the occasion of temptation. But embodied man may, by the power of Spirit, triumph over all evil tendencies.

In this brief paragraph Burton sums up the essential facts of Paul's usage, obscure as it is and not always consistent. It is a great pity that Paul never sat down and gave us a definition of the word. Perhaps he could not have done so, for he was not a systematic, scientific thinker, but an impassioned orator, evangelist, missionary—and strictly scientific or philosophical thinking would have ruined his usefulness as an apostle. Moreover, as Burton notes, even when *sarx* and *pneuma* stand opposed, it is by no means always the same meanings that are contrasted. Partly, no doubt, this is due to Paul's *ad hoc* use of terms—the context and the occasion give color to his language—but partly it is due to the same situation that we find in Philo, where a Greek set of terms has to do service for a series of ideas or concepts derived mainly from the Old Testament. For Paul the scheme runs as follows, and explains some of his obscurities, as he crosses over from one set to the other:

Hebrew:	ruach	nephesh	basar
Septuagint:	pneuma	psychê	sarx
Koinê:	pneuma	psychê	sôma

If, for example, *pneuma* in the Greek sense is contrasted with Hebrew *basar* or with *sarx* in the Septuagint sense, the contrast will be a somewhat different one than we find in the Old Testament itself, where *ruach* and *basar* stand in opposition.

The situation was still further complicated, as Edwyn Bevan has shown in his Gifford lectures on *Symbolism and Belief* (chs. 7-8), when the Latin language became involved. The situation may be illustrated graphically:

	ruach		
	BREATH, WIND	SOUL	LIFE
Hebrew:	ruach	nephesh	chayyim
Greek:	pneuma, anemos	psychê	zôê
Latin:	animus (poet.)	animus, anima	vita

It is no wonder that our modern usage of the terms—derived partly from the Bible, partly from classical literature, partly from the survival of ancient terms through the centuries since and affected by various developments in the modern European languages—betrays a certain amount of confusion, or that we have considerable difficulty in understanding the usage of the ancients, including the writers of the New Testament.

3. *The Fall of Man*

Without stating the fact in so many words, and without any theological elaboration of the doctrine, the New Testament as a whole (even outside of Paul) undoubtedly also takes for granted the Old Testament account of man's creation, his primitive state of innocence, and his fall. For Paul the doctrine of man's sinfulness is cardinal.

According to scripture God created man only a little lower than himself—or than the angels—and set him over the rest of the terrestrial creation, "the works of his hands" (Ps. 8:5-8; Heb. 2:6-8). Man's duty was to tend "the garden of God," conceived as a watered oasis; and of every tree in the garden he might eat the fruit, save of two—the tree of (everlasting) life, and the tree of the knowledge of good and evil. Beguiled by the serpent, first Eve and then Adam ate the forbidden fruit of the latter tree and forfeited their innocence; then, lest they should eat the fruit of the other tree and—in their present state—obtain immortality, they were driven from the garden and compelled to live henceforth in pain, privation, and toil. The serpent, for his punishment, was compelled to crawl on the ground and "eat dust" from that time onward. This ancient tale is told by the Yahwistic writer of Gen. 3 with inspired insight and profound psychological subtlety. There were other accounts of primitive man and of his fall from divine favor, and some of these are reflected elsewhere in the Old Testament; but this is the one that was chosen for a place at the beginning of the Hexateuch, among the "stories of beginnings," and it is the one which through the centuries has set the standard for all Bible readers.

It is the age-old myth of man's yearning for a state of innocence, of plenty, of toilless ease, and of his forfeiture of this primeval estate.

Parallels can be found in Hesiod and Virgil, and even farther afield in the history of religions. In his inmost heart man is aware of the unsatisfactory state in which he now finds himself. He was meant for something better—for innocence, freedom, immortality. He was not born to die—"God made man for immortality" (Wisd. 2:23)—or to struggle for bare survival in an "unfriendly universe," or to be checked and thwarted by his fellows or by his own inner conflicts between will or desire on one hand and ability to achieve on the other. Greek philosophers, and some modern theologians, have attributed this inner discord and discontent to man's finitude and mortality. The Bible, however, never formulated the problem in such terms, though the book of Job at least glanced in that direction. Not finitude, but *sin*— this is what alienates man from God. Even apart from sin man might not, of course, have been immortal (though some theologians have held this view); certainly his finitude, his creatureliness, would still have separated him from God. But apart from sin man could have been the noblest of God's creatures—could, in fact, have continued to be the noblest—and might have enjoyed a state of bliss, founded upon innocence, which should have continued forever.

Speaking generally the Old Testament does not advance beyond this view of the origin of sin. But later on, and especially in such writers as Paul and the author of Fourth Ezra, the problem of the origin of sin receives much more attention—the latter in view of the catastrophe which has overtaken Israel in the fall of Jerusalem and during the dark period since, the former in view of the wholly personal situation in which men find themselves, alienated from God, and under the power of sin. For Paul, brooding over the terrible fact of sin and alienation from God, and reading the story in Genesis as an explanation of this world-wide, age-old condition, it seemed that by Adam's sin the whole universe had become infected, not only mankind but the lower orders of creation as well (Rom. 8:19-23). With sin, death entered the world (Rom. 5:12). Even the stars in their courses had been involved—a view closely related to that of one section of the book of Enoch. And since (*a*) these were either animate beings, as in much of Greek thought, or were under the direct supervision of angelic powers, as in Jewish apocalyptic, and since (*b*) the serpent in Gen. 3 was really Satan, the devil, the tempter and seducer of mankind (one of these heavenly beings, although a fallen one), it was a natural inference (*c*) that man's sin was an episode in the cosmic struggle between the forces of God and the rebellious *kosmokratores* (Eph. 6:12). At least, we may say, some such theory seems to be implied by more than one passage in Paul's letters, though more commonly in the perhaps "deutero-Pauline" epistles, Colossians and Ephesians (cf. Col. 1:13, 16; 2:15; Eph. 1:21; 2:2; 3:10; 6:12). There is no need to attribute Paul's view to Orphism or to Platonism or Neo-Pythagoreanism, or to the general Gnostic doctrine of the "fall of the soul" prior to its birth—or entombment—in this world of matter. Origen of Alexandria was to hold such a view, in the early third century, but the church as a whole repudiated it—and him. Paul's view is not Greek but apocalyptic, with a strong infusion of either private meditation upon Gen. 1–3 or of some type of Hellenized Diaspora Judaism which we may suspect to have existed in the first century but which has left very few traces in surviving literature or archeological monuments.

Paul's doctrine of sin must accordingly be distinguished from that found elsewhere in the New Testament. In the teaching of Jesus sin is not thought of as a cosmic power; as in ordinary Judaism it is simply the totality of actual, concrete sins. The cure for sin is repentance and conversion (Paul almost never uses these words), a fresh start, and the grace or help of God. In the Gospel of John sin takes on a more cosmic aspect. It is related to the whole realm of darkness into which the divine light penetrates—and is not overwhelmed (John 1:5). In the Epistle to the Hebrews sin, or rather "sins," are the ordinary ones, familiar from the Old Testament. The great problem here is not the origin of sin, or of sinfulness, but their removal and the requisite cleansing from defilement or guilt, which the old Aaronic or Levitical priesthood could not effect, but which is now perfectly accomplished by Christ, the great high priest. In other parts of the New Testament similiar views are held—all of which makes the unique emphasis of Paul the more extraordinary.

The classic passage in Paul on this subject is of course the seventh chapter of Romans, which ought never to be read apart from chapters 5 and 6, which lead up to it, and chapter 8, its continuation—not only verses 1-2, which are essential to the sequence of thought, but the whole of the eighth chapter, with its great climax in verses 31-39. In this long section (chs. 5–8) which forms the heart of the epistle Paul's problem is partly (*a*) that of the infection of sin (his use of the first person singular in chapter 7 is not so much autobiographic as typical of human nature—though Paul certainly learned all this through his own experience), and partly (*b*) the problem of the relation of the divine Law to human impotence, disobedience, and inner tension. Obviously God's Law is "holy and just and good" (7:12). How then has it produced the opposite effect to what might have been expected? The Law did not bring about death—sin did that. But like a good medicine to a man so ill that it is poison to him, like wholesome food which he is incapable of assimilating, it had results that were all but disastrous. It was sin (the disease, in our figure) which caused the ensuing "death" of the sick man.

What then shall we say? That the law is sin? By no means! Yet, if it had not been for the law, I should not have known sin. I should not have known what it is to covet if the law had not said, "You shall not covet." But sin, finding opportunity in the commandment, wrought in me all kinds of covetousness. Apart from the law sin lies dead. I was once alive apart from the law, but when the commandment came, sin revived and I died; the very commandment which promised life proved to be death to me. For sin, finding opportunity in the commandment, deceived me and by it killed me. So the law is holy, and the commandment is holy and just and good.

Did that which is good, then, bring death to me? By no means! It was sin, working death in me through what is good, in order that sin might be shown to be sin, and through the commandment might become sinful beyond measure. We know that the law is spiritual; but I am carnal, sold under sin. I do not understand my own actions. For I do not do what I want, but I do the very thing I hate. Now if I do what I do not want, I agree that the law is good. So then it is no longer I that do it, but sin which dwells within me. For I know that nothing good dwells within me, that is, in my flesh. I can will what is right, but I cannot do it. For I do not do the good I want, but the evil I do not want is what I do. Now if I do what I do not want, it is no longer I that do it, but sin which dwells within me.

So I find it to be a law that when I want to do right, evil lies close at hand. For I delight in the law of God, in my inmost self, but I see in my members another law at war with the law of my mind and making me captive to the law of sin which dwells in my members. Wretched man that

I am! Who will deliver me from this body of death? Thanks be to God through Jesus Christ our Lord! So then, I of myself serve the law of God with my mind, but with my flesh I serve the law of sin.

There is therefore now no condemnation for those who are in Christ Jesus. For the law of the Spirit of life in Christ Jesus has set me free from the law of sin and death. (Rom. 7:7–8:2.)

Paul's message is not one of pessimism and frustration, as it would be if the case were hopeless. Instead the very darkness of this inner scene is in some measure due to the brightness of the light outside— it is the foil for Paul's proclamation of redemption, "justification," and salvation. Contrasted with the new life in Christ, the old life of sin and of struggle, with his own debilitated powers, to keep the Law of God seems dark and hopeless. Indeed it *is* hopeless, on this level, for sin is too deeply rooted in human nature (the "flesh") ever to be removed save by a total transformation—the death and resurrection experienced by the Christian in union with Christ. (For this process of renewal, as we shall see, Paul uses a dozen different figures and illustrations, some of which are found elsewhere in the New Testament and other early Christian literature.)

Thus Paul's real contribution to the doctrine of man is a tremendous deepening of the conception of human responsibility, a more profound and more subtly psychological interpretation of the meaning of sin, and a corresponding deepening of the significance and power of redemption. That he was able to make such a contribution, which has left its impress upon vast areas of later theology, especially in Protestantism, was no doubt due in large measure to his own peculiar personality and spiritual experience. He was a "twice-born" man, if ever there was one. The old traditional sequence, derived from the Old Testament and from ancient religion generally, law–obedience–divine favor *versus* law–disobedience–punishment–repentance–forgiveness– restoration to divine favor, was almost obliterated for Paul; it was at least left far behind in his psychological (some would say pathological) reinterpretation of Christian experience. He had fathomed the dark, unplumbed depths of alienation from God, and he had returned, had been brought back to life again by the gracious act of God in Christ. But his new life was no mere restoration or renewal of the old. He was more than forgiven or "acquitted" at the bar of God's justice; he was transformed, reborn, "justified" or "made" righteous in God's sight, a "new man" in Christ; and a wholly "new creation" was the result (II Cor. 5:17).

In Paul we see a representative not only of Judaism but of the whole Hellenistic world of his time, troubled in conscience but more troubled by awareness of its own inner impotence and futility, knowing good but unable to achieve it, held down by evil powers from without (Sin, Satan, Death) and by treacherous forces within which had already handed over the keys to the city of Mansoul to the enemy outside the gates. Paul was a mystic, without question. What he found in the gospel of Christ was something different—certainly in emphasis and in depth—from what many others in his time found there, and from what many other (perhaps most) Christians have found since. And it was this deepening of the conception of human nature which laid the foundations for much of the most significant later work of Christian theologians. Augustine is sometimes credited with being the founder of modern psychology; the title really belongs to Paul.

It is often assumed that Paul's exposition of the doctrine of sin, explaining it by the myth of the fall of man, is representative of the New Testament as a whole, and even of the whole Bible. Evidence for this view is found in references to the universality of sin. But Paul went much further in explaining the origin of sin and in his view of its deep-seated nature, as well as in his view of its relation to the Law, than any other New Testament writer. In the Synoptic Gospels, in the Epistle to the Hebrews, in Revelation, in the Catholic epistles, and scarcely less in John, there is ample recognition of the ubiquity of sin—and even of sinfulness. But only in Paul is sin viewed as the corruption of man's whole nature, to such a degree that human nature is in need not only of redemption and cleansing but of total transformation and renewal. For Paul the sentence of death, which is the judgment of God upon man's sin, not only hangs over the race (all men must die) and over each individual, but has already been experienced by the individual apart from God. "You were *dead* through . . . trespasses and sins" (Eph. 2:1). "You have died, with Christ, and been made alive again," or "you have risen to newness of life," in his resurrection—this is the burden of his proclamation of the joyful news of the "gospel." Even Christ himself, coming in the "likeness" of sinful flesh (Rom. 8:3; that is, in a human nature, though not actually sinning), has to die because of the sin which has infected all humanity.

Nevertheless, dire as the situation is, Paul is no pessimist. The body is no tomb, from which only the soul can be released or raised. Human nature can be redeemed; and in the end, when Christ has won his full victory, even death will be destroyed (I Cor. 15:26). It will then be possible to look back upon the record and recognize that sin has been only a dark and tragic episode, universal for a time, but not permanent. Paul's religion is a religion of redemption, of faith, and of hope.

4. *Specific Sins*

The New Testament contains a number of passages which are in substance lists of sins—the kind of lists which we find in use by ethical teachers in the contemporary Hellenistic world. Such lists are also to be found in Jewish writings of the time, especially in Hellenistic Jewish works. These "tables" of virtues and their contrary vices (usually in the other order, vices and their contrary virtues) were perhaps suggested by the use of framed and hinged wax tablets in the schools; boys were expected to copy and perhaps to memorize the lists. Those duties which had to do with life within the household have been called *Haustafeln,* and a whole series is given in the New Testament epistles (Col. 3:18–4:6; Eph. 4:17–6:9; etc.) But in addition to these specific duties there were also the lists of virtues and vices just mentioned. They are to be found, for example, in Mark 7:21-22; Matt. 15:19; Luke 18:11 (?); Rom. 1:28-31; 13:13; I Cor. 5:9-11; 6:9-10; II Cor. 12:20; Gal. 5:19-21; Eph. 4:31; 5:3-5; Col. 3:5, 8; I Tim. 1:9-10; 6:4-5; II Tim. 3:2-4; Tit. 3:3; I Pet. 4:3; Rev. 9:21; 21:8; 22:15 (cf. also IV Macc. 1:26; 2:15; Testaments of the XII Patriarchs *passim,* etc.).

Taking even these few (20) passages and listing the terms used, the amplitude and variety of the primitive Christian ethical vocabulary will be apparent at once. Many of the words come into Christian use from the Old Testament, especially from the Psalter; some are derived from current religious-philosophical use in the Greek world. The sins here listed include: abusiveness, adultery, anger (two words), arrogance, a base mind, being bereft of truth, bitterness, boastfulness, carousing, clamor, conceit (or conceitedness), covetousness, a craving for controversy, cowardliness, debauchery, deceit, depravity of mind, disobedience, including disobedience to parents, disorder, dissension (two words), doglike behavior (?), drunkenness (two words), enmity, envy, error, evil, evil eye (jealousy? or bearing a grudge?), evil thoughts, extortion, faithlessness (two words), falsehood, false witness, fierceness, filthiness, foolishness or folly (three words), fornication (also rendered immorality in R.S.V.), foul talk, gossip, greed (also rendered covetousness), mutual hatred, being hated by men, hating God, hating good, haughtiness, heartlessness, homosexuality (two words; and also sodomy, as below), idolatry (two words), immorality, improper conduct, inhumanity, implacableness, impurity, ingratitude, injustice, insolence, invention of evil, jealousy, kidnaping, lawlessness, levity, licentiousness, love of money, love of self, lying, malice, malignity, manslaying, murder, murder of father or mother, party spirit, passion (three words), evil desire, slavery to passion and pleasures, perjury, love of pleasure, pollution, pride, profaneness, profligacy, wild profligacy (another word), quarrelsomeness, recklessness, reveling, reviling, robbery, ruthlessness, selfishness, silly talk, sin, slander (three words), sodomy, sorcery, strife (also rendered quarrelsomeness), base suspicion, theft, treachery, ungodliness, unholiness, unrighteousness, wickedness (also rendered evil or injustice), worship of demons, wrangling, wrath—a total of 115 terms, not counting duplications.

That so large a number of terms is to be found in these few passages shows the emphasis which the early church placed upon the moral struggle. That only a few of the terms are found in several lists, and then not in the same order, seems to show that thus far there was no catechetical formula which every Christian had to memorize.

Turning now from the R.S.V. translation to the underlying Greek text, we find that the commonest terms in these lists (which of course do not include all the ethical terminology of the New Testament) are the following:

Fornication or immorality (10 times), with which should probably be listed the words for impurity (3), licentiousness (4), passion (3), adultery (2), and one or two others relating to sins connected with sex.

Slander or abusiveness (*blasphêmia*, 5), with two others (*diaboloi* and *katalalous*, used twice; total 8).

Idolatry (7) with worship of demons (total 8).

Malice (*kakia*, 6), wrath or anger (6), murder (6), theft or robbery or extortion (6), covetousness or greed (5), strife or quarreling (*eris*, 5), lying (4), envy (4), sorcery (4, chiefly in Revelation), reveling and carousing (4), drunkenness (4), jealousy (3), wickedness (3), pride (3), conceit (3).

The only significance these figures possess is relative. No one will assume, for example, that slander was twice as common as lying among the early Christians. In fact, it is not fair to infer from the currency of these terms that those who used them were always guilty of the sins named. Quite the opposite—the language is that of the preachers and teachers of the early church, who were combating these evils; and what was found within the church was certainly thought to be (and probably was) as a landlocked bay compared to the boundless ocean outside. Nor is it necessarily implied that the early Christians were often guilty of them. Yet in the society in which the earliest Christians moved, these things were common—as they are in modern society. What the Christians did, or were at least urged to do, was take a stand against them. At the same time, one can read between the lines and gain a fair picture of that society. Its sins were the sins of the *petit gens* of the great cities of the ancient Roman empire. The church had not yet begun to enter upon its "social triumph," as the late Shirley Jackson Case described it. Paul was quite right; "not many wise, learned, or important" people were found in the Christian community (cf. I Cor. 1:26). The sins excoriated are mainly personal; the highhanded wickedness of "governors and kings," of judges and princes and magnates, is not mentioned (though the mighty of the earth are as prone to personal sins as other men are). Though the *Haustafeln* include duties of masters to slaves, the catalogues of sins do not mention cruelty or brutality or injustice save in general terms. There is no term, for example, for taking a bribe—though this was commonly denounced in the Old Testament. In other words, the sins named are those apparent in a small insulated group within the larger society of the empire. The day would come when the categories of Christian ethics and moral theology would have to be enlarged to include the sins of the governing class, but that day was not yet, was in fact far distant when the books of the New Testament were written. Moreover, the sins named in these typical lists do not imply a unified social group or nation, such as the Old Testament implies throughout. The church was the New Israel, but only ideally; it was a church, not a church nation. This fact, as we shall see, is most important when we come to consider Christian ethics as set forth in the New Testament. Up to the end of our period, and somewhat beyond, the church was still only a sect, though it was eventually to become the "great church" of the later Roman and Byzantine empires.

It is apparent also that the sins denounced and repudiated in the New Testament are not solely those castigated in the teaching of Jesus. The church had now moved out into a different world from that of Galilee in the second quarter of the first century, with its settled system of religious teaching, its ubiquitous scribes, its pious Pharisees, its tax collectors, villagers, and *am ha-aretz*. But the church's teaching appeals, nevertheless, to the "sayings and commandments of the Lord." His example, his words, the whole spirit of his life inspire the apostolic church to apply that spirit to the situation in which it finds itself. In fact, some of the church's teaching is derived from what Jesus himself took for granted without stressing or elaborating. For example, he does not say much (in the surviving tradition, at least) about temperance, but the current teaching of Judaism did—and there were texts of the Old Testament to appeal to, as well. But more than all, there were certain things a Christian, a member of Christ, simply could not do; and this, rather than explicit appeal to written texts or to the oral tradition of Jesus' words, is the real standard upon which Paul and others insisted. What we observe in the New Testament, accordingly, is a principle already at work which was destined to affect the whole development of Christian preaching and teaching of moral doctrine, moral theology, and ethics. To this day it is still the basic principle in the "interpretation" and "application" of the Christian gospel to the conditions and circumstances of life in the world. Not texts, but an example, not even the words of Jesus so much as the spirit of Jesus—this is the main guiding principle of Christian ethical doctrine. There are and have been exceptions enough, but the general principle still holds good, and needs rigorous application today as heretofore.

It is a striking fact that the lists of sins are so much longer, in the New Testament, than the lists of virtues. This is no peculiarity of the early church—though the denunciatory tone of some of the later writings is very marked, going even further than Paul does in specifying the sins of men. It would be interesting to compare other ethical and religious literature containing similar lists. The Old Testament and Judaism furnish examples; other ancient writings, such as those of the Greek and Latin moralists, do the same. Without cataloguing the lists found elsewhere in the ancient world, one has the impression (at least) that the situation is no different from what we find in the New Testament. It is a human and "psychological" feature—sin is more striking than goodness, vice than virtue, and preachers are as a rule more concerned with warning and denunciation than with instruction and guidance in the cultivation of the quieter characteristics and virtues.

An exception must be made in the case of the teaching of Jesus. Although he denounced hypocrisy, greed, false oaths, and other sins, his main emphasis was laid upon the virtues: humility, trust in God (faith), love, perseverance, forgiveness, obedience to parents, renunciation, generosity, prayer, "justice, mercy, and the love of God"— in fact the whole round of virtues as taught in the Old Testament and by the Jewish synagogue. He could say to a man who wished to win heaven by one good deed, "Keep the commandments" (Matt. 19:17). His emphasis was far more upon the positive delineation of the quality of a life devoted to God than upon the negative denunciation of human sins and shortcomings. So much so that he was classed by the "unco' guid" of his day with the sinners; he was called a winebibber and a friend of the outcast, and still worse things (Luke 7:34; Matt. 11:19; Luke 7:39). It is clear from the Gospels that Jesus can scarcely have viewed sin as a dark malevolent power in human life, as Paul viewed it, and that the problem of its origin and spread rarely entered his mind. If Paul was a twice-born man, Jesus was certainly (speaking in human terms) a completely once-born. There are no signs of strain and turmoil, of dark forebodings, of sin repented and still a burden, of the steady awareness of the sentence of mortality which hangs over the whole race descended from Adam—none of this dark view of man's nature and condition can be traced in the Gospels, certainly not in the older elements of the evangelic tradition. Sin is real, but God has provided the remedy. The illness is not chronic, is no cancer eating into the vitals of man's whole nature. Jesus can take an ordinary child and place him in the midst of his disciples and say, "Unless you turn and become like children, you will never enter the kingdom of heaven" (Matt. 18:2-3; cf. 19:14). He can ask his disciples, "Why do you not judge for yourselves what is right?" (Luke 12:57). He can warn his contemporaries, shocked by the collapse of the tower of Siloam, "Unless you repent, you will all likewise perish" (Luke 13:5)—but that is to make it clear that these men were not necessarily hardened sinners, above all other men in the city. At the same time, the proviso "unless you repent" points to the remedy; God judges sin, but God also forgives (Matt. 6:14). He can say to fathers: "If you then"—bad as you are (or even "wicked")—"know how to give good gifts to your children, how much more will your Father who is in heaven give good things to those who ask him?" (Matt. 7:11). There is no "doctrine" of sin here, as there is in Paul. It is only the ordinary Jewish attitude, rooted in Old Testament teaching, and taking for granted the round of Jewish concepts. What is required is repentance, *metanoia, teshubah*—not some radical transformation and regeneration of human nature.

In the dismal situation of our modern world we are inclined to look upon Paul's teaching as more thoroughgoing, since it demands a total transformation of man. Perhaps this is true of modern man, and it may have been true of ancient man; but there is no question that, upon a historical view, Jesus' teaching was not so pessimistic as Paul's; he took it for granted that man is not totally bad but a "mixed" creation, good and bad at the same time. His demand, "Unless you turn and become like children" (Matt. 18:3), is not quite the same thing as John's "You must be born anew" (3:3-8). If it be insisted that Jesus' diagnosis of human ills is not thorough enough, certainly not for the actual situation in which we find ourselves today, the answer is obvious —Jesus' diagnosis has never been accepted, nor his remedy tried. It is idle to infer that since Jesus occasionally healed the sick, and even forgave sinners, without any expression of repentance on their part, therefore he took sin somewhat lightly. The records do not enable us to say that he healed or forgave without any sign or token of repentance; they are too brief for that, and are anything but stenographic reports of events in Galilee. The main tenor of his teaching takes for granted the seriousness of sin, and the necessity of repentance; he was certainly no less in earnest about it than the Old Testament prophets had been. But he did not take the dark view which is forever associated with the mind of Paul and with Paulinism in later Christian history, in the great succession of the twice-born.

Thus within the New Testament there is variety—and tension—on the subject of sin and its relation to the nature of man. Later New Testament writers take one side or the other. The author of the Epistle to the Hebrews is not concerned with sin as a power which must be broken; the angelic hosts are not the dark aeonic rulers whose role in the propagation of sin and the enslavement of the race is so marked a feature of Paul's thought—they are simply the Old Testament "messengers" of the Most High, created *ad hoc* like wind and flame. The sins of men which require expiation are not specified in detail; everyone knows what sins are. Nor is sin a power in the heavens which must be broken by the victorious conquest of the heavenly powers by the Son of God. Instead, it is guilt which must be removed by sacrifice and by priestly intercession—Christ is the great high priest who has ascended above the heavens, and has entered the heavenly tabernacle, even within the veil, in order to make intercession for us (Heb. 4:14). This is a quite different conception from the one familiar to us from Paul. In the Pastorals, in Jude and Second Peter, and elsewhere (e.g. in Revelation), there is a fierce denunciation of the sins of the "latter days"; it is taken for granted that before the Parousia the sins of men will increase, and an almost millenarian delight in the dark outlook prevails. The worse the present situation becomes, the sooner the day of judgment will arrive. The Epistle of James, on the other hand, retains the "moralistic" outlook of Judaism, of popular Greek philosophical ethics—and of Jesus.

5. *The Coming Judgment*

As in the Old Testament, the essence of sin is disobedience. This is the meaning of the classic myth of the Fall. As the ever fuller development of legalism took place, consequent upon the compilation of successive codes, each added to or built upon the preceding accumulation, with no attempt at revision and abrogation of even the most primitive legislation, there naturally came about an ever greater emphasis upon the requirement of obedience, and upon the sin of disobedience. Every infraction of the law is sin (I John 5:17; "all wrongdoing is sin" R.S.V.). And yet it was clear that there were different grades and levels of sinfulness: sins of omission as well as of commission; sins of open and plain error and folly, and also "secret sins," of which the sinner himself was unaware; sins of oversight and neglect, and also sins "with a high hand." The latter, which tally more or less with the later ecclesiastical definition of "mortal" sin, could not be forgiven—the conscious, purposeful, deliberate flouting of the will of God, like the choice of evil by Milton's Satan, "Evil, be thou my good." One difference between the old covenant and the new is that even mortal sin can be repented of, and forgiven, in the Christian view. The "unforgivable" sin of Mark 3:28-30 is the perverse and blind attribution of what is obviously good to motives of evil or to collusion with the devil—Christ's "mighty works" attributed in this case to collusion with Beelzebul. The sin is unforgivable (so most interpreters take it) for the simple reason that, practically speaking, the sinner *cannot repent;* it is a matter of observed fact that one thus hardened in sin and opposed to good will not repent and be forgiven. This is the real "blasphemy of the Holy Spirit," not the chance utterance of some specific formula of malediction, as, alas, too many poor victims of mental illness have assumed.

The conception of *guilt* is fundamentally a derivative from inner experience. It is the consciousness of disobedience, the awareness of broken relations with God, a sense of shame and a feeling that one is in no position to take the initiative in restoring those relations—only God in his mercy and grace can do so. In too much of later Christian theology the conception of guilt and that of sin have been simply identified, with the result that God's initiative in reconciling man to himself had first of all to consider human guilt (as breach of law) rather than the actual state of alienation, infection, or impotence which sin had caused. The Atonement, in some theologies, became an elaborate device whereby God's honor could be upheld and at the same time man could be forgiven and restored to fellowship with him—as if the Almighty had to "save face" in his dealings with us; or as if somehow God kept a ledger, and totted up the overwhelming indebtedness which man owes to the divine "honor." Such a scheme appealed to men schooled in Roman law and concerned with the feudal system of "honor" due to potentates, but it squares ill with the simple and utterly realistic thought of the New Testament. Of course guilt is involved, but the main thing in man's salvation is not the removal of guilt but the actual transformation of a sinner into an obedient child of God. The guilt is removed along with the state of sin and disobedience; "there is therefore *now* no condemnation for those who are in Christ Jesus" (Rom. 8:1). "Since we are justified by faith, we have [rather than, "let us have"] peace with God through our Lord Jesus Christ" (Rom 5:1). For sin unrepented, unforgiven, there remains only the "fearful prospect of judgment" (Heb. 10:27); but God's attitude toward sinners is not that of an angry deity, let alone an offended one—the New Testament is the proclamation of God's grace, God's mercy, God's free forgiveness, from beginning to end. This is true even though Paul seems to imply that there is no possibility of sin after the one divine act of free forgiveness, while the Epistle to the Hebrews insists that there is no possibility of a second forgiveness if the sin nevertheless takes place—a position reversed in the second century and later; the situation in Hebrews was probably a special case, namely apostasy under persecution. And although Paul evidently assumed that those who were "in Christ" (meaning either "Christians," or those who were mystically united to Christ) would not—or could not—commit further sin, his own apostolic experience made it clear that this was too much to expect; his later epistles, and those of the "Paulinists" after him, allow for repentance after further sinning on the part of Christians. The problem became a far more serious one for the later church, when a vast number of ordinary folk became Christians and the high enthusiasm of the early days was no longer common. Traces of this pedestrianizing of the Christian way are apparent even in later parts of the New Testament, where writers of the second and third generation do their best to revive the puritan martyr outlook of the first days.

From the Old Testament, and also from the elaboration of the doctrine in the apocalyptic literature, the New Testament writers drew their conception of the last judgment. Some modern scholars have tried to distinguish between the teaching of Jesus and that of the apostles on this subject—as if our Lord held the prophetic view that God's judgments are a series of crises in world history, or was even thinking only of the crisis of death which each individual has to face. But the expectation of a universal divine judgment is too obviously a part of primitive Christianity to permit such an explanation. From the days of John the Baptist, whose message to his contemporaries consisted chiefly in a prediction of the coming judgment and a warning to prepare for it by repentance and good works, to the days of Domitian and the writing of Revelation, it was assumed that this judgment was approaching. Jesus' teaching did not emphasize it particularly; his conception of the approaching kingdom of God as virtually already present ("realized eschatology") seems to have allowed scant room for a universal judgment. The conception of the Fourth Gospel (the judgment as continuous) does not allow for it either. And yet both in the teaching of Jesus and in the view of the Fourth Evangelist there is a clear recognition of the impending judgment upon the whole world (Luke 10:14; John 5:22). Its place in the sequence of events was in fact indispensable—a world like this cannot continue forever, but must be brought to terms with God (if God is really creator, controller of history, and redeemer of men); on the other hand, God's kingdom, God's reign, which must come eventually, sooner or later, cannot move into the place of this present order without a judgment's taking place. What is evil must be done away; whatever contradicts God's gracious purpose must be removed; sin, suffering, Satan, death—all that stands opposed to God and his gracious will must be confronted with that will and take the consequences. That is what the judgment essentially is—not a dramatic episode at the end of history, but the confrontation of sin and every evil with the goodness, the holiness, the mercy and love of God. Since this is God's world, and he will not abandon it (he cannot abandon it without admitting the defeat of his purposes), there is no other way than the way of judgment, with mercy and forgiveness assured to all who repent from their evil deeds and turn to him to be saved. The figures used by the New Testament to express this great truth are many and various—the light enters the realm of darkness, but is not overcome (John 1:5); the father's love goes out to meet the penitent prodigal and welcome him back to his home (Luke 15:20); the

dying robber on the cross has only to murmur, "Remember me
. . . ," and receives the Lord's gracious promise (Luke 23:42-43);
where sin abounded, "grace abounded all the more" (Rom. 5:20);
Christ even goes to the realm of departed spirits, in one late epistle,
and preaches repentance to those in the prison of the underworld
(I Pet. 3:19). "There is mercy with thee; therefore shalt thou be
feared" (Ps. 130:4 B.C.P.)—that was the high doctrine of the Old
Testament. The same doctrine is evident in the New Testament,
with the inevitable addition, "and be loved," since "perfect love casts
out fear" (I John 4:18).

IX

The Doctrine of Christ

1. *Modern Humanism*

IT has been a favorite view in many circles, during the past century and a half, that Christianity began with a purely human Jesus, a lowly "son of man" who taught a pure ethic of brotherhood and love, was put to death by reactionary ecclesiastics, was believed to have risen from the dead ("the Easter message was the beginning of the Christian faith, whatever the Easter fact"!), and as a consequence of this belief came in time to be deified. Certain tendencies in modern Christianity, both evangelical and Catholic, appeared to favor this view. A vast emphasis was laid upon the humanity of Jesus, not to the exclusion but certainly to the considerable obscuring of the divine nature —a kind of "Jesuolatry," with many features borrowed from early nineteenth-century romanticism and also from earlier Pietism. In Protestant circles this devotion might almost seem to have taken the place of Roman devotion to the saints. Its favorite Gospel was the Fourth, apparently because the "beloved disciple" lay "close to the breast of Jesus" (John 13:25; 21:20); the theological statements and implications of the Fourth Gospel were simply overlooked. And for this popular, emotional type of devotion Paul was a closed book, except for his conversion, an account of which was found in Rom. 7, and for his emphasis on the cross. Many a hymn still to be found in our hymnals (though they are gradually disappearing in the new revisions) reflects this romantic, purely humanistic, sometimes beautiful but often saccharine and overly emotional type of piety.

But the New Testament knows nothing of this type of piety; its conception of Christ is theological, from beginning to end of the sacred volume. As it does not encourage the historian who would "reconstruct" the life of Jesus on a purely human basis and with purely "historical" preconceptions (for the data do not suffice), so it does not encourage a nontheological, purely emotional type of devotion. Back of a "theological" view of Jesus to a wholly—or merely—human "man of Galilee" the New Testament does not permit us to look, even in our oldest sources. From the earliest beginning of Christianity the figure of Jesus was theologically interpreted. The meaning which he bore for Christian faith was a "theological" meaning; apart from that theological meaning or interpretation there were—there could have been—no historical records of his career or teaching. The "purely human" life of Jesus—Jesus as a figure in the world's secular history— can be "reconstructed" only by hypothesis and in imagination. Hence the endless variety in the modern nontheological lives of Jesus, especially in their attempt to reconstruct his "biography."

Similarly the devotion to Christ which the New Testament reflects is theologically conditioned. Its picture of Christ is not the popular nineteenth-century "Man with God is on the throne," but the figure of the Son of God who died and rose again and was exalted by God to his right hand, who has been appointed to be the judge of the living and the dead, and is the divine agent in the realization of all God's purposes. Even the ethical motivation of the New Testament is theological: "Why do you call me Lord [the exalted *Kyrios* of the church] and not do what I tell you?" (Luke 6:46; cf. Matt. 25:31-46). "The love of Christ constraineth us" (II Cor. 5:14 A.S.V.; "controls," R.S.V.; *urget,* Vulgate). This is not some exalted or sublimated variety of human affection but the love of the divine being who humbled himself for us, took the form of a man, lived the life of a slave, and died the death of the cross for love of us sinners. True, there are passages in the Gospels which give us glimpses of the historical figure, Jesus of Nazareth, with almost no theological interpretation. Even the epistles afford such glimpses, though more rarely. But even in such cases the theological interpretation is taken for granted—the authors are not endeavoring to describe the character of the Master or to give us a full account of his earthly life. And it is significant that these passages are sometimes dealt with by later writers as if they provided stumbling blocks and problems; for example, Mark's form of the question addressed to Jesus, "Good teacher," and the reply, "Why do you call me good?" become in Matthew, "What good deed must I do?" and, "Why do you ask me about what is good?" (Mark 10:17-18; Matt. 19:16-17). Even on the subject of the "messianic consciousness" of Jesus, about which so many books and essays have been written since 1890, the Gospels simply do not afford us the data upon which a consistent theory might be based. They were not written for purposes of historical reconstruction or biography; they were written for edification, or rather, in order to proclaim the message of salvation.

And yet there is an element of truth in this modern "humanistic" view. Jesus certainly was a historical figure. The efforts of the "Christ myth" school about 1910 were wasted. Their solution of the problem of identifying, or of dissociating, "the Jesus of history and the Christ of faith" was to assume that Jesus never lived; that the (pre-Christian) concept of a redeemer God became "incarnate" in the "myth" of the crucifixion and resurrection of Jesus of Nazareth; that the real "Christ" was a solar deity who "died" annually each autumn, revived at Epiphany (near the winter solstice), and either became incarnate once more at the spring equinox (Annunciation) or rose from the dead at Easter (that is, about the same time); and so on. Or perhaps the Christ ideal of the New Testament was only the "projection" and "sublimation" of the frustrated hopes of the submerged masses throughout the Roman Empire—a deified carpenter, like Hephaestus, Asclepius, and other craft gods, the appropriate deity of the underpaid working classes of the first century. It is hard to see how such bizarre theories could ever have been taken seriously, or have been put forth by scholars with a real understanding of the history of ancient religion. In contrast with such views the humanistic theory is greatly to be preferred. It at least recognizes the actual situation reflected in our sources—a new religion growing up within Judaism, in closest contact with the old faith and practice, and not at all some artificial construction invented (like certain other ancient religions, such as the cult of Serapis) for political or economic purposes in Egypt, or Rome, or elsewhere in the Greco-Roman world. What this element of truth is, and what its limitations are, we may examine in what follows.

2. *Theological Interpretation in the Gospels*

The necessity of a fresh approach to the Gospels—in fact to the whole New Testament, but especially the Gospels—is growing more apparent every year. It is clear that they are not biographies; that fact has been recognized for some time. For all the efforts that were once made to fit them into the pattern of Greco-Roman biography (for example by the late Clyde Weber Votaw), or the more recent attempts to view them as ancient examples of religious *Kleinliteratur* (for example that of Karl Ludwig Schmidt), as ancient popular hagiographa, circulating in small editions outside the regular channels of literary production—in spite of these efforts the Gospels fit neither pattern very well. Instead, they are the sacred books of a religious movement which came out of first-century Judaism and grew into the Catholic Church—a movement which brought with it, into the Greek-speaking Gentile world, a number of stories about Jesus, anecdotes from his life, examples of his teaching, of his explanation of scripture, and of his controversies with the scribes, above all the brief but majestic account of his death (the basic passion narrative). These stories about Jesus were never wholly isolated from one another; they always belonged to *the* story of Jesus, who was the church's Lord and Savior. The story of Jesus was no biography, but the proclamation of salvation, of God's act in sending him, of the whole process which had begun with his ministry in Galilee, his death at Jerusalem, his resurrection and exaltation, and which was still continuing as the events of the "last days" were now leading on steadily to the eschatological climax—the general resurrection and Last Judgment, and the full and final establishment of the New Age. The story of Jesus was literally the account of what he "began" to do (Acts 1:1)—or of what God had begun to do through him. This was no biography of a great personality, but the first act of a divine drama in three acts, in which the second act was the present, and the third was soon to come. Primitive Christianity was thoroughly supernaturalistic; the "mighty works" which Jesus had wrought upon earth were now being followed by similar mighty works which were being wrought by him in the midst of his church, through the apostles whom he had chosen, and through others. And even greater works than these were anticipated in the future, as even the Gospel of John (14:12) takes for granted. It is this eschatological and supernaturalistic "ethos" of the Gospels which is their most decisive characteristic, and marks them off most sharply from all secular biographies; it even distinguishes them from the "biographical" material found here and there in the Old Testament and in the literature of contemporary first-century Judaism.

It was natural enough, at the end of the nineteenth century and during the opening years of the twentieth, that New Testament scholars should endeavor to recover the "earliest sources for the life of Jesus." Those were the years in which modern historical research came into its own, confident at last of its methods, and ready to deal with whatever material became available. Moreover a theological slogan, "Back to Jesus," rang in their ears—one that seemed to point the way forward to the goal toward which the whole of Protestantism had been moving since the Reformation. But it is now a question whether the earliest sources, taken in isolation, can ever provide us with adequate materials for a biography or even for a satisfactory brief chapter in general history. They leave out of account, if taken in isolation, the whole setting of the stories—not the setting in Galilean Judaism in the twenties of the first century, about which we know almost nothing, but the setting in which they had meaning as told and retold in the early Christian tradition; and likewise their setting in *the* story of Jesus as it was finally put together, in varied form, in our four canonical Gospels and in still others, of which only fragments survive. It is the spiritual Christ, the church's exalted Lord, of whom these stories were told, as incidents from the brief period of his life upon earth; what he is now, as Savior and Lord, is something vastly greater, so that the ordinary, secular biographical perspective is simply out of the question.

It is true that the recovery of these "earliest sources," and of their component elements, the "stories about Jesus," brings him much closer to us, makes his historical figure more vividly real, especially as form history singles out the earliest of them. But it is still not a biography that results from such analysis of the Gospels, nor even the materials for one, save of a quite sketchy and fragmentary sort. Yet we can begin to see the kind of person Jesus was—a wholly unique and entirely dominant person; one who was so completely and utterly possessed by God that he could speak with absolute authority as the

Voice of God and act without the slightest hesitation as God's agent, God's representative, not only exorcising demons and commanding the winds, but forgiving sins (this no ancient miracle-worker, *Wundermann*, from Empedocles to Apollonius of Tyana had ever undertaken to do). It was not that he claimed to be Messiah; his actions and his words left this earthly office (however glorified with quasidivine titles) far behind, and the church's instinct was correct when it took "Christos" for a proper name and left political messianism out of it altogether (messianism was always political, and has been ever since). The religious significance which the church found in Jesus was something far profounder, and attached itself to what was in truth the profoundest fact about him—his sense of God, of close and intimate relation to God, so close as to approach identification.

The process is already at work in the Gospels; it is their presupposition and their setting. For Mark he is both Son of God (which is not a messianic title) and Son of Man (which is not messianic but transcendental); for John he is the incarnate Logos, the Wisdom or Reason or Thought or Word of God by whom the worlds were fashioned, now "made" flesh and "manifesting his glory" upon earth. In Luke and Matthew the Palestinian tradition has left a deeper impress. In Luke the southern, Judean concept of Messiah has been uppermost, and upon this is placed the author's Hellenistic interpretation—Jesus was Savior, Lord, teacher of wisdom, a *theios anêr*, a "divine" man, as well as Messiah. In Matthew the messiahship is more doctrinaire, more transcendent, more completely influenced by the (northern?) Son of Man concept—the Primal Man who is to come on the clouds and judge all mankind. The other elements are present, but this is the concept that most strongly affects and really determines the Christology of Matthew. But back of them all, back of all the divergent emphases found in the tradition, in the early written or stereotyped oral sources and in the finished Gospels, there is the purely religious, nonpolitical, nonsecular evaluation of Jesus; and back of that is the purely religious, nonpolitical, nonsecular, and even otherworldly, transcendent consciousness of Jesus himself, as it is reflected in the very earliest sources. This is not even a subject for biography, but only for autobiography or for such partial disclosure as a wholly unique personality might make in letters, journals, or other intimate writings—but none of these were ever written.

The sayings of Jesus and the anecdotes from his life, selected by an informal process under the pressure of the church's needs and interests, do reflect here and there, it is true, the greatness of his personality. The general impression of his uniqueness is inescapable; it pervades the whole body of evangelic tradition—that is, that surviving part of it which is enshrined in our canonical Gospels. But how to fit all this into the course of history is another question, and one which the first century did not raise, nor the second century, nor the third. Even for the fifth-century church Christ was still the *telos* of history, its climax, completion, and end. As he was the one through whom all things had been made, things invisible as well as things visible, so he would be the judge of the living and the dead. The mode of his incarnate life, as True God and Perfect Man, of two natures which are united inseparably and permanently, and yet unconfusedly and distinguishably—all this lifted him above history; he was "in the world" but "not of the world," as the Fourth Gospel described his disciples (John 17:11-16). It was the nineteenth century (after one or two anticipatory experiments in earlier days) which set about the task of recovering "the Jesus of history." But it is our discovery, in the twentieth, that the task is impossible and can never be accomplished. As Albert Schweitzer said, long ago, "He still eludes us," and we lack not only sufficient data for writing a genuinely historical biography of Jesus but also the pattern which would fit him—he eludes our categories of historical classification for the simple reason that he is wholly unique. He was no more a would-be Messiah who was put to death for his pains than he was a Hindu *avatara* of the Eternal, one in a long series, but specially created for a particular age. All the concepts men have applied to him are inadequate, for they are human, and made out of the stuff of human experience or speculation; he outtops them all, for he is unique, and can accept any one of our human concepts only by first transforming it. And this is as true of the Logos concept as it is of messiahship, or the concept of the Son of Man found in Daniel, Enoch, and elsewhere, or the concept of Lord (*Kyrios*), or the Son of God, or any others found in the New Testament or elsewhere in the early Christian writings.

3. *The Tradition of Jesus' Teaching*

It is not only the career of Jesus, his public ministry followed by the swiftly moving events of the last days in Jerusalem (the two main parts of the story of Jesus as told in the Gospels), which is based upon tradition, and hence can be reconstructed only with minute care and even then often only by hypothesis; the same holds true of his teaching. In the Gospels we stand *in medias res;* the tradition has been handed down for a generation or more, and has been modified to some extent in the process, at least by selection, but also by emphasis and application. The later Gospels make use of the earliest—Matthew and Luke use Mark, though John seems to be independent. How greatly Matthew and Luke modify Mark is apparent to everyone who has made a careful comparison of them. How independent of the Synoptics John is, is equally clear; his type of tradition has only slight resemblances to that of the other three Gospels, while the actual content of the teaching of Jesus is very different. Mark, whose Gospel comes from the period of the earliest crystallization of the tradition· in written form (it probably had a stereotyped oral form long before Mark), is addressed to a martyr church, and the materials selected from the tradition as specially relevant to this situation have also been molded more or less by this purpose. Luke is concerned to present Jesus as a wise and humane teacher, a good man, a "man of God," a prophet, a lover of his kind, an example worthy of emulation in a world far remote from Palestine and eagerly looking for worthy examples to emulate. Matthew thinks of Jesus as the new lawgiver, whose teaching can be—and has been—codified and set forth under appropriate rubrics and titles for the learning and observance of his church. John conceives of Jesus as the incarnate Logos, whose "work" is more important than his teaching, and who "manifests" himself not only in seven great "signs" which (like divine epiphanies) demand belief, but also in his "words" which are "life" (John 6:63*b*). The mystical, theosophical, quasi-theological or philosophical significance of this teaching is apparent at once, and was designed to interpret Christ to the world of the early second century as the full and final revealer of truth, profounder than Thrice-Greatest Hermes, truer than the philosophers of all the schools, and far superior to Moses. *"All* that came before" him were "thieves and robbers" and only misled mankind (John 10:8). On beyond the canonical Gospels, in the second and following centuries (for gospel writing did not cease with the appearance of these four), the apocryphal gospel writers undertook to show that Christ taught celibacy, or the renunciation of marriage (even for the married), or vegetarianism, or Gnosticism, or chiliasm, or whatever seemed to the writer the cardinal doctrine of the Christian faith.

Under such circumstances how can the original and unquestionable features of Jesus' teaching be made out? It is clearly impossible to put all these elements together into one vast, complex amalgam. It is almost equally impossible to single out the largest common denominator, or the elements common to all, and call that the unquestionable historical teaching of Jesus of Nazareth; for the elements neutralize and cancel each other out. Either Jesus did away with the Jewish law (Mark, John) or he did not (Matthew; Luke is silent on this point, but silence apparently gives consent, for the presuppositions of Luke are Jewish). Either Jesus was a "thoroughgoing eschatologist," or apocalyptist (Matthew), or he was not (John). And yet there was something in Jesus' teaching, no doubt, to which appeal could be made in every one of these divergent movements of thought. The situation can be illustrated by a graph, in which several lines move away from a common center without being connected with that center, as in Figure A. In this case the solution of the problem is simple; only project

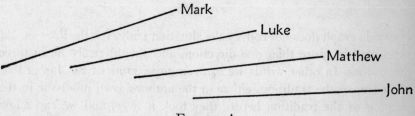

FIGURE A

the lines backward until they meet, and there you find the original, historical teaching of Jesus. But the problem is more complicated, for the lines are curved. They have been deflected by the influences of various kinds which have worked upon the tradition in the course of transmission, as in Figure B. The radii are of different lengths; the process is viewed from different standpoints, for the Synoptics. In John the common center is not a starting point in a historical development, but the focus about which the whole system swings; the perspective is from another dimension—from above, not beside. And yet

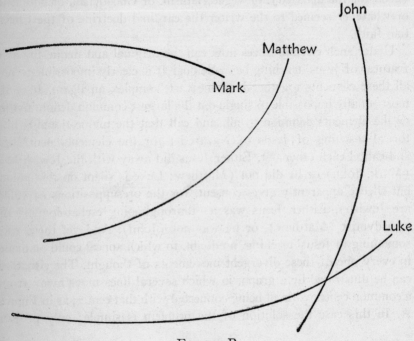

John

Matthew

Mark

Luke

FIGURE B

even this graph does not convey the situation truly, for the lines should be curved in more than one direction, and should really lie in three dimensions. In other words we can recognize *some* of the forces that played upon the tradition, either in the authors' own minds or in the shaping of the tradition before they took it over, and we can allow for this. But we cannot know them all.

For example, there is a strain in the Gospel of Luke, and also in Matthew, which seems to reflect an influence from some such religious philosophy as that of Cynicism, though it is also found in Neo-Pythagoreanism and in other schools and sects. Poverty is a virtue; poverty *per se* is something worth cultivating; the "poor" are blessed, as such;

"the Son of man has nowhere to lay his head"; the birds of the air and the lilies of the field have no anxieties; God clothes and feeds them, and you are of more value in his sight than they—are you not? The point is that you cannot rival the lilies in apparel, nor heap up stores of food for time to come, nor need you; God cares for the birds, and not a sparrow falls to the ground without his knowledge (Luke 6:20; 9:58; 12:22-34; cf. 12:13-21). This praise of poverty, this Franciscan note, strikes many readers in the modern world as strange, improvident, absurd. Most of us are like Alice Meynell, in her poem, and are amazed to find that poverty really goes clad in rags, not in the plain but shining raiment of romance. But why is this note so little stressed in Mark, and not at all in John? That it is authentic seems certain, for it permeates the whole body of Jesus' teaching and guided his life. What we find in Matthew and Luke is not something new and unheard-of, something drawn into the Christian tradition or intruding itself within it under the stress of the poverty and privation of the early Christian communities, either out in the Greco-Roman world (where Cynicism or its popular aftereffects and echoes would be encountered) or in Palestine, especially after the disastrous war of A.D. 66-70. Instead it indubitably goes back to Jesus, and was native and germane to the gospel from the start. Indeed it goes back farther still—the Psalms are full of it, and so is the wisdom literature. What Jesus did, apparently, was to take this principle, already found in the religious ethics of Judaism, and heavily underscore it with reference to the coming end of the age. But it meant even more than this. It was no mere lightening of the ship as the tempest came on—he found peace and strength, as other men have found peace and strength, through renunciation of *things,* and he bade his disciples do likewise. It is not mere trust in riches (Mark 10:24 mg.) but the possession of them (vss. 23, 25) which makes entrance into the kingdom of God difficult. It is not the rich man's contentment with full barns or the fact that the "soul" cannot be provided for by such things that is excoriated in the Lukan parable; it is the folly of the man in failing to realize that life is fleeting, that things mean nothing, that what matters is being "rich toward God" (Luke 12:21). On the lips of a Jewish teacher this would mean that the rich man should have given away his goods as alms or "to feed the poor."

The study of the New Testament demands the use of the historical imagination, especially in the "reconstruction" of the teaching of Jesus —which is the hardest part of New Testament thought or theology. What did Jesus really say? "Blessed are you poor," or "Blessed are the poor in spirit" (Luke 6:20; Matt. 5:3)? Presumably both beatitudes go back to a common origin in the tradition, though there is no reason why Jesus should not have uttered both, on different occasions. This common source is not necessarily Q, but the oral tradition back of Q. Matthew's addition, "in spirit," may have been meant only to safeguard the original meaning of the beatitude; Luke's form of the saying may be due either to his general "proletarianism," or to the social conditions which obtained in Palestine after the war against Rome, which affected the form of the tradition. But back of the saying is something even more—the whole "poverty-piety equation" (as Martin Dibelius called it) reflected in the Old Testament and in the ancient Jewish literature. Indeed, the background of the Beatitudes as a whole (and of the Sermon on the Mount, and of the whole teaching of Jesus) is not merely the social-economic conditions prevailing in Palestine after the war against Rome (through which a large part of the early Christian tradition had to pass, though it was two generations after Jesus), but the religion of the Old Testament, especially of the Psalms. The traditional "poverty-piety equation" was in fact age-old in the East; we can trace it in the old Egyptian popular literature, in early Greece, and elsewhere .The poor but pious man is pleasing to the gods, more pleasing than the rich and unscrupulous and impious (though Pindar and many of the Jewish sages and some of the psalmists rejoiced now and then to find a man who was both rich and pious, and obviously pleasing to God). In the Psalms the equation means this: poverty is the *result* of a religion of entire obedience to God's will, the very opposite of self-seeking, covetousness, pride, and violence, which lead to wealth. The theory implied that if one wished to gain wealth at any cost, even that of the abandonment of religion, it could of course be obtained; but no pious Jew would consider paying such a price. Accordingly, the pious were poor; conversely, one might assume, the poor were pious. Indeed, as a matter of observation, they often were—though at least one psalmist insisted that God never wholly abandoned them or let their children go begging (Ps. 37:25).

This complete, or almost complete, inversion of the ancient eudaemonism of popular Hebrew religion, now surviving from the days before the Exile, may represent a development in religious thought which resulted from the hard conditions of life in the early days of the Second Commonwealth, when Israel was struggling to regain a foothold in Palestine after the Exile; but it seems more likely to be the result of a deeply religious movement, destined to bear fruit, after some further generations of struggle, in Pharisaism and the religion of the "ancient pious men." That Jesus shared in this movement, criticized the extravagance and unreality of certain of its representatives, encouraged his disciples to follow its way of life and to live close to God without concern for this world's goods—this is almost axiomatic for a thoroughly historical interpretation of the gospel. Hence Matthew's phrase "poor in spirit" preserves the true note, whereas Luke's "you poor" *might* be interpreted as pure proletarianism. Jesus represented the *am ha-aretz;* and they were poor because, in spite of their allegiance to Judaism, they had not the leisure—perhaps not even the desire— to observe all the minutiae of the priestly Law and its scribal interpretation, since the requirements of their daily occupations brought them into contact with Gentiles and with Gentile ways of life which were defiling.

One difficulty, today, is that the whole social-economic as well as the political outlook of the modern world is entirely different from that of the New Testament. Our modern social aim is an "economy of plenty," enough for all, so that there will be no poverty. (We fail to achieve this aim, but at least the majority are now coming to recognize it as an obligation upon society.) But in that ancient world, with its narrow margin between production and consumption, between population and the food supply, with recurrent famine and constant privation, all of which was derived immediately from the hand of God, the religious situation was entirely different. Thus we have to reconstruct that situation in imagination, and then limit the interpretation to that specific situation. If later we go beyond this (as we must), then it is essential that we follow the guidance of the *spirit* of Jesus' teaching, rather than the letter. This is no easy lesson for us to learn—especially, perhaps, for us Americans. The hard core of American Protestantism is still fundamentalism, literal biblicism. But fundamentalism plus activism does not equal Christianity.

Or take for example, once more, the so-called "messianic consciousness" of Jesus. Can Christianity (specifically the religion of the New Testament) be derived from one more messianic movement which failed—as all messianic movements are doomed to fail—and which then promptly got shifted over to a transcendental solution of the problem? On the contrary the church has always seen more in Jesus' teaching, character, and aims than that. Indeed, the first disciples found more than that; messianism was only a category (an inevitable one, for them) in which to express their utter devotion to him, but even within the Gospels themselves there are indications that the messianic pattern was inadequate (e.g. John 6:68-69). Something profoundly more religious than messianism (religious as that was for first-century Jews) is indispensable for the adequate explanation of the rise of Christianity—certainly something profoundly more religious than the modern reconstruction known as "thoroughgoing eschatology." And there it is, in the gospel tradition, behind even the Synoptic versions of that tradition.

Or take the miracles, which cannot be rationalized and can only be left where they belong and where they are perfectly natural (that is, in a first-century religious movement), but where they do not even begin to mean what they would in the world today. Their significance is not a breach of the system of law and order which governs the physical universe; there was no such hard and fast system in the thought of people generally in the first century. Instead, as we have seen, their significance is completely eschatological—they are the signs, the harbingers, of the coming age. In the Synoptic tradition they are absolutely not *sêmeia kai terata,* signs and wonders, of which the pagan world was full and of which Judaism could provide examples. Signs and wonders were repudiated; Jesus refused point blank to "do a sign" and thus satisfy the curiosity of his opponents. Instead, the extraordinary and unaccountable things which Jesus did, such as healing the sick, exorcising demons, and even raising the dead, were *dunameis,* powers, mighty works—as the author of the Epistle to the Hebrews used the term, "powers of the age to come," already operative in this age as the new age began to dawn and the great turning point in the world's history drew near.

Thus historical imagination is indispensable for the interpretation of the New Testament, and especially of the Gospels, above all for the interpretation of the gospel tradition, which must be placed in its proper setting and understood against the background of contemporary religious thought in Palestine early in the first century. It will not do to say, "This is how *we* should have understood it, had we been present; therefore the truth of the situation is as follows, namely the situation as *we* would have understood it." This is "historicism," *Historismus,* with a vengeance! This is "modernism," as Ernest Cadman Colwell describes it—the attempt to carry back our preconceptions into the first century and compel the New Testament to speak directly and only to us in the twentieth. According to such a theory everything in Christian doctrine and practice must be carried back—the origin of the sacraments, the trinitarian creed, the Nicene and Chalcedonian Christology, the orders of the ministry, and so on. This is quite as reprehensible as is the opposite effort, to box up Jesus and the origins of the Christian faith in the first century, as one might box a flowing spring, and refuse to acknowledge any relevance to what followed, cutting off the gospel from the church and the movement in Galilee from the vast world historical movement that flowed out across the centuries after the Resurrection. We need a better and more adequate philosophy as well as a richer and more vital historical imagination, we interpreters of the Bible—a philosophy which one might call, perhaps, "spiritual realism," a philosophy which recognizes the continuity of things unseen, and does not insist upon an obvious and open course of development, fully documented, and provable to the hilt by the exercise of a little logic and debate. The true "tense" of religion is always the "present." But you must live in the first-century present while you are there—and in the twentieth when you return. Whatever was true once must be true always, as the *Theologia Germanica* maintained, but you do not get inside that truth merely by quoting dates and documents.

It must no doubt seem to many persons that the final result of the past two centuries of gospel research, especially since the rise of modern historical study, is a sharp dilemma: either total skepticism, or the old-fashioned, literalist, fundamentalist view which takes the Gospels just as they stand without any attempt at the recovery of sources, or of processes of "development" of tradition, or of editorial revision or modification. It is true, we still have the Gospels—*thank God!*— rather than some modern reconstruction of the "life" of Christ which, conceivably, might have been substituted for them. And we are, in reality, no worse off than the early Christians; we are in fact somewhat better off than the earliest of them were, in the days before the Gospels had been written and when only oral tradition was available. The single pericopes, stories, anecdotes, parables, and sayings preserved in that tradition still exist, with all their endless fascination and depth of religious meaning. They still speak to us, as they did to men and women long ago. The relevance and value of their meaning is not dependent upon the successful reconstruction of the life of Jesus, as the solution of a problem in historical research. Moreover, as Rudolf Bultmann insists in his recent *New Testament Theology* (1949), Jesus is not pictured in the Gospels as a "personality"; it was not his personal charm or magnetism that accounts for the rise of the Christian faith, nor were the evangelists (or their predecessors, who handed down the tradition) concerned to depict him as an interesting great man, one of the immortal personalities who have crossed the dimly lit stage of human history. These writings are meant to proclaim a message of salvation, and that message means "life in his name" (John 20:30-31). So with his miracles, so also with his teaching. The New Testament writers were not in the least concerned to assure the proper and adequate "documentation" of the rise of Christianity. There aim was something higher and wholly beyond this—at least something quite different. Taking the Gospels for what they are, for what they aim to be, they are still what they have always been, for the Christian church. Criticism has not only not destroyed them; it has not even impugned their inspired witness.

It is sometimes said that there are only four possible views of the historicity of the gospel narratives (and of the truth of the gospel teaching): skepticism, fundamentalism, liberalism, and Catholicism. But this does not really exhaust the possibilities, for there is a fifth alternative: a sympathetic, imaginative historical interpretation, ne of Jesus' many "trials" (22:28), though, significantly, of Gethsemane (vss. 39-46) there is no suggestion of esence.

is in truth the account of a trial or testing, not a This throws light upon the early Christian view of turn illuminated by the conception. The Lord's Prayer etition, "Lead us not into trial" (*eis peirasmon*, Luke 6:13), where it is inconceivable that God should be t temptation before the believer (cf. Jas. 1:13-14); n of the petition, "Lead us not . . . ," or rather, "Do not . . ." (*mê eisenegkês*). For Jewish religious thought, t is reflected in the Psalms and the wisdom literature, mal meaning of *peirasmos* (e.g. Ecclus. 2:1, "My son, serve the Lord, prepare your soul to endure trial"— . What the "trial" involves is clear from the verses Heb. 12:6, quoting Prov. 3:12, God "disciplines him s, and chastises every son whom he receives." In the trial and tribulation are the lot of the righteous, set r endurance; it is only in extreme cases, where the ly is not inured to such tests, that they become "tempta- e wonderfully dramatic Psalm 73—that is, tempt him , or to say, with the wicked, "God does not see or 94:7).

al or testing of the Messiah has in view his divine in each instance he proves himself the Son of God tempter's suggestion of a short-cut. Like the enemies e Gospels, Satan desiderates outward proof of Jesus' a "sign from heaven" (Mark 8:11; cf. John 2:18). h could be accepted and followed: food would be from the rocks in the wilderness (as water was sup- the desert); the divine preservation of God's chosen r would prove once and for all his supernatural nations would fall at his feet and acclaim him ruler origin the narrative is probably a Christian midrash ages in Deuteronomy (8:3*b*; 6:16; 6:13) from the 's sojourn in "the wilderness" following the exodus e "forty days" (Mark 1:13 and parallels) are like

the Spirit" (cf. Rev. 2–3), and that his present "words" tallied with those spoken of old in Galilee or Jerusalem. This implies that the teaching of Jesus—what we might call the subject of the tradition— was not limited to what men had heard spoken on a hillside in Galilee or in the temple court in Jerusalem or "along the way," but also included utterances of the risen Christ. The "event" of Christ, to use Dr. Knox's term again, was not limited to a few months in Palestine but embraced the whole impact of Jesus, the historical figure and also the superhistorical, the man Jesus and also the Lord Christ, upon the world and especially upon his followers, his church. The possibility of divergence between the later utterances and the earlier must be taken into account; but here too the possibility, or rather the necessity, of establishing a norm is clear. Only, that norm must not be made too narrow—as if Jesus *could* not have said any- thing he might not once have said in a synagogue in Galilee or in a debate with the scribes. After all, Jesus was, to say the least, one of the great creative minds in human history, and we make a mistake if we try to box him up within the six sides of a tiny period or area of first-century Palestinian religion. Some such process as the one just described is inevitable if we are to avoid both a rigid biblical literalism on one hand and total historical skepticism on the other.

The New Testament idea of messiahship is unique. It cannot be derived from, it cannot be reduced to, any mere combination of ante- cedent elements. There was an added element—"not a fourth sound, but a star." This added element was not a purer, more intransigent, more "thoroughgoing" kind of apocalyptic eschatology than Jesus taught, though the traces of that added element are apparent in Mat- thew, and even in Mark. The Messiah was always, as Joseph Klausner rightly insists, the glorious future king of Israel; that is, he was to be king of Israel—a mundane office, however glorified. He was to possess certain divine qualities and qualifications, even certain semi- divine traits. All this was quite appropriate in an Oriental monarch, especially an idealized one. Hugo Gressmann referred to the "court- style" of the ancient monarchies, carried over into the Old Testament and Jewish descriptions and titles of the Messiah. But it is neither the added apocalyptic emphasis nor the eulogistic court style of utterance that makes the New Testament idea of the Messiah unique. It is the *character* of Christ, the human character of the "poor man of Nazareth," that made all the difference. To begin with he was a teacher—but the Messiah was not expected to be a teacher. This is a trait that Matthew, the "Christian rabbi," greatly stresses. Not only that, but he is also a healer, a savior, a son of God—he was all this long before these terms became titles, demanding to be written with capital letters. Even in Paul it is "the meekness and gentleness of Christ" (II Cor. 10:1) that most impresses him, as it did Matthew Arnold. The development of Christology in the New Testament period is of course a conceptual development, and deals with ideas; but back of it is the Christ of experience, whom men were only trying to describe. This Christ of experience was: (*a*) the historical Jesus of Nazareth; (*b*) the Christ—the exalted Messiah or Lord—worshiped by the primitive church (worshiped, and therefore known by them in and through this worship); and (*c*) the Christ foreshadowed in the Old Testament, though the norm was supplied by the historical Jesus, and not by some purely theoretical ("mythological") concept of what a Messiah ought to be and do. It was this norm that was applied, like a magnet, to the Old Testament text, and gathered to itself passage after passage which seemed to yield at last its true meaning; many of these are found among the proof texts of Matthew.

Of course the New Testament idea of the Messiah is eschatologically orientated; how could it be a messianic idea and be anything else? It stands for the *finality* of God's revelation in Christ, the finality of God's act in Christ. There are to be no later Christs; he is not one in a succession of divine *avataras,* but the *only* Son. Such modern poetic (and therefore forgivable) expressions as "the Christ that is to be," "God's word for *this* world is Christ," are simply nonsense, as far as the thought of the New Testament is concerned. The Son through whom God has finally spoken is the unique and only Son, through whom he made the worlds, through whom he sustains them, and whom he has appointed to be the "heir of all things" (Heb. 1:1-4). The uniqueness, and the finality, of God's revelation of himself in Christ could not possibly be stated more clearly or emphatically.

---

4. *The Temptation*

We have stated the need for a fres
we have noted the double emphasis i
search in this field. One is the theologi
which is after all their real historical
recognition that the material in the
is in fact little more than crystalliz
cordingly not only the interpetation
interpretation of his teaching is root
the life of the church, and reflects its
as well as an interpretative process
Gospels. This double feature of t
sections that follow. It is impossible
by page—as one would in a com
illustrate the method, and show how
ment is to be gathered from the Go
strate that what the Gospels tell
valuable than what we should infe
records of the life of Jesus.

The theological significance of
1:12-13; Matt. 4:1-11; Luke 4:1-
is no doubt this: it is the ordeal
himself, endures the trials prop
"strong man" (Mark 3:27), an
Son of God upon earth, even be
"designated," demonstrated to b
Mark the temptation narrative is
tism (1:9-11), a position retai
Mark himself (or the tradition
places where the ordeal might h
35-36, especially 36, where "a m
man" in the Aramaic original
Jesus after his baptism as "ful
and "led in the spirit" (not "
but led by the Holy Spirit); th
or "driven" out (*ekballei*), and
by saying that the devil left h

---

being only o
in the agony
the devil's p
The story
"temptation.
trial, and is i
includes the
11:4; Matt.
thought to s
hence the for
subject us to
especially as
this is the no
if you would
eis peirasmon
that follow. I
whom he love
Psalms, again
before them f
soul of the god
tions," as in t
to forsake Go
care" (cf. Ps.
Here the tr
vocation, and
by refusing the
of Christ in th
divine sonship,
Such a Messia
amply supplied
plied to Israel i
from all dang
powers; and th
of the world. I
upon three pass
account of Israe
from Egypt. T

the forty years of the nation's sojourn, or like Moses' great forty days in the mount (Exod. 24:18), though it was Israel that was tempted—or rather, "tempted" God, put him to the test (Ps. 78:18, 41, 56; 95:9-10; I Cor. 10:9); there is no mention of any "temptation" of or by Moses. And whereas the nation, or many of its leaders and people, succumbed to their trial and even "tempted" God, Jesus the Son of God, the representative of the new Israel, refuses to yield. Israel had been the "son" of God (Hos. 11:1), but only "in a figure"; Jesus was the true Son of God, and so proved himself in each of the successive tests, refusing to "tempt" God (Matt. 4:7), refusing to be concerned over the need for earthly bread (vs. 4), refusing to make obeisance to the devil (vs. 10).

Thus this traditional account, which was no doubt handed down for many years before it was incorporated in the Gospels, shows the crossing of two motifs: the fundamental one the messianic ordeal; the other the dialogue with the devil, or the "catechizing" of the Messiah—as if Satan had been in doubt whether Jesus was really Son of God or not. From the Satanic point of view a Son of God would be expected to use his powers, if he was really in possession of them, for the satisfaction of his own needs, for self-preservation, for the manifestation of himself to the world in order to win the worship and allegiance of men. For it was this Satan who had "set himself in the place of God" (cf. II Thess. 2:3-12). But the devil is not sure; so he "cites scripture for his purpose" (Matt. 4:6; cf. *The Merchant of Venice*, I, 3, 99), and endeavors to elicit the response proper, in his view, to a Son of God. But to no avail; Jesus can quote scripture too—as the scribes were to discover. Jesus' way is not the way of demonstration and compulsion (Matt. 12:19-21; Ep. Diogn. 7:4), but of lowly obedience, confidence in God, and faith. The evil interrogator retires from the scene, baffled and still uncertain. Theologically the meaning of the incident is much the same as that which is presupposed by Paul in his explanation of the crucifixion: the blind and self-deceived *archontes* of the realm of darkness had assumed that thus they could destroy Christ, but they had themselves been defeated and were destined to be dethroned and destroyed (Col. 2:15)—a view which Origen later elaborated in his famous theory of the Atonement. These two motifs are clearly distinguishable:

1. *The ordeal of the Messiah* is briefly recounted in Mark 1:12-13. Jesus is in the "wilderness" for forty days, "tempted by Satan." He is "with the wild beasts"—like Adam in Paradise (though, according to current views, the animals became wild only after the Fall), or perhaps like the Roman Christians in the arena, in Mark's own time. There is no mention of Jesus' fasting, though the final statement, "the angels ministered to him"—as the angel did to Elijah, who also journeyed for forty days in the desert (I Kings 19:5-8)—probably implies that he "ate nothing in those days." The detail is added by Luke, while Matthew says he "fasted forty days and forty nights," and "afterward" was hungry. The setting of the ordeal is accordingly, we assume, a prolonged fast, as in other cases known to religious literature. This ordeal motif is Marcan; the parallel verses in Matthew and Luke, in which they provide the framework of the more detailed story, are only elaborations of Mark.

2. *The dialogue with the devil* appears in Matt. 4:3-10; Luke 4:3-12. Significantly, I think, it is the "devil" in both Matthew and Luke, not "Satan" (the "accuser"; cf. Job 1:9-11; Zech. 3:1; Rev. 12:10) as in Mark. It has been usual to assign these closely parallel passages to Q, which by definition includes all non-Marcan passages common to Matthew and Luke. But Q was not a gospel, and it is a serious question if it was a homogeneous document; also by hypothesis, as a compilation of evangelic material, Q must itself have had still earlier sources, oral or written, and may perfectly well have been composite; while the possibility of common sources of Matthew and Luke in addition to Mark and Q is not to be overlooked. At any rate, the language of the present parallel sections is not that of the rest of the Q material: it is "the devil," not Satan, who conducts the interrogation; he "takes" (*paralambanei,* a word with apocalyptic connotations) Jesus up to the dizzy height above the temple court and to the top of the "very high" mountain; above all, the title under consideration here is "Son of God," which is foreign to Q and unusual in the Gospels. But precisely here lies the main theological significance of the narrative: the Son of God ("*If* you are the Son of God . . .") is invited to declare himself by overt act or sign. It

is the old demand, "Show us a sign from heaven," "What sign have you to show us?" to which Jesus had consistently and persistently refused to respond, from beginning to end of the gospel story, and which Christians in the days of the evangelists were still unable to satisfy. Only faith, not sense, could apprehend his real nature. This lust for "signs" was only another example of

> unfaith clamouring to be coined
> To faith by proof

—and here the demand is placed on the lips of the devil, the *church's* great "adversary" (I Pet. 5:8), and is set forth in all its crassness and blind stupidity.

It has often been suggested that the story must go back, ultimately, to Jesus himself (cf. Luke 10:18-20) and is therefore autobiographic—almost the only autobiographic material in the Gospels. But it seems far more probable that it is a portrait (not a photograph, let alone a stenographic record) of Jesus as he faced his life's task with its problems, one which was sketched by some spiritual genius of the early church. This writer must have been one who was thoroughly familiar with the Old Testament, who in his devout meditation upon the book of Deuteronomy had seen the figure of Christ rise before him, and had heard in imagination the dramatic dialogue which summed up the Lord's whole attitude toward miracles and signs. Finally had come that flash of insight which had revealed to him the inner reason for Jesus' refusal to use his divine powers either to win a following, or to meet his own daily needs, or even, in the end, to save himself from death (cf. Matt. 26:53-54). If it is a "portrait," it is a true one—and a good portrait is always preferable to a photograph, however "authentic."

5. *The Ministry in Galilee*

Luke describes the beginning of Jesus' ministry in almost the same terms he has used in introducing the temptation narrative (4:14; cf. 4:1), "Jesus returned in the power of the Spirit into Galilee." Though he thinks of Jesus' "pneumatic" power in concrete terms (cf. 5:17, "the power of the Lord was with him to heal"), this is manifested first in teaching (4:15-32). The editorial addition in verse *23b*— showing that he has Mark 1:21-34 in mind—implies the miracles of the first day in Capernaum, but this makes all the more striking Luke's primary emphasis upon teaching. Jesus' "power" is also "authority" (*exousia*, vs. 32)—that is, it attests the authority of his divine mission, as the gospel writers consistently assume (cf. even John 3:2). The contrast with Matthew is striking. Luke sets the preaching in Nazareth (4:16-30) at the very forefront of the ministry, as programmatic, and sees in it the fulfillment of the Old Testament prophet's announcement, "The Spirit of the Lord is upon me. . . . Today this scripture has been fulfilled in your hearing." Matthew, on the other hand, is more pedestrian, and sees the fulfillment of scripture in the location of Jesus' work at Capernaum (Matt. 4:13-16); for him the topography is important, for Galilee is the "land of promise" in the new dispensation. (According to Matthew, who follows Mark, Jesus does not visit Nazareth until later—13:54-58.) At the same time Luke omits Mark's description of the content of Jesus' message: "The time is fulfilled, and the kingdom of God is at hand; repent [and believe in the gospel]" (Mark 1:15). Or possibly Luke believes that Jesus' announcement of his anointing with the Spirit and of his mission to the poor, the captives, the blind, and the oppressed (4:18-19) is the equivalent of the message of the kingdom. For Luke the good news of the kingdom of God is certainly eschatological (cf. 10:8-15), and is not limited to Jesus' own mission or to his awareness of it.

The theological significance of the opening words of Mark 1:14 is clear: the imprisonment of John is the signal for Jesus' return to Galilee; the clause "the time is fulfilled" (unless it is textually secondary) probably does not refer to the onward march of the aeons, as it would in apocalyptic, but to the current event of John's arrest. John had been the preacher of judgment to come; his arrest marks the beginning of the end. Hence Jesus begins at once his preaching of "the gospel of the kingdom of God" (which is probably the true reading). Like John, Jesus sets repentance in the forefront of his message, but the rest is different—whereas John had threatened his hearers with the impending doom of the Last Judgment, Jesus is the preacher of the "glad tidings" of God's reign.

According to the sources, Jesus begins his ministry in Galilee as a teacher, taking advantage of the opportunity accorded any layman sufficiently versed in the scriptures to read them in the public service and add an exposition; the organization of the Jewish synagogue at this date was thoroughly "congregational." The beginning of his healing ministry apparently came somewhat later, and as in the experience of other healers was almost accidental. The story in Mark 1:21-28 is perfectly natural—Jesus merely silences a disturber in the synagogue who is "possessed" by an "unclean" spirit, bids the demon come out of the man, and forthwith the spirit "convulses" him and with a loud roar comes out. But the inference drawn by the people present is not that a powerful wonder-worker has arrived in their midst. Instead they exclaim, "What is this? A new *teaching!* With authority he commands even the unclean spirits, and they obey him" (vs. 27). The scene is thoroughly Jewish. It is the authority of Jesus' teaching which is stressed—a feature all the more significant in Mark, where Jesus' mighty works are emphasized more than his teaching. The detail undoubtedly goes back to the old tradition underlying Mark.

From the beginning a whole series of dramatically told cures follow at once: Peter's wife's mother (Mark 1:29-31), the sick and the possessed who are brought to Peter's house at evening (vss. 32-34), the leper (vss. 40-45), the man with palsy (2:1-12). Leaving Capernaum, Jesus journeys about Galilee, preaching in the synagogues and casting out demons (1:39). This is the double pattern for the Galilean ministry as a whole, though Jesus does not restrict himself to preaching in synagogues, but teaches the people wherever they gather about him—for example at the lakeside (Mark 4:1-2). The term Mark uses is theologically important—*ēn* (or *ēlthen*) *kērussôn* (1:39; as in 1:14); Jesus "came preaching." But the verb means even more than that; it really means "heralding, proclaiming" (as in Luke 4:19). This does not exclude "teaching," *didaskôn;* "he spoke to them the word," in 2:2, covers both—yet Mark is surely right in preferring the verb *kērussô*. Jesus is, in this his earliest role, the herald or announcer of the approaching kingdom which is now "at hand" (1:15). It is Jesus' purpose to proclaim this message throughout Galilee, among his own people; to this end he "came out" from

Capernaum at early dawn (1:38). Later exegesis has found here a reference to the pre-existence of Jesus or to the Incarnation. In Jewish idiom God "raised up" prophets, or "sent" them, without implying their pre-existence, except in a purely figurative sense—that is, in the mind and purpose of the Creator. Similarly, Jesus could have said that he had "come out," had appeared before his people, as a prophet or "teacher come from God" (cf. John 3:2). But it seems far more likely, in the context, to mean that he "came out" from Capernaum that morning—he was ready to begin his tour of the surrounding villages.

According to Mark he is already accompanied by disciples, who have been called to "become fishers of men" (1:16-20), and who a little later (3:13-19) are chosen to be "with him" permanently and to go on missions to "herald" the message and exorcise demons. It is sometimes thought that Mark locates the call of the disciples at too early a point in the story, and that the language ("fishers of men") is better suited to the apostolic church. But if Jesus was conscious of a divine mission to proclaim the kingdom of God, to call his people to repentance, to exorcise demons (as the beginning of the establishment upon earth of the divine reign), there is no reason for questioning either the language or the early location.

Early in the ministry Mark provides a location (3:13) which Matthew and Luke use for their presentation of the Great Sermon (on the mount, Matt. 5–7; on the plain, Luke 6:20-49). The sermon is in each case, no doubt, a compilation—in its Lukan form from Q, in the Matthaean from Q and M, with other material as well. In Luke (and therefore in Q, since Matthew also has most of these passages) the sermon begins with the Beatitudes (Luke 6:20-23), supplemented by the Woes (vss. 24-26, peculiar to Luke), goes on with the teaching on love of one's enemies (vss. 27-36), on passing judgment on others (vss. 37-42), on the test of goodness (vss. 43-46), and ends with the parable of the two housebuilders (vss. 47-49). This "sermon" or collection of related sayings found in Q is amplified by Matthew from his source M. As elsewhere in his Gospel, the teaching of Jesus is set forth in a long formal discourse, beginning (like Luke) with the Beatitudes (Matt. 5:3-12, here amplified into a group of nine), the similes of salt and light (vss. 13-16), and then

announcing the major theme of the sermon, according to Matthew—
Jesus' attitude toward the Mosaic Law, as its fulfiller, not its de-
stroyer (vss. 17-20). This statement of the theme is followed by a
series of examples in which the new and deeper interpretation or
"fulfillment" (completion?) of the Law is set forth: the law against
murder (vss. 21-26), against adultery (vss. 27-30), on divorce (vss.
31-32), against false swearing (vss. 33-37), on retaliation (vss. 38-
42), and finally the statement of the "new law" of love for enemies
(vss. 43-48, from Q). A new section in Matthew's sermon opens
with a further elaboration of the theme stated in 5:17-20; as the
rest of the chapter had expounded the true "fulfillment" (or completion) of the Law, so 6:1–7:5 expounds the superior "righteousness" (or practice of religion) which is now required (5:20). Three
characteristic practices of the pious are discussed: almsgiving (6:1-4),
prayer (vss. 5-8; the "Lord's Prayer" is inserted as an example in
vss. 9-15), and fasting (vss. 16-18). Then follow the sayings on
singleness of service or sincerity (vss. 19-24), on trust in God (vss.
25-34), and (again from Q) on the fault of passing judgment upon
others (7:1-5)—likewise a critique of current piety. The chiastic
saying on "casting pearls before swine" has been thought to refer
back to the first section (5:17-42 or 48) or possibly to the second
(6:1-18 or 19), and to be derived from M, where it had a quasi-
legal point, namely "do not waste your words on the stubborn, the
impudent, or the violent"—a thoroughly practical sentiment which
often finds utterance in the Psalms and wisdom literature. Matt. 7:7-29
is a further elaboration (mainly from Q) of the same theme, the
new righteousness, but now in more general terms and without reference to the distinguishing marks of the pious: the answer to prayer
(7:7-11), the Golden Rule (vs. 12), the narrow gate (vss. 13-14),
the test of goodness (vss. 15-20), a warning against self-deception
(vss. 21-23), and the closing parable of the two housebuilders (vss.
24-27).

It is clear that Matthew's sermon cannot be taken, just as it stands,
as a stenographic report of one particular discourse of Jesus; it is a
compilation, not a transcript. Moreover much that it contains is
written out with the needs of the contemporary church in mind, say
near the end of the first century, or, preferably, early in the second.

This is not to deny that Jesus once delivered a "sermon" on the mount or on the plain, but we cannot reconstruct it from the materials available now. The *general* picture of Jesus' activity, the *general* content of his teaching—this is all that we are able to make out. The details are too specifically addressed to the church of the evangelists' own time for us to hope to do more. But this general picture and account of the teaching are sufficient for our purposes. Jesus was no theologian, but a man of the people, addressing his own folk in Galilee, the despised *am ha-aretz* for the most part, with a message of repentance (*teshubah=metanoia*) and of the grace and mercy of God, who was about to set up his kingdom finally and forever over the whole earth. Repentance meant more than "sorrow for sin"; it meant a change of mind, "turning about," "facing the other way"—living a new kind of life, with other purposes and aims than those followed in the past. Much of Jesus' teaching was concerned with this repentance and "newness of life."

Allowing fully, as we must, for certain tendencies or interests which were operative, probably from the very first, in the transmission of the tradition, Jesus' teaching as a whole seems to have been concentrated upon these main themes: (*a*) the proclamation of the reign of God, which is already in process of "establishment" or "coming"; (*b*) the divine requirement of "repentance" on the part of the whole people, a requirement involving not only sorrow for past sins and shortcomings but also the manifestation of "fruits worthy of repentance"; (*c*) the nature of the kingdom, the secret and unsuspected signs of its coming, and its final establishment "in glory," though his restraint in picturing its details is in marked contrast to the exuberance of the apocalyptists; above all, (*d*) the limitless range and universal bearing of the new righteousness, the "fulfillment" of the Law as God really meant it to be understood and observed, as the prerequisite to admission into his kingdom.

As Mark, followed by the other two Synoptists, presents his career, it was not long before Jesus came into conflict with the scribes, the accredited teachers of Jewish religion, and the Pharisees, the lay order or society devoted to full observance of the scribal interpretation and definition of the Law (Mark 2:1–3:30, Mark's first series of controversies). It is therefore probable that the collision with the religious authorities took place at an early date, and that they viewed both his teaching and his cures as unauthorized and dangerous. His cures, in particular, they ascribed to collusion with Beelzebul (3:22-30)— though it is apparent that his chief adversaries were not the local pietists but the "scribes from Jerusalem," who were doctrinaire rigorists and fanatics. Jesus answers the scribes' charge in masterful fashion, but the controversy dogged him all the rest of the way, until finally his enemies procured his death at the hands of the Roman procurator in Jerusalem. It even survived him, as was natural, and had to be faced by the early church in Palestine—hence the embittered and exaggerated form of some of the sayings as we now read them, especially in Matt. 23.

6. *The Titles of Christ in the Gospels*

The Gospels set forth the church's traditions of the life, death, and resurrection of Jesus—and of his teaching. They spring out of the church's own life; their purpose is to instruct, to edify, to confirm, and to guide those who are already believers; in a secondary sense—chiefly in John (see 20:30-31) but also in Luke (see 1:1-4)—they are meant to win converts, or at least to win a favorable hearing for the church's case. In fact the earliest is almost the most theological of the four. Mark's Gospel embodies the tradition as known in a particular church, and it selects and emphasizes this tradition for the benefit of those Christians who are faced with martyrdom; it is the Gospel of a martyr church, the church at Rome, presumably, late in the sixties of the first century. Matthew's Gospel is thoroughly intraecclesiastical in its outlook; it is intended for a settled, more or less peaceful church; its problems concern worship, evangelism, authority—and the hope of the Parousia. Luke's Gospel is an apology, Part I of a two-volume work designed to prove to the Roman authorities that Christians are and have always been a law-abiding group. John's Gospel is face to face with Docetic Gnosticism, which would undermine—and has already partly undermined—the historical foundations of Christianity. What he is concerned to show is the meaning Christ has for the church and for the world in his own time, perhaps early in the second century. This meaning does not depend upon history; for him history is only, as Plato defined time, "the moving image of eternity."

Now all four of these writings reflect not only the external conditions of the period at which each was composed, and the church's reaction to these conditions, but also the church's developing faith. That faith did not develop without tension. The obvious tension between the "Judaizers" and the "Paulinists," for example, of which the Tübingen school made so much (though only exaggerating something which is perfectly evident from the New Testament), is only one among several. There were some which, apparently, never came to the surface—but they were present and very real, just the same. Take Mark's Christology, for example. It is a combination of the traditional "Son of Man" Christology of the early Palestinian group with the "Son of God" Christology of the early Gentile church. How the two could be united, and a bridge flung across the gulf between them, does not appear from Mark, or from any of the Gospels. Paul had made, apparently, no effort to accommodate his thought to the Palestinian Christology—a phenomenon that may suggest further support for Lohmeyer's hypothesis that the "Son of Man" Christology characterized the church in Galilee, and was brought to Jerusalem and combined with the "Messiah" or "Christ" concept later, after Paul's contacts with the church in Judea. By the time Mark took over the (mainly Galilean) traditions of those of Jesus' sayings which he uses, the "Son of Man" Christology had become firmly embedded in them, either as a result of interpreting Jesus' modest self-designation *bar-nasha* in an apocalyptic sense, or as an example of the "Son of Man dogmatic" of the Palestinian church. In any event Mark has a double Christology; the term "Son of God" is pagan in origin, not Jewish, and has behind it much of the noblest and best religious devotion of the contemporary Hellenistic world—just as the term "Logos," which John was to use, enshrined its noblest intellectual contemplations—while "Son of Man" as clearly connotes the apocalyptic figure in the book of Daniel, as interpreted by the writers of the book of Enoch and their school. The later ecclesiastical explanation, that "Son of God" is Christ's divine title, "Son of Man" his human, thus reflecting the doctrine of his two natures, was an explanation quite impossible in the first century. At that time "Son of God" and

"Son of Man" were equally divine titles; each meant a supernatural, heavenly being, though these were very differently conceived in the Gentile and the Palestinian churches. Both titles are very old—much older than Mark, who has not invented them, and who (unlike the other evangelists) hesitates to insert or remove them from the tradition. They are so old in the Christian tradition that one may hazard the guess that they were in use, in some areas, from the very beginning of the Galilean and the Hellenistic churches. They come from a time of which we know nothing—for the origins both of the Christian community in Galilee after the Resurrection and of the earliest Gentile communities (e.g. Caesarea, Antioch, Damascus) are almost totally undocumented.

The other titles are equally old. "Son of David" is almost certainly the title used in the "political" type of messianism characteristic of the South, as the transcendental apocalyptic "Son of Man" type was characteristic of the North. Only, we must not take "political" in too secular a sense—certainly not in the zealot or revolutionary sense. The coming king of Israel was to be a divinely inspired ruler, lowly, humble, the friend of his people, the champion of the poor; a whole series of late Old Testament passages emphasize this sublime conception of the Lord's Anointed (Ps. 72; Zech. 9:9; etc.). There is no reason why the title should not have been applied to Jesus during his lifetime—certainly by those who knew him only by hearsay.

The title "Lord" is really a divine title, as von Baudissin proved. The transition from "Sir" to "Lord" is somewhat parallel to the one from *bar-nasha* to "Son of Man"; in this case, as we have already seen, the intervening step can probably be traced. The oldest surviving bit of primitive Christian worship, *Marana tha,* "Our Lord, come!" (I Cor. 16:22; cf. Did. 10:6) implies clearly enough that at an early date Christ was invoked as *Mar* or *Maran* (Aramaic for "Lord," "Our Lord"). The only possible connotation of the term was messianic, eschatological; it was a prayer for the parousia of Christ in glory—and it was to be offered "until he came." Similarly, the only possible equivalent in Greek for the term *Mar,* in this religious sense as the spiritual, divine head of a religious group, was *Kyrios,* "Lord." Hence it was not necessary for the early church to come in contact with some Hellenistic cult or circle of ideas outside Palestine before the term "Lord" could be used (here Bousset went too far) ; the cultic significance of *Maran* was obvious from the first. The Greek term "Lord" (*Kyrios*) awaited only the conversion of the first Christian believer who spoke Greek as well as Aramaic—and that may have been only a matter of days. But it is also obvious that the title was reserved for sacral or liturgical use; like the others, it rarely gets used in narrative (almost solely in Luke). No one would think of writing, "The Son of God went to Capernaum," or "The Son of Man cast out a demon," or "The Son of David went up to Jerusalem." Luke, however —a thorough Hellenist, as we have seen—does not hesitate on occasion to use "Lord" in narrative. But for one thing, *Kyrios* was also a common Hellenistic term for "Master"; for another, the church's Bible (the Greek Old Testament) made it clear that "Lord" also meant "God," and so there was no danger of confusion. For the Hellenistic (Greek-speaking) Gentile world, on the other hand, both "Christos" ("Anointed," literally "smeared with oil") and "Son of Man" (literally "the son of the [or of "a"] man") were totally incomprehensible and required to be not only translated but interpreted. "Son of David" sounded archaic. Some persons outside the church and the synagogue might possibly have heard of King David, but surely not many; and anyway David had lived a thousand years ago—how could any person living in Palestine ten, twenty, thirty years ago possibly be his "son"?

It is not strange, then, that in the Fourth Gospel the old terminology was more or less abandoned, and that one more appropriate to Gentile circles, especially quasi-philosophical or theosophical circles, was given greater prominence. The term "Logos," already in use, no doubt, since Paul's day in the Greek-speaking churches, affords the key to John's doctrine of Christ. He is the Mediator, not only in redemption but also in creation. He is the Son of God, not in the popular cultic sense but in one which begins to approach the later metaphysical definition. Indeed, John's Gospel as a whole has transposed the evangelic tradition into a metaphysical key. It is the *nature* of Christ that matters now, not only his office, function, title, or personal history. For it is by participation in his divine nature that Christians are saved (cf. II Pet. 1:4): they must eat the "Bread of Life"; be washed in—or drink—the "Water of Life"; see—and walk in—the "Light of the World"; be born again, not by water only but by the Spirit.

Other terms and titles, from the simple survivals of Galilean enthusiasm (such as "the Prophet," "the Teacher," "the Master") to those which were more permanently significant (such as "the Servant"—that is, of the Lord—see Isa. 53), and then on to others still more elaborate (such as "high priest" in the Epistle to the Hebrews, expressing the peculiar literary and philosophical Christology of its author and the group or "area" which he represents)—all these serve to show the great variety in the christological thought in the New Testament, and prove how inadequate any one term or title is when taken in isolation from the others. Every one of those used in the Gospels (or elsewhere in the New Testament) has a religious connotation, and is used here with a religious significance. It is remarkable that no "secular," for example political, title is employed. The thought about Christ, in the Gospels, is accordingly a nascent "theology" of Christ; the religious attitude toward him demands a "theological" statement, definition, and justification.

7. The Theology of the Gospels

We have seen how basic and indispensable to the whole narrative of the Temptation is the concept implied by the title "Son of God." "Son of Man" would not do, in this case. It is a story with a Hellenistic setting—but the "Hellenism" is that of the Greek-speaking, Septuagint-reading, devout and imaginative Gentile church. We must now discuss briefly other crucial events in the Gospels—that is, in the evangelic tradition underlying the Gospels—which were of paramount significance for the growing theology of the early church.

The theological significance of the events in the ministry, as well as of the teaching, of Jesus as these are presented in the Fourth Gospel is clear to every reader. For the author has pointed it out in so many words—words which are sometimes his own and are meant to be understood as his own, but also words which he places on the lips of Jesus. It has often been observed that the style, thought, and terminology of the latter are indistinguishable from the former. For "John" moves in a realm of intellectual activity (largely controversial) and of mystical contemplation for which the purely "historical" view of the past is even farther removed than it is in the Synoptics. In a word the two tenses, past and present, merge into each other. What Christ is now, for the church and for the individual believer, he must always have been—not only in Galilee and Jerusalem in days gone by, but from the beginning of creation. The miracles, the "mighty works" of the Synoptic tradition, are compacted into seven great "signs," symbolic of the "work" of Christ in the world, and of value as manifestations or epiphanies of his divine "glory," which he had with the Father before the world began (17:5). Although the historical element which does survive in John is most valuable, and is in some respects of greater value than that in the Synoptics (for example the date of the Last Supper, or the account of the examination before the high priest), the events have been theologically or "spiritually" reinterpreted. The feeding of the multitude (ch. 6) is no longer a miracle of supplying bread for the hungry, but is interpreted as the Eucharist. The successive Passovers in John are not points in chronology, but merge into one—the chief feast of Judaism, which is to be viewed as transcended, reinterpreted, sublimated in the death of Christ.

These peculiarities of John are easily recognizable. But it is the *Synoptic* tradition which needs to be studied further, from the theological point of view. Though less articulate and often only implied, the significance of the events in the Synoptics is also theological, if in less degree than those in John.

The *Baptism* of Jesus had a twofold significance: (1) It was the prototype, perhaps the inauguration, of Christian baptism. Even in the earliest Gospel, Mark, the story is told in Christian terms (1:9-11): it is a baptism "of repentance, for the remission of sins"; those who received it were baptized (or baptized themselves) "confessing their sins"; in it the Lord himself had been announced as Son of God, and he too had received the gift of the Holy Spirit, in the power of which his lifework had been carried on. (2) At the same time it points out the superiority of Christian baptism to Johannine or Jewish—an emphasis which is more strongly laid in the later Gospels, especially in Matthew and John: "I need to be baptized by you"; "He must increase, but I must decrease" (Matt. 3:14; John 3:30). The whole opening chapter of John is concerned with the question of Jesus' relation to John the Baptist; the question must accordingly have been one of crucial importance for the early church. (3) A further theological question in Matthew (3:14-15) relates to the sinlessness of Jesus: How can he have received John's baptism, which was one of "repentance for the remission of sins"? The answer, unlike those found in later literature, for example in the apocryphal gospels, leaves the problem unsolved, but in a soundly Jewish way: "Thus it is fitting for us to fulfill all righteousness," to do whatever God has declared to be his will. It is not necessary to solve the problem; *our* duty is to obey the requirement of God announced through his prophet, and he has commanded all men to repent and be baptized.

In the Fourth Gospel the question does not arise. John's baptism is no longer thought of as a "baptism of repentance for remission of sins"; in fact John's whole appearance was for the purpose of preparing the Jews for their coming one, for the declaration (as messenger) of his arrival, and for his "manifestation to Israel"—"I myself did not know him; but for this I came baptizing with water, that he might be revealed to Israel" (1:31).

The *Temptation,* which follows immediately (in Mark, and presumably in the older tradition, though the Fourth Gospel omits it), we have already discussed. Its theological significance was (1) Jesus' refusal to do "signs and wonders" and prove himself a "Son of God" in the classical sense, or even to exercise his divine power in order to satisfy his own needs or save his own life, and (2) the ordeal of the Messiah, by which he "proved himself" victor over hunger, privation, the wild beasts, and even Satan.

The *ministry* of teaching and healing was the proclamation of the coming kingdom, the full and final realization of God's reign; and it was "new teaching, with authority and power" (*exousia* means both; see above), as Mark notes (1:27). It was "the word of God with power" (cf. Luke 4:32). Jesus taught with prophetic authority—the phrase must not be watered down; it means that he was the very Voice of God, and that if one refused to hear him it was at his peril. The "signs following" were "mighty works," supporting the authority of the prophet and also providing evidence of the arrival (or at least of the near approach) of the divine reign: "If it is by the finger of God that I cast out demons, then the kingdom of God has come upon you" (Luke 11:20). The two went together, the proclamation and the mighty works. The implied theological inference is that Jesus was already inaugurating the kingdom—though various conceptions were entertained of it and of him, and many of these have survived in the gospel tradition. Matthew goes even further in his thinking: the kingdom is *Christ's* kingdom (e.g. 13:41), practically identical with the church—at least manifested in the church—and the teaching of Jesus is the new Law, supplementing and completing the old (5:17-20). Jesus is a second and greater Moses, the lawgiver of the new covenant —an idea not far removed from that of the Epistle to the Hebrews, though there the center of interest is the priesthood and the sacrifices, not the Law as a whole or as a code governing conduct. This estimate of the Law which Matthew assumes is of course a far remove from that of Paul. Here are several distinct "areas" of thought into which early Christianity moved, exploring the significance of Christ and his teaching for Judaism, for God's earlier revelation, and for the Christian church.

The *confession of Peter* (Mark 8:27-30) carries its own theological implication. At last one of the disciples, the first to be called and the one destined to be the first to see Jesus after the resurrection (I Cor. 15:5; Luke 24:34), the natural spokesman of the group, had penetrated Jesus' secret. The "hardening" of the nation and even of the disciples (which Mark stresses) was not too great for Peter to perceive who Jesus really was: "You are the Christ," the Messiah (Mark 8:29). But even Peter did not rise to the full height of his own faith and intuition; he still thought in earthly terms, as the sequel shows (vss. 31-33). The great paradox, fundamental to Mark's Christology, is that Jesus both was and was not the Messiah—his true nature was *divine,* as Son of Man and Son of God. And the astonishing, unbelievable, but true paradox is that this divine, heavenly "Son of Man" had to suffer rejection and death at the hands of sinners. Peter had not grasped this—no disciple had, before the Crucifixion (Mark 9:32). But so are the ways of God, and such was the way the Son of Man "went" (Mark 14:21). The church, which in Mark's day is still intently looking forward to Jesus' coming in glory, knows that he is the heavenly Son of Man; but Peter did not know this at the time of his confession. His faith was only dawning.

The *Transfiguration* (Mark 9:2-8) has sometimes been viewed as an antedated resurrection appearance—somewhat as John 21:1-14 is a postdated and transformed pericope, which is better preserved, though still not in its original form, in Luke 5:1-11. The theory is possible, but not very probable. Even Matthew has no inclination to "write up" his account of Jesus' postresurrection appearance on "the" mountain in Galilee (28:16-20) in this fashion. Whatever its origin, the incident has in its present form the theological implication which a later writer drew (II Pet. 1:16-21). It was a preview of the "majesty" of Christ, a foregleam of his "power and coming"; it was preliminary to and pointed forward to the coming of Christ "in glory," at the Parousia (not only at the Resurrection). Luke represents Jesus as engaged in conversation with Moses and Elijah (Luke 9:30-31), and discussing his own *exodos* which was soon to take place. But this surely is an afterthought, born of devout inquiry and imagining. Albert Schweitzer and others have proposed that in the true order of events the Transfiguration should precede the confession of Peter. But Mark's instinct was sound; the Transfiguration was the divine attestation of Peter's faith, and its transformation. Jesus is not only Messiah; he is the heavenly Son of Man (8:31) and also the Son of God (9:7). Peter's too mundane, too human (8:33c) faith had to be enlarged and transformed—as had that of the other disciples, and that of the early apostolic church in the days following the Resurrection.

The theological significance of the *passion announcements* (Mark 8:31; 9:31; 10:32-33; etc.) is clear. Jesus accepted the fate which confronted him. He died because he willed to die. He died because there was no other way, if he was to be faithful to the mission laid upon him—it could not be "that a prophet should perish away from Jerusalem" (Luke 13:33). He died as all other prophets had died, including John, until their blood cried out for the judgment of heaven (Luke 11:49-51). He died because it was the divine will; mysteriously, inexplicably, God had decreed it (*dei genesthai;* cf. Mark 8:31; 9:11; 13:7, 10), and in some equally mysterious way God would use his death for the salvation or "ransom" of "many" (Mark 10:45). In the account of the Last Supper the same tone of mystery prevails (14:17-25); indeed Mark represents Jesus as journeying to Jerusalem in the same mood of mystery: "They were on the road going up to Jerusalem, and Jesus was walking ahead of them; and they were amazed, and those who followed were afraid" (10:32)—then follows the third passion announcement. C. H. Turner argued that the original text ran "*he* was amazed," but this is unnecessary. According to Mark, Jesus' own mind was clear as he faced the mysterious future. It was the disciples who were amazed, at his boldness in going up to the very stronghold of his enemies and of the Roman authority. The theological significance of all this is quite clear.

The Arrest, Trial, and Crucifixion are the heart of the passion narrative. Their theological significance is that this is the climax of the earthly life of Jesus. Although efforts have been made to uncover the earliest form of the passion narrative—presumably the oldest continuous block of tradition in the Gospels—the best we can hope to do is to get back to an earlier, pre-Marcan form, perhaps the original Roman form of the story. "Earlier" is not the same as "earliest." And yet this earlier form lies some way back of the present account in the oldest of our Gospels (Mark 14–15). What is important is that it too has a theological significance, and would scarcely pass for a plain chapter of historical prose in some elaborate "History of Palestine in the First Century." The whole bearing of Jesus, his refusal to speak, his acceptance—and rejection—of the title "Messiah," with the substitution of "Son of Man" in glory and "coming on the clouds of heaven" (if this is really pre-Marcan)—all this is theologically motivated. Jesus was almost as one "whom a dream hath possessed." He died, not as the champion of the poor (so Bacon), or as a revolutionist (so Eisler), or as a disturber of the peace (so the priests, as represented in Luke 23:2, 5), but as the one whom God had chosen to be "faithful unto death," and whose death was somehow indispensable for the salvation of "the many." The dramatic modern interpretations are usually fanciful, for they neglect this essential note in the very oldest source we possess. The note is theological, of course, which means that it reflects the attempt to grasp the meaning of the event from a purely religious point of view—from the point of view of God, we might say. It is the climax of a whole long history, the history of salvation—not just of the earthly life of Jesus, but of the longer process of God's dealings with mankind. This "theology" is not peculiar to Mark, or the Synoptics, or the four Gospels, but characterizes all Christian reporting and reflection upon the event of the Cross. In Paul's account of his own earliest preaching to the Corinthians he reminds them that *in primis* he passed on to them the common Christian *kerygma* of Jesus' death "for our sins in accordance with the scriptures" (I Cor. 15:3), followed by his resurrection "in accordance with the scriptures." From the very first beginnings of the Christian faith the death of Christ was a problem; its solution was found in the scriptures.

It is clear that there is also one other theological note in the Marcan passion narrative—Christ was the first of his own glorious company of martyrs. What this meant to a martyr church, and to individual Christians faced with the prospect of martyrdom, can easily be perceived as we read the story.

The *Resurrection* is told in a variety of ways in the Gospels. If there were only one account, or if the story were told in one uniform way, we should suspect invention. It is obviously based upon tradition, and a very multiform tradition at that. The resurrection appearances are not limited to one person or place; hence we need not choose between "Jerusalem or Galilee." Paul even includes the risen Jesus' appearance to himself in the list which he gives (I Cor. 15:8). And there are others in the New Testament, either related (as in Acts 7:55-56 or Rev. 1:10-20) or referred to (note what I Cor. 9:1 implies as to the qualifications of an apostle). In fact appearances of the risen Jesus, especially to martyrs in the presence of death, but also to the devout in hours of exaltation, continued for a long time—indeed have never ceased in the long history of the church.

The earliest conception of the resurrection of Christ was, as Johannes Weiss made clear in his *History of Primitive Christianity* (Bk. I, ch. 2, pp. 23-40), that he was raised "from the dead" rather than "from the grave," and that he thereupon became the glorified, heavenly Messiah. It was then that he "entered into his glory" (Luke 24:26); in the earliest tradition, surviving in Luke (24:1, 13, 33, 36, 44, 50-51—note the time implied) and in the Epistle to the Hebrews (see below), the Resurrection and the Ascension were probably viewed as one event. Only later were the great "forty days" (Acts 1:3) intercalated—and elaborated in such apocryphal writings as the second-century Epistle of the Apostles. Only later, likewise, was emphasis laid upon the "physical" resurrection, the empty grave, the corporeality of Jesus' resurrection body, his eating with the disciples, the tangibility of his transformed flesh, and so on. Here the resurrection of Christ is being used as concrete, tangible proof of survival, and even, perhaps, as the answer to the very natural question, "What will *our* resurrection body be like?" Since it is to be like his (cf. I John 3:2), the picturesque elaboration of the concept of Christ's resurrection body has a quite understandable motive—though see the protest in John 20:17. But Paul takes it for granted, as the well-known common *kerygma* which will be as familiar to the Christians in Rome as it was to himself, that Christ was designated *"Son of God in power* [according to the Spirit of holiness] by his resurrection from the dead" (Rom. 1:4). Paul was writing this in the middle of the first century; that is, about twenty-five years after the Resurrection, and several years before the writing of any of the Gospels.

All of which is to say that the earliest understanding of the Resurrection was theological—that is, eschatological. The picturesque account in Acts 1:6-11 retains the primitive note, though the story is elaborated: "This Jesus . . . will come. . . ." That the Resurrection was God's act of reversal of human judgments; that God "ordained" this way of saving mankind (or the elect, or believers), and of transferring his Son from earth to heaven; that the Resurrection was the beginning, in full earnest, of the "coming" of the divine kingdom, and would be followed presently by the parousia of Christ in glory, the last judgment, and the inauguration of the New Age—all this is presupposed or reflected in the earliest sources we possess for primitive Christianity, and is taken for granted throughout the New Testament.

Among later New Testament writings, the Epistle to the Hebrews does not mention the resurrection of Christ. It might be assumed that the author takes that central fact of Christian faith for granted; if he does so, he certainly does not lay the emphasis upon it which we find in Paul and the Gospels. To that extent, then, the Resurrection is not central to the Christian faith for this writer. But it seems more probable that Hebrews represents an area of Christian thinking for which the thought of the Resurrection was absorbed into the larger idea of Christ's exaltation; Christ is the great high priest who has "passed through the heavens" (4:14), who is even now "above the heavens" (7:26), seated "at the right hand of the Majesty on high" (1:3; cf. 10:12). That the actual fact or possibility of resurrection is neither denied nor ignored is evident from 6:2; 11:19, 35; only, it is not connected with or made dependent upon the resurrection of Christ. In the area reflected in Hebrews the doctrine had thus taken its departure directly from the primary meaning of the Resurrection, which was the exaltation of Jesus to glory rather than his physical resuscitation or transubstantiation or "metamorphosis" (Mark 9:2). This movement of thought was accordingly in an opposite direction from that represented in the Gospels with their strong emphasis on the Resurrection as an event in time, and in the later additions to the Gospels, which emphasized the physical or material actuality of Christ's risen body (for example his eating honeycomb, added to Luke 24:43, or the disciples running up to touch Jesus, added to John 20:16).

That this interpretation owed something to the quasi-philosophical cast of the whole theology of Hebrews is probable, but at least it seems clear that primitive Christian theology was not entirely or everywhere centered in "the fact of the resurrection." The greater fact was the triumphal progress of the martyred Christ to the throne on high, this entrance "behind the curtain" (6:19). It has often been pointed out that the Gospel of Luke, and perhaps John 20 (that is, the Gospel of John without the appendix), represent the ascension of our Lord as taking place at once, on the day of his resurrection; the longer period ("the great forty days") is derived from Acts 1:3. And it might be argued that this is the conception held by the author of Hebrews. It is more probable, however, that in the view of the author of Hebrews the resurrection and ascension were *identical,* one and the same act, and that this act took place in the transcendental realm, unseen by mortal eyes; it was by his *death* that Jesus entered into the holy of holies of the temple not made with hands (9:11), or—in the figure used earlier in the book—ascended far above the heavens, where he sits enthroned in glory at the right hand of God.

The church might have done well to retain this emphasis or interpretation in its statements of doctrine, instead of stressing the physical resurrection. That it did not do so is undoubtedly due to the Gnostic peril in the late first and second centuries, when not only the reality of the Resurrection but also the reality of Christ's human nature was called in question or denied—the Aeon Christ returning to the Father (or to the Primal Source of Being) had no occasion to resume a physical nature, even in a transformed or "spiritualized" state, from which he was now wholly free. Even the phantom of the human body, the "likeness" of mortal nature, was to be left behind in the realm of darkness. But it was unfortunate for all later Christian teaching that the Gnostic crisis gave such a reactionary turn to primitive teaching (the emphasis in the Gospels is pointed more or less in this direction), with the result that the interpretation set forth in Hebrews was left at one side—a landlocked bayou beside the on-rushing current of developing Catholic dogma.

The *Virgin Birth* is found nowhere in the New Testament outside the Gospels of Matthew and Luke. The attempt to read it into such passages as Gal. 4:4 ("born of woman") or Rev. 12 (the child of the woman) or the Old Latin text of John 1:13 (*"who was* born, not of . . . the will of the flesh . . ."*) represents an impossible kind of exegesis. In Luke the story hinges on six words (in Greek): in 3:23 the words "as was supposed" (two in Greek) are obviously an addition to the genealogy; in 1:34 the words "since I have no husband," or more literally, as in the King James Version, "seeing I know not a man" (four words in Greek), are most improbable, in view of Mary's betrothal and prospective marriage, and the story reads more naturally without them. The Annunciation is the divine message to the bride of Joseph that she is to bear a son, and this son is to be the Messiah. How all this will come about—not the birth of a son, for that was to be expected, or at least hoped for, by any Jewish bride, but the extraordinary destiny of the one to be born—is explained in what follows:

> The Holy Spirit will come upon you
>   [as upon the blessed women of old],
> And the power of the Most High will overshadow you;
> Therefore the child to be born will be called holy,
> The Son of God (vs. 35).

The theological implications of this story in its original form (as I view it) are clear enough, and are thoroughly Jewish—as the idea of a virgin birth was not.

The origin of the story must be sought in, or behind, the Gospel of Matthew (1:18-25), as one of its numerous "midrashic" elements.

For Matthew, or for the type of Christian teaching which he represents, the Old Testament (the *Greek* Old Testament, as a rule) contains abundant prophecies of Christ; again and again he notes that "all this took place to fulfill what the Lord had spoken by the prophet" (1:22; cf. 2:15, 17, 23; 8:17; 12:17; 13:35; 21:4; 26:56; 27:9). For him the Old Testament could almost be used as a "source" for the life of Jesus, as we might infer from 2:15 or 2:23. As a rule, however, he takes a datum in the tradition and then finds a passage in Old Testament scripture which foretold it—2:15 and 2:17-18 may be exceptions. Moreover, a close examination of Matthew's language shows Old Testament influence throughout, not only in the text of crucial passages but in subtle nuances of expression (e.g. 28:2-4, where some such verse as "the keepers . . . shall tremble," Eccl. 12:3, probably lies behind the tale; or 28:16, "the mountain to which Jesus had directed them"—cf. Gen. 22:2, 14 Septuagint). We are not surprised, then, to find the account of Jesus' birth in 1:18-25 written up in midrashic style, and based upon the "prophecy" found in Isaiah 7:14—in the Septuagint, not in the Hebrew. The quasi-ascetic tone of the story is matched by other passages in Matthew—for example in 5:28; or in 5:32, the exception clause, repeated in 19:9; or in the strange sayings quoted in 19:10-12. In the Gospel of Matthew second-century Encratism is already in the offing, and the whole ethos of Hellenistic spirituality.

If we consider the Virgin Birth as the belief is reflected in the New Testament, then, we find it to be a doctrine which is secondary and inferential, a doctrine derived from a text of the Old Testament and supported by it, a feature in the story of the life of Christ which entered the tradition at a relatively late date—and entered it as a doctrine, not as a part of the primitive *kerygma* which is basic to the Gospels. How widely influential the doctrine became is clear not only from later writers, and from the Apostles' Creed (*ca.* A.D. 150 and later), but even from the New Testament. The Old Latin text of John (see above) reflects its influence, and so do the early interpolations into Luke—interpolations made at so early a date that all surviving manuscripts, versions, and quotations in the Fathers contain them. The strange readings of Matt. 1:16, making Joseph the father of Jesus, which are found in some manuscripts and versions may possibly be derived from the original text of the genealogy; but they are more probably due to later heretical tampering with the text. In any case, if the genealogy did say that Joseph was the father of Jesus, the explanation, in a Jewish setting, was simple—he was his "legal" father. Thus no conflict would exist with vss. 18-25.

The theological significance of the Virgin Birth is accordingly twofold: the fulfillment of prophecy, and the divine nature of Christ—though how this was guaranteed by the supernatural mode of his conception is not stated.

8. *The Christology of Paul*

There are certain great "key" passages in Paul's letters which deserve careful study, not only for their own sake but for the light which they shed upon Paul's thought as a whole and upon Gentile Christianity in general. One of these, and the most important of them, is Phil. 2:5-11. It has sometimes been thought that the passage is quoted by Paul from some early creedlike hymn. But the thought and the language both tally so completely with Paul's thought and language as a whole that this view is unnecessary. If Paul was quoting these verses, he may well have been quoting himself—as he may also have done in I Cor. 13. His thought naturally took wings, on occasion, and soared to loftier levels. A mind nurtured on the Old Testament would not find this difficult; and if now and then he burst into poetry, like that of the prophets and psalmists, or into exalted rhythmic prose, like much of the Old Testament prose, this should not surprise us. The example of a modern Christian preacher like the late G. A. Studdert Kennedy, who would often swing into verse, very frequently his own earlier poems, sometimes a poem created at the moment—such an example helps us to understand Paul better.

The passage in Phil. 2 is poetic, both in style and theme. The pattern of thought, the "scheme"—that of a heavenly being (not God, but next to God, and certainly divine) who comes to earth to redeem mankind—has antecedents in more than one area of ancient religious thought. The late Canon Streeter pointed out the parallel in Buddhist thought, for example, in his lectures on *The Buddha and the Christ.*

The theology of the Hellenistic age recognized the work of "saviors" and "founders," the hero gods (e.g. Heracles, or Asclepius) who out of their "love for man" (*philanthropia*) chose to undergo suffering or to remain upon earth and cure the ills of mankind. The later Gnostic theology of the redeemer who comes down to earth to release the souls held in the dungeon of matter—all this is well known, and the Gnostic "pattern" is probably much older than Gnosticism. It is in connection with such hopes and yearnings for redemption—not from matter, as among the Gnostics, but from sin, disease, death, and all evils—that the later Old Testament and ancient Jewish conceptions of a coming Messiah are to be interpreted. Only, in this case the evils from which redemption was longed for included political servitude, economic oppression, and other purely this-wordly conditions which were interpreted as a present denial of the sovereignty of God and his reign over his people. Much the same may be said of the "eschatology" of Virgil and other Roman poets of the early empire. One may say, in fact, that the longing for redemption—whether out of this world or within its limitations, whether of the individual or of mankind, or of a part of mankind, the elect—was a characteristic note of the religion of late antiquity, from the fourth century before Christ and onward, almost throughout the Mediterranean world and the Near East.

Christianity—that is, Christ—came in answer to this longing. "The hopes and fears of all the years" were met in the coming of Christ. No wonder if the "pattern" of expectation became clearer as its fulfillment was realized! Nowhere else is the motivation of divine redemption carried further: it springs from the love of God himself; the humiliation of the Son, the Redeemer, is a self-chosen way of renunciation, and he had a real option in so choosing, for he declined to share the pride and ambition of the other heavenly beings, who aspired to seize the throne of God and set themselves up as the real rulers, *archontes,* of the cosmos; moreover, his humiliation and self-impoverishment was complete, for Christ chose the life of a slave, and died a slave's or a criminal's death on the cross—no redeemer god of the ancient religions had done this! No one ever dreamed that the Jewish Messiah would do this! And the unity of will and purpose between the supreme God and the "self-emptying"

Son was nowhere stressed as in the Christian gospel: "Therefore God has highly exalted him . . ." (vs. 9). The Gospel of John carries the motivation even further: "*God* so loved the world that he *gave* his only Son . . ." (John 3:16). The passage in Phil. 2 is no extraneous element in New Testament Christology, but sets forth in sublime terms the fundamental "pattern" or concept which lay at the very heart of Gentile Christianity from the first, the main principle of its creed as a religion of redemption.

In elaborating this principle Paul makes use of an age-old myth, the revolt of the angels, as the background of Christ's self-humiliation, since it does not belong to his human and historical choice of a way of life (contrast the groping toward a Christology to be seen in the temptation narrative of Matthew and Luke) but is carried back to his "pre-existent" state—the "mind" that was "in Christ" was his from the very beginning (vs. 5). In contrast to the titanic heavenly powers—Satan? Hesperus? Lucifer? "Wormwood"? the Titans of Greek myth? or "the angels that did not keep their own position"? (see Jude 6; I Enoch 6–16)—in contrast to these rebellious cosmic spirits in the dim and distant prehistory of the heavenly world, Christ's obedience and self-renunciation were rooted in the very core of his nature. For, as we may translate verses 6-11,

a

Though he lived a divine existence
  [that is, as a divine being, only a little lower than God;
  so the ancient myth pictured the "sons of God"],
He did not reach out to seize equality with God
  [as the rebel angels did, aspiring to seize the throne
  of the Most High; *harpagmon* cannot be meant to
  suggest the story of Adam's fall, in spite of the language of Gen. 3:5, "Ye shall be as God . . ."—though
  there were speculations which made Adam a cosmic
  figure],
But he emptied himself
  [or "impoverished himself"—humbled himself, made
  himself of no account, stripped himself bare even of the
  prerogatives that were rightly his, as Son of God],
And took the form of a slave,
And was born in the likeness of men.

b

Then finding himself in human form
He [still further] humbled himself,
And became obedient, even unto death
  [even to the extent of dying],
Even death on a cross.

c

Therefore God has highly exalted him.
And has bestowed on him the name [*Kyrios,* Lord]
  which is above every name,
That at the name of Jesus every knee should bow
In heaven and on earth and under the earth,
And every tongue confess that Jesus Christ is Lord,
To the glory of God the Father.

It is noteworthy that Paul does not introduce this passage as a piece of *didachê,* perhaps new or at least not very familiar. He uses it homiletically, and apparently assumes that his readers are already familiar with the doctrine: "So if there is any encouragement in Christ, any incentive of love, . . . any affection and sympathy, complete my joy . . . by being . . . of one mind . . . in humility. . . . Have this mind among yourselves, which you have in Christ Jesus, who . . ."—this is his introduction (vss. 1-5). And immediately after the great passage Paul goes on once more with his exhortations (vss. 12-18). It is this almost casual way of introducing the passage that surprises us most. Every Christian—at least every Gentile Christian— already knows the teaching and is thoroughly familiar with it!

"Christ Jesus" is a more solemn title, with Paul, than "Jesus Christ," which was to him practically a proper name—a double name, like "Titus Livius" or "Horatius Flaccus" or "Joseph Barsabbas." In "Christ Jesus" there is a lingering reminiscence of the origin of *Christos* as a title; it suggests "Messiah Jesus," "the Anointed One, Jesus" or "Jesus the Anointed by God." And the importance of the title in this passage is clear; for to Paul, and no doubt to the vast majority of Gentile Christians, "Christ" was a pre-existent divine being—not God, but certainly divine. (It is impossible, as we have said, to require the Christians of the first century to speak the language of Nicaea or Chalcedon—though they doubtless would have done so had they lived in the fourth or fifth century.) To Paul, and to Gentile Christianity in general, Jesus was both Messiah and Lord. He had pre-existed "in a divine form," as one of the great spiritual beings in the presence of the Creator, probably as the greatest of these, *the* "Son of God"; then he became man, lived a lowly human life, indeed a life of degradation and of suffering (an utter paradox for the Messiah), died on a cross, and was buried; then God raised him from the dead, exalted him to a position far higher than the one he had formerly held, in fact made him "Lord," so that at the name of Jesus (*Kyrios Jesus,* I Cor. 12:3) every knee should bow, in heaven and on earth and in the regions below, and every tongue confess that "Jesus Christ is Lord," to the glory of God the Father. The "name which is above every name" (vs. 9) is obviously the title *Kyrios* (vs. 11).

But Christ is not only the Redeemer; he is also the Creator (that is, the agent of God in creation), the "image of God, the first-born of all creation," and the head of the church, the "first-born from the dead" (that is, the head of the *new* creation as he had been the head of the old). This idea is set forth in another great "key" passage in the Pauline epistles, Col. 1:13-20:

He has delivered us from the dominion of darkness
And transferred us to the kingdom of his beloved Son,
    In whom we have redemption, the forgiveness of sins.
He is the image of the invisible God,
    The first-born of all creation;
For in him all things were created,
    In heaven and on earth,
    Visible and invisible,
    Whether thrones or dominions or principalities or authorities—
All things were created through him and for him.
He is before all things,
    And in him all things hold together.
He is the head of the body, the church;
He is the beginning, the first-born from the dead,
    That in everything he might be preëminent.

> For in him all the fullness of God was pleased to dwell,
> And through him [Christ] to reconcile to himself [God] all things,
>> Whether on earth or in heaven,
> Making peace by the blood of his cross.

Somewhat more doubt has been cast upon this passage than upon the one in Phil. 2; but for our present purpose it is not important to decide whether Paul wrote the words, or Timothy, or some other person. The passage is certainly Pauline; and, more important than that, it reflects first-century Gentile Christianity, the type of christological doctrine which, even at this early date, was steadily moving in the direction of the later Catholic creeds. Once more it is clear that the passage is not introduced as a bit of new and esoteric *didachê* but comes in almost casually in support of Pauline exhortation (*parainêsis*): "May you be strengthened with all power . . . for all endurance," since God "has qualified us to share in the inheritance of the saints in light" (vss. 11-12). Then, following the passage, the epistle continues right on with the same sort of exhortation (vss. 21 ff.)—but taking for granted now the fact of reconciliation (vs. 20) in such a way as entirely to exclude the notion that verses 13-20 can be a later interpolation into the chapter.

The doctrine of Christ the "image" of God is related to that which is set forth in the opening verses of the Epistle to the Hebrews (1:3), though not so subtly stated. It is a corollary of the redemption, already described in Phil. 2 and elsewhere, that Christ was also the agent of God in the creation; Christ is not now one among other divine, angelic, pre-existent beings about the throne of God; he is simply and completely God's Son—the "beloved Son" (vs. 13). As Athanasius was to point out in his *De Incarnatione,* the Redeemer could be no other than the Creator, no secondary, alien, or substitute being; and the logic of this passage simply affirms the same view, but in inverse order—the Creator (God's agent) is also the Redeemer. Even the *archontes* of the cosmos, whether good or evil (some of them had later revolted) were created through and for him (vs. 16). Surely the Nicene Creed does not go beyond this, for in the Nicene Creed it is God the Father who is "Maker . . . of all things visible and invisible"; nor does John 1:3, "All things were made through him, and without him was not anything made." Moreover, not only did he (as God's agent) create the whole universe, but he sustains it: "In him all things hold together"—that is, "con-sist," *sunestêke* (vs. 17). Finally, it was in him that the whole "fullness of God" (*pan to plêrôma*) was pleased to dwell—he is completely and absolutely God, as completely and absolutely as it is possible for human nature to contain deity. He was no half-god, no *theios anthropos* or "divine man," no prophet or temporarily inspired man, one who bore God to men; in fact the language *could* be interpreted (as it was by Docetists and others) as if deity took the place of humanity in him. Instead of his "bearing God to men," it was God who indwelt him (as vs. 20 shows), and *through him* God reconciled all things to himself (cf. II Cor. 5:18-19). The doctrine is all but identical with that of the Prologue to John (especially John 1:14, 16, 18). Since the major concept is Hellenistic, not Jewish, it seems certain that the doctrine could not have arisen in the old milieu of Palestinian Christian Judaism—though there are scholars who affirm that this was possible. But the important point is that it was characteristic of *Gentile* Christianity, and this at a date long before the end of the first century. Moreover the language, the "pattern" of thought presupposed, and the "framework" of ideas were all perfectly natural in the world of Hellenistic religion and theology.

The language of this passage suggests another "key" passage in Paul's letters, I Cor. 15:20-28:

But in fact Christ has been raised from the dead,
   The first fruits of those who have fallen asleep.
For as by a man came death,
   By a man has come also the resurrection of the dead.
For as in Adam all die,
   So also in Christ shall all be made alive.
But each in his own order: Christ the first fruits, then at his coming those
    who belong to Christ.
Then comes the end,
   When he delivers the kingdom to God the Father
   After destroying every rule and every authority and power.

For he must reign until he has put all his enemies under his feet.
The last enemy to be destroyed is death.
   "For God has put all things in subjection under his feet."
   But when it says, "All things are put in subjection under him," it is
      plain that he is excepted who put all things under him.
[But] when all things are subjected to him,
Then the Son himself will also be subjected to him who put all things
      under him,
That God may be everything to every one.

Here the thought is concerned, not with the creation of the universe and the new creation of the church, but with the historical
process of Christ's victory over sin and death, the reconquest of the
rebellious province of disobedient human and demonic wills and its
reincorporation in the divine empire, and the final submission of all
things to God—the consummation of God's reign or "kingdom." Even
the King's Son, the noble young Prince, after leading the armies of
God to a complete victory, will himself be subject to the King, that
God may be "all in all" (K.J.V.)—that is, "everything to every one"
(R.S.V.).

The pattern of thought presupposed in this passage is quite obvious,
and is more or less the political one just described. It is not the age-
old *mythos* of Phil. 2, nor the metaphysical-theological one found
in Col. 1, but in its essence the idea is the same. Christ volunteers to
go behind the enemy's lines, that is to enter human life, die and rise
again, and thus as the "first fruits" (vs. 23; cf. the "first-born" in
Col. 1:18) "make alive" all those who belong to him. Victorious over
sin and death, he is now reigning as God's viceroy in the revolted
province—for the war is not yet won. *All* God's enemies must be subdued or destroyed, and "the last enemy to be destroyed is death" (vs.
26, of special relevance to the subject of the chapter). This military
figure is not to be isolated from Paul's other metaphors, though for
him, from first to last, Christ's earthly life was viewed as a continuous
conflict with the forces of evil. Nor is it to be separated from Paul's
total view of history, with its long and tragic episode of sin and death,
and the crucial and climactic subepisode of the Law. We can diagram
it somewhat as follows:

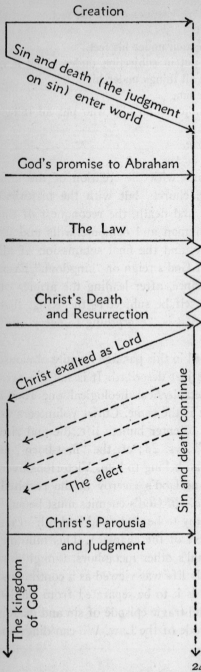

a) Described in Jewish, Old Testament, theological terms, the facts of sin and death are the great contradictions of God's rule over his own universe. The Law, far from saving men from sin, only made them aware of their sinfulness, and indeed deepened their guilt. At last Christ came into the world in order to save men from sin and death—to effect what the Law never could. He is now exalted and enthroned at God's right hand, but presently the Parousia and the Judgment will take place, and the final full realization of God's universal kingdom.

b) Described in terms perhaps more understandable to Gentile readers, Christ came to earth in order to release men from their enslavement by the wicked rulers of this present darkness. These are the wicked *stoicheia tou kosmou,* the "elemental spirits of the universe," who revolted against God and hold mankind in thrall—the evil *archontes* of this present age, the star spirits and nature spirits and heathen gods who inspired the wicked political rulers who put Christ to death, and threaten even now the extinction of his church (Eph. 6:12). But their ultimate victory is impossible, for in principle they are already defeated and dethroned. Far from being their victim, with the *titulus* above his head on the cross the proclamation of his folly (*Jesus Nazarenus, Rex Judaeorum*), Christ had really defeated them. They had taken on as antagonist one whom they knew not; his weakness was only for the moment, part of his human disguise, and their blindness had led—was now leading—to their utter destruction. Thus he "disarmed the principalities and powers and made a public example of them, triumphing over them in it" (the cross), or perhaps "in him" (Christ, if "God" is the antecedent of "he"; Col. 2:15).

Such language may strike modern readers as mythological—as indeed it is. For ancient religion *mythos* was the perfectly natural expression of what lay beyond the range of exact scientific or philosophical definition; this was the sense in which Plato had employed the term, and this was the purpose for which he had fashioned his superb "myths." In popular religious thought, Jewish as well as Greek, the use of myth was inevitable, in the absence of either philosophical or dogmatic theology. And even today, as throughout the history of the Christian church, much of the language of faith is still of this character; at certain high levels of apprehension it is impossible to avoid the use of analogy, of anthropomorphism, of parable and picture and dramatic representation.

9. *The Religious Basis of Christology*

Thus the New Testament reflects a long process of christological development, in which we cannot altogether make out the various "stages" but only some of the "areas" penetrated by the church's advancing thought. The earliest levels or stages—or areas—are wholly Jewish. Jesus is "a prophet mighty in deed and word" (Luke 24:19), "the prophet Jesus from Nazareth of Galilee" (Matt. 21:11). He is the long-expected Messiah (John 1:45), the Son of David, the King of Israel (Mark 10:47; 15:32), the Savior of his people—the one who was expected to "save" or rescue them, not to die for them (as we have seen, there is little evidence for any Jewish expectation of a "dying" Messiah in the New Testament period). He is "the" prophet like Moses (John 1:21; 6:14; Acts 3:22), popularly conceived on the basis of Deut. 18:15. He is "the one to redeem Israel" (Luke 24:21) and restore the kingdom of David (Acts 1:6). Much of this language reflects popular enthusiasm on the part of Jesus' large following during the ministry in Galilee and Judea.

After the Resurrection a new stage was begun in the development of Christology. Jesus was not Messiah after all—or not *merely* the Messiah—but the apocalyptic Son of Man, exalted to heaven, and the Lord of his cult (*Mar, Maran*). Whether or not these two titles were localized, the one (Son of Man) in the North, the other (Lord) in the South, we cannot say; but the hypothesis seems to fit the data.

From *Mar* or *Maran* to *Kyrios* was a short step, and carried with it immense consequences, not only because of its cultic significance but also because *Kyrios* was the Septuagint rendering of the name of God *YHWH* in the Old Testament (see above, pp. 130-37). Whether this step was taken within or outside Palestine, say at Damascus or Antioch, we cannot tell; clearly a "Greek" (a person who ordinarily spoke Greek) could read the Septuagint inside Palestine—many others besides the Ethiopian treasurer of Acts 8:27.

The great christological title of primitive *Gentile* Christianity was "Son of God," with its age-old associations, and with overtones which commended it to the purest and devoutest piety of the pagan world. That it had no "metaphysical" implications, at first, is probably true, though it was not difficult to read them into the term. A purely human Jesus who *became* Son of God might do for a time, or in some circles (or areas), but not permanently. If he is *now* Son of God, there must have been something in his *origin* which related him to God; that is, he must have "come" from God, he must be derived from God—or, in our language, he must have been pre-existent.

Mark probably does not follow this line of thought to its conclusion, though some eminent scholars hold that Mark really does view Jesus as pre-existent. The title "Son of God" is certainly of profound significance in this earliest Gospel, written on Gentile soil, and embodying the traditions of a Gentile, Greek-speaking church. Nor is it certain that Matthew and Luke so view him. Nevertheless the title, like those of "Son of Man" and "Lord," contained within itself the suggestion; and the inference was sure to be drawn sooner or later, under the impulsion of Christian devotion, evangelism, and apologetic preaching.

In Paul, Hebrews, and John (including the Epistles of John) Christ is clearly pre-existent, either as a Son of God in the company of heaven, or as the reflection or effulgence of the divine glory, the one through whom God created and upholds the worlds, or as the divine Logos, with God, and himself "God" (*theos,* not *theios*) from the beginning.

The affirmations of the New Testament set serious problems for the later church, as the history of doctrine during the early centuries makes evident. The great problem was how to maintain the monotheistic idea of God—not in spite of these affirmations, but in such a way as to include the richness and depth of the Christian experience of God in Christ and in the Spirit which underlay these affirmations. The final result was the dogma of the Blessed Trinity and the christological affirmations of Nicaea, Constantinople, Ephesus, and Chalcedon. These were not ventures in speculation, but, as their very language indicates, simply statements which *ruled out* various conceptions or attempted definitions which infringed or invalidated the language of scripture and of religious experience, especially of worship. The long battle with Gnosticism and, following it, the equally severe struggle with Arianism were both motivated by loyalty to scripture and history. If Gnosticism had triumphed, the historical element in Christianity would have vanished. If Arianism had triumphed, a system not incompatible with Hellenistic syncretism might have prevailed—at least a system which would have contradicted the implications of the last and highest reaches of New Testament Christology.

It is not uncommon for students of the New Testament to read into it views derived from these later conflicts, either positively or negatively—that is, views which are either favorable to the later growth of dogma or critical of it. But the New Testament must be taken as it stands, if it is to be properly understood; and although one cannot be oblivious of the direction in which thought is moving in its various areas, the future must never be allowed to determine the past.

In the field of christological doctrine the New Testament owes somewhat less to the Old Testament than it does in any other field. That is, here the departure from, and the advance upon, the Old Testament and contemporary Judaism was most marked. Yet even here, as we have seen, the Old Testament supplied an indispensable element. But the fundamental drive in the whole development of Christology was not exegesis, nor yet loyalty to the data of history—for example the sayings of Jesus—but the living spiritual experience of Christians. It was the realization of the new life in Christ which led Paul and many others to take high, and ever higher, views of the nature of the one in whom and through whom this "newness of life" had been made possible and was now being effected. The christological development of the New Testament is fundamentally and thoroughly religious, not philosophical, metaphysical, or speculative, nor yet purely historical or factual. Its center was not a movement through a series of inferences, nor yet the declarations ("claims," as they used to be called) which the historical Jesus had once made in the temple court in Jerusalem or elsewhere. Not deliverances of factual data, whether historical or metaphysical, but the necessary inference men drew from their own experience—this was the driving force in the development of New Testament Christology. Here again we see faith seeking an intellectual expression, *fides quaerens intellectum,* but without ceasing to be faith at any point, from first to last.

The title *Christos* soon became a proper name in the Greek-speaking church; so Paul uses it constantly, sometimes in the form "Jesus Christ," sometimes "Christ Jesus," sometimes with "Lord," sometimes with the article—as if it were still a title. The proper name "Jesus" continued in use, presumably, in the Aramaic-speaking churches in Palestine and the East, though supplemented with titles like "our Lord" (*Maran*) and "Master" (*Ribbon, Ribbona*—in the New Testament usually *Rabbi* or *Rabboni*), if we may judge from surviving fragments. But everywhere, East and West, it was in Christian worship that the old titles not only survived but remained true, came true again and again, and received ever fresh emphasis and meaning. Their use in preaching and writing is equally certain, and also the fullness of meaning which they retained, with still deeper meanings added from further study, chiefly of the Old Testament, and reflection; but preaching and writing were secondary to worship, since in worship, as the early Christians realized, Christ was a present Lord, meeting with his own wherever and whenever they assembled in his name (Matt. 18:20). He was *still* the Teacher, Master, Prophet, Son of David, Messiah, Lord, Savior, Son of Man, and Son of God. And although, as T. R. Glover once remarked, no one would ever have thought of singing, "How sweet the name of Logos sounds," we have ample evidence that such titles as "Christ the Wisdom of God" and "Christ the Power of God" were dear to Christian hearts, and were used in Christian worship—even as they are used to this day, as for example in the hymn "Strong Son of God, immortal Love."

X

The Doctrine of Salvation

1. *The Antecedents*

THE good news of the gospel was addressed to a world which was profoundly conscious of its need for salvation. In this respect it was a very different world from ours—though the need for salvation was really never greater than it is today, in a human society threatened with total self-destruction. Jewish apocalyptism was one symptom of this yearning. Though the main emphasis, in the first century, was upon the need of salvation for the world as a whole, the individual was not forgotten. Hellenistic mysticism and spirituality, even Hellenistic philosophy—not to mention the spread of the Eastern cults and the revival of astrology, magic, asceticism, theurgy—are likewise symptoms of the same deep-seated hunger and unrest. In Hellenistic mysticism it was naturally the need for individual, personal salvation which was most strongly stressed. Men had become acutely aware that they were *not* "at home in the universe," and the repeated cry, "What must we do to be saved?" (cf. Acts 16:30), was the expression of this profound longing. Hilaire Belloc's lines might have been written by an ancient Hellenistic poet, any time after, say, 250 B.C.:

> Strong God which made the topmost stars
> To circulate and keep their course,
> Remember me; whom all the bars
> Of sense and dreadful fate enforce.

Coming to such a world, or rather, arising within it, the Christian church with its inspired message, the gospel, and its divine revelation, which God had made in his Son, provided a way of salvation. In fact, if we can trust our interpretation of the language of Acts, "the Way" was a name for the church before the term "church" or even the term "Christian" came into use (Acts 9:2; 19:23; etc.). This originally meant, in all probability, a way of belief and worship or of religious practice (*derek,* in the Jewish religious sense); but in the wider Hellenistic, Greek-speaking world, "way" undoubtedly meant "way of salvation." The Greek world, which is the world of the New Testament as a whole, was familiar enough with ways of life—Stoic, Cynic, Orphic, Pythagorean, Indian, and other. What the Greek world longed for was not another way of life, or of living, but a way of salvation.

The Christian doctrine of salvation goes a long way back for its antecedents and its earlier prehistory. The Old Testament is a sacred history of a specific salvation. God's creation of the world, his choice of Israel, his redemption of Israel from Egypt, his covenant with his people, his punishment of his people, his forgiveness and restoration of his people, his preservation of his people—this is a *Heilsgeschichte* (story of salvation) from beginning to end. So far was this idea carried that the structure which was finally built about the Hexateuch (and perhaps even the Octateuch) and continues down through Chronicles, at the end of the Hebrew Bible, is the continuous story of God's dealings with his world, with Israel his people, with the world through Israel, and with Israel and the rest of the world (in combination) in terms of salvation. His word to Israel was salvation, *shalôm,* the word with which the later Mishnah ends. The nearest Greek word for this was not "peace" (*eirênê*) but "salvation" (*sôtêria*), the whole state of welfare or well-being of the people in right relations with God; and the nearest English word to this is likewise "salvation," viewed as a state rather than a single act or a series of acts. Thus what men longed for in the Hellenistic age was in truth something that men had always longed for, certainly in Hebraism and Judaism, only now more acutely, and without those satisfactions of personal peace and salvation in obedience to *YHWH* which the Psalter, for example, with its beautiful archaic outlook, reflects on page after page. Yet even this satisfaction was only partial, could never be more than partial, in a world like this present one.

The Old Testament conception of salvation thus involved the idea of covenant, the "agreement" between God and man, graciously proposed by God and guaranteed by his "goodness and truth"—his faithfulness, his fidelity to his word and to his own character. Israel was to be God's people, and God was to be exclusively their God; no other gods were to be worshiped. The exclusiveness worked both ways; and Israel alone was to be God's people; at least this was the early view, as in Amos 3:2; the later view, as in Second Isaiah, broadened and modified this (see Isa. 19:24-25). In return for Israel's loyalty and obedience God guaranteed his people survival, food, protection from enemies, and all the blessings of peace and prosperity. This primitive eudaemonism, this ancient principle, "Be good [obey, meet God's requirements] and you will be happy [you will receive his blessings]," is fundamental to the conception. Only rarely in the history of the world's religions has the idea received as complete an exposition. Naturally the idea broke down in practice. Either the guarantees were not made good—for the prophets this inference was unthinkable —or, much more probably, in fact undeniably, Israel had sinned and thus prevented God from carrying out his side of the agreement. The later prophets of the classical age, looking more deeply into the problem, insisted that what was needed was not merely repentance and restoration but a deeper motivation, a "new" covenant, written not on tablets of stone but upon the human heart (Jer. 31:31-34; Ezek. 37:26; Isa. 55:3). Israel, redeemed long ago from Egypt, must be redeemed once more, from exile; in fact the redemption must go further than that —men need to be redeemed from sin, which means from actual sinning, not from some abstract "principle" of sin, and from the consequent alienation from God. At the same time not only Israel but all the nations of mankind, including even Israel's age-old archenemies, Egypt and Assyria, must be included in the new agreement between God and man (Isa. 19:19-25). Righteousness or justice and the practice of true religion must become universal, as God is the God of the whole universe; Israel cannot find peace or salvation apart from the rest of mankind.

This conviction marked a great shift in emphasis and orientation from the ancient, primitive eudaemonism still surviving in the preexilic age. In retrospect Israel's sufferings could now be seen to have been not only the punishment for Israel's own sins but also the punishment for the sins of other peoples, and not only punishment, blind and automatic (like a Greek *nemesis*), but discipline, motivated by divine pity and love—discipline for Israel, but also an atonement for the sins of other nations as well, and an example which was to be restorative, saving, redemptive for all mankind. Nowhere in scripture has this insight come to clearer expression than in Second Isaiah (Isa. 53). Not only were the children no longer to be punished for their fathers' sins (the "deuteronomic" view, deeply rooted in ancient thought, as the parallels in Greek epic and tragedy show), but each individual must pay the price of his own sin—as Jeremiah held (31:29-30; cf. Ezek. 18:2-4). But even more than this. The nation (as in Isa. 53) or the individual (as perhaps in Ps. 22, etc.), suffering in consequence of, or "for," its own sins and also as a consequence of, or "for," the sins of others, was really making "an offering for sin." The suffering was redemptive. Its closest analogy was the ritual of sacrifice in the temple; yet it accomplished what, in the view of the prophets, at least, the temple sacrifices sometimes failed to achieve—satisfaction, the restoration of right relations with God. The full expression of this idea in the Epistle to the Hebrews, as interpreting the death of Christ and what was thus effected for all mankind, only draws together into one the lines upon which thought is already moving in the post-exilic prophets of the Old Testament. But the ancient eudaemonism, rooted in the temple cultus and its whole system of ideas, including the covenant, was not so easily set aside. The author of Hebrews shows how seriously a Greek-speaking first-century Christian, nurtured on the Septuagint, could take the sacrificial ritual—though he probably never saw a temple sacrifice and knew no more about it than what he read in the Old Testament.

The primitive eudaemonistic idea came to full expression likewise in apocalyptic eschatology, as we have already seen. This is God's world; whatever in it contradicts his rule must be done away, including sin, suffering, death; God must take his great power and reign over Israel and over all the world; he must either come himself as King, or send his "Anointed," the (King) Messiah, to be his vicegerent; Paradise must be restored, and the primeval state of the world when "God saw everything that he had made, and, behold, it was very good" (Gen. 1:31). Everlasting life, either forfeited by primitive man or else never attained by him (Adam and Eve in the Garden), must be achieved—that is, granted by God to his faithful or at least, most assuredly, to his martyrs (so Dan. 12:2-3)—hence the resurrection of the dead. The wicked must be punished—hence the survival, or revival, of the idea of a final judgment, not in the afterlife (as in Egyptian religion, in Orphism, and in later religious movements) but here on this earth. Thereafter God and his people will dwell together in peace, and all the blessings hitherto withheld by sin—or by the devil, or by the demons—will at last be realized. "Salvation" is the final state of a redeemed and transformed world with God as its sole ruler.

2. *Salvation as Act and State*

In a word, "salvation" as understood in the Bible is *eschatological*. It is "the last of life for which the first was made"—the full and final realization of all God's purposes, for the world, for Israel, and for the individual, after all frustrations and obstacles (human, demonic, material, or spiritual) have been removed or overcome. *Sôtêria* is not only an act of "saving" but a state of being saved—that is, preserved— a continuous condition of welfare and well-being in the sight of God and under his blessing. The saving act is only the inauguration of the state of salvation, whether it is viewed as release from unhappy conditions, as restoration to a former state of freedom and divine favor, or as the beginning of something new and better than has ever hitherto been achieved.

Paul uses a dozen different metaphors in his attempt to convey the rich meaning of this new state of well-being; "justification" (or acquittal at the bar of God's justice) is only one of them. We are adopted as sons. We are redeemed, as prisoners are redeemed, or slaves, or debtors—or even as a slave accumulates savings at a temple and is eventually "purchased" by the god with the funds thus made over to him, and so is set free, though he is still the slave of the god (and thus Paul is "Christ's slave"). We are "reborn." We are "translated" out of the kingdom of darkness into the kingdom of light. We are re-created (the creation story in Genesis is repeated in us) and so are now "new" persons in Christ. We die with Christ, are buried with Christ (in baptism), are raised with Christ (through his resurrection), to live henceforth "in" him and "by the power of his resurrection."

We have arrived at maturity, and are no longer under "tutors" and taskmasters. The bill of charges (or the indictment) against us has been canceled. We have been "reconciled" to God—who was never our enemy, though we were his—and have received the "forgiveness" of our sins. We have been "transformed" by the gift of the Holy Spirit, the Spirit of God, or of Christ, and have been "sealed" for the day of "redemption." We are "united" with Christ, who dwells within us— the body is "dead in trespasses and sins," but we are alive in spirit. "I live; yet it is not I who live, but Christ lives in me"—"Christ within, the hope of glory!" Almost every page of Paul contains, or echoes, one or more of these figures or symbols. They are not so much figures of speech as of thought; there is no hard and fast scientific formula for describing, let alone for defining, the state of salvation and its achievement. The realization of its meaning depends upon a depth of experience which is, in its fullness, quite incommunicable in human language. Like the appreciation of beauty, or the apprehension of truth, it must be directly and personally experienced. All that another, even an inspired apostle, can do is to hint at its richness and depth of meaning—as by these various metaphors—and then leave it to the Holy Spirit, the guide into all truth, to make known to the individual believer in his own experience all that the Christian salvation means. This is characteristic not only of the understanding of the rank and file, the ordinary believers to whom the message is addressed. It is true also of the original apprehension of the apostle himself, who pauses to exclaim, more than once, over the surpassing and really incomprehensible goodness of God, the wealth of his grace, the amazing depth of his design, the infinite resources of his wisdom, mercy, and power.

At the inmost core of the Christian religion, and an indispensable condition of its true and full expression, lies a type of experience which can only be described as mystical. These things cannot be stated in words; they cannot be completely described, let alone rationally explained and accounted for. Why all this took place; how it took place; how and why salvation, both as act and as state, depends upon Christ, and especially upon his death—to these questions the early church has no complete answer. The best explanation it can offer is analogy. The analogy which most readily suggested itself—to almost anyone in the ancient world, but especially to a Jew, whose religion was enshrined in the Old Testament—was naturally that of sacrifice. All over the world, and from time immemorial, the way of access to God had been thought to open only through the presentation of gifts; an invisible sovereign must be approached in the same way as a visible, earthly one. When this sovereign was offended, or when his subjects were guilty of disobedience, special gifts and offerings must be presented. For ancient Judaism, as for ancient Greek and ancient Roman religion and for many others, a "bloody" sacrifice was viewed as much more precious, much more effective, than an "unbloody" offering, such as cakes, fruit, or the like. For the blood was the life (Lev. 17:14), and the presentation of a *life* was the highest, noblest, completest conceivable offering one could make to God. Men already looked upon the deaths of martyrs as in some sense "making atonement" for the sins of their people (IV Macc. 6:29; 17:22; Pal. Sanh. 11. 30c, 28). Thus it was the most natural step in the world—in the world of the first century—for the answer to the question, "Why did Jesus die?" or "Why did God's Messiah have to die?" to take the form, "He died for sins—for *our* sins— in accordance with the scriptures" (cf. I Cor. 15:3). The psychological consideration "We are forgiven" was not simply an inference, "Christ died for our sins; *therefore* we are forgiven." Instead it worked simultaneously, in Christian experience, with the conviction that this was the meaning of Christ's death. Indeed it was probably one of the antecedent factors leading to that conviction: "Our sins really *are* forgiven; we are certain of this, with an assurance which no animal sacrifice, no acts of penitence, no practice of piety has ever sufficed to give us; the explanation can only be that Christ's death has really effected what all our previous practice of religion— whether sacrifice, acts of penitence, or deeds of piety—has only dimly reached out toward." The "logic" of the Atonement is accordingly not merely rational, or categorical, but "psychological," experiential, deeper than reason and understanding. It is a matter of faith, not of logical explanation or even of rational description.

It is not surprising, then, that no one metaphor can convey the full meaning of this fundamental doctrine of Christianity and of the New Testament. Nor is it surprising that later theologies, taking some one metaphor as absolute and complete in itself, went off on tangents and ended by caricaturing what is, in the New Testament, the indispensable presupposition of the whole process—the goodness, the mercy, the love of God. For the New Testament the Atonement is God's act; Christ is "put forward" by him as an offering for sin (Rom. 3:25) or as an expiation or as a reconciliation or as a place of reconciliation (*hilastêrion*). God "accepts" the offering; but the will of the Son and the will of the Father are never in opposition—hence Hebrews lays such stress upon Christ's "obedience" (5:8)—or even very clearly distinguishable. What the Father wills, the Son wills; what the Son wills is in perfect accord with the will of the Father (see especially John 17). It is inconceivable, in the realm of New Testament thought, that God should ever have "averted his gaze," even for an instant, as the Son took upon himself the full penalty for human sin; or that Christ should bear the "wrath" of God deserved by sinners; or that Christ might, let us say, have been transported to the far side of the moon or to some distant star and there have been put to a hideous death because other human beings had incurred the vengeance of heaven— such artificial and unreal ideas are a travesty of the New Testament doctrine. That doctrine is really inexplicable apart from the experience of salvation, the new life in Christ, the "new covenant," the awareness of being forgiven, in Christ and through Christ, and the experienced sense of fresh power and of peace with God—in brief what the Epistle to the Hebrews calls a cleansed conscience (9:9, 14; 10:22).

This is the background of Paul's doctrine of "justification by faith." Acquittal in God's sight, divine forgiveness, the new life in grace— these are not steps on the way to be achieved by human effort, by the "works" of the Law. God treats the penitent sinner *as if* he were already righteous—even as a father treats a penitent child *as if* he were already obedient and responsive. God can do this because he sees more possibilities in the situation than human eye can discern. The human parent of course sees more in the situation of the penitent child than any other person can see; but his insight is only a dim, distorted vision, compared with the penetrating insight of the divine searcher of hearts. And the miraculous and unpredictable fact turns out to be that the penitent sinner responds to this treatment—"responds," we say, as we say that a difficult case "responds" to proper medical treatment; but the sinner is still saved by "grace," not by his own effort. In fact, the response is far profounder, far more radical, far more complete than anything the ancient formula of law-obedience-reward could show. It is Jesus' gospel of free access to God, stated now in the terms of Paul's forensic, legalistic frame of thought; it is the gospel of the "last days," and its setting is thoroughly eschatological—perhaps no one would have time enough for a long life of perfect obedience to God's commandments—and it is at heart a mystical experience of release, renewal, restoration, and growing intimacy of fellowship with God, in Christ.

The doctrine of justification by faith (its full title in Reformation theology is "Justification by Faith only, apart from works of the Law") has sometimes been stated as if it were the whole of the gospel, or of the religious thought of the New Testament. It has been stated, at times, in such a way as to cut the nerve of the social message of Christianity, and more than one false inference has been drawn from it. But in spite of all this the Pauline doctrine is unquestionably grounded upon the central experience of the Christian religion, and is an expression of the fundamental terms and conditions of the Christian salvation.

3. *The Atonement*

It might have been expected that the death of Christ would occasion speculation over the problem of suffering in human life, and especially the question of divine justice in human affairs. So it might have done, had Christianity been a philosophical school; but the answer of the New Testament (that is, of the early church) was purely religious (nonphilosophical). Christ died because it was so foretold of him in scripture—which meant it was the will of God—because he willingly accepted death, and refused to run away (John 7:35) or to save himself (Mark 15:31), because according to the divine plan his death was for the benefit of "the many" (Mark 10:45). The explanation was religious, as we have said, not philosophical. Moreover the answer was found where it had already been given, long before, in scripture (Isa. 53). The Lord had "laid on him the iniquity of us all"—and "with his stripes we are healed." The background and setting of the problem, for the early church, was totally different from what it would have been for a group of philosophers—say the disciples of the martyred Socrates. For such a group of philosophers the presupposition would have been: *either* a good God in control of a universe where everything went entirely according to his will, and always for the best, and where martyrdom, like other suffering, was most unfortunate, but quite meaningless; *or* a blind, inscrutable *Moira* overruling all events; *or* a world where the gods had abdicated, and *Tychê* ruled by whim and caprice. With any such background, however philosophical men might be, the problem was insoluble—though there are many traces in later Greek thought of the idea that Socrates died a martyr, and that his lot in the other world was certainly blessed. But it was the wholly religious, or biblical, background of the event, as the early Christians reflected upon it, which made all the difference and transformed what might have been a dark, impenetrable mystery into a luminous intuition of God's purpose for revelation and redemption.

Yet there was a still remoter background to the event of Calvary, as the first Christians viewed it—the background likewise of the sublime vision of the inspired poet in Isa. 53. The conditions and circumstances which led Christ to his death were not only the blind authorities in Palestine (Acts 3:17), or the evil powers in the spiritual world (Col. 2:15), but the whole fact of human sin, from "man's first disobedience" to the present. This was something more—and less—than penalty for human wrongdoing. Sin was still thought of in primitive terms, as a kind of blight or infection (*miasma*) which spread over the sinner's neighborhood, involved even physical nature in its effects (Rom. 8:19-22), and passed on to the sinner's posterity. Just as in Greek tragedy, where a similar primitive outlook survives, the relatively innocent are borne down by the consequences of sin along with the wrongdoer himself. In Sophocles' tragedy, Oedipus is as confident of his innocence as Job was (cf. *Oed. Col.* 266-67, 275, 521-22) ; and yet since he shares in the consequences of primeval guilt—the sin of his ancestors—he too is guilty (*Oed. Tyr.* 1374, 1381-82, 1433). The order of nature has been disturbed, even by his unwitting sin, and the pest spreads throughout Thebes. It is not enough that the guilty should be sought out and punished—how could the *original* wrongdoers be punished, in the Greek tragedy, since they were long dead? Instead, a powerful rite must be enacted to cleanse the present "sinner" (Oedipus) and to transform his harmful presence into a blessing for the city

(Athens; *Oed. Col.* 466 ff., 1518 ff.). And it is not so much that Oedipus is "guilty" in some forensic sense, whether because his ancestors' guilt has been "imputed" to him, or because he is the only living representative of their line (or the only one caught in the chain of inherited "guilt"), or because of his own unwitting crime—the great point is not the solution of a problem at law but the cleansing of a whole land and people from the *pollution* that has resulted from the sin. Oedipus is a polluted being, one to be avoided and shunned as if he bore some infectious plague, like smallpox or leprosy. So far as the gods are concerned his personal innocence does not matter—any more than it does in the case of a person who has come down with smallpox or has contracted leprosy. And while his state of pollution continues he is abhorrent and detestable in the sight of gods and men alike. Bloodguiltiness was thus a physical reality. That it had been incurred involuntarily, unwittingly, even innocently, made not the slightest difference.

It is this profound ancient view of sin, rather than the casual and superficial modern view—which often reduces it to a mere state of private alienation from God, with consequent mental distress (the "psychoanalytic" equivalent) or with attendent external but still private misfortunes—it is this ancient view rather than the modern which the New Testament consistently take for granted. The crime against justice in putting the Innocent One to death was fully recognized; "the wrath" (of God) which had finally overtaken his rebellious people was the necessary, indeed inevitable, consequence of their rejection of the one whom God had sent them (I Thess. 2:16). Nevertheless God had permitted the crucifixion. That God might be unjust—this was unthinkable! Since God had permitted it, had indeed foreseen it and still allowed it, had, even more, planned it—this could mean only that, instead of being simply the final and grossest miscarriage of justice in all the world's long history, the death of Christ was the means which God had chosen for removing the sin that had led to it (somewhat like Oedipus' rite of cleansing and reconciling—though Christ was "without sin," Heb. 4:15, etc.). Not moral wrongdoing, then, with an exactly proportioned penalty, as in later Western theology and jurisprudence, but "infection of nature"—this was the really primitive conception of sin, and the one which the whole Bible, Old Testament and New

Testament alike, presupposes. And it is this primitive conception, with its profound connotation of the social nature of wrongdoing, which provides the background for the New Testament doctrine of the Atonement, so far as the doctrine emerges at this earliest stage of Christian theology. Some of the later theological theories (such as the "imputation" of sin to Adam's descendants and the "imputation" of mankind's sin to Christ, or the exact balancing of Christ's suffering with the "guilt" of the human race—in general all "forensic" or "Western" theories of the Atonement) would have been impossible and could never have arisen had the church retained its really primitive outlook and the thoroughly biblical, thoroughly Greek pattern of thinking in which its first efforts at formulation were expressed.

4. Further Inferences

As we have seen, the term "salvation," as used in the Bible, has an eschatological reference—it is the final state of well-being which God intended for his creatures and for his servants from the beginning. He "saves" them repeatedly, in the Old Testament. He saves them once for all, through Christ, in the New Testament. But all God's saving acts, even his final act in Christ, lead on to the *state* of salvation which he has planned for them from the beginning, but which has not hitherto been realized because of human sin. The New Testament arrives at this conviction, not by way of logic: "You know all this, having now been told it; *therefore* proceed to assume that your sins are forgiven, and enter the new life." Instead forgiveness and the new life are coeval—as in that strange order of words in Luke 7:47, "Her sins . . . are forgiven, for she loved much; but he who is forgiven little, loves little." It sounds almost as if love were cause, not consequence, of forgiveness—and so sentimentalists incline to take it—when in fact, the hidden springs of love and forgiveness well up from a deep common source, the goodness and mercy, the redeeming and restoring love of God, who loved us before ever we loved him (I John 4:10, 19; Rom. 5:8, 10).

It is because salvation is not only a hope but a realized hope, not only a "far-off, divine event" but a matter of experience, that the term takes on the richly varied meanings given it in the New Testament. In the gospel of Jesus it is still fundamentally "the hope of Israel" (Acts 28:20), the coming reign of God; but this was far from being a political or social dream. In Jesus' teaching it was filled with the rich content of his own religious life. God is not only King but Father. Judaism already recognized this, but of the two Jesus laid far more stress upon the term—and the idea—Father, and gave to it a fuller meaning than other teachers had done. God is our Father in heaven who is *also* King of all the world. His fatherhood is primary and personal; his kingship is, not secondary, but certainly official. His forgiveness of the sinner is direct and immediate, without reference to any offering of sacrifice, and is conditional only upon repentance—though even this is sometimes, in the gospel tradition, taken for granted rather than described. One may "enter into life" not only hereafter, in the age to come, but already, here and now, with the full expectation of salvation in the Day of Judgment and in the everlasting kingdom beyond.

For the early Christian church in Palestine, salvation was still thought of in this twofold way, as an eschatological event but also a present experience. Christ was the Lord of his church, of his cult, present with his followers in their common worship; but he was also at the right hand of God, and would come in glory and power before long to judge the world, rescue his own (his "elect"), and establish the kingdom of God in outward magnificence and splendor. Let men repent, therefore, before that day arrives, and prepare for the divine judgment which will then take place. "Salvation" is the state of "being saved," in preparation for that day (Acts 2:40), as well as the state of bliss that will follow it. The formula is thoroughly biblical, and takes for granted the ministry and "mighty works" of Jesus, his death, resurrection, and exaltation (Acts 4:12, etc.). Whether any profounder meanings were seen in it we cannot say—the documents for this period are late and secondary. Presumably the experience of the earliest Christians included visions of the risen Christ (like Stephen's, Acts 7:55-56), mighty hours of prayer and of spiritual exaltation (2:1-11; 4:23-31; etc.), "signs and wonders," works of healing, restoration, conversion—all interpreted eschatologically as proofs of the nearness of the Parousia, of Christ's immediate coming in power and glory. The early Palestinian Christians had a sense of impending great events; they were living in "the last days"; they were the new or true

Israel, living in the brief period which formed the interval between the beginning of the era of salvation and its full realization (though, as we have already seen, the interval was really one where the two ages overlapped, not—as in "thoroughgoing eschatology"—a hiatus between them).

A deeper meaning, at least the application of the idea to a profounder area of human need, was found by the early Gentile Christians, for whom Christ was not only Teacher, Prophet, Messiah, Head of a community of worshipers, and expected Judge of mankind, but also a present Lord and Savior. He was *Kyrios* in a fuller sense than the cultic *Maran* of the Palestinian Christians, *Sôtêr* in a spiritual and otherworldly sense, and "Son of God" in a sense somewhat more "metaphysical" than "Servant" or "Child" of God in the Old Testament and in Jewish piety. Although many of the Gentile Christians had no doubt once been attached to the Jewish synagogue as "God-fearers" (*theosebomenoi*), and some even as proselytes, it is scarcely to be supposed that every convert to Christianity had come under the influence of Judaism. And it cannot be thought that every convert was required to prepare for baptism by auditing a course of lectures in Old Testament theology or in Judaism; or that every pagan convert to Christianity would forthwith forget all the old familiar religious associations of such terms as *Kyrios, Sôtêr,* and Son of God, and would understand them henceforth in an exclusively Jewish sense. The contrary was the case, as we may infer from what Paul and other writers take for granted, and from the basis of "common Gentile Christianity" which the later books of the New Testament presuppose. For example, there is no doubt that "Son of God" was a title of Christ among Gentile Christians before Paul began his missionary career. It is understood in Mark, our earliest Gospel, written presumably after Paul's career had ended, in a quite non-Pauline sense—that is, without the precise shade of meaning which Paul gave to it. In Mark the Son of God goes about healing the sick, exorcising demons, and performing other "mighty works." The type of piety—the experience of salvation —which lies behind the earliest theology of the Gentile church is one in which "supernaturalism," miracles, the powers of the Spirit, the hunger for immortality (and the assurance of its satisfaction), the warfare between flesh and spirit (and the victory of the spirit), were already significant factors.

Undeniably a new religious ethos was arising in the world, and the new religion addressed itself to the situation which it found among the Gentiles. Certain things which it could take for granted in Jewish Palestine could no longer be taken for granted in the world outside. The belief in one God and one only; the lordship of Christ, not only over his community, but over the whole world, visible and invisible; his victory, not only over local demons and their vile plagues in the villages of Galilee, but over the elemental, cosmic spirits who ruled the high places of the universe and in defiance of God had led mankind astray and into bondage; the danger not merely of contamination with idolatry, but of mortal infection through eating meat obtained from heathen temples (the leftovers from heathen sacrifices)—all this was part of a new world, with new dangers, requiring new remedies, new procedures, new emphases in thought, devotion, and practice. Paul did not create, nor was he the first to face, the problems that arose for Christianity in its new environment. In this new setting "salvation" still meant the future eschatological act of divine redemption, both of the world and of the individual; but it meant, even more, the state of safety, welfare, and well-being of those who were "in the world but not of the world," who lived as citizens of another country, and as metics or exiles in this world. The eschatological emphasis was far from being abandoned, but the problems—and the solutions of the problems—of Christian living in this present world involved an entirely new emphasis and orientation. Salvation meant safety in the midst of moral and spiritual dangers, the assurance of final victory in a never-ending contest with present evils, including, before long, hostile neighbors, hostile public officials, and eventually a hostile world state. The Christian was beset with foes, without and within, not least his own immature and scantily nourished religious and moral nature. But of such stuff martyrs were made, and saints; and the church triumphed, in the end, with its tattered armies of indomitable heroes—plain men and women who had caught a glimpse of what life might be, under God, and could become, in Christ.

Further inferences were drawn as fresh problems arose. One might suppose that the burning question for all Gentile Christians in the fifties and sixties was the permanent validity or invalidity of the Mosaic Law. We derive this impression from the quantitative extent of Paul's letters in the surviving literature of the first century. It *was* a burning question for Paul, and for some others. The Galatians, for example, had apparently been led to suppose that over and above their experience of salvation in Christ and through the Spirit they required, for final "perfection," the added practice of Jewish rites. Paul's pen—or his secretary's—scorches the paper as he writes his refutation of this preposterous theory. In Romans he again develops the idea; for he is writing, not to deal with concrete problems, as in the Corinthian letters, but in order to introduce himself to the Roman Christians, whom he has never seen; and so he writes out of his heart and deals with religious issues as they appear to him, and sets forth a theodicy upon which his whole presentation of the gospel can be based. Nevertheless, in spite of the famous Tübingen theory, and others like it, it is quite doubtful if the rank and file of Gentile Christians in the first century were as strongly drawn to Judaism as Paul seems to imply, or felt the tension caused by a transition from "legalism" to the religion of the gospel as keenly as Paul did. For one thing, the majority had not been nurtured upon the religion of the Mosaic Law; for another, most persons knew nothing of such inner wrestlings and strivings, such plunges into the depths and such soaring to the heights as Paul experienced. For Paul was a mystic born into a rigid creed, destined to find release of soul only in revolt, and satisfaction of mind only in a new, transforming faith. Paul's struggle over the Law is reflected in Rom. 7—though the details of this chapter cannot all be autobiographical. The struggle is idealized, as Augustine idealized his own conversion, and other writers their spiritual experiences, when recalled long after the event. The general character of the situation is clearly reflected in the opening verses of the chapter—this is the part which is so often overlooked in our modern psychoanalytic interpretation of sanctity. But our modern psychoanalytic interpretation inclines to leave out mysticism, the sense of rebirth, the new power that comes, not from a full "analysis" and a careful probing of sin or of long-forgotten emotional disturbances, but from consecration, the new life in Christ, the power of an endless life brought to bear upon a mortal one, the powers of the age to come already operative in this age—and operative not merely upon the level of external things, conditions, and events, but upon soul and spirit, the whole inner constitution of man.

It is one of Paul's boldest figures, and one which at the same time displays his characteristic logic (which often moves *per saltem,* and leaves out the intervening steps), that is found in Rom. 7:1-6. Law is binding only upon the living; at death a person is freed from its regulations and restraints (vs. 1). Similarly, or rather in fact by application of this very principle, since Christians "have died to the law through the body of Christ," they are no longer bound to observe its rules (vs. 4). But he confuses his argument by the illustration he chooses—the right of a widow to marry again (vss. 2-3). He is not thinking of the practical situation, as when in I Cor. 7:8 he advises widows to remain unmarried, in view of the approaching end of the age; the present reference is purely theoretical and logical—but illogical. For in strict logic it is the dead man who is freed from the obligation to observe the law, not his surviving wife; but Paul already has in mind the parallel he wishes to draw (in vs. 4): "You have died to the law . . . so that you may belong to another"—that is, to Christ. It is now the dead husband who is free from the law and at the same time may "remarry"—that is, belong to Christ—though the term "belong to" is more appropriately said of the wife. It is sometimes thought that this purely verbal or analogical type of inference is characteristic of rabbinism, and that Paul imbibed it in his course of study at the feet of Gamaliel in Jerusalem. But it is more than that. It is Oriental picture thinking; it is the kind of inference a poetic or mystical type of mind often instinctively pursues. Preachers sometimes follow it, but in cold type it is far less cogent than in the warm utterance of the exhorter. What Paul is trying to convey is that the new life in Christ leaves sin behind it; whatever analogy may help to bring this out clearly is seized and pressed into service. It is the general effect, the over-all argument, which is persuasive, not the minutely detailed, finely chiseled logic of the case.

As we have already noted, Rom. 7 should never be read apart from Rom. 5–6 and 8. The old life of struggle and defeat—and of ever renewed struggle—is long past; "in Christ" Paul is a new person, and has been so for a long time. Perhaps he idealizes; elsewhere he admits that he has not yet attained, though he has been taken hold of by the Lord—and the Lord's hand is strong and firm (Phil. 3:12). Perhaps his inner transformation was not as complete as he supposed, or wished; perhaps it never is, for any of the saints. Perhaps he went too far in assuming that the same experience was shared by other Christians, who would accordingly know at once what he meant by the words in which he describes the heights and depths of his own inner life, his freedom from the Law, his "death" to its demands, the new principle of life in the Spirit, or "justification" at the bar of God's judgment. His experience with some of these pedestrian Christians must have been thoroughly disillusioning to him. Later generations did not understand him; probably his own did not—though they preserved most of his letters. He was a towering, valiant soul, a spiritual genius whose wide-ranging inner experience has been understood by a few, here and there, during the centuries since—and understood in some slight measure by countless others—but often misinterpreted by those who understood a little and then assumed that they comprehended the whole. For Paul salvation was both a future good and the present guarantee of it; even more, it was the future good and also the present realization of that good, here and now in this present life. It was the "power of God for salvation," for everyone who believed (Rom. 1:16). It was an inner renewal which broke the power of the "flesh" (human nature apart from God, bereft of grace, and infected with sin) and set one free to do the will of God by virtue of the new power of the indwelling Spirit, the indwelling Christ.

5. *Spirituality*

First-century Gentile Christianity moved amazingly far in this direction, as we see from Paul, from John, and from the Epistle to the Hebrews. But it did not move too far. We can observe the extent of this "area," and of its penetration by early Christianity, from the contrast between the New Testament and Philo with his unique and characteristic type of piety—that is, his conception of salvation.

In the doctrine of Philo of Alexandria the Old Testament conception of the sovereignty of God is carried, under a philosophical impulse, to its absolute extreme. God is not only "of purer eyes than to behold evil" (Hab. 1:13), "the high and lofty One that inhabiteth eternity" (Isa. 57:15), but absolute being, and beyond definition. Hence only negative terms can be employed in describing him—he is *not* this, *not* that, since our human concepts are inadequate for positive statements about him. It is probable that mystical experience lies behind this high, transcendental philosophy; Philo certainly makes use of a number of "mystery" terms current in religious circles in the ancient world, though without implying, any more than Paul does, that he was ever initiated in a pagan cult—that idea is preposterous. Yet for all his mysticism Philo began by trying to explain—or to explain away—the crude ideas of God still surviving in the earlier parts of the Old Testament, and the traditional, sometimes poetical, language found in the later books. (If he had only known the method of historical criticism, most of his problems would have disappeared.) His indebtedness to older and still current philosophies, for example to Stoicism (especially the allegorization of myth, but also its ethical terminology), to Platonism (the doctrine of the reality of "ideas," of the "ideal" world), and likewise to Neo-Pythagoreanism (the body the prison of the soul, etc.), was very great, though he was also a philosopher in his own right, as Harry A. Wolfson is the latest to demonstrate. His philosophy was a combination of divinely revealed truth with human speculation—a combination eagerly sought in the Hellenistic age, and destined to be enormously influential upon later patristic and medieval theology.

As absolute being, God has no direct contacts with the world. Philo "cannot think of the infinite as manifested in the finite" (E. Caird). Yet God as creator and maintainer of the universe *must* be related to his creation; this relation takes place through his Powers, chief of whom (or of which) is the Logos. According to the Stoic distinction, the Logos is both *endiathetos* (innate in the mind as thought or reason) and *prophorikos* (expressed, uttered, spoken as word); whether "uttered or unexpressed," the Logos is—for Philo as for the Stoics —the rational principle immanent in man and in the universe. The Logos is both the reason which sustains all things (Wisd. 6–12; cf. Col. 1:17, "in him all things hold together," *sunestêke*) and the spoken word of Gen. 1 and elsewhere in the Old Testament: "And God *said*, Let there be light, . . . a firmament, . . ." and all created things. Thus the Logos is the mediator between God and the created universe, and the agent through whom it was brought into existence and is still maintained (cf. Heb. 1:2-3a). In describing this first and foremost of the divine Powers, Philo uses a variety of figures, some of them derived from scripture. The question arises, especially for Christian students, whether or not Philo thought of the Logos as personal. The answer seems to be both Yes and No. As an angelic being (thinking scripturally) the Word of God has no more substantial existence than the angels of the Old Testament or the spoken word of God. And yet even in the Old Testament the "word" of God is sometimes almost a thing apart from the divine Speaker—for example, "My word . . . shall not return to me void" (Isa. 55:11). And when the word and the wisdom of God are identified, and wisdom is thought of poetically (as in Prov. 8:22-31; cf. Wisd. 7:22 ff.), the philosophical—and also primitive—idea of the *demiurge* comes uppermost; the Logos is then referred to as a person or being distinct from God. Yet for Philo the fundamental principle is surely that the Logos, like the creation which it sustains, is completely dependent upon God, and could not conceivably exist apart from him (if God ceased to be, neither the creation nor the Logos would survive). The problem was certainly considered by Philo, as when he makes the Logos say: "I stand between the Lord and you [like Moses—cf. Deut. 5:5], I who am neither uncreated like God nor created like you, but midway between the two extremes, a hostage to both sides" (*Who Is the Heir of Divine Things* 206 = ch. 42). This may sound "meaningless," as Dr. Nairne observes; but what Philo has in mind is the *logos endiathetos,* created (like thought) yet not created ("like you"); independent to the extent of being capable of expression, utterance, projection, as a divine command; not a physical creation, but an intellectual creation; and yet wholly dependent upon God and inseparable from him. The Logos, like God himself, can be defined only (a) poetically, by a wealth of figures or analogies, or (b) metaphysically, by a series of negations—"not uncreated, . . . not a creature like you."

Since Philo shared the Neo-Pythagorean, Orphic, ascetic views of the body current once more in the Hellenistic age, reviving now and destined to affect all later Greek (or Greco-Roman) philosophy and religion, he looked upon man as "a soul defiled by a body." Only by abandoning his physical nature, and indeed much of his sinful, defiled personality, can man be saved—not, as John stated it, "in the world" but "not of the world" (John 17:11, 15, 16), but saved "out of the world" (cf. I Cor. 5:10; 3:15). With such a doctrine of salvation neither the Old Testament nor the New can agree. The body is sacred, made in God's image; it is even the "temple" of God or of his Holy Spirit (I Cor. 3:16-17; II Cor. 6:16); it must be preserved, sanctified, saved —hence Paul's doctrine of the spiritual "body." In holding a doctrine of pure incorporeality Philo went so far in the direction of Greek syncretism, Gnosticism, or what was later to become Neo-Platonism, that he left behind him, in principle, the bounds of Judaism. Paul, John, and the author of Hebrews, though they have many contacts with Philo, never went as far as he did in the direction of pure "spirituality."

Philo may have influenced the author of the Fourth Gospel, and perhaps the author of Hebrews; more likely the influence which they undoubtedly reflect was derived from the type of philosophy or "school" of spiritual exegesis of the Old Testament which Philo represents. It is most unlikely that he influenced Paul—and yet there are resemblances. In fact Paul's very similar ideas and likewise the examples of his exegesis clinch the argument that it was not Philo who influenced the New Testament but the "school" or type of philosophy which he represented. And this was very widespread indeed, not limited to Alexandrian Judaism but found elsewhere in the Jewish Diaspora, one may assume, and fairly ubiquitous among inquiring religious minds and "seekers after God" in the first century. It was the "ethos" to which we have referred—the longing of the spiritually minded for another world, a "city which has foundations, whose builder and maker is God" (Heb. 11:10), a commonwealth (*politeuma*) in heaven (Phil. 3:20), with release from fate, death, moral weakness, and all those deprivations and denials of man's inner freedom which the old religions (traditional Judaism included) only amplified and increased.

There may be a natural immortality of the soul; some passages of the New Testament seem to assume that there is—for the soul must survive death if it is to face the final judgment—but the ancient world in general was far from convinced of it. Hence the rites, the mysteries, the philosophies and cults that undertook to guarantee it. Coming into that world, primitive Christianity brought the message of its gospel: "Christ is risen!" (cf. Mark 16:6; I Cor. 15). "If any one is in Christ, he is a new creation" (II Cor. 5:17). "In him was life, and the life was the light of men" (John 1:4). It is surprising how little of formal statement of the content of salvation is to be found in the Gospels, even in John, the most Hellenistic of the four. Yet the whole spirit, the whole tone—and the overtones—of the Fourth Gospel convey the sense of realized salvation, here and now, which is to continue hereafter. "This is eternal life, that they know thee, the only true God, and Jesus Christ whom thou hast sent" (John 17:3). This knowledge is not something formal or factual, but personal; it is not even the mysterious *gnosis* of the Gnostics, an esoteric lore including cosmology, cosmogony, the nature of the soul, and so on, with "salvation" viewed as release from the flesh or from the body or from the realm of matter. Salvation is still related to the old eschatological hope—the dead will rise (John 5:25); the new life is now dawning, the era of the Spirit (4:23-24). But the true knowledge which Christians possess (unlike Paul, John does not use the word "faith") is something immediately effective and transforming. It is nothing less than the awareness of eternal life, here and now, and already partially realized under the conditions of this life. All this is in Christ, from Christ, in utter dependence upon his word, his person, his own victorious life in which he had "overcome the world" (John 16:33), defeated "the prince of this world" and all the powers of darkness (12:31; 14:30; 16:11). By sharing in him, by partaking of his "flesh," sacramentally or mystically (6:25-58), the eternal life which was with God from the beginning is conveyed to those who are "born anew" (3:3; 1:13) in Christ. This conception of salvation, though not universal in the second century, certainly laid the foundation for later Catholic theology, with its doctrine of the Incarnation, the sacraments (baptismal regeneration and the real presence of Christ in the Eucharist), and eternal life as the consequence of participation, sacramentally, in the incarnate life of God the Son.

XI

The Doctrine of the Church

1. *The Eschatological Community*

WE are now in a position to begin to see (*a*) what was basic and fundamental to both Judaism (as the formal religion of the Old Testament, in its first-century form) and early Christianity—that is, what primitive Christianity took for granted, without question or argument, as true in the revealed religion of the past—and (*b*) what was new and distinctive in the thought of the New Testament. And yet what was new in it was new primarily by way of emphasis, and took for granted the principle that the new was the "fulfillment" or completion of the old—and ought therefore to be accepted by all believers in the old.

It was only gradually, and as the result of the first stages in the separation of church from synagogue, with its accompanying controversy and persecution, that the church came to view itself as the New Israel, the True Israel, the Remnant foretold by prophecy, the congregation of the Messiah; for the concept still reflects the conditions within Palestinian Judaism. The church was at first only a "sect" within Judaism; these were "Christian Jews," not "Jewish Christians," a particular group of messianists who recognized in Jesus of Nazareth, especially in the risen and glorified Jesus, the true Messiah of Israel. In all other respects they viewed themselves as loyal, faithful Jews— as the book of Acts makes clear, and as one may read between the lines of Paul's letters, and as the Synoptic Gospels (Greek and Gentile though they are) reflect the situation in the Palestinian communities in which the Synoptic tradition had been handed down. In other words the earliest conception of the church which we are able to trace is an *eschatological* conception. The church is the community of those who have recognized and accepted Jesus as Messiah and Lord, They do not make up the church—they only belong to it. The church *is* the eschatological community; it is the "church of the latter days," indeed of the "last" days, since the anticipated interval between the resurrection of Christ and his final parousia is thought to be extremely brief. The New Testament doctrine of the church illustrates conspicuously the three principles which have been stressed throughout this volume: (1) eschatological orientation (relevance to the future); (2) the Jewish background, even the Jewish nature of the primitive community; (3) the process of transition to a fuller expression in terms of Hellenistic religious concepts.

The New Testament doctrine of the church is thus a "high" doctrine, as contrasted with modern theories which would make of early Christianity simply the loosely organized, or wholly unorganized, group of the "followers" of Jesus. The earliest Christian group was made up of "followers" of Jesus, true enough; but they were persons who (*a*) already belonged to the privileged society of Israel (either by birth or as proselytes), were members of the sacred covenant, and also, therefore, inheritors of the promises; and who in addition were (*b*) followers of Jesus as the promised Messiah, or "Messiah designate," and as members of his fellowship were (either in anticipation or in actual realization) already members of the New Israel, the Israel of the latter days, destined for admission and membership in the kingdom of God which was about to be set up in place of the present world order. Before the Crucifixion they could "rejoice" that their names were "written in heaven" (Luke 10:20), that they belonged to the elect of the coming messianic time, that among the many who were "called" they belonged to the few who were "chosen" (Matt. 22:14). They might easily assume, therefore, that they were entitled to inquire which among them was to be "greatest in the kingdom" (Mark 9:34; Matt. 18:1); two of their number might even naïvely request the privilege of sitting at Christ's right and left hand "in his glory" (Mark 10:37). After the Crucifixion and the Resurrection, when Jesus had entered "into his glory" (Luke 24:26), they were still members of the messianic community, whose full manifestation was now expected to follow the "return" of the Risen Lord in "power and great glory" (Matt. 24:30).

For the church was now viewed as not only the New Israel, but the True Israel, the "holy remnant" which had inherited the promises and privileges of the old People of God. The church was indeed the people of God in a special and final sense; the old "Israel after the flesh" (I Cor. 10:18 A.S.V.) was supplanted by the new, true Israel "after the Spirit." Only those were now members of the true Israel who had been admitted upon a basis of faith, not upon the basis of physical descent from Abraham or by virtue of circumcision and observance of the Law. This new development of ideas we find in Paul, but it is taken for granted by Paul as something commonly known and recognized by all Gentile Christians. It may accordingly be assumed that the principle goes back a long way before Paul, and was probably the common view of the earliest "Hellenist" Christians, even in Palestine, and certainly in Antioch and elsewhere—in fact wherever the gospel had been presented to and accepted by pagans without their first becoming proselytes to Judaism (Acts 8:4-17; 8:26-39; 10:1–11:18; 11:20-21).

The popular nineteenth-century view that Jesus "founded" the church has no more support in the New Testament than the equally popular view (in secular circles) that Jesus was the "Founder" of a religion known as Christianity. Neither Pentecost, nor the Resurrection, nor the Last Supper, nor the Sermon on the Mount, nor the appointment of the Twelve, nor Jesus' own baptism, nor his birth, marked the "birthday of the church." It had no date of birth, for it was continuous with the Old Covenant, and was in strict continuity with the "Israel of God" known from of old. A first-century Christian would not have understood the question, "When did Jesus found the church?" As much of a precise dating of the emergence of the church as one can find in the New Testament is probably the "late" passage in Matthew (16:18): "On this rock I *will build* my church." This seems to point forward, probably to the Resurrection, when Peter was to be the first witness of that fact (I Cor. 15:4-5); certainly in Matthew's view the church had not yet been "founded" when Jesus uttered these words. And yet the Resurrection was not the "founding" of the church, but a new and indispensable stage in its realization, the crucial stage (as the New Testament views it) in the transition from the old earthly Israel to the new spiritual fellowship.

2. *The Ministry*

The earliest form of the ministry was likewise thoroughly Jewish. The apostles were "emissaries" of the local church as well as of the risen Lord (cf. Acts 8:14; 11:22-30; 13:3; 15:33; etc.: "they sent . . ."). The ministry of the "deacons" in Acts 6:1-6 (they are not called deacons, but this is the traditional term) was intended, according to the author of Acts, to set the apostles completely free for "prayer and . . . the ministry of the word"; the Seven were to supervise the "daily distribution" of food—presumably among the complaining Hellenists (Greek-speaking Christian Jews). The view of Johannes Weiss, that they were the heads of the Hellenist wing of the Jerusalem church, as the Twelve headed the Hebrew (Aramaic-speaking) wing, is not improbable. That they did not confine themselves to the work of charitable ministration is clear from what follows: Stephen worked miracles, disputed in the synagogues, and preached; Philip preached in Samaria, on the route to Gaza, at Azotus, and up along the coast to Caesarea. In brief, the book of Acts itself represents the Seven as evangelists (cf. 21:8) and not merely as charity officers of the Jerusalem church.

In Acts 15 "the apostles and the elders" appear. Elders are everywhere characteristic of Jewish organization; they are not synagogue officers only, but the elders of the Jewish community, whose function in public worship (whenever they are called upon to function) is only a natural part of their office in the community. The popular idea that the ancient synagogue was organized like a modern Protestant congregation, with a minister and a vestry or board of elders or deacons, is quite inadequate. The head of the Jewish congregation was a layman or a group of laymen—the "elders" of the community, who were literally older men. The "ruler of the synagogue" was not unlike the modern "president" of the synagogue, of the congregation. The "preacher" was not really a preacher, but an expounder of scripture, and he might be either a layman or a scribe or perhaps a priest. A "rabbi" (the later title of the scribe) was primarily a teacher, and was not a priest at all. His "ordination" (a later rite) was not to the priesthood (which was impossible; one had to be born a priest), but to the office of teacher, expounder of the Law, and guide to the congregation. Thus in a way he was a "preacher," but not in the modern Christian sense, with a sermon each Sunday and other addresses in between, though the Reformed Synagogue of today does approximate the current Protestant system. Thus the elders of the early Palestinian Christian church were presumably the older men in the community, gathered about the apostles as the elders of Israel had surrounded and assisted Moses (Exod. 19:7; 24:1-18). Their duties included the decision of serious questions—as here in Acts 15, the terms of admission of Gentiles to the church.

It must be recognized of course that the book of Acts views the conditions within the early Palestinian Christian community, including its ministry, from the vantage point of later decades, presumably from the time of Domitian—perhaps, more explicitly, from the last decade of the century. Moreover, it presents the history from an apologetic angle; Luke is endeavoring to prove, both in Volume I (the Gospel) and in Volume II (the book of Acts), that neither Christ nor his followers have been revolutionists, that Christianity (as a sect in Judaism) is entitled to the same protection afforded by the government to that ancient and well-known *religio licita*. Hence Luke may be suspected of underlining the Jewish nature of the early Palestinian church. Underlining, yes; but not of creating his facts. For the whole New Testament supports the view that the earliest Christianity was Jewish, that its earliest doctrines arose within the Jewish pattern of religious thought, that its very vocabulary was Jewish, and remained Jewish in considerable measure even after it launched itself independently in the Roman world. Its Greek was mainly "Jewish Greek," as its Bible was the Greek translation of the Hebrew scriptures; its earliest prayers were Jewish prayers, revised and amplified; its organization and ministry were patterned, not upon Greek or secular models—let alone the "mystery religions"—but upon the Jewish synagogue. For all these reasons, and still others that might be given, Luke was undoubtedly right in representing early Palestinian Christianity as he does in Acts 1–15. Where he goes beyond the evidence of his own early sources (which are embedded in these chapters), and tends to become "programmatic," it is in describing the spread of the church as the result of an official propaganda emanating from Jerusalem, with the Jerusalem church in control of the whole Christian movement—as Rome controlled the secular *orbis terrarum*. This may have been, doubtless was, the situation within Palestine—that is, in Jewish territory—though the "ecumenical" epistle in Acts 15:23-29 is addressed to "the brethren who are of the Gentiles in Antioch and Syria and Cilicia." The authorities of the Jerusalem church would naturally parallel those of orthodox Judaism: the high priest, the other priests, and the Levites had charge of the temple worship; the high priest, the sanhedrin, the scribes and elders, exercised that modicum of authority still retained, for most administrative purposes, under the Romans; the Christian "apostles and elders" form the Christian sanhedrin, presided over by the Christian high priest, James the brother of the Lord. Thus the *local* polity of the Palestinian church was presbyterian, while the ideal polity of the church as a *whole*—as represented by the mother church in Jerusalem—was episcopal. But this was by no means either a "monarchical" or a "monarchial" episcopacy (as advocated by Ignatius a few years later). James the Lord's brother is not really a high priest, nor an archbishop, nor even, perhaps, a bishop—let alone a pope. He is simply the presiding officer of the Jerusalem presbytery. And when Matthias was chosen to take the place of Judas (Acts 1:15-26), the act was that of the whole body—and was therefore congregational!—or rather of the Spirit, present in the body and exercising his choice through the casting of the lots—and therefore charismatic!

When we turn to other books of the New Testament, we find a variety of terms in use, a variety which continues in the other earliest Christian writings outside the canon. Paul's epistle to the Philippians, for example, is addressed "To all the saints . . . at Philippi, with the bishops and deacons" (Phil. 1:1). In I Cor. 12:28 a list appears: apostles, prophets, teachers, workers of miracles, healers, helpers, administrators, speakers in various kinds of tongues. From such evidence, and more of the same kind found elsewhere in the earliest Christian literature, the late Canon B. H. Streeter concluded that a wide-ranging variety characterized the ministry of the church during the first century of its history. Each of the various areas had its own type of ministry, some patterned on the synagogue, others freer (the "charismatic" type, for example), and none bound by any preconceived or officially designated order which had been planned in advance. Perhaps Streeter went too far; perhaps some of the details in his evidence need to be revised—or abandoned. But the general argument of his famous book is incontrovertible, and is supported by the research and the conclusions of other scholars. One chief value of his work is that he made it impossible any longer to argue that one sole and exclusive type of ministry prevailed from the start, or had been authorized in advance by our Lord, or that only one type could be viewed as classical and normative, in contrast with which all others were only local or temporary aberrations. No old-fashioned assumption that the "primitive" ministry was *either* presbyterian *or* episcopal *or* congregational *or* "charismatic"—a view which even Lightfoot, Hort, Hatch, and a whole series of eminent scholars had not succeeded in dislodging in the English-speaking world —can now be maintained, thanks to Streeter. Even conservative scholars (like Bishop Kenneth E. Kirk or Dom Gregory Dix) now recognize that there was variety—that is, variation—though the fundamental or central office of the apostolate is not questioned. Indeed the prevailing view now is that the whole early ministry was "functional"—a view which Paul himself suggested in the verses that follow our last quotation from him (see I Cor. 12:29-30). Nothing could be antecedently more probable. The church of the first century was a missionary church, and had to adapt itself to conditions as they already existed. Moreover it was a liturgical church, at a date earlier than we used to assume. The purely "pneumatic," ecstatic, "charismatic," enthusiastic, Spirit-guided worship of some of the Pauline churches—for example in Corinth— must have been exceptional. Paul himself discouraged their excesses (I Cor. 12–14). A sober Palestinian congregation of Christian Jews worshiping in their "ecclesia" would have no more need for an "interpreter of tongues" than for a modern rural dean or for a Roman archdeacon of the days of Jerome! Above all, the eschatological outlook of the early church made for much less emphasis upon a settled, amply supported ministry than one finds later on, even as early as the Didache (chs. 11–13, 15). The center of the church's life was not found in officialdom, in an ecclesiastical hierarchy or a state-church bureaucracy, as in medieval Rome or Byzantium, or elsewhere. The center of the church's life was in worship. Here men came into real and living contact with the heavenly *Kyrios Christos,* who existed both in heaven and in the midst of his ecclesia here on earth; back of Paul's mystical "in Christ" is this vital experience of the Christian worship, as Wilhelm Bousset pointed out.

The "functions" of the ministry were thus twofold: (1) the conduct of the common worship, including the prayers—some of them fixed, as in the synagogue, some of them free, as Justin Martyr implies (*Apol.* 65:2, 67:5; cf. Did. 10:7)—but also including the reading of scripture, its exposition in homilies, evangelistic preaching, and at least the overseeing, if not the actual administration, of the sacraments, Baptism and the Supper; and (2) the administration of affairs belonging to the community in its relations with the civil authorities, the adjudication or settlement of differences between church members, the discipline of offenders. These functions of the church's officers or ministers are not all stated in so many words in the New Testament; but they may be read between the lines, or inferred back from the duties actually laid upon the church's ministers as soon as church orders, manuals, directoria, and collections of canons came into use. The Pastoral epistles contain many directions for the ministry, and it is not illegitimate or unreasonable to infer that some of them must have been in force long before the date (*ca.* A.D. 95-105) of those post-Pauline documents.

The "charismatic" endowments of particular individuals or congregations can scarcely have been general or common, though there is evidence that "prophets" continued their functions long into the second century, at least in remote places (Montanism, the Didache). Paul's great principle prevailed—the true test of prophecy as of glossolaly was whether or not it served the welfare of the whole church, the whole congregation (I Cor. 12; 14). The soberer gifts of administration and exposition were as much the expression of the Spirit's guidance as the more spectacular gifts of "tongues" and prophecy. Moreover, everything (in the church's worship) must be done "decently and in order" (14:40). Wherever the stately service of the synagogue formed the background of Christian worship, it may be assumed that Paul's final admonition would be effective. Whether or not this was so in Corinth remains a question. They were a turbulent congregation, as Clement's epistle implies (I Clem., *ca.* A.D. 98). It can scarcely be supposed that "speaking in tongues" was common throughout the early church. The author's interpretation of the phenomenon at Pentecost in Acts 2 is generally thought to read too much of later Gentile behavior into the record.

Though there are very few references to ordination (e.g. I Tim. 4: 14), the custom of solemn designation and appointment, or delegation, by the laying on of hands, was a common religious practice, and must have been followed from an early date (cf. Acts 13:3). (Jewish ordination to the rabbinate seems to have been later.) But the laying on of hands was not restricted to ordination. The Lord had laid his hands on the sick and healed them. So did the apostles. And yet the appointment of the apostles by the Lord himself is not described in the New Testament as accompanied by this manual act (cf. Mark 3:14; Matt. 28: 18-20; John 20:22-23; Acts 1:8). But the absence of specific reference to ordination is quite characteristic of the New Testament, which is by no means a collection of documents for the constitutional history of the Christian church. The endless arguments over "valid" and "invalid" ordination which have distressed all Christendom for the past three centuries—the very term "valid" is a lawyer's invention, and was thrown into the controversy by Roman legists—have no foundation, nor any solution, in the New Testament. But all historical probability is certainly on the side of those who assume that some such form as the laying on of hands accompanied ordination, from the time that ordination took place (e.g. Acts 6:6). But that this proves the *modern* theory of "apostolic succession"—which is very different from the ancient theory—is another matter. Apostolic authority was very real; it is written all over the New Testament epistles, and the book of Acts as well. The delegation of such authority is also taken for granted, as in the Pastoral epistles. But the theory of succession is later, both the ancient theory of succession in sees with its guarantee of a sound tradition of doctrine, and the medieval or modern theory of tactual succession, guaranteeing validity in sacramental ministration. Neither theory had any place in the eschatological community of the New Israel, the "church of the latter days" which eagerly awaited the return of the Lord from heaven, the last judgment, and the inauguration of the reign of God in full and final splendor upon a transformed earth.

3. *Baptism*

The origin of Christian baptism seems to have been "the baptism" of John (Acts 10:37). Various theories of the significance of John's baptism have been held, all the way from that of a Greco-Roman or Hellenistic ceremony of lustration (approximately Josephus' view) to a national cleansing before the arrival of the Messiah and the Day of Judgment; John has even been viewed as an Essene. It was, presumably, like all Jewish baptisms, self-administered. Although the New Testament describes it in quasi-Christian terms (e.g. Mark 1:4-5), its primary significance as a "baptism of repentance" seems indubitable. Whether the remission of sins was only symbolized or was sacramentally "sealed" by the rite is not clear; perhaps the remission of sins is only a Christian "tag," added in the course of tradition to the phrase "baptism of repentance" (*baptisma metanoias eis aphesin hamartiôn*), though it is difficult to understand either the baptism or the repentance without reference to sins. What else were John's hearers to repent of? Was it "sinful*ness*"? That is too modern, too Protestant, and for the first century too Pauline a conception to suit the situation; moreover the account in the earliest Gospel rules it out (Mark 1:4, "sins"; vs. 5, "confessing their sins"). To suppose that John's "baptism" was a mechanical process of confession-baptism-remission is to ignore both the primitive realism of ancient religion and the specific Judaism of John. The three steps all sprang from, were motivated by, and were consequent upon the initial act of repentance. God forgives men's sins upon repentance, but repentance is not without confession—the acknowledgment not only of "sinfulness" but of the actual sins. The self-baptism in the waters of the Jordan betokened, symbolized, in some sense probably made effective the inner cleansing which repentance inaugurated. Our tendency is to inquire the precise order of thought and of performance; what concerned John's hearers, and no doubt John himself, was the total act of confession-baptism-remission, the whole act which was inspired by repentance or "turning" (*teshubah*) from one's sins. And this total act, inspired by repentance, had reference to the coming judgment—it was a "messianic," or, better, an "eschatological" event; it was the appropriate response to John's proclamation of the coming Judge.

Ever since the earliest Gospel was written, and probably ever since the Christian tradition was first handed down—that is, ever since the earliest Christians were required to take some attitude, favorable or unfavorable, to John—that prophet's appearing and message have been interpreted from a Christian point of view. He has been uniformly described as the "forerunner" of Christ, the prophet who heralded the coming of the Greater One and "prepared" the way for him. That John did *not* himself recognize Jesus as the Messiah (contrast John 1:26-36) is clear from the older tradition preserved in Q. But it is a serious question if the "Coming One" whom John announced was really the Messiah, and not, rather, the heavenly Judge.

A comparison of the three Synoptic accounts of John's message (Mark 1:7-8; Luke 3:16-17; Matt. 3:11-12) makes it probable that in the oldest form of the tradition his "messianic" preaching was summed up as follows:

I baptize you with water . . . , but he who is coming . . . is mightier than I, whose sandals I am not worthy to carry; he will baptize you *with fire.* His winnowing fork is in his hand, and he will clear his threshing floor and gather his wheat into the granary, but the chaff he will burn with unquenchable fire.

John's message was a message of fire—of impending judgment. He took up where Malachi left off, the last of the prophets in the Old Testament canon (4:1):

> Behold, the day cometh,
>   it burneth as a furnace;
> and all the proud,
>   and all that work wickedness,
>   shall be stubble:
> and the day that cometh shall burn them up,
>   saith the Lord of hosts,
> that it shall leave them neither root nor branch.

This judgment was to be executed by the "coming one," either "my messenger," "the messenger of the covenant," or the Lord himself (3:1-3, 5,), who will "suddenly come to his temple," and will be "like a refiner's fire." John is a prophet of judgment, like Malachi; it is only later Christian interpretation which has made him the forerunner of Christ—so much so that Matthew even places on John's lips words which belong to Jesus (3:3), while the Fourth Evangelist, in a polemic which runs all through his opening chapters, has John pass from the stage of history with an incomparable "last line" of perfect testimony, "He must increase, but I must decrease" (3:30).

The striking feature of John's baptism was his requirement of the rite on the part of born Jews, who had presumably suffered no defiling contacts with idolatry. They were to undergo the same "washing of repentance" that proselytes received at the time of their acceptance of the Jewish law and initiation into Judaism by circumcision. But the words of the prophet were authoritative (Mark 11:27-33; Luke 7:28), and had to be accepted as "from God." In order to "fulfill all righteousness" (Matt. 3:15), to do all that God had declared to be his will, it was necessary for everyone—Jew and pagan alike—to repent and be baptized "for the washing away of sins." That John's movement long survived his death is clear from Acts 18:25; 19:3, and also from the polemic in John 1-3. Its still later survival, among the Mandaeans, or the various "baptist" sects described by Epiphanius, is further evidence of its great influence and wide spread in the first century. By the fifth century, however, this influence had waned, or had been confined to one sect (if the Mandaean religion is that old); the theory that John's followers looked upon him as the Messiah is about on a par with the view, ridiculed by Jerome, that the "Herodians" believed Herod to be the Christ.

If we attempt to sum up the evidence of the New Testament on the subject of baptism, fully recognizing the incompleteness of the data and the uncertainty of later interpretation upon some points, we may say:

1. Many early converts, especially in Palestine, had already received the baptism of John. To them baptism meant the symbolic—but real—washing away (or "putting away") of their sins.

2. Many, especially in the pagan world, had already been baptized as proselytes to Judaism. To them it meant the removal of defilement contracted through contact with idolatry.

3. The origin of the distinctively *Christian* practice goes back to the earliest apostolic days—naturally without an explicitly formulated theology, for there was no such thing as theology, and indeed no need was felt for one, in the Jewish or Christian Jewish world at that time.

4. The original meaning of the rite was *a washing away of sins,*

following repentance, as in John's baptism, and as in the case of Jewish proselyte baptism, though it could not long remain at this level. The whole significance of Christian baptism, as distinct from others, was that it was "in [not into] the name of Christ"; that is, it made a man a Christian, not a Jew or a follower of John; and this meant that he became a disciple of Christ, was committed to follow his teaching, to look forward to his coming as the glorified Messiah, to spread his gospel, and to submit his whole way of life to "the commandments and ordinances of the Lord." This was no doubt the point at which baptism became *the sacrament of initiation* into the church, the New Israel, and hence was required of all—Jews as well as Gentiles, followers of John, and all others. From now on baptism was the normal mode of admission into the Christian body, and it is so represented in the book of Acts and in the Gospel of John and elsewhere in the New Testament.

5. Paul's great contribution was the opening up of profounder depths of meaning in the Christian experience of salvation. As Johannes Weiss held, his theology was "a theology of conversion and of mission," and his great doctrine of the church as Christ's body, and likewise his description of salvation in terms of rebirth, led directly to the later Catholic doctrine of baptismal regeneration. It was Paul, no doubt, or the Gentile Christianity associated with him, that made of baptism the *sacrament of regeneration,* of a new life. The Christian "died with Christ" and "rose again in newness of life"—the parallel between Christ's death, burial, and resurrection and the immersion of the convert and his emergence as a Christian is the clue to this great metaphor of Paul (Rom. 6:3-11). At any rate, this is a third stage in the development of the doctrine of Holy Baptism in the New Testament, and seems to be derived from Gentile Christianity, probably from Paul.

6. At the same time, and later, in "common Gentile Christianity" outside the Pauline sphere—and to some extent even within it—the older language continued in use. Justin wrote, a century after Paul, "I will relate how we dedicated ourselves to God *when we had been made new* through Christ." The undertaking to live the Christian life, morally and devotionally, come first, as it does in later practice, when

people were urged to defer baptism until they had first proved their ability to live without grave sin, and when sponsors were required to attest the previous conduct of the candidate. All this looks as if the church generally did not take the Pauline doctrine in full earnest, and as if the doctrine had proved somewhat too heroic or too confident for the majority of Christians.

7. Finally, the whole New Testament, and following it the earliest noncanonical Christian literature, stresses the *ethical* presuppositions of the rite. Not only must the candidate for baptism renounce his sins, and prove himself a disciple of the Christian way, but after his baptism he must hold most loyally and tenaciously to his Christian profession. There was no second baptism, and, for many teachers and groups of Christians, no "second chance" of any kind, if a man fell away into sin or apostasy or gave way under the stress of persecution (Heb. 10: 26-39). Here the ethical standard and the test of true faith go hand in hand—and the rigidity of the requirement (as Paul Wernle pointed out long ago in his book, *Der Christ und die Sünde bei Paulus,* 1897) is largely owing to the refusal of Paul to recognize, at least in theory, the possibility of postbaptismal sin. But the church had to recognize it, practically, and so devised a system of penitence, of confession, penance, and restoration, which would meet this situation. And it did so— contrary to the popular modern assumption—without lowering the "heroic" ethics of Paul, or of the New Testament in general, or of Jesus himself as set forth in the gospel.

Much of our reconstruction of the history is by hypothesis; so is our modern interpretation of the meaning which baptism held for the earliest Christians, at many points. But it is hardly possible to exaggerate the importance of the rite, in more than one area of primitive Christianity; and it seems to have been stressed equally in Christian Jewish and in Gentile Christian circles. It was the mark of the Christian and set him off from other men. In this sense he was baptized "into" Christ—that is, became a Christian, a follower of Christ's "way," a member of his cult, and henceforth belonged to him. That, I believe, is what being baptized "in the name of Christ" or "into Christ" would mean to almost anyone who heard the term in the first century.

4. *The Eucharist*

The word Eucharist ("thanksgiving"), though not used of the Lord's Supper in any passage in the New Testament, is found with this meaning in such early writings as the Didache (ch. 9), the letters of Ignatius (Philad. 4; Smyrn. 6), and the *Apology* of Justin (I. 66) who uses it of the consecrated elements over which the thanksgiving has been pronounced. The language is undoubtedly old, and its meaning is embedded not only in the accounts of the Last Supper but also in the stories of the feeding of the multitude.

There are four accounts of the institution of the rite, three in the Synoptic Gospels and one in Paul (Matt. 26:26-30; Mark 14:22-25; Luke 22:15-20; I Cor. 11:23-26). Since Matthew and Luke are dependent upon Mark (the theory of a special source followed by Luke in his passion narrative is very questionable), the sources amount in fact to two, though both are traditional and go back some way behind the dates of Mark (*ca.* A.D. 68) and First Corinthians (*ca.* A.D. 55). Since they do not greatly differ, it is to be supposed that both have a common origin in the tradition of the primitive Palestinian church.

PAUL	MARK
For I received [*parelabon*] from the Lord what I also delivered to you, that the Lord Jesus on the night when he was betrayed took bread, and when he had given thanks, he broke it, and said,	And as they were eating, he took bread, and blessed, and broke it, and gave it to them, and said,
"This is my body which is broken [omit "broken"? or read "given"?] for you. Do this in remembrance of me." In the same way also the cup, after supper,	"Take; this is my body."
	And he took a cup, and when he had given thanks he gave it to them, and they all drank of it.
saying,	And he said to them,
"This cup is the new covenant in my blood.	"This is my blood of the [*new?*] covenant, which is poured out for many.

Do this, as often as you drink
it, in remembrance of me."

For as often as you eat this
bread and drink the cup,
you proclaim the Lord's death
until he comes.

Truly, I say to you, I shall not
drink again [omit "again"?] of the
fruit of the vine until that day
when I drink it new in the kingdom
of God."

A comparison of these two earliest accounts with those found in Luke and Matthew will disclose at once the fact that the narrative was traditional; Matthew retains the Marcan account with the least revision: " 'Take, *eat;* this is my body.' . . . a cup . . . , saying, *'Drink of it, all of you* [this is narrative, in Mark]; . . . for many *for the forgiveness of sins . . . this* fruit of the vine . . . drink it new *with you* in *my Father's* kingdom.' " Luke's account paraphrases—he is the Hellenistic historian telling a vivid and sublime story. He transfers the saying at the end, Jesus' vow not to drink wine until he drinks it new in the kingdom of God, to the beginning of the narrative, gives it an appropriate introduction (vs. 15), and makes it refer to the Passover, not merely to the wine. (It is noteworthy that the same textual phenomena are observable; some manuscripts omit the word "again.") Then in verse 18 the vow is repeated—clearly Luke thinks of Jesus as *not* participating in the Passover meal nor drinking the wine, though verses 7-14 equally clearly emphasize Jesus' anticipation of it. The "longer reading" (vss. 19*b*-20) closely resembles the narrative found in First Corinthians and probably represents an early attempt to complete what must have looked like a fragmentary and incomplete account of the institution of the Supper. Indeed, Luke left a lacuna here, if he omitted verses 23-24 of Mark—though he went on with his own prophecy of the betrayal, Luke 22:21-23, which is based on Mark 14:18-21. *Why* Luke omitted the equivalent of Mark's verses 23-24, if the "shorter reading" is to be preferred, we cannot tell, though the sacrificial language may have repelled him, both on historical and on religious grounds. It has often been remarked that Luke had no doctrine of the Atonement. Further evidence for this observation is provided in verse 27, just below, where Luke pointedly paraphrases and softens Mark 10:45.

A comparison of Mark and Paul suggests that although the Pauline narrative is the earlier in writing it is scarcely older in its form; the Pauline narrative has been molded by Paul himself or by those who handed down the tradition before it came into his hands. "My body which is for you" (or "broken," or "given," for you) is non-Synoptic and expresses the Pauline doctrine of the representative or corporative idea—the Christian disciple is "in" Christ, and the Lord's death is also his death, since he "died with Christ" and "rose with him." The identification of the covenant with the "new" covenant (presumably the one announced by Jeremiah) is peculiar to Paul's interpretation of the rite, and is undoubtedly the source of the variant readings in the Synoptic passages where this word is introduced. Above all, Paul's twice-repeated solemn command to repeat the rite is wholly non-Synoptic and cannot be reconciled with Jesus' clear anticipation of the immediate coming of the kingdom of God. Paul still retains the eschatological idea, but it is reformulated; it is the coming of Christ, not the kingdom, that is essential. The rite is to be repeated during this interval, this *Zwischenzeit,* between the Crucifixion and the Parousia, for the very purpose of "proclaiming the Lord's death." There was every reason for repeating the rite. Indeed, the earliest church had repeated it, and it was now the distinctive feature of Christian worship on every Lord's day (every "first" day—the term "Lord's Day" probably came later). Only, what had come down to Paul as custom and observance he set forth as command, just as Matthew formulated the words "Drink of it, all of you," out of the simple narrative statement of Mark, and as any ancient writer would have done. There is thus no need to accept Alfred Loisy's view that the command to repeat the rite (let alone the rite itself or the narrative of its institution) had come to Paul by divine revelation; the word *parelabon* is the most natural in the world for Paul to use in describing what had come down to him by tradition.

Even this brief survey of the New Testament data must make it clear that the original narrative of the Last Supper lies some way back of both the Synoptic and the Pauline forms of the narrative. It was one of the narratives most likely to be modified in the direction of current usage (like the Lord's Prayer, and for the same reason); by the same token it was one of the narratives least likely to be either manufactured or transformed out of recognition. The tradition in this case was more widely based, less dependent upon individual memories, and yet inevitably forced to fit the needs of the worshiping community; for its whole significance lay not in its preservation of a historical recollection of an incident in the passion narrative, but in its explanation of the origin of the distinctively Christian rite of fellowship—first of all with the Lord, and then, in him, with one another, with the group. In a word, both narratives, Synoptic and Pauline, are etiological, and both reflect current usage and its langauge—Paul with more interpretation than the Synoptists' accounts. But even back of the simpler of the two basic narratives lies a tradition which had carried on the story for twenty-five or thirty years—in Mark's case for nearly forty. If the later Synoptists show modifications of the Marcan narrative, and if Mark and Paul show decided divergences, as they do, it is certainly natural to assume that modifications had also taken place during the period prior to Paul as well as prior to Mark. Here was a tradition, rooted in practice and not only in *kerygma* or *didachê,* and therefore subject to the kind of modification which rite and practice always undergo, even during comparatively brief intervals. What the *origin* of the rite was, exactly what words Jesus said to his disciples at the Last Supper, and just what those words meant—these are questions for the historian, but questions which the historian may never be able to answer. As a general principle, since rite is always subject to interpretation, and since the language of rite and liturgy invariably tends to grow ampler, it may be suspected that the briefest possible form of the narrative and the least explanatory is to be preferred as the older, the more authentic and original.

If one may venture to suggest his own conviction in so disputed a matter, I believe that the Lukan narrative (with the shorter reading, omitting vss. 19b-20) stands closest to the original form of the tradition. It was not the institution of a rite for all time to come; it was not an "acted parable" of Jesus' approaching sacrifice; it was the story of Jesus' last supper with his disciples (not a Passover meal—here Luke follows the revision of the passion narrative that Mark had made), and it told how Jesus was aware of the impending tragedy in which he and his disciples were now involved. The whole chapter is dominated by this tone and outlook. Jesus will not drink of the cup—which is the cup of rejoicing, or of salvation, and which at the Passover time, especially, signified the coming redemption of Israel and Israel's joy over the deliverance—for the time to drink that cup is *after* the redemption, not before. Therefore he "will drink it new in the kingdom of God," rather than now face to face with death. As to the bread, "This is my body"—broken, as his body will be broken (not on the cross, for he does not anticipate crucifixion, but in death, perhaps by stoning, perhaps by the bastinado, perhaps by Roman swords or spears, if there is a riot)—this broken bread symbolizes what is to come to pass on the morrow. And the rite, so far as it is a rite, based upon this simple symbolism, is one of union and fellowship of the disciples with their Master. It is a covenant, in this sense and to this degree. Whatever comes, now, they too are to share in it. Come death—they are to stand by him and face the issue. Come victory—they will share that too. But these thoughts are not expressed in so many words. The breaking of the bread, and the simple statement of Jesus, "This is my body," are enough to convey the idea. And out of the idea grew, quite naturally and legitimately, the whole eucharistic idea or doctrine of the Christian church.

Fundamentally the Eucharist is a rite of fellowship, of union and communion, first with Christ, then with one another, in him. The partaking of the "spiritual" or "mystical" or "real" body and blood of Christ only emphasizes and makes more clear what was implicit yet undeniably involved in the setting, the mood, the action, and the words of Jesus in the upper room, the night before he suffered. Around this rite has gathered, through the centuries, an inexhaustible wealth of devotion in all the churches—from the first century to our own. What has kept it alive and growing has been the realization of what is supernaturally and really present *here,* not some historic commemoration like the anniversary of a battle or of the Declaration of Independence. The beginnings of this devotion and its effect upon the tradition of the origin of the rite we can observe in the New Testament, and more clearly, just over the horizon of the New Testament, in the words of Clement, Justin, Irenaeus, and other early Christian writers, though they can now no longer affect the form of the tradition but only its interpretation. Nevertheless, the unique formula contained in the Didache and the total absence of any account of the "institution" in the

Fourth Gospel are facts which must be taken into the reckoning by the historian. They must also be evaluated by the theologian. It is evident that the meaning of the Eucharist, even in the New Testament, is not dependent upon a strict conformity to some one form, or formula, of tradition. John is quite as eucharistic as Paul—even more so—and he is more eucharistic than the Synoptics, yet John has an account of the Last Supper which completely omits the "institution." One might almost gather that the "institution" took place in Galilee, at the feeding of the multitude. (Does not Albert Schweitzer hold that the feeding of the multitude was an "eschatological sacrament"?) What the formula in the Didache implies we can hardly make out. Was it really eucharistic, or only a late surviving Christian Jewish table benediction? In either case, the outlook of the tract is eucharistic, though in a tone very different from John, or Paul, or even the Synoptics; one might guess that it tallied in a measure with the views and practice of the author of James.

But the inference from all these facts is obvious. The doctrine of the Eucharist, as found in the early church, certainly in the New Testament period, does not depend upon a rigid formula, or a strictly guaranteed and invariable tradition, or even upon a precise historical datum. In this respect it is like the doctrine of baptism—which does not depend upon any specific "institution" of the rite by Jesus, or upon any formula. Quite frankly, the only formula is the postresurrection one in Matt. 28:19, and that seems "late"; we should not have been surprised if the "institution" of the Lord's Supper had likewise been assigned to the period after the Resurrection, where Oscar Cullmann would appear to locate it. The rite as actually practiced and handed down in the church is something greater and more significant than even the New Testament data can explain. The narratives of the "institution" are later revisions of the earliest tradition, which we can therefore reconstruct only in hypothesis. And what lay behind the church's earliest tradition of the event is even more hypothetical. The stories are, as we have said, obviously etiological—of the kind with which the ancient historian and especially the historian of ancient religion are constantly familiar. But that does not mean that the origin vanishes into thin air. The explanation may not be adequate, but this does not mean that the thing never originated at all. Nor does it imply a foreign borrowing, for example from pagan mysteries. Nothing is more unlikely than such a theory, both in view of the date and place of origin of the Eucharist, its earliest form (quasi-Jewish), and the character of the mystery rites (with which the most ardent champions of the theory of borrowing seem to be the least familiar). Finally, the rite has the characteristic New Testament variety of interpretation: for Paul it is the Christian proclamation of the Lord's death "until he comes"; for John it is the communication of the "living bread," the flesh of Christ which he gives "for the life of the world"; for others it is the "new covenant," taking the place of the old, the new Passover, fulfilling and supplanting the old and conveying gifts and graces which the old could never convey but only promise.

A still oft-debated question is whether or not the Last Supper was a Passover meal. The Synoptic accounts, as they stand, plainly state that it was, and that our Lord ordered the preparations which were made by the disciples for the observance in the upper room—though the Lukan account, as we have seen, is compatible with the view that Jesus did not actually partake of the meal (22:15). The Johannine account, and the whole chronology of the passion narrative in John, presuppose that the supper took place before the Passover. Although there is much emphasis in John upon the identity of Christ's death on the cross with the sacrifice of the Passover lamb, as the "lifting up" of the unbroken body of the true Lamb of God, it is doubtful if this symbolical interpretation occasioned a shift in chronology from the Synoptic account; it is more probable that the symbolism rested upon the fact that Jesus actually died on the afternoon when the Passover lambs were slain (though the truth may be that he died earlier still). Moreover, the Synoptic accounts, basically that of Mark, contain data which are incompatible with the view that the meal was the Passover: the arrest of Jesus was planned to take place before the feast (Mark 14:2); those who come to arrest Jesus are bearing arms (vs. 43), which was forbidden during the feast; the trial takes place at night following the Passover meal; and so on. In fact, the narrative contravenes Jewish juridical procedure at many points, at least at fourteen; while the account of the supper itself bears little resemblance to the Passover—there is no mention of the lamb, the seder, the traveling attire to be worn by the participants, and other marked features of the Jewish observance, and at the end the group have no difficulty in leaving the city (vs. 26), though this was impossible in the middle of the night.

The probability is that the oldest account of the supper, as found in the pre-Marcan passion narrative, described it simply as Jesus' last meal with his disciples. He and they had come up to Jerusalem for the Passover, but the feast had not yet arrived. It was thus *at Passover time* that Jesus died—probably Paul was not the first or only early Christian to refer to his dying Lord as "our passover," who "is sacrificed for us" (I Cor. 5:7 K.J.V.). It was this identification—a theological and devotional identification, to begin with—which led to the view that the Last Supper was itself the Passover meal.

Some have thought that the supper was a *kiddush,* a meal shared by a religious group on the eve of Sabbaths and festivals, and intended to "sanctify" them for the observance. Some such groups were known by the name *chaburah* or "fellowship," especially in Pharisaic circles. But the theory does not take sufficient account of the character of such an observance by pious Jews, nor of the nature of the *chaburoth* or "fellowships." These fellowship groups were composed chiefly of older men; they met for study early in the afternoon preceding the Sabbath or festival (the Jewish day began at sundown). The *kiddush* proper, certainly as it eventually came to be observed in Judaism, was a ceremony or set of prayers, chiefly *the* prayer, of preparation for the ensuing day, after which the meal of fellowship was partaken. If the Last Supper was a *kiddush,* its leading features are absent from the New Testament narratives—the afternoon of study and the concluding prayer or prayers. It is very doubtful if anything as formal as this can represent the situation underlying the gospel narratives.

Nor does the eucharistic language used elsewhere in the New Testament, for example in the accounts of the feeding of the multitude, reflect such an observance. The language is rather that of the early Christian rite, used to describe what seems to have been essentially a common meal, and no more. But "no more" does not imply the absence of all religious significance from the meal, certainly not in a Jewish setting and situation; every Jewish meal had religious significance, and began and ended with thanksgiving (in Greek, *eucharistia*). If the early evangelic tradition retains echoes of Jesus' characteristic words or gestures in the breaking of the bread (e.g. Luke 24:35), this fact does not point back to the Last Supper so much as it does to the common meals of the Lord and his disciples during the months of his ministry in Galilee—the two disciples at Emmaus were not thought of as present in the upper room. The language of Acts (e.g. 2:42, 46) may not be eucharistic, nor even refer specifically to the common meals of the Lord with his disciples during his ministry, but is only a way of saying that the early disciples in Jerusalem after the Resurrection ate their meals together. Even Acts 20:7, 11 may not describe a eucharist (certainly 27:35 does not), and yet the background of all early Christian meals was the table fellowship not only with each other but with the risen and exalted Lord, still present in the Spirit with his own; and on the level of history it was the remembered fellowship of Jesus with his disciples in the old days in Galilee.

It seems inevitable to conclude, therefore, that the narratives of the "institution" project backward into the event in the upper room the practice and the ideas of the contemporary church—which means, not that there was *no* Last Supper, or that the ideas which had gathered about the rite were new and revolutionary (borrowed from the mystery religions!), but only that the tradition had been modified somewhat in the course of transmission. The profoundly religious and personal meaning of the Last Supper contained more implications than even the New Testament church was destined to fathom or express. That these implications were understood and interpreted in the light of the Old Testament was not only natural but inevitable, since the Old Testament was the Bible of the early church. The very language of the "institution" reflects this influence: for example, "blood of the covenant" or of the "new covenant"; "do this"; "memorial" or "in memory of" or "in remembrance of." But so does the language of Christian worship in general, as in Rom. 12:1; 15:16; Phil. 2:17; I Pet. 2:5; Heb. 13:10, 15, 16, etc. It is not possible to identify each of these Old Testament allusions with the Eucharist—all Christian worship is a continuation and "fulfillment" of the worship rendered to God under the Old Covenant. Thus in the Didache the leaders of the church are referred to by titles derived from the Old Testament, while the church's earliest ordination prayers allude to Moses and the elders rather than to Christ and the apostles—clear evidence of the continuity between Jewish and Christian worship as well as organization.

What we are to make of the "love feast" (*agápê*) of the early Christians is one of the still-unsolved questions of New Testament research. Presumably it was a continuation of the primitive fellowship meal, but it had come to have—in a purely Hellenistic environment—more emphasis laid upon the meal than upon the religious rite which inaugurated or concluded it. In I Cor. 11 Paul refers to the meal partaken of by the Corinthian Christians in which, apparently, the recital of the "institution" or at least a reference to the Last Supper had a part, but in which the scandalous and unbrotherly behavior of the participants robbed the meal of its sacred character. For Paul the entire meal was—and should be—a religious observance, quite distinct from meals "at home" where the hungry could eat their fill. It was a "supper of the Lord" (*kyriakon deipnon*), whose sacred significance was to be impressed upon those present by a recollection of the words of the Lord "on the night when he was betrayed." But when they came together merely to eat and drink, as at a communal banquet, this was no "Lord's supper" (vs. 20). Perhaps this gives us the clue to the *agápê* of Jude 12—it was a mere fellowship meal, potentially good, like other "fellowship meals" in the Greco-Roman world of that time, observed by guilds, trade unions, burial societies, and other organizations; but it was not the Lord's Supper. To transform a fellowship meal into a supper of the Lord it was not enough simply to recite the words of "institution" somewhere in the program of the feast; the *whole* meal was to be sacred, in remembrance of the Lord and as the proclamation of his death. And what Paul desired was that every fellowship meal of Christians should have this character—"as often as you eat this bread and drink the cup"—"do this, as often as you drink it." In the course of time the *agápê* was abandoned, for all its old associations (not only the fellowship meals described in Acts but also the common meals of the disciples with the Lord during his earthly ministry); it proved, in the Hellenistic world, too mundane, too secular, and was therefore incompatible with the sacred Supper or Eucharist, the church's most solemn hour of worship and communion with the exalted but present Lord.

There are other features of the New Testament Eucharist which deserve notice: almsgiving, the collection and presentation of alms, characteristic of the Pauline churches but undoubtedly going back to the primitive community in Jerusalem (perhaps connected with the daily ministration to the needy as practiced in that church; almsgiving was a marked feature of the Jewish practice of religion, and equally characterized the Christian Jews); the provision of food, not only for the banquet of the community but also for the needy; the kiss of peace, the symbol of fellowship and of brotherhood, which long survived in various Christian rites and is observed even now by some Christians; the weekly observance of the rite, "on the first day of the week," presumably from the earliest time, though we cannot precisely date it. Presumably, also, even from the first there was something formal about the service. If we may argue backward from the later use, and if we take into account the influence of Jewish usage, there would be a lesson or lessons from the scripture, one or more psalms, a discourse (mainly exposition of scripture), prayers, perhaps even the reading of letters or epistles from other Christian communities or from apostles or evangelists. It has been thought that the passion narrative, which was probably the earliest consecutive story of Jesus to be put together out of discrete pericopes of oral tradition, was read or rather recited at the Supper (Gal. 3:1 has been thought to prove this); but this is only a hypothesis, however probable, and cannot be proved. The arrangement of the passion narrative in Mark, as Loisy observed, seems to reflect a series of hours of devotion, as if for some very early Holy Week or at least Good Friday, Holy Saturday, and Easter; early as this would have to be, to get into Mark, it is not impossible, and the evidence seems convincing. That the whole of the Gospel of Mark is arranged upon a lectionary scheme for a Christian Jewish church year is likewise a defensible view. This feature has already been observed in John and Matthew, and is not impossible in Mark as well; the early church was no "religious society of Christians" but a continuation of the Jewish synagogue under new conditions and with an expanded creed; it was in fact the Christian synagogue, and in its earliest manifestation in Palestine was the Christian *Jewish* synagogue.

At what point in history the observance of the Eucharist was transferred from evening to morning we cannot say. The factors involved would seem to have been chiefly (*a*) the separation from the *agápê*, which naturally came in the evening, when the laboring people of the

Roman world ate their chief meal of the day, and also when the Last Supper had taken place; and also (*b*) the separation of the Christian ecclesia from the Jewish synagogue, since the Hellenistic ecclesia would observe the method of reckoning time current in the secular world, rather than the old Jewish method, which began the day at sundown. The beginning of "the first day of the week" was now Sunday morning, not Saturday evening. A further motive for the transfer would undoubtedly be (*c*) the reverence and devotion which centered more and more in the rite. As time went on, the Eucharist came to be thought of in relation to the Resurrection rather than the Last Supper—a feature given classical expression in the Eastern liturgies, with far more emphasis than in the Western—and Christ's resurrection had taken place early on "the first day of the week" (Matt. 28:1, which is correctly translated in R.S.V., "after the sabbath, toward the dawn").

As the Eucharist became the chief and most distinctive Christian rite, moral and even ceremonial conditions were soon laid down for the communicants, as we may learn from Paul (I Cor. 5; 11) and also from the famous letter of Pliny (Bk. X, ep. 96). The Christians bound themselves by an oath (*sacramento*) not to commit theft, robbery, or adultery, not to break their word, and not to deny a deposit when it was demanded. Incest (or adultery, I Cor. 5:1), promiscuity, greed, robbery, idolatry, reviling, drunkenness (vss. 9-13; cf. ch. 6)—such sins destroy the fellowship, and the only recourse is excommunication (5: 13*b*). Even the eating of meat which has been offered to an idol and then has been sold in the market, not to say public banqueting in a heathen temple (ch. 8), is forbidden: "You cannot drink the cup of the Lord and the cup of demons. You cannot partake of the table of the Lord and the table of demons" (10:21). All of the Jew's instinctive abhorrence of idolatry comes out in these passages with added force. The "puritan" element in early Christianity was no importation of Hermas or Tertullian in the second century; it is plainly visible in the letters of Paul.

5. *Primitive Catholicism*

It is a far cry from the New Israel, the "congregation of the latter days," in the thirties or forties of the first century to the "holy catholic church, the communion of saints" of the later apostolic creed. Nevertheless the two concepts are related, and the emerging catholicism of the second century has antecedents in the first. No doubt the development of the doctrine of the church in this direction took place more rapidly in some areas than in others. As we have seen, this is true of the development and formulation of other doctrines, and of doctrinal growth as a whole. The development of doctrine was not like the unfolding of the science of geometry by Euclid, or like the carrying out of a well-laid plan—say the invasion of Normandy. The functions of the ministry, and even its forms, as we observed above, were (to all external appearance, at least) adventitious, experimental, determined by various needs, such as the care of the church's dependents, and adapted to local conditions. If one believes, as I certainly do, that the development of the ministry was in accordance with the mind and will of God, it must be viewed as the result of divine overruling and of the guidance of the Holy Spirit—rather than as the setting up of a predetermined organization. The church did not sail with sealed orders, to be opened at Lat. x, Long. y. The *principle* of the ministry was there from the beginning, for the apostles were the emissaries of Christ himself. So were some of the factors involved in its development, for example the Jewish community organization, including the "ministry" of the synagogue—that is, the "function" of conducting public worship. So also was the general picture of the Old Testament ministry, with priests, Levites, elders, the high priest, and other functionaries.

The importance of this factor is reflected in the very terms retained in the early Christian literature. The book of Acts (14:23) represents the apostles as having "appointed elders . . . in every church," even as Titus (1:5) is directed to do. In the Epistle to the Hebrews the "clergy" are described by the general term of "leaders" (13:7), and not "priests," who belonged to the old dispensation; the Christians' only priest is Christ—indeed he is the one true high priest (3:1, etc.). But in the Didache the settled ministers of the local church are "high priests," deserving the support of the congregation (13:2). The Gospel of Matthew (23:8-10) disapproves the use of such titles as "rabbi," "father," and "master" (as clerical titles?), since they are all of divine application and reference. From the context (vss. 5-7, 11-12) one may infer that they were sought after by Christian leaders, who were the "opposite numbers" of the Jewish scribes (vss. 2-3). The passage, like the Gospel of Matthew as a whole, must be late; the evidence seems to prove that the titles "rabbi," "father" (*abh*), and "master" (*rab* or *rabban*) were not in common use until after the reorganization of the Jewish schools in the period following the fall of Jerusalem in A.D. 70. But the passage also shows—as do many others in Matthew—how great an influence the synagogue exercised, not only upon the Palestinian gospel tradition but also upon the developing church. It is not only unlikely that a "charismatic" type of ministry was the sole or even the chief type to be found in Christian Jewish congregations; it was impossible that the settled and orderly organization of the church should be achieved along these lines. The first steps, fortunately, were taken under the influence of the synagogue. What we see in places outside Palestine, for example the "bishops and deacons" in Philippi, probably represents an accommodation of the Jewish-Christian type to the conditions found in a purely Hellenistic environment. When a further step is taken, as by Ignatius early in the second century, the "monarchial" bishop is still a local supervisor (*episcopos*); but the church has grown in numbers, and quite naturally one head of the local congregation or group of congregations is to be preferred to several. (The theory that the church in Alexandria was headed by a "collegium" of presbyter-bishops is not very strongly supported by the evidence, and in any case may have been only a local peculiarity—like the "collegium" of the Dutch church in New York, or the "senate" of a university.) The stages in the development were doubtless not uniform throughout the world, and in any event we are not able to reconstruct the process in detail. But it is clear that by the middle of the second century the form and organization of the ministry were fairly fixed, and that the process of development had led more or less steadily in the direction of the later catholic order. The words of the Anglican Prayer Book are sufficiently accurate: "From the Apostles' time there have been these orders of ministers in Christ's Church,—Bishops, Priests, and Deacons." "*From the Apostles' time*" does not necessarily mean "inclusive of that time," but rather "since"; nevertheless, the actual existence of these orders in apostolic days is amply clear from the New Testament. "Bishops and deacons" were addressed at Philippi; "priest" ("presbyter"="elder," not *hiereus*) is probably an even older designation—as old as the earliest community of Christian Jews in Palestine. The far later development of the papacy in the West, as of the patriarchates in the East, is not even hinted in the New Testament, though there were Jewish ethnarchs at Alexandria and elsewhere, while the high priest in Jerusalem exercised a certain degree of ecumenical authority over Jews everywhere. Only the most resolute special pleading can find support for the Roman papal claims in the New Testament (e.g. Matt. 16:17-19; Acts 12:17; etc.). As a matter of fact, Antioch nearly succeeded in making Peter its pope before Rome did.

As with the ministry, so with worship. The guiding, steadying factor was the synagogue service (rather than the temple worship, except for the immediate neighborhood, Jerusalem and the near-by towns). The use of a fixed calendar of lessons from the Law and the Prophets in the synagogue may not be older than the third century, but the probability is that it was older. The widespread familiarity of Jews with the Old Testament was probably due more to hearing the lessons read at worship than to private study, though the synagogue itself was as much a "house of study" as it was a "house of prayer." The same was no doubt true of Christians. The great passages which they pondered and memorized and recited and meditated upon were not only the "messianic prophecies" in the Old Testament. They were familiar with other parts as well, so that an ingenious early Christian preacher—like an ingenious rabbi—could find new truth and meaning (with a Christian reference) in familiar but hitherto not much regarded verses, words, or turns of expression. The New Testament is full of echoes of the Old Testament. Not only the words printed in blackface or uncial type in the standard editions of the Greek text, but many more words and phrases contain allusions to, or at least reflect the style of, the Greek Old Testament, as the commentaries point out. Moreover the calendar of festivals taken over from Judaism, and revised and supplemented by the church, carried with it certain lessons which were familiar to the readers of Paul's epistles; his "midrash" upon the rock in the wilderness (I Cor. 10: 1-13) is an example. This particular Old Testament lesson was presumably read sometime between Passover and Pentecost, or soon after. The early Christians were equally familiar with the Psalms, as the New Testament writers clearly assumed their readers to be. The great tradition of the use of the Psalter in Christian worship—of course with a Christian interpretation—apparently goes back to the earliest beginnings of that worship. The "hymns" of the early church, such as the canticles in Luke 1–2 and the paeans of Revelation, are obviously modeled upon Jewish psalmody. In fact there was a continuous tradition of religious poetry in Israel, long after the conclusion of the Old Testament Psalter, as the Psalms of Solomon, the psalms incorporated in the apocalyptic writings, and the snatches of song in First Maccabees and elsewhere in the Apocrypha clearly show; the early Christian church entered upon this inheritance and carried on the tradition. Paul's "psalms and hymns and spiritual songs" were no doubt of this kind (Eph. 5:19; cf. I Cor. 14:26).

The early history of the Eucharist is a part of the same story. Whether or not it originated as a common meal, with prayers, in preparation for the Sabbath or for festivals, it was certainly observed in many—probably most—parts of the church as the commemoration of the Last Supper of Jesus and his disciples. The "catholicizing" of this rite was no importation from the pagan mysteries, though mystery language came to be applied to it early enough. The central meaning of the common meal was that Jesus the Lord (*Kyrios Iêsous*, I Cor. 11: 23) was present with his own, "wherever two or three are gathered" in his name (Matt. 18:20). In the Greco-Roman world, even more than in Jewish Palestine, it was inevitable that this rite of union and communion with the "Lord" Christ, the heavenly Son of God, should receive special emphasis. Not that it imitated the banquets in the temples of Serapis (which were scarcely communion services!) or the meals in the Mithraic centers (which may have been later, and anyway had a very different connotation); but this rite met the yearning for union with God which was widespread throughout the whole Hellenistic world. The eucharistic language of the Didache (chs. 9–10) is presumably archaic, and shows what an "undeveloped" rite would be like, say around A.D. 130. The main currents of liturgical development flowed farther west and south; Syria and the East remained attached to primitive, Judaic, eschatological ideas for a longer time, if we may judge from the Didache (and of course we may perhaps *not* so judge). But for all the high eucharistic language of other regions, and the growth of eucharistic doctrine, it was Ignatius of Antioch in Syria who described the rite as "the medicine of immortality" (Eph. 20:2;

ca. A.D. 110) ; and it was the Fourth Gospel which referred to the body of the Lord as "bread from heaven," "the true manna," the "flesh" of Christ given "for the life of the world" (John 6, *passim*). Compared with such florid language the oldest prayers in the Roman liturgy seem plain and unadorned—for example, "Command these offerings to be carried by the hands of thy holy angel to thine altar on high, in the sight of thy divine Majesty . . ."

As with the ministry and with worship, so with the educational work of the early church, to take a third crucial example of its growth. The work of the church's "teachers" has never been adequately recognized, either in the ancient world or the modern. They are referred to often enough in the New Testament, not only in the epistles but in the Gospels. It was they, apparently, who handed on the gospel tradition— the teachers, rather than the "evangelists" or preachers—and had some share in giving it the fixed and final form it possesses in the four Gospels. It was they who instructed new converts in the teachings of their adopted faith, and not only in the Christian faith but also in Christian morals. The "catechism of primitive Christianity" which some have seen in the background of the epistles certainly existed, though it was no written document, like Luther's or the Anglican or the Westminster. Nor may it have been a uniform oral body of instruction; and yet, as Archbishop Carrington and others have shown, the "pattern of sound words" which is referred to more than once in the New Testament does seem to be reflected in various sequences of ideas, words, and turns of expression. In the main it was apparently based upon similar Jewish instruction, and took for granted the combinations of passages from Leviticus and Deuteronomy which were in use in the Jewish schools or in domestic religious instruction. The early church did not neglect religious instruction; that is clear from Hebrews, First Peter, and James, not to mention the strong didactic element in Paul's letters —which were of course far more "occasional" in nature, and less formal. As for the Gospels, Matthew might almost be described as the first religious educational text in Christian history—and back of Matthew the sources Q and M (M *may* be only further revision, amplification, and codification of Q) were certainly formal enough. They set forth the teaching of the Lord in his own words, and also undertook —as did the finished Gospel of Matthew—to set forth the rules, likewise in words of Jesus, for "life in accordance with the commandments and the sayings of the Lord." Somewhat as Ben Sira made a collection of his grandfather Jesus' sayings for the benefit of those who would live "orderly in accordance with the Law," though dwelling in an alien world far from the Holy Land, so Matthew drew up a "gospel." This was in five books, each with its narrative and its didactic parts, for the guidance of the Christian disciple and of the organized church. It was a kind of early "Master's Guide for His Disciples," and its immense influence upon all later Christian literature shows how well it met the need—not only of its own time but of all later Christian generations.

The "development," accordingly, of Christian religious instruction is no late product of "institutionalized" Christianity, as opposed to an earlier free, "charismatic," noninstitutional religion or religious movement; instead it was a feature in Christian life from the first. In Palestine it was so because the church was the *Christian* ecclesia or *synagogê,* parallel to the Jewish one, and really derived from it; outside Palestine, in the Gentile world, it was so because there was even greater need for it. Converts from paganism needed even more instruction than converts from orthodox Judaism; and they needed instruction in morals quite as much, if not more, than in doctrine.

All these factors—ministry, worship, instruction—showed the steady growth of the church in the institutional direction. And that growth began at a very early stage. It was no relapse from the first high enthusiasm and the eschatological hope which made such a development necessary. Of course during the first weeks or months following the original Easter Day one could hardly look for a fixed and settled ministry, liturgical worship, and formal religious instruction. But within a very short time, partly under the influence of surrounding Judaism, partly under the influence of the Old Testament, partly as a result of simple human necessity, the "functions" of ministry, liturgy, and instruction found form and expression in the Christian groups. The "growing catholicism" of the second century really had its roots far back in the first.

XII

New Testament Ethics

1. *The Jewish Background*

A NEW understanding of the New Testament and of early Christianity is dawning upon us today. The older views, both orthodox and rationalist, often took it for granted that Jesus was the "Founder" of a new religion, Christianity; that the Gospels are the "records" of his "life," while the epistles, the book of Acts, and Revelation are the "records" of the early church; and that the total collection of inspired or "canonical" books set forth fully and for all time the rules and regulations to govern the church's faith and life. Today we are beginning to realize—what the church fathers and even the Schoolmen assumed—that Jesus took Judaism and the Old Testament for granted, and addressed his teaching to those who were nurtured in that faith; that the apostles were not bent upon establishing a corpus of canon law valid for all time, or a "liturgical norm" which should control catholic worship throughout history; and that the ancient church was perfectly correct in viewing the Bible as a whole (the Old Testament, including the "Apocrypha," supplemented by the New Testament books) as the vehicle of the divine revelation which had been given "in many and various ways" and had finally, consummately, been made in Christ the Son of God.

Again, it has been taken for granted that the New Testament contained, at least implicitly, a finished theological system, complete with cosmology, ecclesiology, and even social or political ethics. In truth its "cosmology" is simply that of the Old Testament, slightly modified—wherever traces of cosmological thinking can be found (e.g. Rom. 1; Heb. 1)—by the common and widespread influence of Hellenistic thought, which had been largely influenced by popular Platonism and

Stoicism. Its "ecclesiology" is still in process of maturing, and reflects various stages reached in different areas towards the end of the first or early in the second century. Its "ethics" is a blending of traditional Jewish ethics, modified in emphasis by the teaching of Jesus and the apostles, popular Stoicism, and the religious "wisdom" of Hellenistic (Diaspora) Judaism, already engaged in gathering up the best of current and ancient teaching—there are Cynic parallels to the Sermon on the Mount, as well as Jewish or rabbinic. The unique or distinctive element in New Testament ethics is anything but a system. It voices, both in Jesus' sayings and in Paul's letters, a powerful protest against received standards; and this ethics of protest was primarily individual, not "social" at all—as for politics, it reflects an almost purely apolitical point of view. Men are not to be saved in the world, or as a world, but out of this present world (John 17). The message was centered in the expectation of coming judgment: What kind of behavior will see you through that crisis? What will avail when you stand before the Son of Man (Luke 21:36)? "Save yourselves from this crooked generation" (Acts 2:40).

In fact a thoroughly "biblical" ethics must necessarily sit lightly to the present order—throughout vast tracts of biblical thinking man is not considered as a political or social being at all, let alone as an economic. Instead of guaranteeing a safe and secure political and social order, or an economic system of peace and prosperity, the New Testament is not in the least interested in these things. It is not only the "social gospel" of the early twentieth century, or modern "liberalism" since the middle of the nineteenth, that has gone astray at this point, but orthodoxy as well. Men have assumed that if only the teaching of the New Testament were fully carried out and put in practice—or if it *could* be put in practice, a hundred per cent—we should then have a utopian society here upon earth. The only questions that remained to be answered were the really fundamental ones: whether or not Jesus really intended his teaching, for example as recorded in the Sermon on the Mount, to be put in practice; or whether the church or the state was the best instrument for achieving the end of a Christian society; or whether mankind could achieve this blessed end with or without divine grace; and so on. Actually the New Testament makes no such promises, contemplates no such goal. If ever we are to take the New Testament, or the Bible as a whole, in complete seriousness, there must be a complete reorientation of human life; and some of the concepts and ideals most dear to modern man will have to be let go—or drop into a minor place. Political liberty, democratic citizenship, the rule of the majority, economic security, in fact the whole scheme of things envisaged in modern political idealism, good as much of it may be, can no longer be identified with the teaching of the Bible, either of the Old Testament or of the New. The religion of the Bible—despite all the "political" interpreting of Old Testament prophetism and of the teaching of Jesus, popular since about 1880—is simply not concerned with politics at all. And it may be true, indeed it probably is true, that our modern preoccupation with politics and economics is a very one-sided interpretation of the meaning of human life. Once we get past the present international and world-wide "time of troubles" (to use Professor Toynbee's term), which began with the breakup of Western society in the sixteenth century, and has been accompanied by endless wars and bloodshed as nations have fought for territory or markets and by the prostitution of modern science, culminating in the atomic bomb, then we may begin to see that the essential values of human life, and the essential meaning of human life here and hereafter, do not depend upon a just and secure political system, and that man is not essentially the "economic man" or the "political man" but potentially the child of God, born upon earth but destined to be reborn for eternity.

It has been a serious handicap to much modern Protestant interpretation of the Bible that it completely divorced the New Testament from the Old, and set "Law" and "Gospel" in irreconcilable opposition, with the inevitable consequence that first-century Judaism—which it identified with "nomism," the religion of the Law—was misrepresented, misinterpreted, and entirely rejected. What should have been, and is, the indispensable background and setting for the interpretation of the life, teaching, and mission of Jesus, for the interpretation of the whole phenomenon of primitive Christianity, the mission and work of the apostles, and the teaching contained in the epistles—all this was either ignored or treated as purely negative, photographically "negative," its white patches black, and its black white.

Jesus did not (so far as we know) set out to "reform" or to "revolutionize" Judaism; he simply took it for granted as the religion of his people, based upon the Torah of God, the religion of priests and law-givers, of prophets and psalmists and wise men. But he reorientated and "fulfilled" it—that is, completed it—and taught his followers to live solely for God and his divine reign which was soon to be established over the whole earth. It is within the area or circle of Judaism that the gospel took root; there is nothing "Aryan" or extraneous about it, and very little that is "Hellenistic" in the sense of non-Jewish. (Hellenistic Judaism, which was to be found even in Palestine, had already been influenced in some measure by the religious thought of the Greco-Roman world.) The original gospel of Jesus was based upon the Law and the prophets; the conception of the coming reign of God is fundamental alike to prophecy and to the message of Jesus.

2. *The Agrarian Protest*

The "ethics" of the gospel are Jewish through and through. Not that they are identical with those of the Pharisees, or of any one Pharisaic teacher; Jesus was an individual, and unique. The ethics of Jesus are, in fact, agrarian—whereas, as Louis Finkelstein has shown, those of the Pharisees were mainly urban. But the background of Judaism as a whole, especially as it is reflected in the Old Testament, was agrarian, and had been so for a thousand years; before that, it had been nomadic—anything but urban. The unworkableness or "impracticality" (impracticability) of the gospel, of which so much is heard today, is true only in our overgrown urban and industrial society; in a purely rustic society like that of most of Galilee in the first century the charge could not be. made. Parallels to the Gospels are to be found in many an ancient Jewish source—especially, for example, in First Enoch, which was apparently a Galilean or north Palestinian collection of apocalyptic material, traditions, poems, visions, and hortatory wisdom sayings. The gospel is, in fact, the greatest agrarian protest in all history, and the last great protest against the oncoming tide of industrialism, power politics, and the whole economic reorientation of human life which was represented first in the ancient world by the great empires, and since then, except for the brief interlude of the Dark and Middle Ages, has steadily come to dominate the whole human scene.

Most of us are too familiar with the New Testament—or with the traditional ecclesiastical interpretation of the New Testament—to recognize this. But we can understand a similar protest when it is raised in an unexpected quarter, in the poems of a "court poet," the friend of a wealthy patron, a man who owed his position and much of his influence to Maecenas and the Emperor—Virgil of Mantua, the Italian countryman. In his long poem on country life, *Georgica,* which is almost a "Farmer's Almanac" and "Guide to Agriculture" combined, he describes the conditions that once prevailed, and still prevail in large measure, in the country, and then contrasts what one found in the towns—or, more chronologically stated, what has taken place since rural life gave way to urban. The theme is common in the Latin poets, and is found in other writers—which makes it all the more striking, since it proves that many men realized what was taking place in the world, with the total "politicizing" of the human race.

> For God himself decreed
> Our life should not be soft; 'tis skill alone
> Awakes the fields, 'tis care awakes man's wit,
> Lest slumbering torpor should weigh down his world.
> Ere Jove had reigned, no tiller tamed the soil,
> No sign marked field from field or bound the waste;
> Men toiled for common store; the land itself
> Bore freely, more when no man sought his own.
> To serpents black he gave their savage sting,
> Bade wolves to plunder, bade the seas to swell;
> From dripping leaves wild honey fell; but fire
> He hid, while wine that once had run in streams
> Held back—that men by taking careful thought
> Might slowly master arts, might learn to seek
> The ripening corn in furrows of the field,
> By striking flint produce the hidden fire.
> Then rivers felt the weight of hollowed tree;
> Then sailors named and numbered all the stars—
> The Pleiads, Hyads, Arctos, Lycaon's sons;
> Then men began to snare wild game, and trap
> The birds, while hunters with their baying hounds
> Drew circles round the dark deep forest glades;
> The casting net they spread upon the stream,
> Sweeping the depths, or dragged the salty sea.

Harsh iron and the noisy sharp-toothed blade
Now conquered wood—no longer split by wedge.
Thus came the various arts: toil conquered all,
Unceasing toil, and driving pinch of want.

First Ceres taught mankind to plough with iron—
The holy acorn and arbutus groves
Had failed: Dodona now refused them food.
But soon upon the corn fell withering blight;
Corrupting mildew sapped its tender stalks,
While lazy thistles spread throughout the fields—
Thus adding labor to its fragile growth.
The harvests die; rough weeds and thorny scrub
Spring up abundant, burrs and brambles all;
Amid the shining stand of growing grain
The luckless darnel, barren oats gain sway.
Unless with hoe your soil is harrowed long
And greedy birds are driven off with cries,
Unless the shadowing boughs are sharply pruned
And freshening showers won from heaven with vows—
Alas, in vain shall you behold the store
Of other men, but in the lonely wood
Console yourself by shaking down the oak. (I. 121-59.)

It is hardly too much to say that the outlook of Virgil is not remote from that of the Bible; there are phrases and even passages in his poems which make one suspect that he had read the Old Testament. Nor is it remote from that of Jesus—what takes place "in kings' houses" is totally different from what takes place in the homes of the poor; wealth, the pursuit of power, war, even industry, are all inimical to the best interests of men. The change that had come over human life since the primitive days was as greatly resented by Jesus as by Virgil. The urbanization, industrialization, and "politicizing" of the race are, on the whole, rejected alike by the Bible and by Virgil. From Hesiod down, classical literature contains repeated expressions of this rejection. (Aristotle, it is true, defined man as "a political animal"; but that did not mean the mass man, the puppet of "political" leaders, the human being doomed to be transformed into a rabid nationalist, warring against his fellow men for a slogan or a flag. Aristotle meant a man fit to live in a city, *polis,* a creature by nature gregarious—as man has always been, since the earliest times—and perhaps qualified to be a citizen of Athens.) The great myths, echoed by Virgil, which Hesiod had set down—the revolt of the Titans, the four ages of mankind, the revolution of Zeus, and so on—these all described, or could at least be interpreted as describing, the same phenomena that are described and explained in the Bible by the myths of man's expulsion from Eden, the rival offerings of Abel and Cain, the tower of Babel, Noah's ark, the choice of Lot, and others. What we refer to as "the Fall" was really a myth (that is, a tale, as Plato defined it, which must be resorted to for lack of a precise scientific or logical explanation) accounting for the necessity of eating bread "in the sweat of thy face" (Gen. 3:19)— primitive man ate fruit which grew naturally on the trees. The slaying of Abel explains the conflict between agriculture and nomadism; the tower of Babel, man's revolt against the divine rule, a revolt which centered in and was headed by a city; Noah's flood, the divine vengeance upon the accumulated wickedness of man's inventions; the choice of Lot, the evil consequence of forsaking a pastoral mode of life for an urban; and so on.

It was only a later theological interpretation which read into the story of man's expulsion from the idyllic oasis of Eden various theories of the origin of sin (and of death, its consequence), of human depravity, and the like. In its original form the story was far simpler and more naïve—and truer. The story, viewed as "myth," is still true. Somewhere along the way, at some point in the long annals of humankind— probably at several points, among various peoples—men ceased to be nomadic and pastoral, and became agricultural; at some point, or points, agriculture gave way to industry, and life became urban, not rural. Whether or not the origin of evil (or of sin) can be traced to the beginnings of urban life—or earlier, if agricultural—may be questioned. But the point is that sometime or other men began to prey upon their fellows, and the old gregariousness gave way to rivalry, avarice, exploitation, and war. Here was the point of entrance of *political* evil (sin and death, in the symbolism of the myth) into the world. This is a fundamental biblical concept, and the whole Bible is influenced by it, more or less; and it certainly forms a large element in the cosmological and world-historical background presupposed by the doctrine of the kingdom of God.

This "sociological" interpretation of the story of the Garden of Eden and of man's expulsion is far more probable, I believe, than the psychoanalytic, which sees in it a myth of human birth. In the latter, for example, the beginning of sin has been wrongly placed; sin follows the expulsion, so that one might paraphrase Paul and say, "I had not known sin if I had not been born!" But in the story of Eden—the myth of transition from primitive life to civilized, from an easy life in the forest or on the oasis to the hard life of tilling the soil—the "sin" is only an act of disobedience, required as the trigger to set the action going; yet even so it is nothing very extraordinary or unnatural, given human curiosity, human self-indulgence, human love of ease. (The great myths of human or demonic pride and rebellion, such as the fall of Satan, or the tower of Babel, are far profounder in their interpretation of the root source of human sin.) Freud's theory would perhaps apply better to Plato's doctrine of the fall of the soul in a pre-existent state, or to the Orphic or Pythagorean doctrine of reincarnation; but here also there are difficulties.

Thus there is a fundamental disturbance at the heart of the scriptural view of the world—an anxiety and dissatisfaction and unrest. The Bible does not represent the world as perfect; it was "good" on the day of creation (Gen. 1, *passim,* especially vs. 31), but it did not remain so. Nature is subservient to the purposes of God, but is not the full and final expression of his will, let alone of his nature. As the earth is not a perfect sphere but a spheroid, as its orbit is not a circle but an ellipse, as its rotation is not smooth and even but a slow wobble, causing the precession of the equinoxes and the shift of its axis from the Pole Star, so the world of human wills is not a perfect representation of the divine plan or a full realization of the divine purpose.

3. *The Ethics of Jesus—and of Paul*

The agrarian background of Jesus' ethics (or what Martin Dibelius called the "patriarchal" background) is reflected even in the metaphors and similes that he used. In the selection from his teaching—sayings, parables, expositions of the Law, eschatological warnings, and "beatitudes" or macarisms—which Matthew gives in the Sermon on the Mount this is perfectly clear. The figures of speech, the examples selected, the persons addressed by the Teacher all belong to the Galilean village or countryside: the tasteless salt flung into the street, the single lamp that lights up the whole house, the village blasphemer with his string of oaths and terms of abuse, the temple pilgrim setting out with his one gift to present before the altar, the village judge and the jailor, the local ruffian and hoodlum swift to strike, the king's man or garrison trooper who compels the peasant to carry his baggage or to yield up his mantle, the sinner's field wet with the same rain that falls on his righteous neighbor's, the local tax collector, the birds of the air and the lilies of the field (the bright anemones springing up in profusion beside the country lane), the child crying to be fed, the fruitful trees and the unfruitful, the two housebuilders, one wise and one foolish. There is nothing here about kings and their councils, let alone parliaments and assemblies; nothing about armies and tribute, not even about the Roman army of occupation in Palestine, and the question of submission to this invasion and denial of the theocratic rule assumed in the Torah; nothing about civil or criminal law, the administration of government, the function of courts, the rights of the people, the duties of statesmen and administrators, the merits of various constitutions! Aristotle would have been greatly puzzled by these chapters, supposing he had thought them worthy of examination.

Jesus was no philosopher investigating the logical bases of ethics, or endeavoring to work out a system which should be applicable to all men everywhere, in every age, under whatever conditions of society, of political organization or of economic order, might then prevail. Instead he was carrying on the tradition of biblical ethics, enriching, deepening, and "completing" the teaching of the Law and the prophets (Matt. 5:17). The biblical ethics, as we have seen, was fundamentally agrarian, not urban, with many surviving traces of nomadic ethics. It was among the "poor of the land" that he lived and worked. His trade of "carpenter" not only was that of builder (*tektôn*) but also included that of smith, joiner, and village artisan. Justin Martyr was probably right— he made plows and yokes (*Dial.* 88:8). By trade and vocation, and also by his own interest, he was associated with agricultural life. The farms and meadows of Galilee were not in some remote region, but came up to the edge of the village; thus the village was in closest contact with rural life. The same outlook was found, for the most part, in the older elements of the wisdom tradition as it circulated in Judaism— as it had circulated, in fact, for two thousand years or more throughout Egypt and the Near East, an international fund of ethical lore. It is significant that the subject matter of Jesus' ethical teaching is identical with that of the Jewish wisdom teachers, and of the early scribes.

His *gospel*, the proclamation of the nearness—practically the arrival —of the reign of God, was not paralleled in either wisdom tradition or in scribal teaching. Far from it! This was the unique and distinctive thing in Jesus' message. But the immediate coming of the kingdom of God made doubly urgent the requirement of repentance, already stressed by John the Baptist; and the "fruits of repentance" were the changed heart and the good deeds, "worthy of repentance," which those who were to enter God's kingdom must manifest in their daily lives. This was no "interim ethic," but the thorough practice of religion and the sincere behavior demanded of all who were to become members of the *Malkûth Shamayim* which was about to appear. Thus the *didachê* followed the *kerygma*, the teaching followed the proclamation, as logically and inevitably as in all biblical announcements: Judgment is at hand; repent! Turn from your evil ways! Cease to do evil; learn to do well! Seek peace; speak the truth with your neighbor; in everything obey the will of God! This is the relation in which ethics stand to eschatology—and indeed to religion—throughout the Bible, and especially in the gospel of Jesus. For—it cannot be repeated too often!— biblical "repentance" does not mean mere "sorrow for sins" but an actual turning away from them, turning about (*teshubah*) and facing in another direction, turning to the Lord and accepting his way and his will. In place of the former evil deeds, good deeds must now be done, as proof and confirmation of a changed life.

There is of course in all this no idea of "earning" salvation by one's good works. It is only a shallow caricature of religion which would criticize this as a doctrine of "merit." You repent of your evil deeds, and begin the practice of good deeds, because it is the will of God— and your salvation depends upon *him*, not on the things that you do. So the picture of the Pharisee thanking God that he was "not like other men" (Luke 18:11), or of the surly son who repented and finally did the will of his father (Matt. 21:29), or of the unsuspecting righteous souls whose good deeds have all been done to the heavenly King (Matt. 25:31-46) is entirely compatible with the gospel of repentance and grace, and by no means implies a theory of "merit and reward." The Gospels have to be read—each Gospel has to be read, even Mark and John—as if Paul had never lived. It is a great mistake to interpret the evangelic tradition from the point of view of Rom. 7, or of the Epistle to the Galatians! Even the saying "Great is your reward in heaven," though probably a late item in the gospel tradition, is thoroughly consonant with its general tenor; compare Luke 12:32 (L), "Fear not, little flock, for it is your Father's good pleasure to give you the kingdom." There is no conflict here with the Pauline point of view, for the "reward" is not really earned, but given—God will "give" you the kingdom (cf. "I choose to *give* to this last," Matt. 20:14). The reward is still a matter of grace, not of desert—God gives so much more than anyone could possibly earn, even in his utmost deserving! But as there is no conflict with Paul, by the same token it is equally unfair to set up Paul's polemic against the self-sufficiency of legal observance as the standard of interpretation, and then to read the Gospels exclusively in its light. The normal Jewish response, and likewise the Christian Jewish, is the still later one of the Epistle of James (2:18-26): "Show me your faith apart from your works, and I *by* my works will show you *my* faith. . . . A man is justified by works and not by faith alone. . . . For as the body apart from the spirit is dead, so faith apart from works is dead." This may not be entirely anti-Pauline, and it is certainly not a precise formulation of the gospel point of view, for it reflects a later controversy over faith versus works. But it certainly takes for granted the whole biblical doctrine that if a man repents—that is, turns away—from sin and believes in God, his new life must manifest itself in a new pattern of behavior, a new "walk" with God, of which the outward and visible sign is good works. These "good works" are not mere ceremonial practices (Luther, one suspects, was thinking more of his own past life than of the Bible when he inserted this idea; and so perhaps was Paul), but represent the whole pathway of obedience, humility, loyalty, fidelity, devotion, trust in God, and of lovingkindness, mercy, gentleness, generosity, forgiveness, and patience with one's fellows which marks the daily behavior of the consecrated and truly devout man. The "good works" of the gospel are not the mere saying of prayers, or the observance of periods of fasting, or occasional gifts of alms, or regular attendance at public worship, but the "deeper" or "weightier" things of the Law—justice (righteousness, uprightness in God's sight), mercy, and faith (Matt. 23:23).

How can there be any conflict between the gospel and Paul? Those theological interpretations which made out a conflict, or at least a tension, between Paul and Jesus (they were much too common in Protestant circles forty or fifty years ago!) simply ignored the fact that Paul was castigating a type of religion, exemplified in his own life before his conversion and hence seen largely in the light of a later revulsion, which undertook to "establish its own righteousness," whereas the gospel tradition took it for granted, as Jesus had taken it for granted, that "righteousness" was something far profounder than mere acquittal at the bar of the divine judgment, and was centered in utter devotion and personal abandonment to the will, the goodness, the love, and the mercy of God. It was a life which corresponded with such faith, obedience, and devotion; and its highest level was complete trust in the salvation which God would give—not which man would earn.

And yet there is certainly a shift in emphasis as the Christian tradition passes from Jesus to Paul. Jesus' religion is Judaism, of a high and noble kind, the consummation of all biblical revelation; Paul's is a Christ-centered mysticism, a religion of salvation conceived more specifically in terms of the current Hellenistic-Oriental quest for salvation from "this present evil world," from a sin-infected realm of "flesh" (if not from evil "matter"), from the bondage to death and subservience to the elemental powers of the cosmos whose rebellion against the Supreme God and his rule had carried mankind with them. Paul is no "theologian of a mystery cult"; but he undoubtedly does think of Christ, and of the salvation wrought by him, in terms of that longing for salvation which pervaded the whole pagan world under the early empire. This new emphasis was more than an accommodation to current ways of speech; Paul the Diaspora Jew had probably absorbed this anxiety and longing from the world about him during his earliest years. It was no mere product of his troubled adolescence, reaching a climax of despair just before his conversion—as used to be the popular explanation of Paul's "psychology"—though his own peculiar and unique religious experience undoubtedly *led* to his conversion, prepared him for it, and determined the form it was to take. Paul, the scrupulous, the troubled, the anxious, was probably just like that from his earliest years. If Philo was right in saying that "of all men the Jew was the most conscientious in the world," Paul was all this—and more. He had the "chronically troubled conscience" of the mystic born in a quasi-legalistic, ceremonious religion, of one whose perfectionist impulses could never be satisfied with the round of external observances inculcated by his ancestral faith. In addition to this he shared the spiritual malaise of many of his contemporaries, especially in paganism, for whom none of the received rites and regulations of civic worship brought satisfaction, and who demanded a more personal assurance of salvation, a more positive revelation, and the certainty of survival in a blessed life to come. One thinks of other tender consciences in the ancient pagan world, of whom Aristides the Sophist in the second century was typical; and there must have been multitudes of other men and women to whom the mystery cults, or the healing shrines, or various philosophies, or even, to some extent, astrology and magic brought solace and relief. Added to all this, Paul's outlook was urban, cosmopolitan, not rural. He could never have endured a quiet life in the hills of Galilee. Instead of the gorgeous lilies of the field or the chattering birds nesting in the thickets or the poor sparrow fallen to the ground or the shy foxes in their holes, Paul sees nature under a curse, "groaning in travail together until now" (Rom. 8:22), existing in bondage, waiting for the revelation of a more glorious era and the manifestation of the "sons of God" (Rom. 8:19). It is no wonder that Paul's ethics have a different orientation from those of Jesus, and that the old agrarian, biblical, traditional emphasis has been partly supplanted, partly supplemented from Pharisaic (urban) and Stoic (urban) outlooks, terms, and norms.

4. *Apocalyptic Ethics*

The fundamentally agrarian outlook of the Old Testament, of Judaism, and of Jesus is found also in the apocalyptic literature and its traditions. The very language of the apocalyptic hope is rural, and the conceptions of coming bliss are the reverse of conditions now prevailing. (*a*) The calendar has gone wrong, in Enoch (I En. 80:2-8), as was natural and inevitable since twelve lunar months do not make a solar year. But the grave seriousness of the situation was not apparent in the cities, where the traders with their goods and their contracts carried on as usual; the real crisis faced the farmer, for the seasons were awry, the harvest now came when the seeding should begin, and the festivals (still basically agricultural) were all at the wrong time of year. Something had gone wrong in the heavens—the moon had slowed down, or the stars were slipping from their accustomed courses! This was surely a naïve, rustic explanation; a little astronomy, and an intercalary month, could have cured the trouble—and did cure it, in due course, when the added month was more scientifically devised and made official—not in the country but at Jerusalem. So likewise (*b*) with the pictures of imagined bliss in the Age to Come; these are fundamentally agrarian, and the reverse of the conditions now prevalent. Instead of poor harvests, abundance; instead of blight, murrain, and mildew, sound ears in every sheaf; instead of a brief, toilsome life for the tillers of the soil, a long life, like that of the patriarchs, or even that of the men of old who lived before the Flood; instead of painful childbearing, and the hazards of infancy, and barren wedlock—fatal to the countryman—there would be abundance of offspring, born without pain, and maturing with amazing health and vigor. The crops, the herds, the flocks would all exemplify the changed conditions. And instead of war, that ancient curse to the dweller on the soil, who was always the first to suffer from invasion and pillage, peace would prevail over the whole earth. It takes no great gift of imagination to understand the conditions of life among those who dreamed these dreams, or to interpret their vision of the blissful future as the compensating reversal of present ills in the great age about to come.

The ethics which accompany these agrarian dreams are the traditional rustic virtues with their usual sanctions and imperatives—as old as the Egyptian moralists, or Hesiod, or the oldest portions of Proverbs, or the still older ethical elements in the popular traditions underlying the Old Testament as a whole. This was not a scientific, philosophical ethics, but popular, age-old and fundamentally religious: Do good and you will prosper, because God is in control of things! Or, if you are not prospering, find out what is wrong; examine your ways and your doings! This message the prophets had driven home to their contemporaries through century after century. But the apocalyptists opened up still another alternative—nature itself might be under a curse. Their clue they found in the verse of Genesis, "Cursed is the ground for thy sake"—for man's sake, or perhaps on account of the demons (3:17). Then pray God that the demons may speedily be vanquished and his world brought back to its original, pristine state as soon as possible! Or pray that he will soon take his great power and reign, and establish the New Age at once—"in your days, in the days of your children" as the familiar synagogue prayer phrased it! The precise "time of the end" was variously calculated, by "weeks of years," or by decades, or in other ways; but the basic and dominant character of all apocalyptic was the reversal, or the abolition, of the present world order and the inauguration of one completely under the control of the divine sovereignty.

That Jesus shared this outlook up to a point, but excluding the attempted calculation of "the times," is apparent from the Gospels. That Paul also shared it is probable, though he added to it a special emphasis derived from current Hellenistic religious thought, and gave to it his own peculiar, personal orientation, derived from his own private speculations and interpretations. This special emphasis and orientation are both apparent from his epistles. But on the ethical side it is evident that Jesus stood closer to the biblical tradition, lived closer to the soil, and made greater use of the motives and aspirations of the country dweller than Paul with his urban outlook and his cosmopolitan experience and terminology.

5. The Central Concept

The profoundest conception underlying the ethical teaching of both Testaments is that of the family. It is also the one toward which modern political theory is tending, as philosophers of government endeavor to find a more secure basis for political thought and action than in the older theories (such as the social contract, the class war, the safeguarding of the rights of property, or even democracy—conceived as an end in itself). The primitive conception of the family viewed it as having a supernatural basis in the genius, the life force, resident within it; this was incarnate in the *paterfamilias,* and descended from generation to generation—as for example in the Roman empire, centered in the Augustan house with its *Genius Augusti,* which that emperor made the pivot of the whole state cult and also of the imperial administration. This ancient conception belonged to, or rather implied, a system of power, of *mana,* rather than of *tabus* and prohibitions. Its positive side is equally to be seen in Israelite law and custom. And it was this primitive concept which biblical ethics singled out, sanctified, and made basic.

If, therefore, we are to isolate one idea which is more basic to New Testament ethics than the rest, it will be the idea of the family. Christianity arose among "the ancient lowly," for whom the family—rather than the state, the corporation, a common trade, or even the religious community—was the fundamental unit of society and the primary standard of reference for ethical behavior. Moreover it inherited an age-old tradition of ethical thought and language from the Old Testament, from Judaism, and, in somewhat less degree, from the ancient world in general. Of course the New Testament contains no systematic ethical philosophy, no formal exposition of the Christian "ideal." It simply sets forth the way of life of those who are "being saved" (Acts 2:47), the standards of behavior expected in members of God's kingdom, or, in Paul's language, what is "fitting [that is, appropriate] among saints" (Eph. 5:3; cf. Phil. 1:27). Its ethics are all fundamentally and profoundly religious. All this is preliminary to a recognition of the central emphasis in both Jesus' teaching and that of Paul. Jesus' "ethics" are ethics of the kingdom of God—and God is the heavenly *Father.* Paul's "ethics" are ethics of the nascent church —but the church is "the body of Christ" (Col. 1:24). Both concepts reflect, and transform, the old idea of the covenant of God with Israel. But all three ideas, covenant, kingdom, and church, are in essence ideas of a group specially related to God, conceived as the "people" of God or the "family" of God.

The covenant idea is at its basis a survival of the idea of the large patriarchal family or clan. The ethics of the covenant are the traditional ethics of family loyalty, obedience, love of neighbor (not of foreigners), preservation of the family (hence the strange marriage laws of the Old Testament), purity of descent within the family, regard for property within the family and clan, consideration for the poor, mercy to debtors (within the covenant), purity of tribal worship, and so on. Not that the religious ethics of the Old Testament stop with these regulations, but they lie very near the beginnings of that development. And when we consider the higher reaches of Old Testament devotion, as in the Psalms, or the pleading cries of the prophets to their sinful people, it is the idea of Yahweh as the King, the Father, even the Husband of erring Israel that is stressed. God is the King of Israel—and of all the earth—and God has chosen Israel to be his own "inheritance." The pattern of thought underlying the covenant idea is patriarchal, and the duties that go with the covenant are similarly conceived. God is the merciful, gracious *Shayik* of his people, merciful to the obedient, stern and intolerant of the disobedient.

What is true of the covenant idea is equally true of the kingdom idea. It is, as we have already seen, no idea of an Oriental monarchy, with a remote and unapproachable ruler at its head. It is the reign of one whom men may deeply and genuinely love, as a Father; and the corresponding duties are centered in loyalty, love, and obedience. Jesus widens the idea of God's kingdom to include many who were looked upon as hopeless outcasts by the religious authorities of his day. He may even have drawn a wider circle—the evidence shows that he did so, on occasion—to include devout pagans and heathen. But his "ethics" are still ethics of the family of God. The new messianic community, the group specially devoted to preparation for the coming of God's kingdom, had its own requirements, some of which were stricter and more severe than those of ordinary Judaism. To the scandal of the scribes, he insisted that family loyalty might have to yield to a higher loyalty to the kingdom of God (Luke 14:26). At the same time he stressed care of parents in the face of certain *ex parte* rules (e.g. Corban, Mark 7:9-13) which absolved sons from the care of their dependent fathers or mothers. The apostolic church cherished his sayings, and it also added to them—guided by his spirit, and speaking in his name—certain rules for missionaries which in effect set up a double standard. It then turned about and applied these to all Christians (e.g. Matt. 10:5-42), since every disciple was a missionary. Yet over all the sayings of the gospel—even over such sayings as "How hard it will be for those who have riches to enter the kingdom!" (Mark

316

10:23-27), "Sell all that you have, . . . and come, follow me" (Mark 10:21), "He who loves father or mother more than me is not worthy of me" (Matt. 10:37)—over all these sayings with their implied duties of renunciation and sacrifice stands the gracious assurance, "Fear not, little flock, for it is your Father's good pleasure to *give* you the kingdom" (Luke 12:32). This is the heart of Jesus' ethics, and the mainspring or central motive of all his revision, re-interpretation, or re-emphasis of the traditional round of duties. If the kingdom and its requirements are superior to the ties and duties of kindred, family, and home, it is only because the kingdom is itself a more perfect family, the reign of God our Father.

Finally, the same central emphasis is to be found in the idea of the church, which is the "family of God," from whom every fatherhood —or family, *patria*—"in heaven and on earth is named" (Eph. 3:15); it is "the household of faith" (Gal. 6:10); it is the "body of Christ" —but Christians may be "members" of this body, as they are members of a family. And the duties that go with such membership are family duties, raised to a new and transcendent level. As Christ loved the church and gave himself up for it, so Christians must be prepared to lay down their lives—if that is required—"for the brethren" (Eph. 5:25; I John 3:16). All the way up to that high, heroic motive of utter love and self-abandonment the Christian scale of values in human conduct springs from this central idea of union and communion with Christ, who is "the head over all things for the church, which is his body, the fullness of him who fills all in all" (Eph. 1:22-23).

It is clear that no concept of racial or national solidarity, no "ideal" of personal self-cultivation of the gentleman, the citizen, or the patriot, the ideal philosopher of Plato, or Aristotle's *megalopsychos* ("great-hearted gentleman"), or the wise man or sage of the Stoics, the saint or ascetic of the Pythagoreans, the perfect observant of the scribal law (the Pharisaic ideal), could compete with Jesus' simple but intransigent gospel of the kingdom, or with Paul's more mystical concept of the church as the body of Christ. In the glowing light of the New Testament these other concepts and ideals faded out, and the allegiance of Christians could be offered to none but God, Christ, and the heavenly kingdom. The result, in that ancient world, was privation, ignominy, even martyrdom. But, for Paul at least, and for some others, all other things, all lesser, human values were "counted loss" for the sake of knowing Christ—and being known by him. It was this quality of utter devotion, of inspired enthusiasm, which transformed the Christian ethic from rules of a code into self-sacrificing zeal for complete consecration and sanctity. "Ethics" were pedestrian; here was something which set men on fire.

6. *Specific Duties*

And yet rules are necessary, in human life, even in the transfigured life of the "family of God." Paul's converts probably needed more rules than he realized—and he gave them, in the end. The Gospels, especially Matthew, show how the sayings of the Lord were taken as rules, codified, classified, and given specific application. The "hortatory" parts of other New Testament writings reflect the same tendency, and need. All this was perfectly natural and inevitable, as the church grew into an institution separate from the synagogue, and represented no "fall" of early Christianity from the high level of the gospel. Paul's "walk by the Spirit, and do not gratify the desires of the flesh" (Gal. 5:16) and his substitution of ecstatic devotion for rules of behavior, which he identified with "law," represent a daring innovation in religious teaching, safe enough for a saint but hardly safe for the generality of mankind, even of believers. It is like Augustine's "Love, and do what thou wilt" (*Commentary on John's Epistles* VII. 8), which sounds like a rule but is really antinomian—except upon the highest level of personal devotion and consecration. The generality of mankind forget the premise, and do what they will. There is nothing like either principle, Paul's or Augustine's, in the teaching of Jesus. In Augustine's case, certainly, the saying is not nearly so profound as it is often supposed to be—a characteristic little jewel turned off by Augustine's sparkling fifth-century rhetoric.

Those modern churches which for a century and more have substituted the Pauline maxim and the theory of conversion for the slow, patient practice of ethical indoctrination and moral teaching are now reaping the harvest. The almost total lack of discipline in modern Protestantism is notorious, though this feature of present-day life is not limited to Protestantism. The situation is the more tragic in view of the growing barbarism of modern society; no age of mankind has ever seen such cruelty, inhumanity, and savagery as ours. Upon this dark scene the church ought to turn the pure light of another world, from a higher level of existence and of achieved sanctity and self-discipline; but the modern church has given up teaching "mere morals." Not so did the church of the first century, or of the fifth, or of the thirteenth, or of the earlier Protestant period! In the first, second, and third centuries the church stood out from the mass of society, and was held together by a body of independent conviction which was moral as well as doctrinal. The church of the first three centuries could criticize and condemn the world, for it was not of the world. The apologists, like Aristides the Christian, could point to the moral conduct of their fellow believers as something difficult and above the ordinary (*Apology* 15–17). Even pagans who were critical of the church recognized the difference. "See how these Christians love one another" (Libanius). The martyrs, far from being accidentally selected victims of persecution, were specially chosen by the Christians, specially trained for their ordeal, and put forward to be the representatives and witnesses of the church. It will not do to dismiss the New Testament ethics—or, for example, the Epistle of James—as a mere "survival from Jewish legalism" or a "relapse into mere moralism."

The virtues which Jesus stressed were those emphasized in the Jewish ethics of his time; what he did was deepen the emphasis upon some virtues, criticize the inconsistency, extravagance, and professionalism of certain contemporary scribal expositions of the Law, and place the whole demand of ethics in a new setting. The assurance of the immediate coming of the reign of God gave a new sanction to the highest imperatives of "righteousness." And he did all this, not as a teacher of ethics or "wisdom," or even of religion—though the "wisdom" element in his teaching is obvious—but as the prophet, herald, and agent of God in the establishment of his kingdom. As his highest term for God was "Father," so his all-embracing description of perfect discipleship was "childlikeness"; both were terms derived from the family. "Unless you turn [the Semitic word for "conversion" or "repentance"] and become like children, you will never enter the kingdom of Heaven" (Matt. 18:3). "To such belongs the kingdom of God" (Mark 10:14). The characteristic of the child which Jesus emphasized was not immaturity, helplessness, or obedience, but receptivity. In relation to God the strongest, maturest, most self-reliant must become as a little child, as the psalmist had said (Ps. 131:2).

Associated with this religious-ethical attitude is a whole group of virtues: humility, single-mindedness, sincerity, honesty, responsiveness, purity of heart, poverty in spirit, peaceableness, generosity, readiness to forgive, contentedness, trust in God, mildness of speech, restraint in judgment, nonresentment, love of neighbor, and love even of enemies. The whole round of terms descriptive of the character requisite in those who are to enter God's kingdom (the new "righteousness" of the Sermon on the Mount) is derived mainly from the Old Testament and the old Jewish piety; what is distinctive is the selection, the emphasis, and the setting—that is, in relation to the approaching kingdom. True, Jesus had nothing to say to the judge on the bench or the Roman procurator or the tax collector about their duties. Jesus was concerned with the men he knew, in the circle of their environment, faced with their problems and responsibilities. He lived among the lowly, the *am ha-aretz,* the "people of the land," and to them he devoted himself —"the lost sheep of the house of Israel" (Matt. 15:24; cf. 10:6). If his gospel was ever to be applied in other situations, it could only be by applying fundamental principles, not by quoting texts. And so deep and broad was his teaching that the process of further application is easy. After all, a judge on the bench, a military administrator, or a civil servant is still a man, and cannot excuse himself from the duties of honesty, humility, singleness of heart, and obedience to God. What Jesus did was drive home the importance, the indispensableness of right motives. "If your eye is sound, your whole body will be full of light" (Matt. 6:22). It is what you *see,* and how you see, that determines what you will do, what kind of a life you will live. Not murder only, but anger, is forbidden; not false witness only, but scurrilous abuse; not forswearing of oaths only, but the lying that makes oaths necessary; not divorce for one cause or another, but any "putting away" of one's wife; not adultery only, but the lustful look (Matt. 5: 17-37). This widening and deepening of the law's application is made with the assurance that it represented the real and primary intention of the divine lawgiver. Divorce, for example, was a concession to human weakness, allowed by Moses to the fathers; but from the beginning it was not so—God meant one man and one woman to live together in lifelong fidelity (Mark 10:2-9).

The saying about desire (Matt. 5:28) is sometimes viewed as an intrusion of pagan asceticism into the gospel tradition: "Every one who looks at a woman lustfully has already committed adultery with her in his heart." But the parallelism with the preceding and following interpretations of the old Law is exact—the teaching is concerned with motives which lie behind acts. It does not forbid the natural desire of a young man for a young woman, or her desire for him, which leads to marriage; for the desire here denounced is one that involves adultery. *Gunê* means wife as well as woman, and Dibelius is right in translating it in this passage by "married woman." What is forbidden is the "adultery of the eyes," which was likewise forbidden in Pharisaic ethics. But since *gunê* means "wife," the Encratites and other groups in the early church which forbade marriage (I Tim. 4:3) found justification for their views in this verse, as did those who required Christian married couples to live as if sex did not exist, in anticipation of the next world (Luke 20:34-35). It is possible that such views had already affected the tradition found in Matthew, for there are other traces of ascetic teaching in this Gospel (1:25; 19:10-12; etc.). But the fundamental Jewishness of the saying seems certain, and should be understood as forbidding the indulgence of the eyes and of the imagination, the covetous desire for another man's wife (forbidden in the Decalogue, Exod. 20:17); instead of this desire's being innocent, at least until carried out in act, even the unguarded gaze is itself adultery "in the heart," and is included in the other commandment, "Do not commit adultery." The Jewishness of this interpretation is evident from the familiar caricature of the Pharisee who runs into a stone wall as he walks past a woman, looking the other way (Sotah 22b). To "turn away the eyes from beholding vanity"—that is, from committing sin—was the aim of the pious (cf. Ps. 119:37); God himself, according to the prophet, was "of purer eyes than to behold evil" (Hab. 1:13). There was even a later rabbinic saint who had closed his eyes to idolatry for forty years, and when he died they covered the pagan statues along the street where the funeral procession was to pass. Such an extreme case shows that the principle lying behind the practice was genuinely Jewish, and not an instrusion of pagan ascetic ethic into the gospel tradition. The possibility of influence from the surrounding world in which this principle received expression is not to be denied (cf. the Essenes), but the state of the evidence does not permit us either to affirm or deny its existence in this case.

Other examples might be taken, illustrating the same principle: the words about the use of oaths, presumably in court (Matt. 5:33-37); or the validity of vows, especially in relation to other duties, such as the care of one's parents (Mark 7:9-13); or the accumulation of wealth (Luke 12:22-34); or the division of an inheritance (Luke 12:13-21). In every case what Jesus does is lay bare the inner motive behind the outward deed, the real orientation of the soul toward God or possessions or other persons. The great characteristic of his teaching is its depth, and also its surpassing realism. No other teacher ever searched more deeply into the hidden recesses of men's hearts in examining their conduct, character, or motives. This is still true of his teaching, centuries after, and makes it the harder to understand why the modern church is so little interested in "morality."

Paul's lists of the virtues in Gal. 5:22-24 and elsewhere—"the fruit of the Spirit"—are similarly couched in Jewish terms, in the "Jewish Greek" of the Septuagint and of synagogue piety. But here also there is a difference in tone and in emphasis, a freshness and vitality which raised the terms to a new pitch and set their practice in a new key. It is not only true that Paul was influenced to some degree by popular Greek philosophical ethics, especially Stoic; what is more important is the echo of Jesus' teaching which Paul reflects. This very list in Gal. 5 is characteristic: love, joy, peace, patience, kindness, goodness, faithfulness, gentleness, self-control—and the total conquest or "crucifixion" of the "flesh" with its passions and desires. Compare also II Cor. 6:6-10. This is a series of "objectives" in ethical living set forth by an enthusiast, a mystic, a man whose whole outlook on life had been transformed by the vision of Christ. It is a "religious" ethic, through and through. Its highest example is the self-humiliation of the Son of God, who "though he was rich, yet for your sake . . . became poor" (II Cor. 8:9), whose whole career, in the other world and in this, was one of lowliness, self-abasement, self-sacrifice (Phil. 2:5-11). And when Paul writes out specific directions for his converts, living in this world, and faced with pedestrian, everyday problems, he still carries over into practical advice the vision seen on the mount: the Christian is not as other men, but is a redeemed, transformed person, who belongs to Christ and is to manifest outwardly his inner transformation. The terms were traditional; the spirit was new.

It surprises some readers that Paul has little to say about pride and humility, though one cannot say he never refers to them (see Phil. 2:8; Gal. 6:1; etc.). But at least he does not stress humility, or child-likeness, as Jesus did. Nor is the precise proportion or balance of Jesus' ethics reflected by Paul. For one thing, of course, the two situations were totally different—the farms and villages of Galilee on one hand, and the vast, teeming centers of population in the Greco-Roman world on the other. But the question goes further: Why are some important virtues and vices not mentioned at all in the New Testament? Gambling is not mentioned, nor the manufacture and sale of weapons (which Maimonides considered in his *Mishnêh Torah*), nor civic responsibility —except for civil obedience, or subjection to lawful rulers (Rom. 13:1-7; Mark 12:13-17). The answer must be that the New Testament is concerned with principles more than with details of application; with the right spirit behind all ethical behavior; with salvation in the age to come, when earthly relations—even marriage and the family (Mark 12:25)—will cease; with the specific problems, especially in Paul's epistles, which had arisen in various communities, so that no formal and exhaustive statement of all Christian ethics was called for. Moreover the New Testament simply presupposes the Old Testament revelation, and takes for granted the reader's familiarity with the Bible—whose rules of conduct were still binding, except when specifically abrogated. It is impossible to understand the New Testament without the Old; and it is equally impossible to isolate New Testament ethics and treat them as a complete system, when they constantly presuppose the Old Testament, and require the Old Testament for their fullest interpretation—their very language is Old Testament language. It is impossible likewise to sever the relations between the New Testament ethics and the piety encouraged by contemporary Judaism.

But the answer must go further still. Above all, the New Testament is concerned with a new vision of life and a new spirit of endeavor. That vision men beheld in Christ. That spirit came from him. The New Testament ethics are, in the ultimate analysis, not philosophical or humanitarian at all, but religious, and supernaturalistic. The virtues are not self-achieved, but are the "fruit of the Spirit," and flow out from a transformed inner life. The goal is not self-perfection, or even self-edification, the *ataraxia* (inner peace) or *apatheia* (inner unconcern or detachment) of the pagan saint or sage. The goal is likeness to Christ, "that I may know him, and the power of his resurrection, . . . becoming like him in his death, that if possible I may attain the resurrection from the dead" (Phil. 3:10-11). The grace of God is taken for granted, and so, at least in John and in the New Testament epistles, is the inner renewal, rebirth or regeneration—though it is carried to an extreme in the very latest books, and human nature is thought to "partake" of the divine (II Pet. 1:4), a thoroughly Hellenistic view. Hence the reorientation of life: "Out of [the heart] are the issues of life" (Prov. 4:23; cf. Mark 7:14-23). And hence too the apostolic counsel: "Whatever is true, whatever is honorable, whatever is just, whatever is pure, whatever is lovely, whatever is gracious, if there is any excellence, if there is anything worthy of praise, think about these things" (Phil. 4:8).

Reference Index

General Index

Abel and Cain, 306
Abh, 295
Adam, 170
Adôn, 134
Adonai, 110, 131
Adultery of the eyes, 321
Aeon Christ, 229-30
Agápê, 291
Age to come, 313
Agrarian protest, 303-7
Alexander, 107
Ambrose, 40
Am ha-aretz, 179, 199, 216, 320
Anagkê, 122
Anawim, 15
Andrewes, Lancelot, 44
Anemos, 169
Angels, 25, 101, 105
Anima, 169
Animus, 169
Annunciation, the, 230
Anti-Semitism, 94-97
Apatheia, 324
Apocalypse, the, 24, 90-91, 92
Apocalyptic, 17, 24-25, 60, 64, 91, 105, 125, 129, 184, 218, 249
Apocalyptic ethics, 312-14
Apocalyptism, 104, 106, 121-22, 246, 314
Apocrypha, 77, 123
Apollo, 68
Apollonius of Rhodes, 79
Apollonius of Tyana, 150, 192
Apologists, 64, 73, 74
Apostasy, 184
Apostles, 38, 64, 89, 271, 294
Apostles' Creed, 231
Apostolic succession, 276
Apostolic writings, 64, 77
Aquinas, 40
Arabia, 34
Archontes, 104, 209, 233, 237, 240
Areas of thought, 24-26, 60
Arianism, 243

Aristarchus of Samothrace, 79
Aristides the Christian, 319
Aristides the Sophist, 312
Aristophanes of Byzantium, 79
Aristotle, 166, 305, 308, 317
Arius, 141
Arnold, Matthew, 206
Arrest, the, 226
Arrian, 48
Articles of Religion, 78-79, 118
Ascension, the, 227
Asceticism, 40, 231, 246, 265, 321
Asclepius, 189, 233
Ataraxia, 324
Athanasian Creed, 138
Athanasius, 77, 141, 237
Atonement, 35-36, 183, 252, 254-57, 283
Augustine, 15, 18, 37, 44, 57, 120-21, 125, 147, 175, 261, 318
Augustus, 103
Authority of Jesus, 76, 213
Authority of revelation, 63, 69, 76
Avatara, 193, 206

Baalism, 127-28
Babylonian ideas, 107
Bacher, Wilhelm, 204
Bacon, Benjamin W., 226
Baptism, 89-90, 276-81
Baptism of Jesus, 222-23
Barnabas, 92
Bar-nasha, 219
Barth, Karl, 27
Basar, 162, 164, 169
Baudissin, W. W. von, 131, 219
Baur, Ferdinand Christian, 19
Beatitudes, the, 198
Beelzebul, 100, 149, 183, 217
Belloc, Hilaire, 246
Ben Sira, 299
Bevan, Edwyn, 169
Bewer, Julius, 88
Biblia, 81